Ultimate Microsoft Dynamics 365 CRM for Enterprises

Unlock the Power of Microsoft Dynamics 365 CRM to Automate Your Business Processes and Drive Digital Transformation

Vidit Vikas Gholam

www.orangeava.com

First Published: March 2025

Published By: Orange Education Pvt Ltd, AVA®

Address: 9, Daryaganj, Delhi, 110002, India

275 New North Road Islington Suite 1314 London,
N1 7AA, United Kingdom

ISBN (PBK): 978-93-48107-82-4
ISBN (E-BOOK): 978-93-48107-27-5

Dedicated To

My Beloved Parents

Mr. Vikas Gholam and Mrs. Vinita Gholam

And

My Grandparents
Mr. Shantaram Bhatade, Mrs. Sumitra Bhatade and
Mr. Shankar Gholam, Mrs. Laxami Gholam

About the Author

Vidit Vikas Gholam is a Microsoft Certified Trainer (MCT) and Microsoft Certified Professional with a bachelor's degree in Computer Engineering. He is a software developer specializing in Dynamics 365 CRM, Power Platform, and Azure. He has extensive experience architecting and implementing innovative solutions for product- and project-based companies. He excels at solving complex business challenges using Microsoft cloud technologies, enabling organizations to enhance workflows, streamline processes, and achieve tangible results.

Starting his career with Dynamics 365 CRM, Vidit has developed a deep understanding of various functionalities within the platform, including Dynamics 365 Sales, Customer Service, Field Service, and Azure integrations. He has successfully delivered client solutions across the United States, Europe, and Australia, helping businesses unlock the full potential of Microsoft technologies.

A dedicated and active member of the Microsoft community, Vidit is an experienced speaker who has presented at major Microsoft technology events, including large-scale conferences in the United States, as well as in-person and virtual Dynamics 365 community events in India. Through these engagements, he has shared practical insights on optimizing business operations and adopting innovative technologies.

Vidit is also passionate about mentoring professionals, enabling them to excel in Dynamics 365 CRM and Power Platform. His enthusiasm for lifelong learning and his ability to solve intricate business challenges, have earned him recognition as a trusted expert in the field.

Beyond work, Vidit enjoys writing and engaging with the tech community. His dedication to learning, teaching, and sharing his expertise continues to inspire professionals and students to thrive in the rapidly evolving world of technology.

About the Technical Reviewers

Nishant Rana is a seven-time Microsoft Most Valuable Professional (MVP) in Business Applications, recognized for his extensive expertise and significant contributions to the Microsoft Dynamics 365 ecosystem. With over 18 years of experience, he has been an integral part of the journey from Microsoft CRM 3.0 to Dynamics 365, excelling in areas including analysis, design, development, team leadership, and architectural solutions. He is also a KingswaySoft SSIS MVP, further solidifying his position as a thought leader in the integration domain. As a Microsoft Certified Professional in Dynamics 365, Power Apps, Azure, SharePoint, and .NET, Nishant brings a multifaceted perspective to solving business challenges with technology. Throughout his career, Nishant has worked with renowned organizations including Microsoft, DXC, First Abu Dhabi Bank, and KPIT Cummins. Currently, he serves as Technology Lead at Delta Insights, where he collaborates with his team to deliver tailored Dynamics 365-based solutions to clients.

Amit Prajapati has over five years of experience in designing and implementing solutions across Dynamics 365 CRM and Microsoft Azure platforms. He specializes in integrating data-intensive enterprise applications with cloud technologies, focusing on automation and process efficiency. His passion for innovation led him to explore advanced data management and CRM integration techniques, aligning business objectives with cutting-edge technology.

Amit has successfully led technical consultancy, solution architecture, and development teams across diverse industries, including manufacturing, IT consulting, finance, and healthcare. He has delivered impactful projects for global clients in the USA, Australia, and Singapore. Additionally, Amit holds Microsoft certifications in Dynamics 365 and Power Platform, reflecting his commitment to continuous learning and expertise in his domain.

Acknowledgements

First and foremost, I would like to express my deepest gratitude to my parents and my younger brother, Tanish Gholam, for their unwavering support, belief in me, and encouragement throughout my life. Your contributions to my educational journey have been instrumental in shaping the person I am today.

I am sincerely grateful to my organization, CloudFronts Technologies, for being a pillar of my professional growth. A special note of thanks to Mr. Anil Shah, the CEO of CloudFronts, for fostering a culture of continuous learning and development. I also extend my gratitude to my mentors and managers, Priyesh Wagh and Amit Prajapati, for their invaluable guidance, advice, and direction. I also thank my colleagues at CloudFronts for their collaboration and support, which have significantly contributed to my achievements.

I would also like to express my heartfelt thanks to my extended family; my uncle, Deepak Bhatade, my aunts, Deepa Bhatade and Lata Bhatade; my paternal uncles, Santosh and Vishwas Gholam, and my aunt, Jyoti Khake. Their constant support and encouragement have been a source of strength throughout my educational journey.

I am deeply indebted to Dr. Naresh Dhanawade and Mr. Deepak Khake for their mentorship and invaluable guidance during my educational journey. Their insights and encouragement have been pivotal in my growth.

I extend my gratitude to my friends for always being there, offering support, and cheering me on every step of the way. Their belief and constant encouragement have made this journey even more meaningful.

Additionally, I would like to acknowledge the publisher and their team for their unwavering support and dedication to bringing this book to life.

Finally, I want to express my gratitude to my cousins Yukta, Parth, Vedang, Daksha, Anvi, Saanvi, Saee, and Devansh, for always cheering me on and being a constant source of joy and inspiration.

DID YOU KNOW

Did you know that Orange Education Pvt Ltd offers eBook versions of every book published, with PDF and ePub files available? You can upgrade to the eBook version at **www.orangeava.com** and as a print book customer, you are entitled to a discount on the eBook copy. Get in touch with us at: **info@orangeava.com** for more details.

At **www.orangeava.com**, you can also read a collection of free technical articles, sign up for a range of free newsletters, and receive exclusive discounts and offers on Print Books and eBooks.

PIRACY

If you come across any illegal copies of our works in any form on the internet, we would be grateful if you would provide us with the location address or website name. Please contact us at **info@orangeava.com** with a link to the material.

ARE YOU INTERESTED IN AUTHORING WITH US?

If there is a topic that you have expertise in, and you are interested in either writing or contributing to a book, please write to us at **business@orangeava.com**. We are on a journey to help developers and tech professionals to gain insights on the present technological advancements and innovations happening across the globe and build a community that believes Knowledge is best acquired by sharing and learning with others. Please reach out to us to learn what our audience demands and how you can be part of this educational reform. We also welcome ideas from tech experts and help them build learning and development content for their domains.

REVIEWS

Please leave a review. Once you have read and used this book, why not leave a review on the site that you purchased it from? Potential readers can then see and use your unbiased opinion to make purchase decisions. We at Orange Education would love to know what you think about our products, and our authors can learn from your feedback. Thank you!

For more information about Orange Education, please visit **www.orangeava.com**.

Table of Contents

CHAPTER 1
Introduction to Microsoft Dynamics 365 CRM

Introduction

In this chapter, we will start with the basics of Microsoft Dynamics 365 CRM. We will understand Dynamics 365 CRM and why it is such a powerful tool for businesses. We will explore Model-Driven Apps and their flexibility and scalability in Dynamics 365 CRM. We will also learn about Dataverse, the data platform that makes everything in Dynamics 365 work together smoothly.

Next, we will learn about key modules: Dynamics 365 Sales for managing sales processes, Dynamics 365 Project Operations for handling project management, Dynamics 365 Customer Service for building strong customer relationships, and Dynamics 365 Field Service for optimizing field service tasks.

By the end of this chapter, we will have a good grasp of these essential components, establishing a solid foundation for more advanced topics in the following chapters.

Structure

In this chapter, we will discuss the following topics:

- Understanding Dynamics 365 CRM
- Understanding Dataverse
- Sales Module: Introduction to Dynamics 365 Sales
- Project Module: Introduction to Dynamics 365 Project Operations
- Field Service Module: Introduction to Dynamics 365 Field Service
- Customer Service Module: Introduction to Dynamics 365 Customer Service

Understanding Dynamics 365 CRM

Dynamics 365 is a suite of intelligent business applications designed to help organizations set up their operations, enhance customer engagement, and drive growth. These applications cater to various business needs, including finance, operations, customer service, and marketing.

Some of the major Dynamics 365 apps include:

- Dynamics 365 Sales
- Dynamics 365 Marketing
- Dynamics 365 Customer Service
- Dynamics 365 Field Service
- Dynamics 365 Finance
- Dynamics 365 Supply Chain Management
- Dynamics 365 Project Operations
- Dynamics 365 Business Central

In this chapter and subsequent ones, we will focus on Dynamics 365 apps that form the CRM suite, Dynamics 365 Sales, Marketing, Customer Service, Field Service, Project Operations. In this chapter, our focus will specifically be on Sales, Project Operations, Fields Service, and Customer Service.

Before we explore Dynamics 365 CRM, let us first understand what CRM actually is.

Customer Relationship Management (CRM)

Customer Relationship Management (CRM) is a system that helps businesses manage and organize customer information in one place. It gives teams easy access to the data they need, improving how they work and connect with customers.

In the past, businesses used spreadsheets, emails, and paper files to store customer details. This made it hard to find and share information, slowing down marketing, sales, and customer service.

Today, CRM systems collect and combine data including contact details, purchase history, and customer interactions. This creates a clear, complete picture of each customer, helping teams work together to build stronger relationships and improve customer experiences.

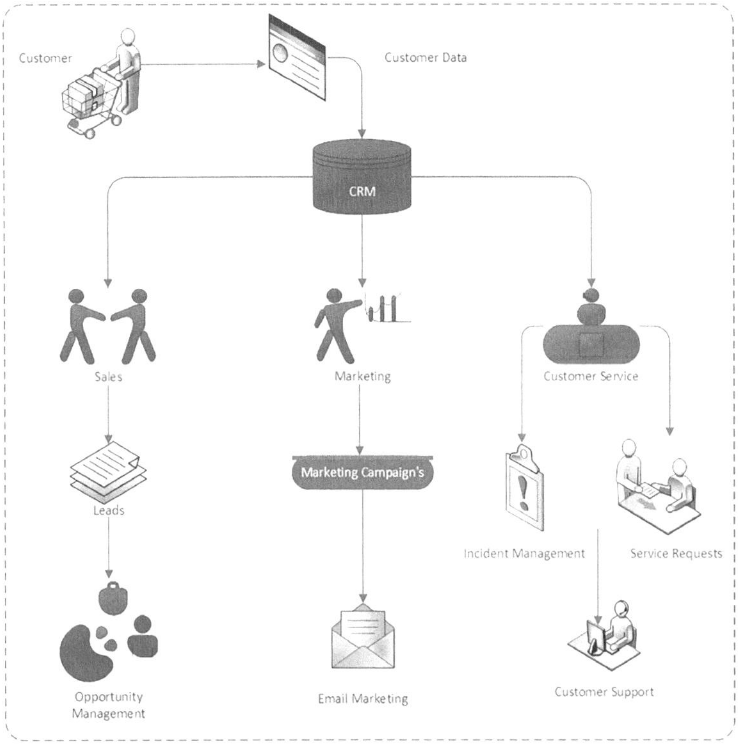

Figure 1.1: *Customer Relationship Management*

Figure 1.1 is a simplified flowchart illustrating the typical processes and components involved in a Customer Relationship Management (CRM) system.

In this flowchart:

CRM system is the central hub that manages all customer-related activities, including:

- **Sales** handles lead generation, opportunity management, and sales tracking.
- **Marketing** deals with marketing campaigns, email marketing, and lead nurturing.
- **Customer Service** encompasses case handling, customer support, and issue resolution.

Each component interacts with the CRM system to ensure seamless customer relationship management, from initial contact through sales and ongoing support.

Evolution Timeline of Dynamics 365 CRM

Before we learn more about Dynamics 365 CRM, let us look at its brief history and how this SaaS product has evolved over a decade.

- **2003**: Microsoft launches Microsoft CRM 1.0, an on-premises software solution for improving customer relationships, managing sales processes, and enhancing marketing campaigns.

- **2005**: Microsoft releases Dynamics CRM 3.0, a critical milestone in its history. This version was rebranded as part of the Dynamics suite and built on the .NET framework, laying the foundation for its future adaptability and scalability.
- **2010**: Dynamics CRM gains traction, offering modules for sales automation, marketing automation, and customer service. Microsoft introduces Dynamics CRM Online, a cloud-based version for greater accessibility.
- **2013**: Dynamics CRM 2013 introduces a redesigned UI and enhanced mobile capabilities, increasing its popularity among businesses.
- **2015**: Microsoft announces plans to transition Dynamics CRM into Dynamics 365, integrating CRM with ERP functionalities for a unified business platform.
- **2016:** Dynamics 365 is officially launched, combining CRM and ERP under one platform. It introduces modular apps for Sales, Marketing, Customer Service, Field Service, and Project Service Automation, allowing businesses to pick and choose functionalities that meet their needs.
- **2018**: Microsoft invests in Dynamics 365 CRM, introducing new features and tight integrations with Office 365, Azure, and the Power Platform.
- **2020**: Dynamics 365 CRM remains a leading choice for businesses seeking modern CRM solutions. Microsoft continues to update and innovate Dynamics 365 CRM to enhance customer experiences.
- **2021:** The introduction of low-code tools in Dynamics 365 enables users to create and customize applications with minimal coding, opening the platform to a broader range of users and use cases.
- **2024**: The release wave 1 brings exciting innovations, including Microsoft Copilot for Sales and enhancements to Dynamics 365 Customer Service and Field Service. These updates reinforce Dynamics 365 CRM's position as a comprehensive solution for managing customer relationships and driving business growth. These are just highlights! You can explore the release plans using Reference 1.

What Are Release Waves?

Release waves are biannual updates from Microsoft that introduce new features and enhancements across Dynamics 365 and the Power Platform. These waves occur in the first and second halves of each year (referred to as Wave 1 and Wave 2) and ensure the platform remains innovative, secure, and aligned with modern business needs. Release Wave 1, for example, focuses on AI integration, user experience improvements, and enhanced capabilities for Sales and Customer Service, making it a key update for users.

Figure 1.2 showcases the suite of CRM and ERP apps within the Dynamics 365 ecosystem, along with the Power Platform tools used to manage, customize, and analyze data within these apps.

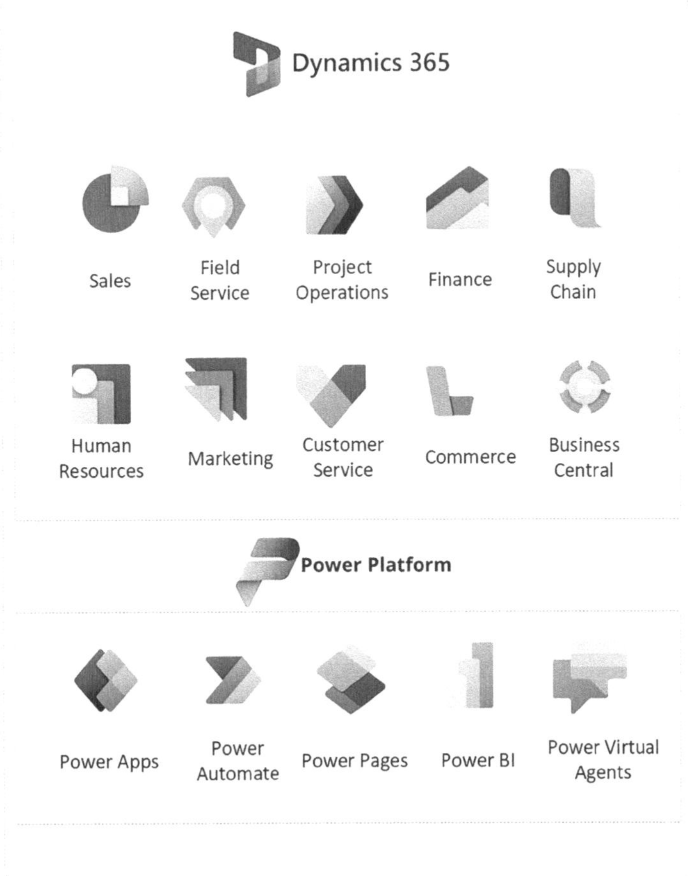

Figure 1.2: *Dynamics 365 Application Suit*

Now that we have covered the history of Dynamics 365, let us take a brief look into the data model and various Modules within Dynamics 365. Microsoft Dynamics 365 uses the Dataverse (formerly known as the Common Data Service) as its core data model.

Understanding Dataverse

Dataverse, formerly known as Common Data Service (CDS), is a pivotal component of Microsoft's Power Platform and Dynamics 365 ecosystem. It provides a secure and scalable data storage solution that allows users to manage and store data used by business applications. With Dataverse, data from multiple sources can be brought together into a single store that can be used in Power Apps, Power Automate, Power BI, and Dynamics 365 applications.

Key Features of Dataverse:

- **Data Storage**: Dataverse provides a structured and secure data storage solution, organizing data into tables (formerly known as entities). These tables can store a variety of data types, including numbers, text, dates, and more complex data types such as files and images.
- **Standard and Custom Tables:** It includes a set of standard tables that cover typical business scenarios, but also allows for the creation of custom tables to fit specific business needs.
- **Data Integration**: Dataverse supports data integration from various sources, including external databases, spreadsheets, and other business applications. This integration capability ensures that all relevant data can be consolidated and accessed from a single platform.
- **Security**: It provides robust security features, including role-based security, row-level security, and field-level security. This ensures that sensitive data is protected and only accessible to authorized users.
- **Business Logic**: Dataverse supports the implementation of business rules and logic directly at the data layer. This includes workflows, business process flows, and calculated fields that help automate business processes and ensure data integrity.
- **Scalability and Performance**: Built on Azure, Dataverse offers high scalability and performance, capable of handling large volumes of data and complex business processes.

For more details on Dataverse, see **Reference 2**; for a visual representation, see **Reference 3**.

Dynamics 365 CRM offers a suite of modules designed to cater to various aspects of customer relationship management. These modules include Sales, Customer Service, Field Service, and Project, among others. Each module is tailored to address specific business functions, such as lead management, opportunity tracking, case resolution, scheduling and dispatching, project planning, and execution.

Sales Module: Introduction to Dynamics 365 Sales App

The sales module in Microsoft Dynamics 365 CRM is designed to enhance the sales process for organizations. It offers a set of tools to manage the entire sales cycle, from lead generation and opportunity management to order processing and invoicing. The sales module includes the following key features:

- **Lead Management**: Capture and qualify leads from various sources such as web forms, emails, Microsoft marketplace, LinkedIn, and so on. Assign leads sales representatives and track their progress through the sales funnel.

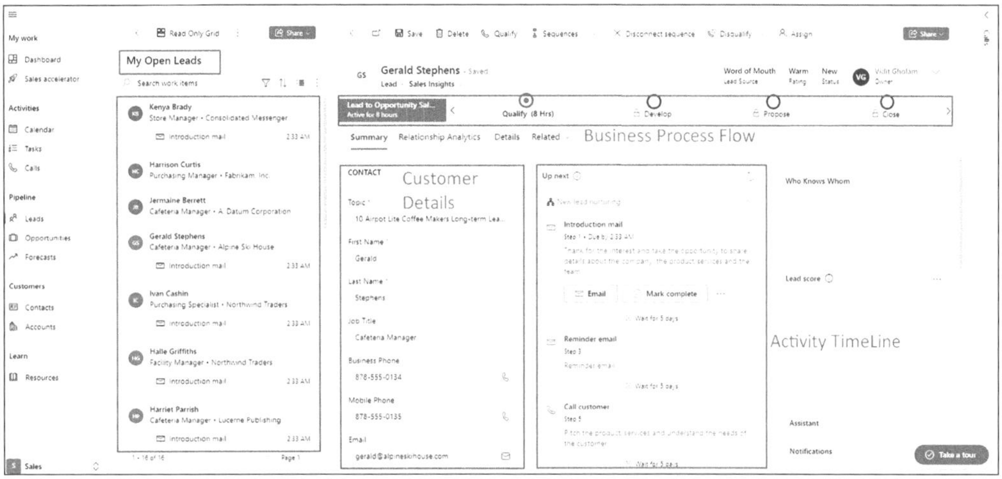

Figure 1.3: *User Interface for Leads in Dynamics 365 Sales*

- **Account and Contact Management**: Maintain records of customer accounts and contacts. Access detailed information about customer interactions, purchase history, and preferences to build stronger relationships.

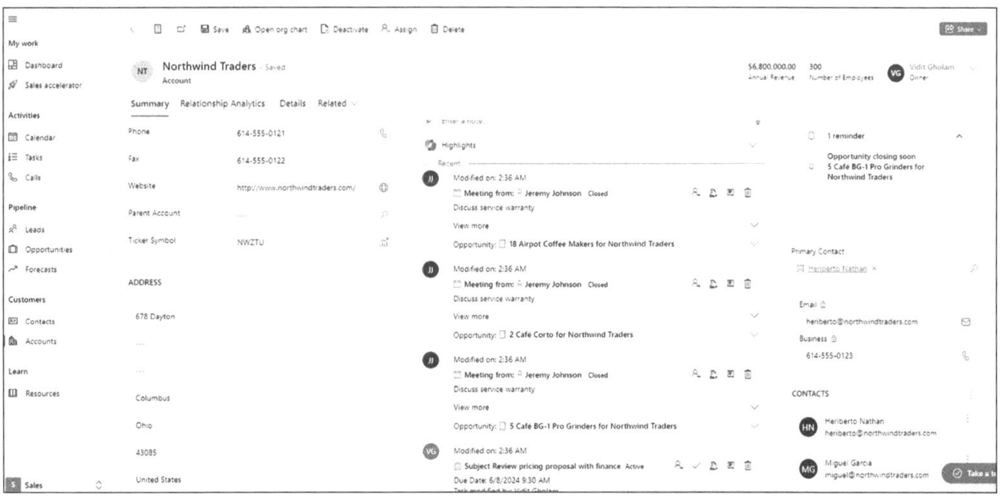

Figure 1.4: *User Interface for Accounts in Dynamics 365 Sales*

- **Opportunity Management**: Convert qualified leads into opportunities. Track and manage opportunities through different stages of the sales process, from initial contact to closing the deal. For detailed information on opportunity management, refer to **Reference 4**.

Figure 1.5: *Deal Tracker View in Dynamics 365 Sales for Opportunities*

- **Sales Forecasting:** Utilize advanced forecasting tools to predict future sales performance. Generate accurate sales forecasts based on historical data and current opportunities.

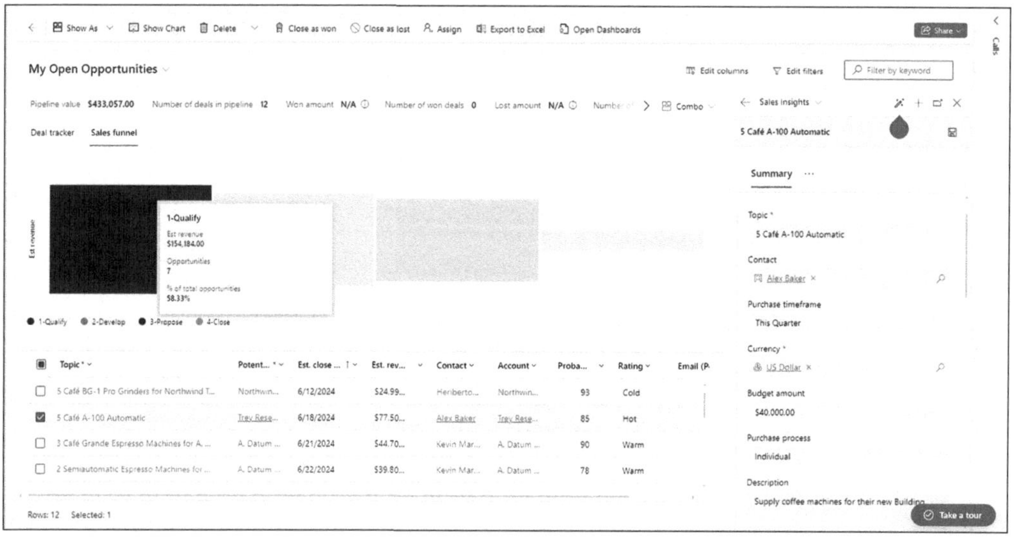

Figure 1.6: *Sales Funnel View in Dynamics 365 Sales for Opportunities*

- **Product Catalog Management**: Manage a centralized product catalog with detailed information about products and services. Create price lists, discounts, and bundles to offer customized solutions to customers. For detailed information about the product categories, refer to **Reference 5**.

- **Quote Management**: Generate professional quotes for customers based on selected products and pricing. Track the status of quotes and convert them into orders when approved.
- **Order and Invoice Management:** Create and manage sales orders, including tracking order fulfillment and delivery. Integrate with inventory and supply chain systems to ensure timely order processing. Generate and send invoices to customers based on completed orders. Track payment status and manage accounts receivable. For detailed information about order and invoicing, please refer to **Reference 6**.
- **Sales Insights:** Utilize built-in analytics and reporting tools to gain insights into sales performance. Monitor key metrics such as sales pipeline, win/loss ratios, and sales trends, using out-of-the-box and custom dashboards.

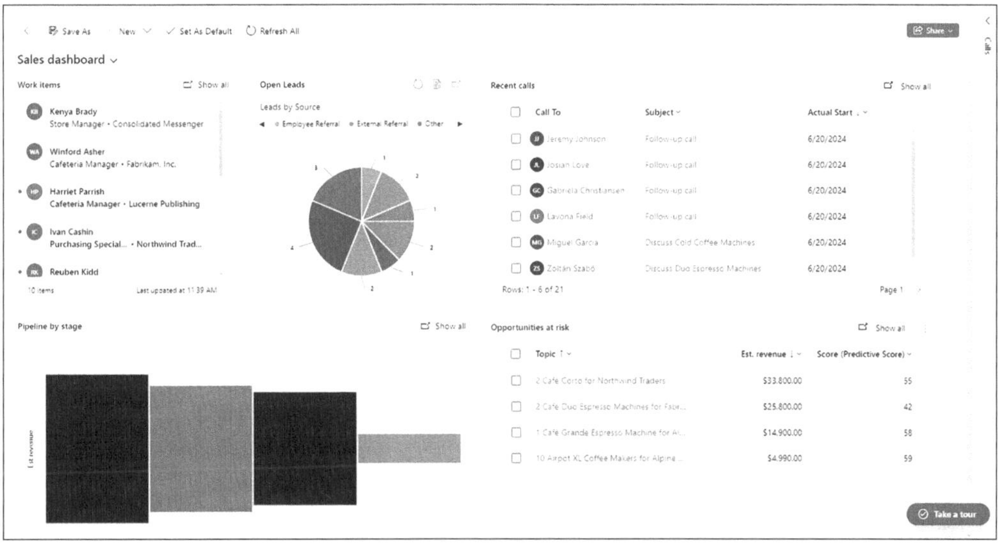

***Figure 1.7**: Sales Dashboard in Dynamics 365 Sales*

- **Mobile Access:** Access sales data and perform key tasks on the go with the Dynamics 365 mobile app. Enable sales representatives to stay productive and responsive while in the field.

Sales Business Process Flow

The sales process flow in Dynamics 365 Sales initiates with the creation of a lead, typically sourced from various channels such as marketing campaigns, website inquiries, or referrals. Once a lead is qualified, it seamlessly transitions into an opportunity, signifying a potential deal worth pursuing. During this conversion, the customer and contact information captured in the lead record is automatically populated into corresponding account and contact records within Dynamics 365 Sales, ensuring data consistency and accessibility.

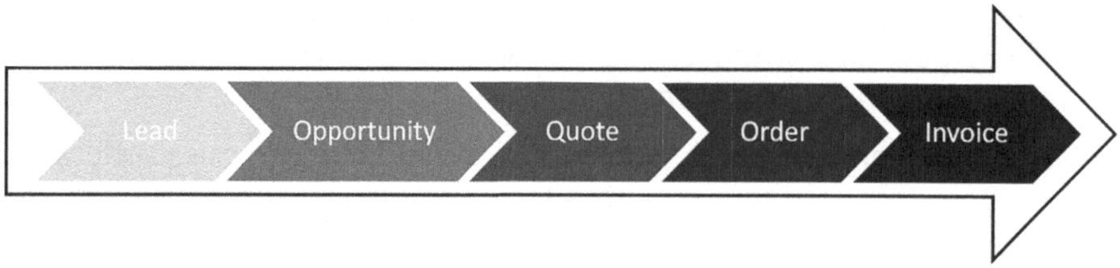

***Figure 1.8(a):** Sales Business Process Flow in Dynamics 365 Sales. These images are referenced from https://learn.microsoft.com/*

Following the creation of an opportunity, the sales team prepares and submits quotations tailored to the customer's needs and requirements. These quotation records are linked to the associated opportunity, providing a clear overview of the sales pipeline. Upon acceptance of a quotation by the customer, the respective quote is marked as "won," signaling a successful sale, and consequently, the opportunity is also marked as "**won**." Conversely, if a quotation is rejected by the customer, it translates into a lost opportunity, providing valuable insights for future sales strategies.

Subsequently, upon successful deal closure, orders are generated based on the accepted quotations. These orders initiate the order fulfillment process, wherein products or services are delivered to the customer as per the agreed-upon terms and conditions. Invoices are then generated against these orders, facilitating the billing and payment process.

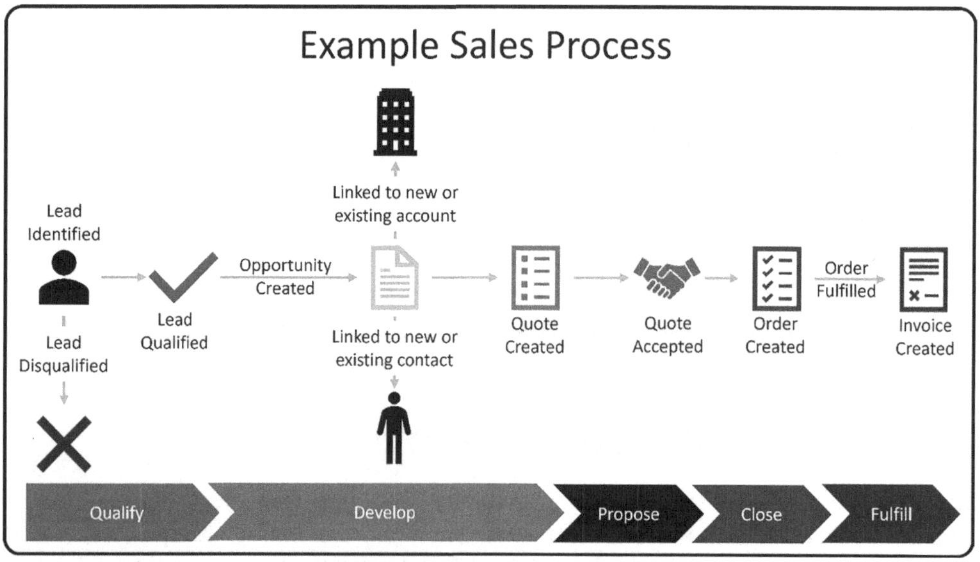

***Figure 1.8(b):** Detailed Sales Business Process Flow in Dynamics 365 Sales. These images are referenced from https://learn.microsoft.com/*

Throughout this entire sales journey, Dynamics 365 Sales provides a centralized platform for managing customer interactions, tracking sales activities, and driving revenue growth, ultimately fostering a seamless and efficient sales experience for both the sales team and customers alike.

Note: *A complete training course on the fundamentals of sales module is linked in Reference 7.*

Project Module: Introduction to Dynamics 365 Project Operations App

Project Operations in Dynamics 365 is a module designed to streamline project management processes. It consists of various aspects such as project planning, resource management, time tracking, expense management, invoicing, and reporting.

Let us examine each of these aspects:

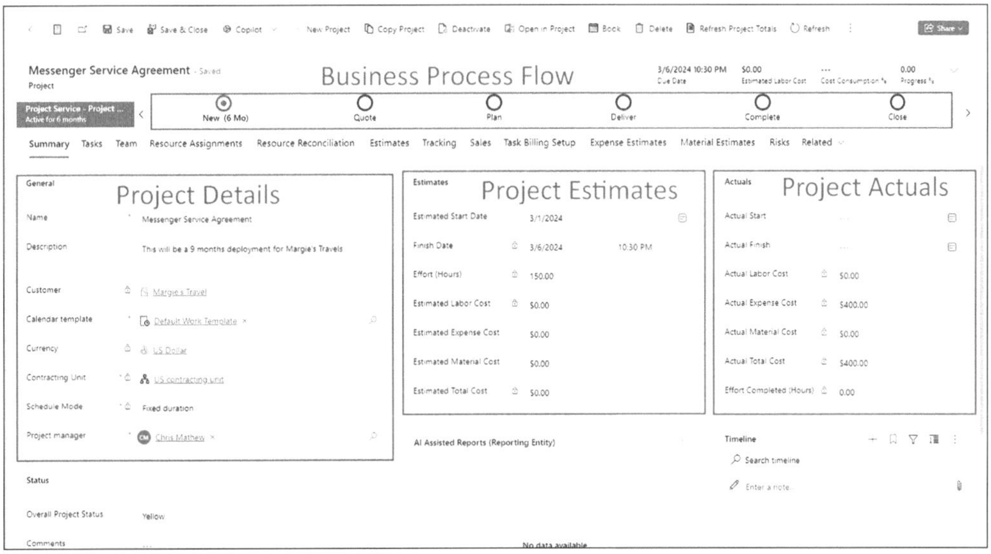

Figure 1.9*: Project Details in Project Operations*

- **Project Planning:** Dynamics 365 enables users to create and manage project plans efficiently. They can define tasks, set timelines, establish dependencies, and identify milestones within the system. This feature provides a structured approach to project execution, ensuring clarity and alignment across team members.

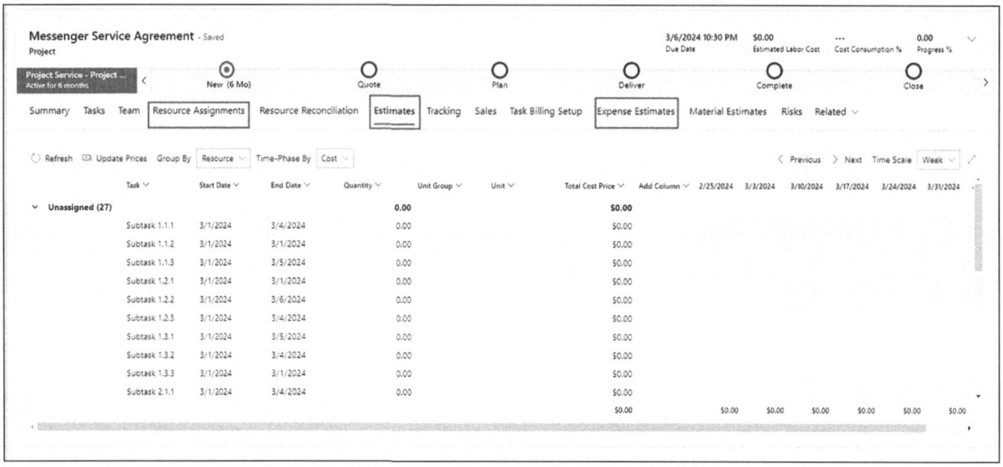

Figure 1.10: *Other Project Parameters*

Figure 1.10 illustrates project parameters including **`Resource Assignments`**, **`Project Estimates`**, and **`Expense Estimates`**.

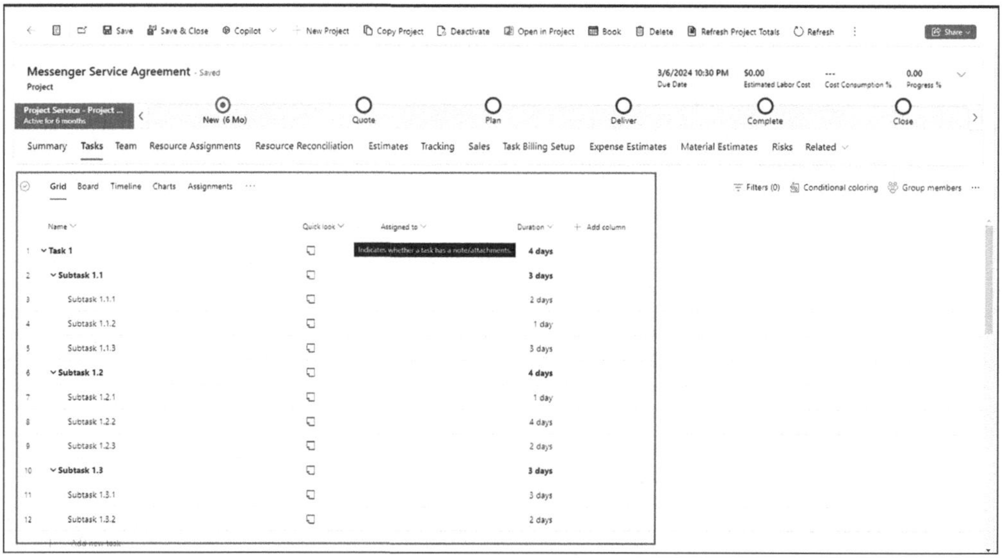

Figure 1.11: *Project Plan in Project Operations*

- *Figure* 1.11 shows **`Project Tasks`**. Tasks serve as the building blocks for managing work within a project. They define specific activities, set timelines, and allocate resources needed to achieve project milestones. By organizing tasks hierarchically and linking them to deliverables, teams can track progress, manage dependencies, and ensure projects are completed efficiently and on time.

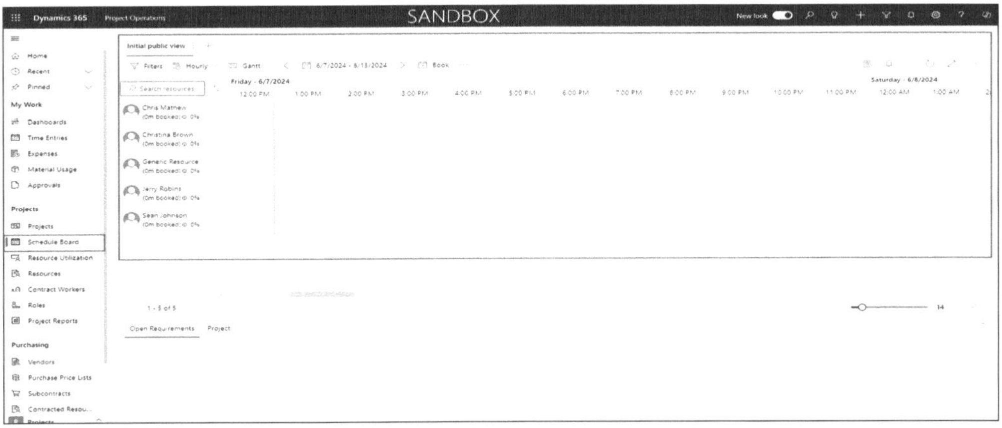

Figure 1.12: *Resource Allocation and Bookings in Project Operations*

- **Resource Management:** Efficient allocation of resources is critical for project success. Dynamics 365 facilitates the optimal allocation of resources based on factors such as availability, skills, and workload. With visibility into resource capacity and demand, project managers can make informed decisions to ensure resource utilization is maximized.

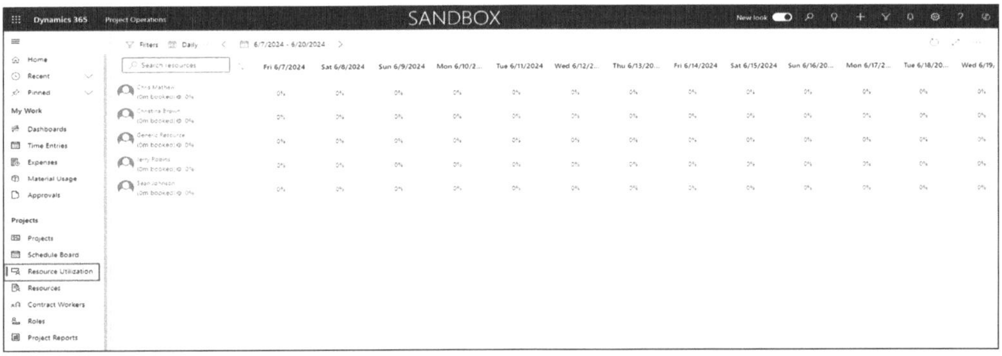

Figure 1.13: *Resource Utilization in Project Operations*

- **Time Tracking**: Accurate time tracking is essential for monitoring project progress and billing clients correctly. Dynamics 365 allows employees to log their time spent on various project tasks. This data is then used for project costing, billing, and performance analysis, ensuring transparency and accountability.

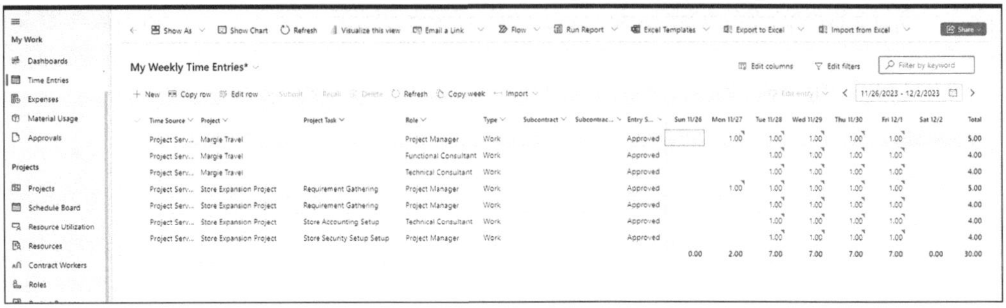

Figure 1.14: *Time Entry Management in Project Operations*

- **Expense Management**: Managing project-related expenses can be cumbersome without the right tools. Dynamics 365 streamlines this process by enabling users to capture and reimburse expenses incurred by employees or contractors. From travel expenses to equipment purchases, all expenses can be tracked and managed within the system.

Figure 1.15: *Expense Entry Management in Project Operations*

- **Reporting and Analytics:** Provide insights into project performance, resource utilization, profitability, and other key metrics through customizable dashboards and reports.

Project Operations Process Flow

1. Just like in sales, the process flow of project operations begins with creating a lead.
2. Qualify the lead to an opportunity.
3. Quotes are associated with the opportunity.
4. The quotes have two types of quote lines: Fixed Price, and Time and Material.
5. Fixed Price lines have milestones associated with them.
6. Time and Material lines have invoice schedules associated with them.

7. You can also add projects to these lines to get a proper project estimate and, hence, quote profitability.
8. Once the quote is accepted and marked as won, a Project Contract (sales orders are called project contracts in project operations) is created.
9. All the quote lines automatically transfer to the contract and become actual project contract lines.
10. Now, the actual project lifecycle begins with time, expense, and material entries being submitted.
11. These entries are approved by the project managers.
12. Once approved, actuals are created for these approved entries.
13. Project contract milestones are marked as ready to invoice.
14. From the Project Contract, a Proforma invoice can be generated.

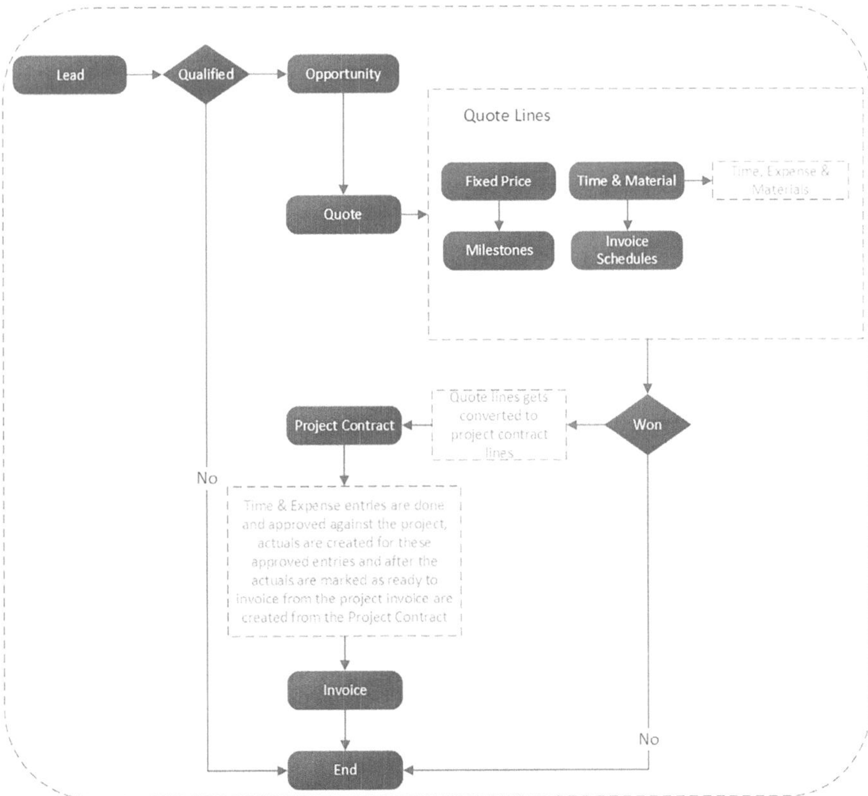

***Figure 1.16:** Process Flow of Project Operations*

Note: *A complete training course on Getting Started with Project Operations is linked in Reference 12.*

Field Service Module: Introduction to Dynamics 365 Field Service App

Field Service in Dynamics 365 is a robust module designed to help organizations manage their field operations efficiently. Whether you are dealing with routine maintenance, repairs, or complex installations, Dynamics 365 Field Service ensures that your field technicians are equipped with the right tools and information to deliver exceptional service. This module integrates seamlessly with other Dynamics 365 applications, allowing for a comprehensive approach to customer service and operational management. At its core, Dynamics 365 Field Service helps companies with their service operations, from scheduling and dispatching to managing work orders and inventory.

Figure 1.17: *Field Service User Interface in Dynamics 365*

Let us discuss some of the features of Field Service:

- **Mobile Accessibility**: Field technicians can access work orders, customer information, and inventory data on their mobile devices, enabling them to perform their tasks efficiently and update job statuses in real time.
- **Inventory Management**: Track and manage inventory levels, ensuring that technicians have the necessary parts and tools to complete their tasks without delays.
- **Customer Communication**: Keep customers informed throughout the service process with automated notifications, providing them with real-time updates on technician arrival times and service progress.
- **Service Agreements**: Manage service contracts and agreements, ensuring

that all service commitments are met and that customers receive the agreed-upon level of service.

- **Work Order Management:** Create and manage work orders for various service requests, ensuring that all necessary details are captured and communicated to the field technician.

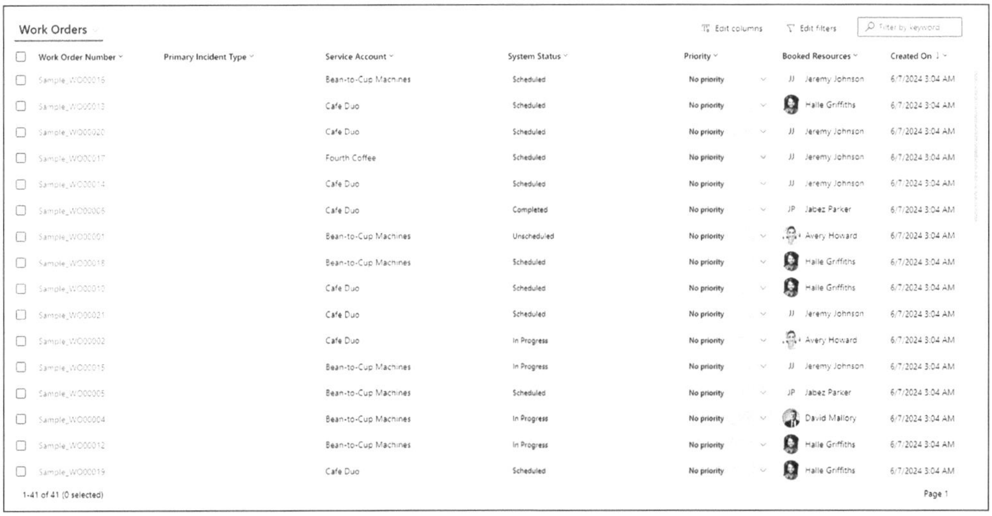

Figure 1.18*: Work Orders in Field Service*

- **Scheduling and Dispatching:** Utilize advanced scheduling tools to assign the best-suited technician based on skill set, location, and availability. Optimize routes to reduce travel time and costs.

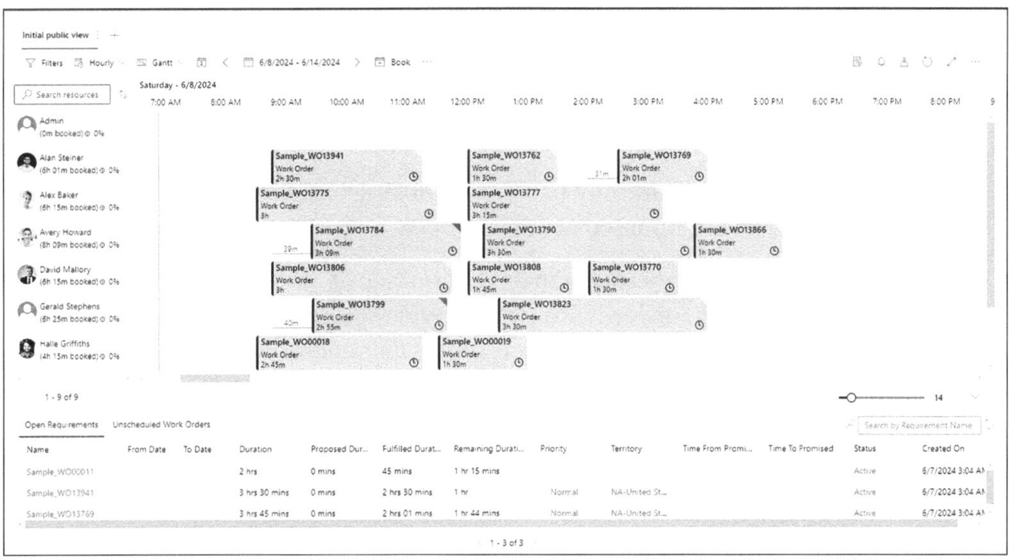

Figure 1.19*: Schedule Board in Field Service*

- **Resource Management:** Allocate and manage resources effectively, ensuring that your team is utilized to its fullest potential and that service requests are handled promptly.

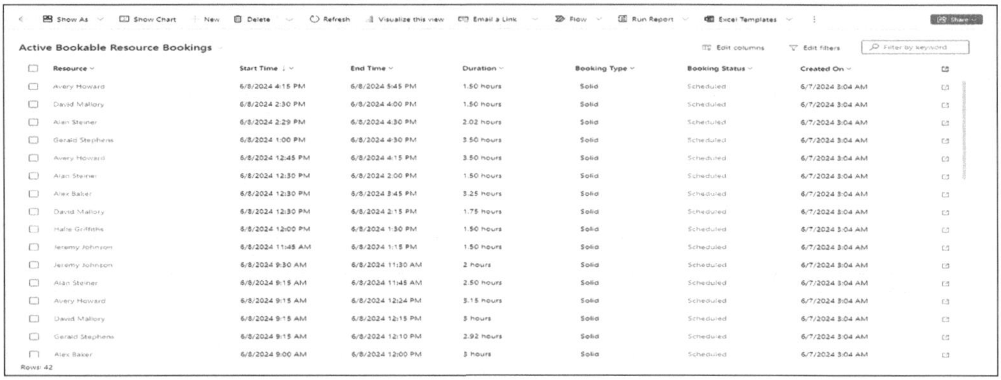

Figure 1.20: *Resource Management in Field Service*

Business Process Flow in Field Service

The business process flow in Dynamics 365 Field Service typically follows these steps:

1. **Service Request Creation**: A service request is initiated by a customer or automatically generated by a connected IoT device indicating a potential issue.
2. **Work Order Generation**: The service request is converted into a work order, detailing the nature of the service, required parts, and any specific instructions.
3. **Scheduling and Dispatching**: The work order is assigned to a suitable technician based on availability, skills, and location. The technician receives the work order details on their mobile device.
4. **On-Site Service**: The technician arrives at the customer location, performs the required service, and updates the work order status in real time.
5. **Inventory Management**: Any parts used during the service are recorded, and inventory levels are updated accordingly.
6. **Completion and Reporting**: Once the service is completed, the technician updates the work order with the service details and obtains customer confirmation, if required. A service report is generated and shared with the customer.
7. **Billing and Follow-Up:** The completed work order is reviewed, and billing is processed. Follow-up activities are scheduled if necessary, ensuring ongoing customer satisfaction.

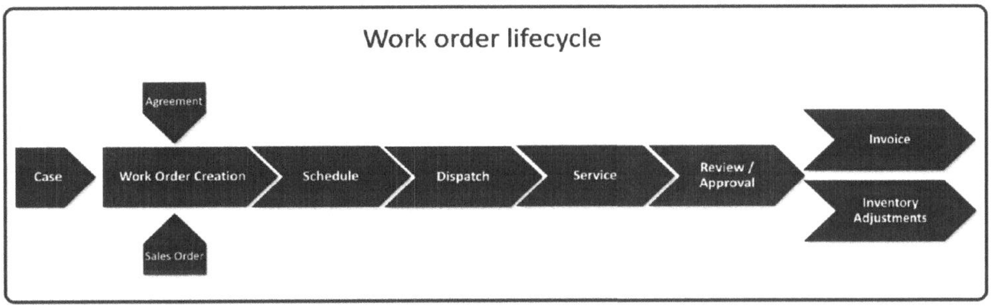

Figure 1.21: *Business Process Flow of Field Service*
The image is referenced from https://learn.microsoft.com/

Note: *A complete training course on Fundamentals of Field Service is linked in Reference 13.*

Customer Service Module: Introduction to Dynamics 365 Customer Service App

Dynamics 365 Customer Service is a powerful module designed to help organizations deliver exceptional customer support and enhance customer satisfaction. This module provides a comprehensive set of tools for managing and resolving customer inquiries, issues, and service requests efficiently. By centralizing customer interactions and data, Dynamics 365 Customer Service ensures that support teams have the information they need to deliver timely and effective solutions.

The primary goal of Dynamics 365 Customer Service is to create a seamless and personalized experience for customers. It achieves this by integrating various communication channels, automating routine tasks, and providing insightful analytics. Whether it is through email, phone, chat, or social media, this module enables support agents to engage with customers consistently and effectively, ensuring that no inquiry goes unanswered.

Let us look at some features of the `Customer Service` module:

- **Case Management:** Track and manage customer issues from initial contact through to resolution. Cases can be automatically routed to the appropriate agent based on predefined rules, ensuring efficient handling of inquiries.

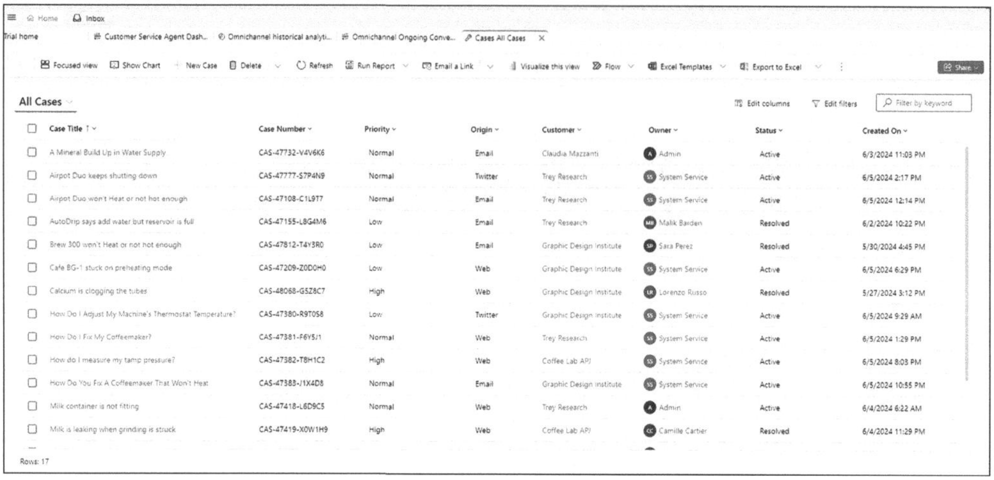

Figure 1.22: *Case Management in Dynamics 365 Customer Service*

- **Service Level Agreements (SLAs):** Define and manage SLAs to ensure that customer service standards are met. Monitor SLA performance and receive alerts when service levels are at risk.

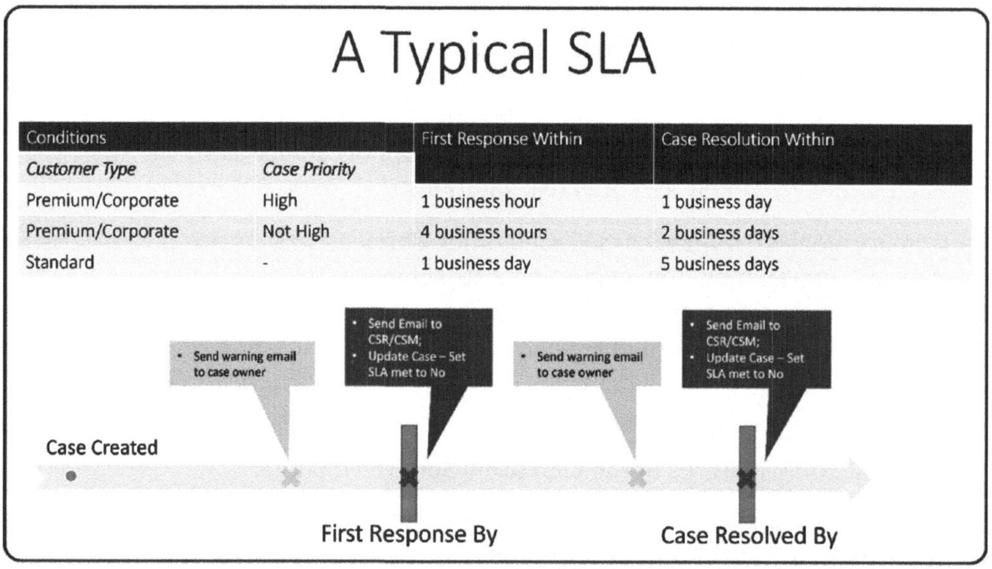

Figure 1.23: *Managing SLAs in Dynamics 365 Customer Service*
The image is referenced from https://learn.microsoft.com/

- **Omni-Channel Engagement:** Support customers across multiple channels, including email, phone, chat, and social media, from a single interface. This ensures a consistent and unified customer experience.

Figure 1.24: *Omni-Channel Engagement in Customer Service*

- **Knowledge Base**: Create and maintain a centralized repository of knowledge articles that agents can use to resolve issues quickly. Customers can also access this knowledge base for self-service support.

Figure 1.25: *Managing Knowledge Base in Customer Service*

- **Queue Management**: Organize and prioritize customer inquiries into queues, enabling support teams to focus on high-priority issues and manage workloads effectively.

Business Process Flow in Customer Service

Managing cases in Dynamics 365 helps teams handle customer issues quickly and effectively. Each step, from creating a case to resolving it, is designed to make the process smooth for both the support team and the customer. Here is a simple overview at how cases are created, assigned, and resolved to provide great service.

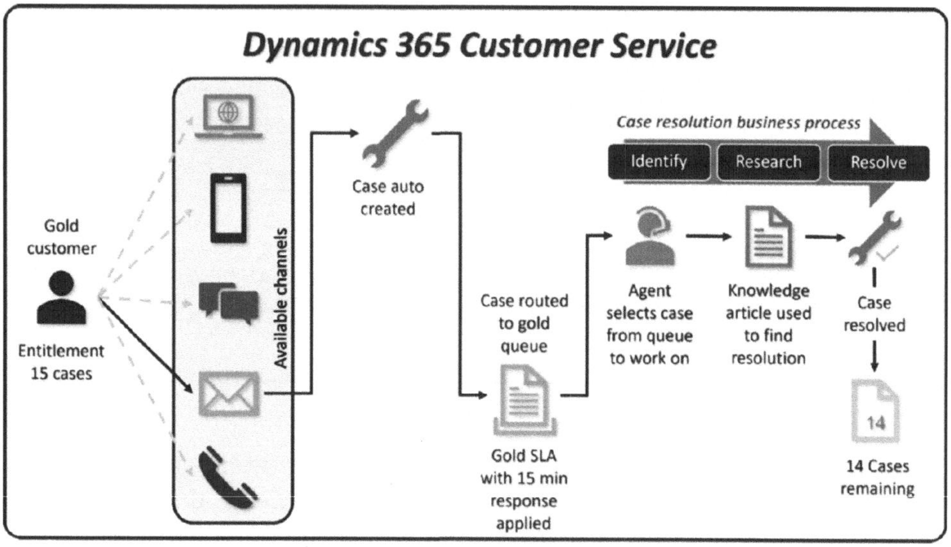

Figure 1.26: *Business Process Flow of Dynamics 365 Customer Service*
The image is referenced from https://learn.microsoft.com/

1. **Case Routing**: The case is automatically routed to the appropriate support agent or queue based on predefined rules and criteria, ensuring that the right person handles the issue.

2. **Case Management**: The assigned agent reviews the case details, contacts the customer if necessary, and begins working on a resolution. The agent may use the knowledge base, consult with colleagues, or escalate the case if needed.

3. **Customer Communication**: Throughout the case resolution process, the agent keeps the customer informed of progress via their preferred communication channel. Automated notifications and updates ensure that the customer is always in the loop.

4. **Resolution and Closure**: Once the issue is resolved, the agent updates the case status and provides the customer with a summary of the resolution. The case is then closed, and any necessary follow-up actions are scheduled.

5. **Feedback and Reporting**: After the case is closed, customers may be prompted to provide feedback on their experience. This feedback is used to improve service quality. Additionally, performance metrics are tracked and analyzed to identify areas for improvement.

Note: *A complete training course on Fundamentals of Customer Service is linked in Reference 14.*

Conclusion

In this chapter, we covered the essentials of Microsoft Dynamics 365 CRM, exploring its significance for businesses and the role of Model-Driven Apps in tailoring the system to specific needs. We also introduced Dataverse, the robust data platform behind Dynamics 365, and provided an overview of key modules including Sales, Project Operations, Field Service, and Customer Service, each designed to address distinct business functions.

With this foundation, the next chapter will dive into the prerequisites for setting up Dynamics 365 CRM. It will provide step-by-step guidance on creating user accounts, setting up environments, managing security roles, and configuring essential features to ensure a successful implementation.

References

1. Release plans for Dynamics 365, Power Platform, and Cloud for Industry - Dynamics 365 | Microsoft Learn
2. More details on Dataverse: https://learn.microsoft.com/en-us/power-apps/maker/data-platform/data-platform-intro
3. Visual Representation of Dataverse: https://danikahil.com/2023/04/microsoft-dataverse-concepts-explained.html
4. Opportunity Management in Dynamics 365 Sales: https://learn.microsoft.com/en-us/training/modules/explore-dynamics-365-sales/7-describe-opportunity-management-process
5. Product Catalog in Dynamics 365 Sales: https://learn.microsoft.com/en-us/training/modules/explore-dynamics-365-sales/6-describe-product-catalog
6. Order & Invoicing: https://learn.microsoft.com/en-us/training/modules/explore-dynamics-365-sales/9-describe-sales-order-processing
7. Training Course - Fundamental of sales module: https://learn.microsoft.com/en-us/training/paths/learn-fundamentals-of-microsoft-dynamics-365-sales/
8. Project Management in Project Operations: https://learn.microsoft.com/en-us/training/modules/get-started-project-operations/6-project-management
9. Resource Management in Project Operations: https://learn.microsoft.com/en-us/training/modules/get-started-project-operations/7-resource-management

10. Time tracking in Project Management: https://learn.microsoft.com/en-us/training/modules/get-started-project-operations/8-time-tracking
11. Expense tracking in Project Management: https://learn.microsoft.com/en-us/training/modules/get-started-project-operations/9-expense-tracking
12. Getting Started with Project Operations: https://learn.microsoft.com/en-us/training/modules/get-started-project-operations/5-sales-management
13. Fundamentals of Field Service: https://learn.microsoft.com/en-us/training/paths/learn-fundamentals-of-microsoft-dynamics-365-field-service/
14. Fundamentals of Customer Service: https://learn.microsoft.com/en-us/training/paths/learn-fundamentals-microsoft-dynamics-365-customer-service/

CHAPTER 2
Setting Up Microsoft Dynamics 365 Environments

Introduction

This chapter provides a hands-on guide to setting up Dynamics 365 CRM. We will begin by walking through the creation of user accounts to ensure everyone on your team has access to the system. Then, we will do an overview of the licensing options for Microsoft Dynamics 365.

Next, we will guide you on setting up your Dynamics 365 environments. Using examples from Project Operations and Sales, we will see how to configure the basic requirements for these applications. We will also cover setting up security roles and permissions within the Dynamics 365 environments. This includes defining and assigning roles and managing field security profiles to ensure appropriate access to sensitive information.

Data management is another key topic. We will learn how to export and import data within Dynamics 365. By the end of this chapter, we will understand how to set up and manage Dynamics 365 CRM, from creating user accounts and understanding licensing to setting up environments and managing data. The information and knowledge covered in this chapter will serve as a foundation for the next chapter, where we will explain the complete Sales to Billing cycle. This process involves both Sales and Project Operations features, highlighting how these modules work together.

Structure

In this chapter, we will discuss the following topics:

- Creating User Accounts
- Overview of Licensing

- Creating Dynamics 365 Environment
    - Power Platform Admin Center
    - Create a Dynamics 365 CRM Environment
- Users, Teams, Business Units, Security Roles, and Permissions
    - Users Set Up in Dynamics 365 CRM
    - Teams Set Up in Dynamics 365 CRM
    - Security Roles Set Up in Dynamics 365 CRM
    - Business Units in Dynamics 365 CRM
    - Field Level Security in Dynamics 365 CRM
    - Setup Dynamics 365 Project Operations
    - Setup Dynamics 365 Sales
- Data Management in Dynamics 365 (Exporting and Importing)

Creating User Accounts

A user account in Dynamics 365 CRM is essential for enabling individuals to access the system and perform their designated tasks.

Creating user accounts for Dynamics 365 CRM involves several steps, which include configuring user settings in the Microsoft 365 Admin Center.

Setting Up Microsoft 365

To get started with Dynamics 365, you typically need a Microsoft 365 subscription. To get a Microsoft 365 subscription follow these steps:

1. Go to the Microsoft 365 Business Signup page (see **Reference 1**).
2. Select a plan as per your requirements, such as Microsoft 365 Business Standard.

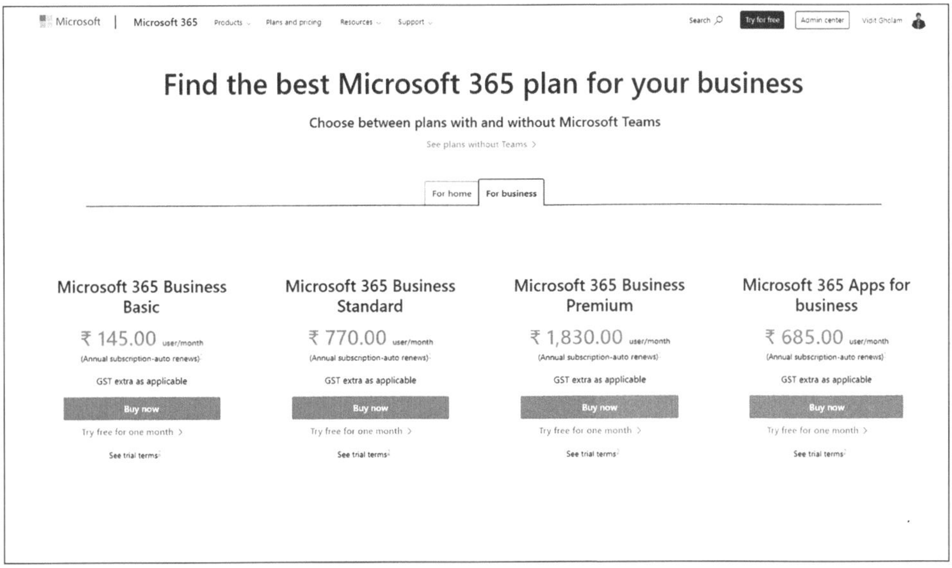

***Figure 2.1**: Microsoft 265 Plans*

3. Enter your business information, including your organization's name, address, and contact details.
4. Create a new Microsoft account by providing an email address and setting a password.

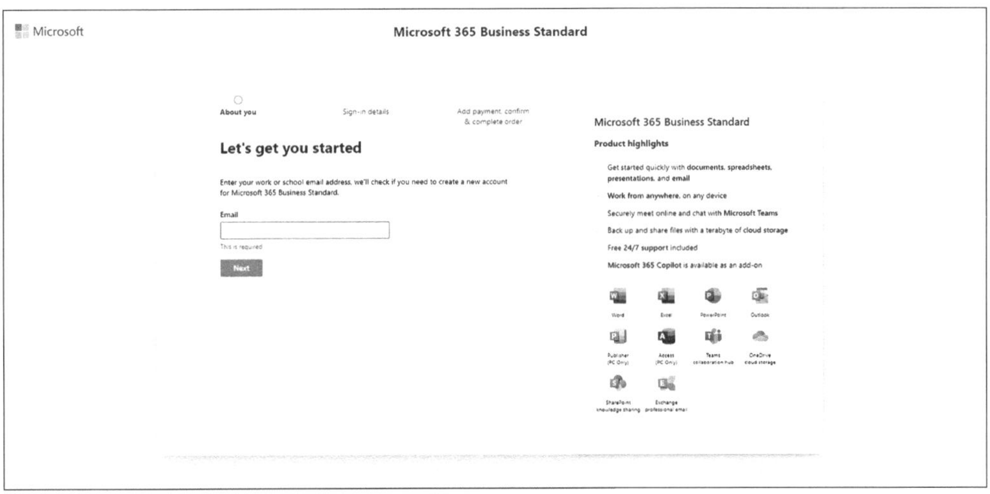

***Figure 2.2**: Customer Details Screen*

- Follow the prompts to complete the setup. You will be provided with an admin account for managing your Microsoft 365 subscription.
- After setting up your Microsoft 365 subscription, you can navigate to the **`Microsoft Admin Center`** to create user accounts.

Microsoft 365 Admin Center

Go to admin.microsoft.com and sign in with the admin account credentials created during the signup process while setting up Microsoft 365.

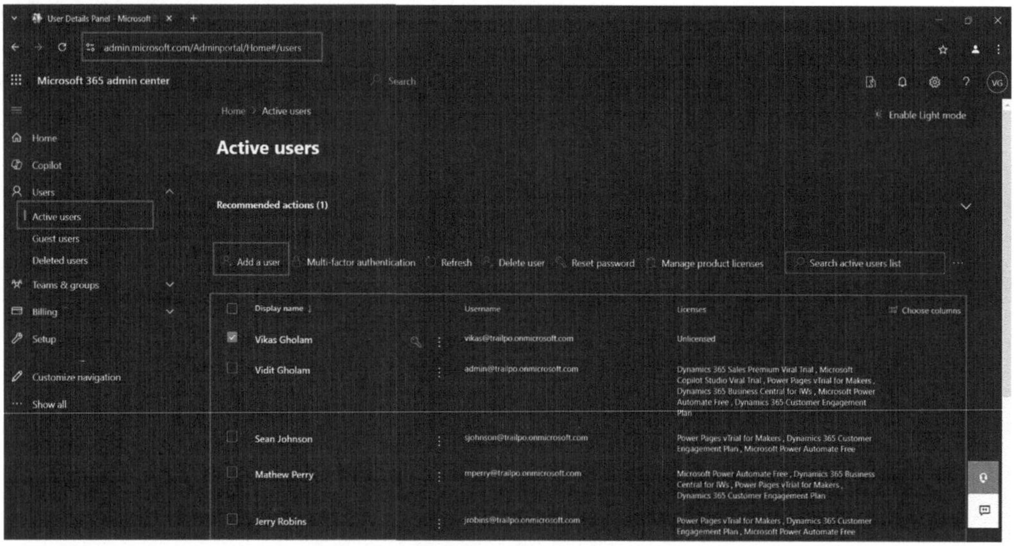

***Figure 2.3**: Microsoft 365 Admin Center*

- In the left navigation bar, you will see the following options:
    - **`Active Users`** are individuals who have been assigned a Microsoft 365 license and have full access to the services and applications included in their subscription. These users are typically employees or members of the organization.
    - **`Guest Users`** are external users who are granted limited access to specific Microsoft 365 resources. This feature is often used for collaboration purposes, allowing partners, vendors, or customers to access certain files or join Teams meetings without having a full Microsoft 365 account within the organization.
    - **`Deleted Users`** are user accounts that have been removed from the active user list. These accounts are typically retained in a "soft delete" state for a period (usually 30 days) before being permanently deleted. This grace period allows administrators to recover the account if necessary.
    - Under **`Active Users`**, click **`Add Users`**. Fill in the required fields such as **`First name`**, **`Last name`**, **`Display name`**, and **`Username`**.
- Choose the domain for the user (for example, user@yourcompany.onmicrosoft.com).

- Set password options (auto generated or manually create a password).
- Choose whether the user must change the password on the first login.

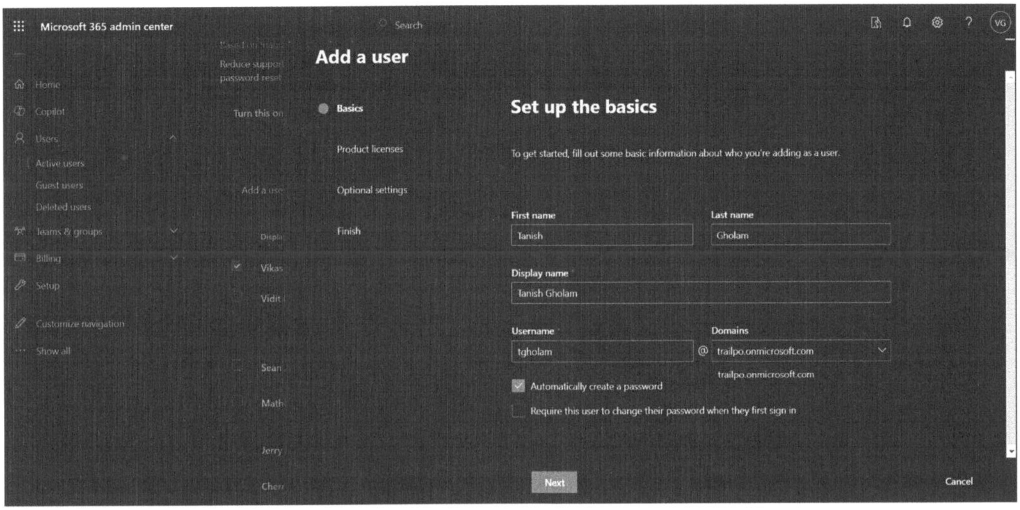

Figure 2.4: Adding User

- Select the appropriate license for the user (licensing is covered later in this chapter).

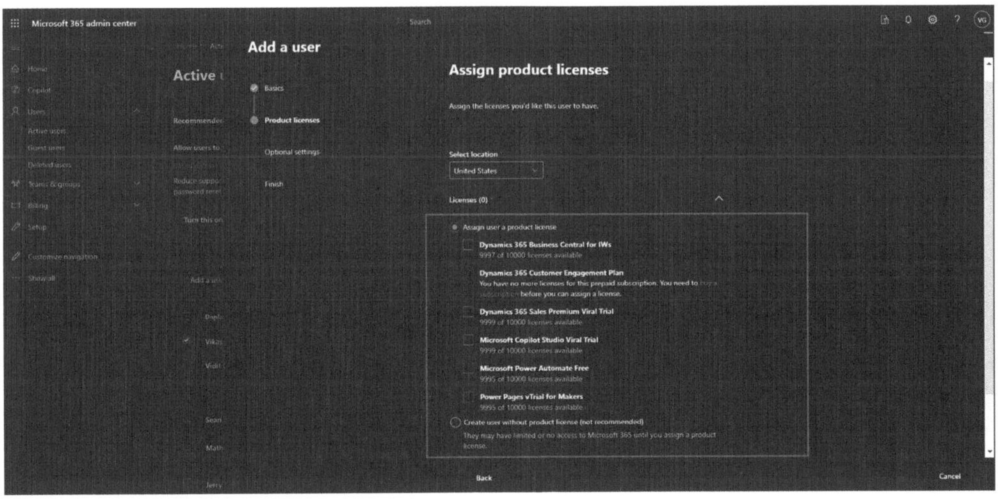

Figure 2.5: Assign Licenses

- You can set administrative privileges to the user if necessary and fill in the user details.

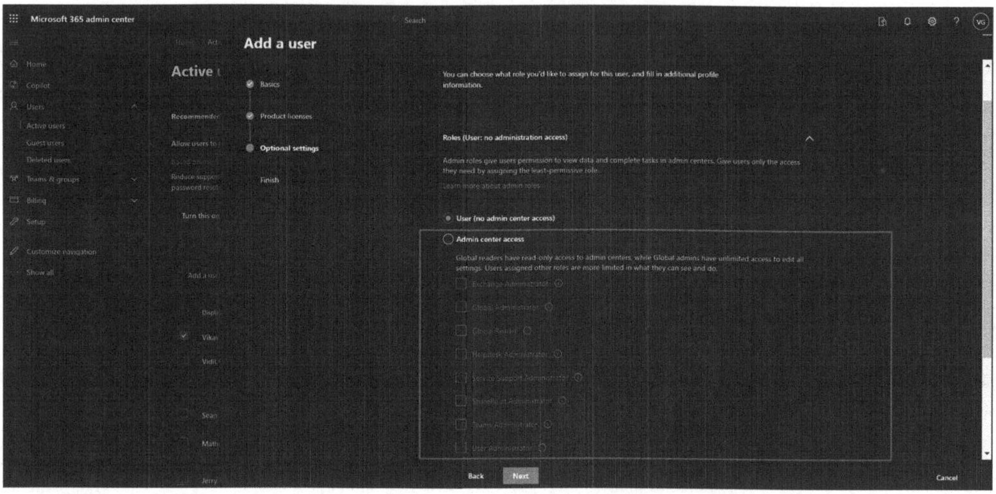

Figure 2.6: *User Privileges and Details*

The following figure illustrates the user information page:

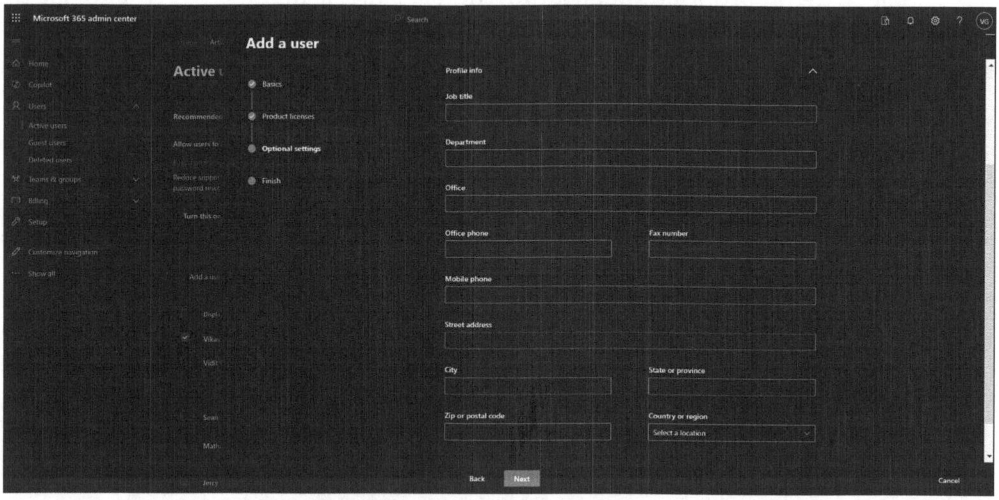

Figure 2.7: *User Information Page*

  - Complete the steps and click **`Finish`** adding to create the user.

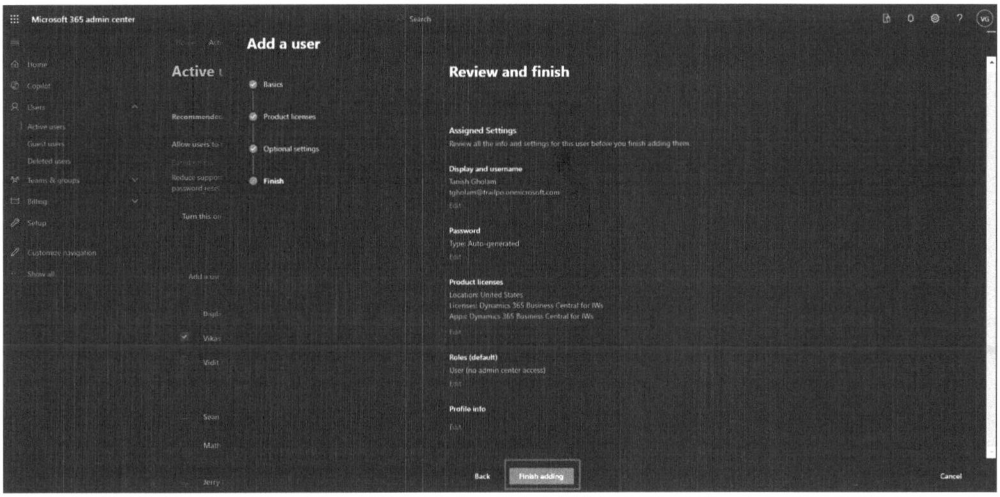

***Figure 2.8**: Adding a User in Microsoft Admin Center*

Now that we have learned about creating user accounts for getting started with your Dynamics 365 CRM journey, let us look at the licensing for Dynamics 365 CRM.

Overview of Dynamics 365 CRM Licensing

Licensing for Dynamics 365 CRM is structured to provide flexibility based on the specific needs and roles within an organization. What licensing you choose depends upon various factors, such as which app/model you are implementing, Sales, Project Service, Field Service, Customer Service, and more.

Dynamics 365 offers a variety of licenses to cater to different business needs and user roles. Here is an overview of the main types:

- **Subscription Licenses: User**

  This is for individual users who need access to the Dynamics 365 services. It is further categorized into:

  - **Full User Access Licenses (User):** For users who need extensive access to the application, such as sales managers or customer service reps.
  - **Additional User Access Licenses (Team Member):** For users who require limited access, such as team members who only need to view data and reports.
  - **Device:** Ideal for shared devices used by multiple workers on the shop floor or in a retail environment.

  - **Organization:** These are scenarios where an entire organization needs access to the services.
- **Assigned Licenses:** These are tied to specific users and provide access to various Dynamics 365 applications based on the role and needs of the user.
- **Unassigned Licenses:** These licenses are not tied to individual users but are available for anyone in the organization to use as needed.
- **Full Application Access Licenses:** These licenses provide access to individual Dynamics 365 applications, including Sales, Customer Service, Project Operation, and more.
- **Cross-Application Access Licenses:** These allow users to access features across multiple Dynamics 365 applications without needing separate licenses for each.
- **Capacity Licenses:** These are for additional storage or other capacity needs beyond what's included with the user or device licenses.
- Each license type is designed to offer flexibility and scalability to businesses, ensuring that users have the right tools to perform their roles effectively.

Let us delve into the specifics of Dynamics 365 licenses with some examples to make it easier for you to understand. We will begin by gaining an understanding of the various subscription licenses for Dynamics 365 CRM.

Dynamics 365 User Subscription Licenses

Dynamics 365 offers various user subscription licenses tailored to different user roles and needs. The primary license types are as follows:

- **Enterprise**: For full access to all capabilities, ideal for core users. For example, "`Dynamics 365 Plan`" gives access to all applications.
- **Professional**: For users who need to access specific business apps fully. For instance, "`Dynamics 365 Sales Professional`" is tailored for sales teams.
- **Team Members**: For light users who need to perform basic tasks such as time/expense entry and HR record updates.

Following are the licensing details for `Dynamics 365 Sales`, as of 2024 (see **Reference 2** for more information).

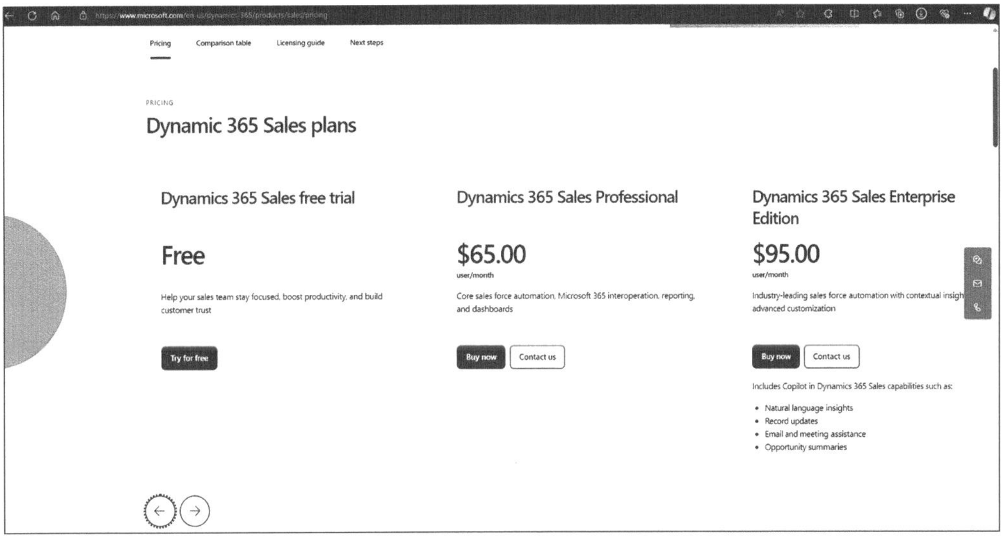

Figure 2.9: *Dynamics 365 Sales Licensing Details*

- **Dynamics 365 Team Members License:**
  - This is a light-use license that allows users to view and report on Dynamics 365 data and take part in workflows.
  - For more details, please refer to the link from Reference 3.
- **Power Apps/Power Automate Licensing:**
  - For users who need to create or run standalone applications with Power Apps or automate workflows with Power Automate.
- **Dynamics 365 Attach Licenses:**
  - These are discounted licenses for users who need a second Dynamics 365 app. For example, a user with "**`Dynamics 365 Sales`**" might add "**`Dynamics 365 Customer Service`**" as an attached license.
- **Dynamics 365 Capacity Add-Ons:**
  - For additional storage or sandbox environments. An example is the "**`Dynamics 365 Extra Storage`**" add-on.
  - These licenses are designed to be mixed and matched to fit the unique needs of your business and its users.

Buying a Dynamics 365 CRM Licenses

Purchasing Dynamics 365 CRM licenses can be typically done in two types:

- **Contact a Microsoft Partner or Reseller (Recommended)**

  Microsoft Partners and Resellers are authorized to sell Dynamics 365 licenses. Contact them to discuss your organization's requirements and get assistance with purchasing licenses.

- **Self-Service Purchase**

  If you prefer not to contact a Microsoft Partner or Reseller and want to purchase Dynamics 365 CRM licenses directly, Microsoft provides options for self-service purchasing through their online portals. Here's how you can do it:

  - **Access Microsoft 365 Admin Center:**
    - `Sign In`: Go to admin.microsoft.com and sign in with your admin credentials which you just created at the beginning of this chapter or use an existing admin account if you already have one.
  - **Navigate to Purchase Services**
    - Go to `Billing`: In the left-hand navigation pane, click `Billing` > `Purchase Services`.

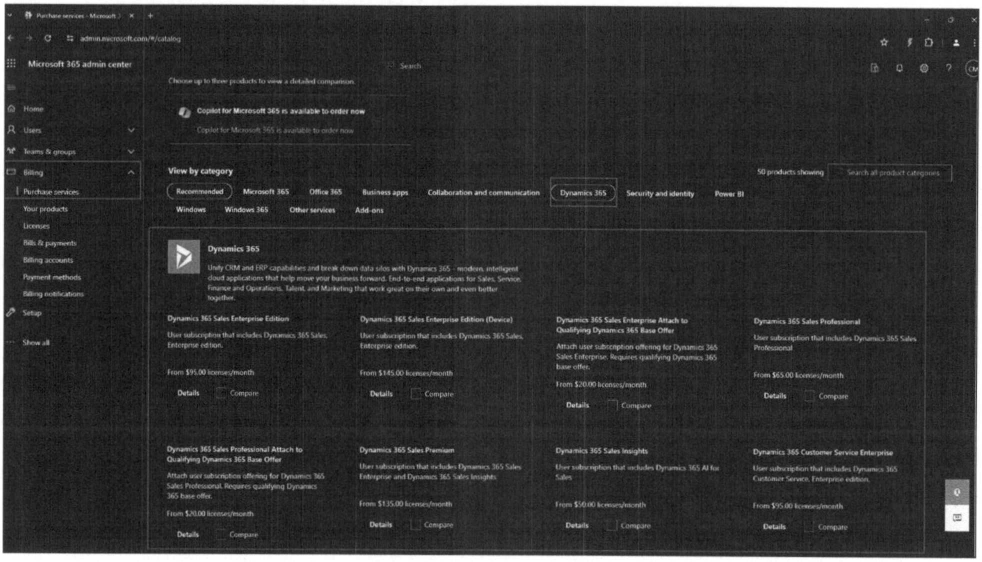

***Figure 2.10**: Purchase Services in Microsoft Admin Centre*

- **Select Dynamics 365 CRM Licenses**
  - **Choose Products**: Browse or search for Dynamics 365 CRM licenses you wish to purchase, such as Dynamics 365 Sales, Customer Service, or Team Member licenses.

  - o **Add to Cart**: Select the licenses you need and add them to your cart.
- **Review and Purchase**
  - o **Review Details**: Check the details of the licenses in your cart, including quantities and pricing.
  - o **Proceed to Checkout**: Follow the prompts to proceed to checkout and complete the purchase.
  - o You will be able to see all the purchased licenses under the license option in the admin center.

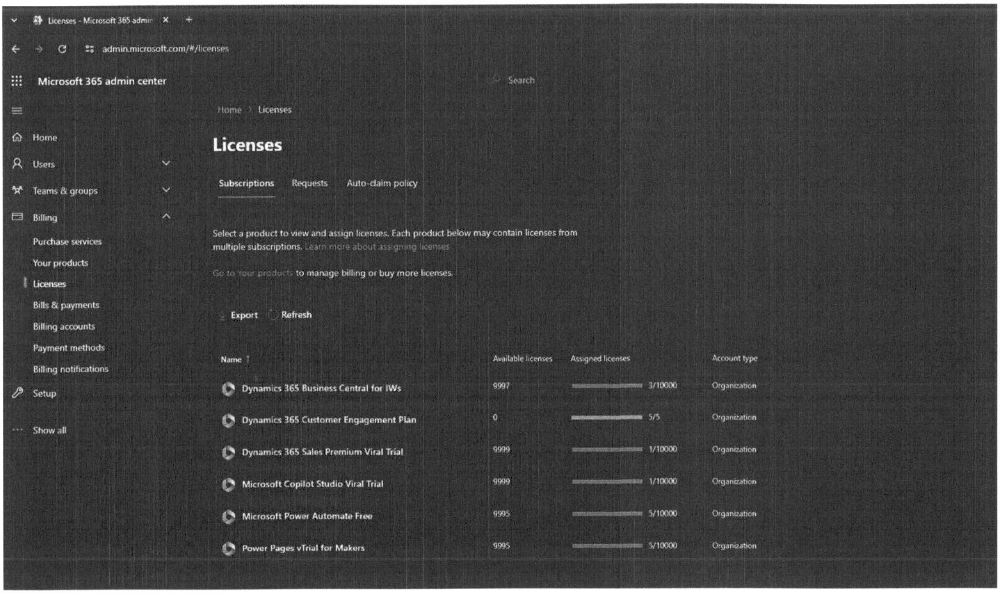

Figure 2.11: *Purchased Licenses*

- **Assign Licenses to Users**
  - o **Assign Licenses**: After purchasing, go to **`Users`** > **`Active users`** in the Microsoft 365 Admin Center.

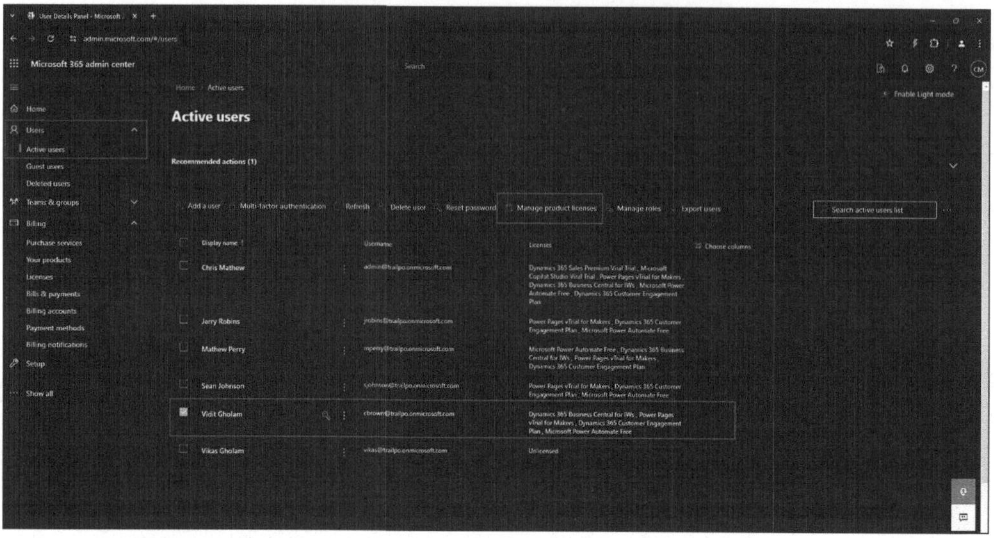

Figure 2.12: *Assigning Licenses to Users*

- **Assign Licenses**: Select the user(s) you want to assign licenses to, then assign the purchased Dynamics 365 CRM licenses.

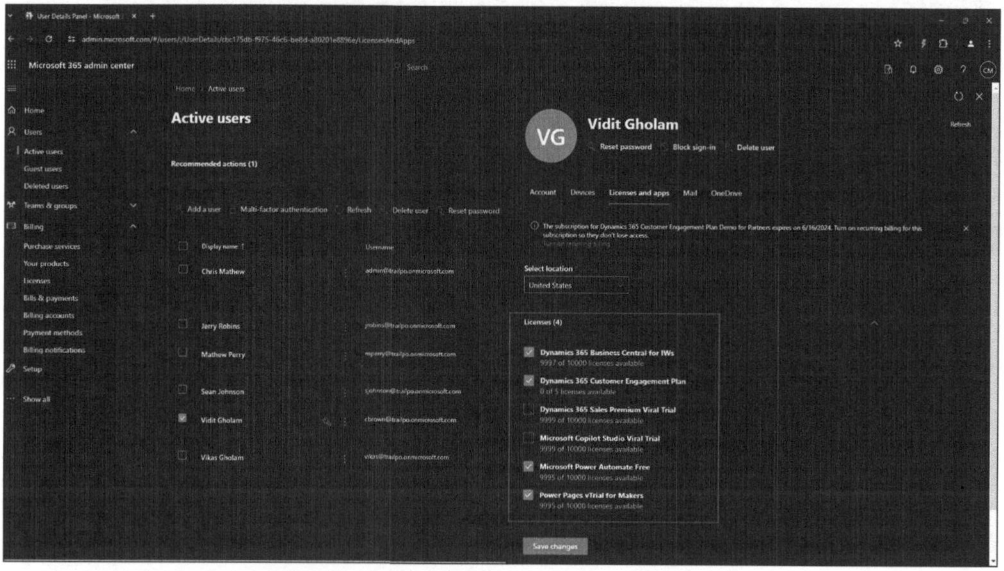

Figure 2.13: *Assigning the Purchased Licenses to Users*

For more details on the licensing in Dynamics 365 and Pricing, refer to **References 4** and **5**.

Disclaimer: *Microsoft Dynamics 365 licenses can vary depending on the region due to differences in local pricing, regulations, and support. Prices are adjusted based on regional economic conditions and currency exchange rates, so the cost may differ* *from one country to another. Additionally, regional data privacy laws, like the GDPR in Europe, can affect where and how your data is stored and processed. Microsoft also provides localized features and language support tailored to specific regional needs. All the licenses and costs in this book are with respect to the United States region, please make sure to go through the available licenses and services specific to your regions.*

It is also important to note that licensing for Dynamics 365 is subject to frequent updates and changes. To ensure you are working with the most current information, we recommend referring to the official Dynamics 365 Licensing Guide referenced in Reference 20. This guide provides the latest details on licensing options, pricing, and any recent updates, helping you make informed decisions about which licenses best suit your business needs.

Free Trials: *Microsoft offers free trials for various Dynamics 365 models, allowing users to explore the specific functionalities of each model.*

- *Sign Up for a Free Trial: Visit the official Microsoft Dynamics 365 website and sign up for a free trial (https://www.microsoft.com/en-in/dynamics-365/free-trial). You will need a Microsoft account to create an account, and once registered, you will get access to a full set of features for a limited period.*
- *Complete the Setup: Once signed up, you can configure your trial instance by selecting which Dynamics 365 modules you'd like to try, such as Sales, Customer Service, or Field Service. You will also define your organization's name and some basic setup details.*
- *Admin Role: The account you use to sign up will automatically be granted the System Administrator role, which provides full access to all features and settings of your trial environment.*

With this trial environment, you can begin exploring the capabilities of Dynamics 365 CRM. If you need to manage users or assign roles, you can do so through the Microsoft 365 Admin Center, where you can add users and configure permissions.

Now that we have successfully created user accounts and covered the basics of licensing, we are ready to move on to the next part: setting up a Dynamics 365 environment.

This is where we will configure the system and start utilizing the features of Dynamics 365. This section explains how to create and set up your environment.

Let us get started!

Creating a Dynamics 365 Environment

To begin creating an environment, you will use the **`Power Platform admin center`**.

Power Platform Admin Center

The Power Platform Admin Center is a portal that enables administrators to manage Microsoft Power Platform products, including Dynamics 365, Power Apps, Power Automate, and Power BI. This centralized management hub offers a wide range of functionalities to help oversee environments, applications, and data integrations.

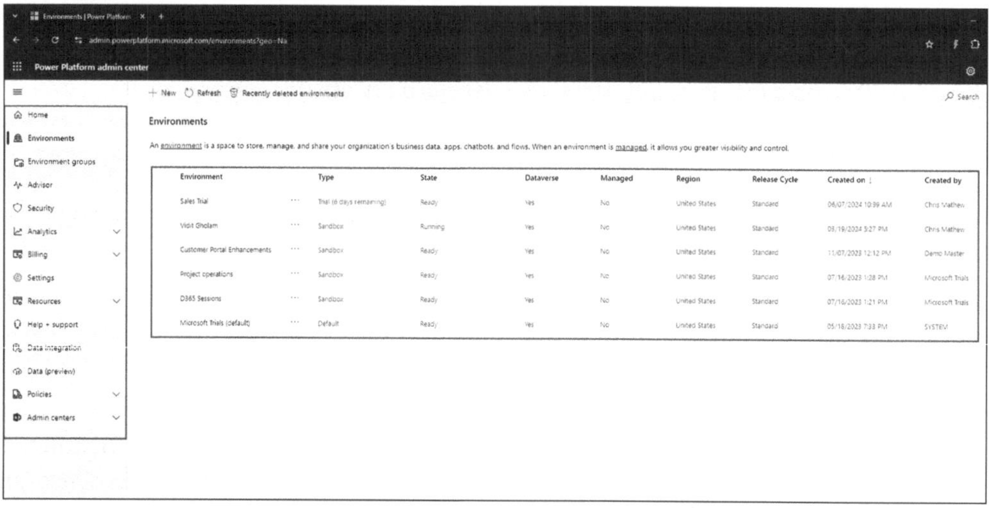

Figure 2.14: *Power Platform Admin Center*

Following is the list of functionalities that **`Power Platform admin center`** offers.

Create New Environments:

1. Administrators can create new environments for development, testing, or production purposes. This includes selecting environment types such as Production, Sandbox, Trial, and Developer.

    a. **Production**: The live environment used for daily business operations with real data.

    b. **Sandbox**: A non-production environment for testing, training, and experimenting with changes.

    c. **Trial**: A temporary environment (usually 30 days) to explore and evaluate features before purchase.

    d. **Developer**: An environment for developers to build and test custom apps, plugins, and integrations.

2. Environments can be configured with a Dataverse database, specifying base language and default currency. When creating a new environment in Dynamics

365 CRM, selecting a base language and currency is crucial as they define the default settings for the environment:

a. **Base Language**: Determines the default language of the user interface, labels, and system messages. Once set, it cannot be changed, but additional languages can be enabled later for user preferences.

b. **Base Currency**: Sets the default currency for financial transactions and reports. While multiple currencies can be added later, the base currency serves as the foundation for currency conversion and reporting.

3. Environments With or Without Dataverse Database

   The decision to create an environment with or without a Dataverse database depends on its intended use:

   a. **With Dataverse**:

      i. Choose this option if you plan to use full Dynamics 365 apps, such as Sales, Customer Service, or Field Service, which need a place to store customer records, transactions, or other business data.

      ii. It's also required when you want to connect different systems, automate tasks, or store related data (for instance, linking customer orders to their details).

      iii. In short, use this for a complete, functional system that works with all Dynamics 365 features.

   b. **Without Dataverse**:

      i. This option is suitable for simpler needs, such as testing or building basic apps that don't need to store large amounts of data within the system.

      ii. It's commonly used when apps only pull data from outside systems or use external storage, saving costs by not including Dataverse.

      iii. Think of it as a lighter version for specific, less complex tasks.

For most business use cases, environments with Dataverse are essential, but choosing one depends on how much functionality is needed. In this chapter, we will be creating an environment with Dataverse.

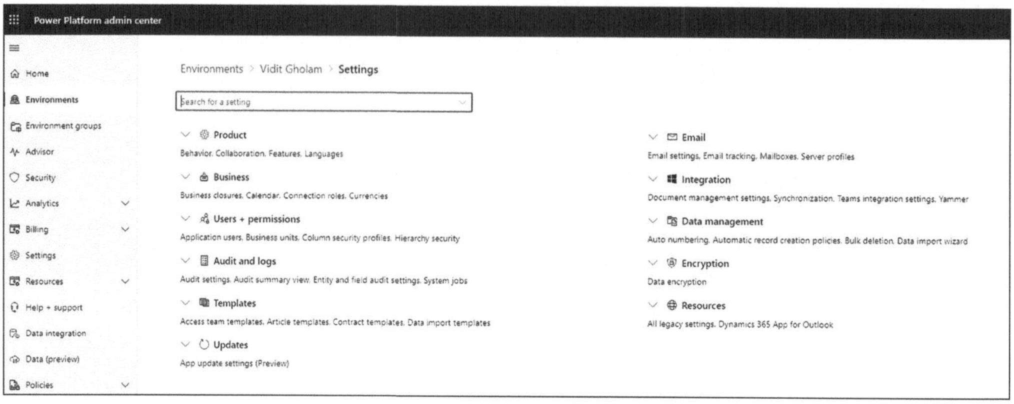

***Figure 2.15**: Environment Settings in Power Platform Admin Center*

User and Security Management

- **User Management**: Add and manage users, assigning appropriate roles and licenses to ensure they have the necessary access to Power Platform and Dynamics 365 applications.
- **Security Roles and Permissions**: Define and manage security roles, controlling access to data and features based on user roles within the organization.
- Implement field-level security and record-based security to maintain data sensitive information.
- **Data Policies:** Configure data loss prevention policies to control data sharing across connectors and environments.

Data Integration and Management

- **Data Integrations**: Set up and manage data integrations between Dynamics 365 and other external systems or services. Use connectors to integrate with a wide range of data sources, ensuring seamless data flow and consistency.
- **Dataverse Management**: Manage Dataverse databases, including schema definition, data import/export, and data quality monitoring.

Analytics and Insights

- **Monitor Usage**: Access detailed usage reports and analytics to understand how Power Platform and Dynamics 365 applications are being utilized within the organization.

  Identify trends, monitor application performance, and make data-driven decisions.
- **Capacity Management**: Monitor and manage storage capacity, ensuring that environments have sufficient resources to operate efficiently.

Creating a Dynamics 365 CRM Environment

Let us begin creating an environment.

Step 1: Access the Power Platform Admin Center

Go to the `Power Platform admin center` and sign in with your admin credentials.

Step 2: Create a New Environment

a. **Navigate to Environments:** In the left-hand navigation pane, click Environments.

b. **Create New Environment:** Click `+ New` to start creating a new environment.

c. **Enter Environment Details:** Enter a name for your environment (for example, "`Sales Environment`" or "`Project Operations Environment`" or "`{Company Name} _ {PROD/UAT/DEV}`").

d. **Type:** Select the type of environment. Options include Production, Sandbox, Trial, and Developer.

e. **Region:** Choose the region where the environment will be hosted. (Please note as mentioned earlier in this chapter, Dynamics 365 services may vary from region to region)

f. **Purpose:** Optionally, you can add a description or specify the purpose of this environment.

g. **Configure Database:** Add a Dataverse Database, check the option to add a Dataverse database.

h. **Language:** Choose the base language for your environment.

i. **Currency:** Select the default currency for your environment

j. **Security Groups:** Assign a security group to your environment. This can essentially be a M365 group, such as Global Admins or Sales Admins. If you don't want to assign any security group, you can select None as an option.

   i. It is recommended to assign a security group, assigning a security group to a Dynamics 365 environment is a smart way to control who can access it.

   ii. A security group is like a list of people who are allowed to use the environment. For example, you could have a group for sales team members or administrators.

   iii. By assigning a security group, only the people in that group can access the environment, making it more secure and organized.

iv. It also makes managing access easier–just add or remove people from the group, and their access updates automatically.

v. If you don't assign a group, everyone with a license might get access, which could cause security or privacy issues. So, assigning a security group is a good way to keep the environment safe and manageable.

k. **URL:** Set the URL for your Dynamics 365 environment.

All these steps are shown in *Figure* 2.16 and *Figure* 2.17.

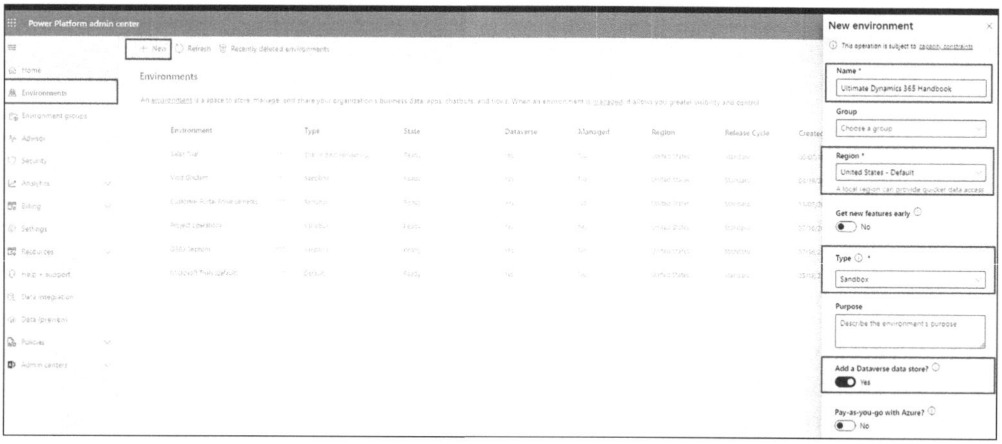

***Figure* 2.16**: *Creating Environments in Power Platform Admin Center*

Step 3: Enable Dynamics 365 Apps:

a. When you create an environment in the Power Platform Admin Center, you can install and configure applications, such as Dynamics 365 Sales and Customer Service (see *Figure* 2.17) when creating an environment, even before assigning user licenses. This is possible because the process of creating an environment and installing applications is separate from the process of assigning licenses to users. Here is how it works:

i. The environment creation process involves setting up the infrastructure and configuring the settings where Dynamics 365 applications will run. This includes choosing the region, setting up a database, and installing the applications you plan to use.

ii. You can install applications such as Dynamics 365 Sales, Customer Service, Field Service, and more, within the environment. Installing these applications makes them available in the environment, but users cannot access or utilize these applications until they have the appropriate licenses assigned.

iii. After setting up the environment and installing the necessary applications, you need to assign the appropriate licenses to users. Only users with the required licenses will be able to access and use the installed applications.

b. **Click Save:** After filling in the necessary details, click Save to create the environment.

c. It will take a few seconds time to get the environment configured and ready.

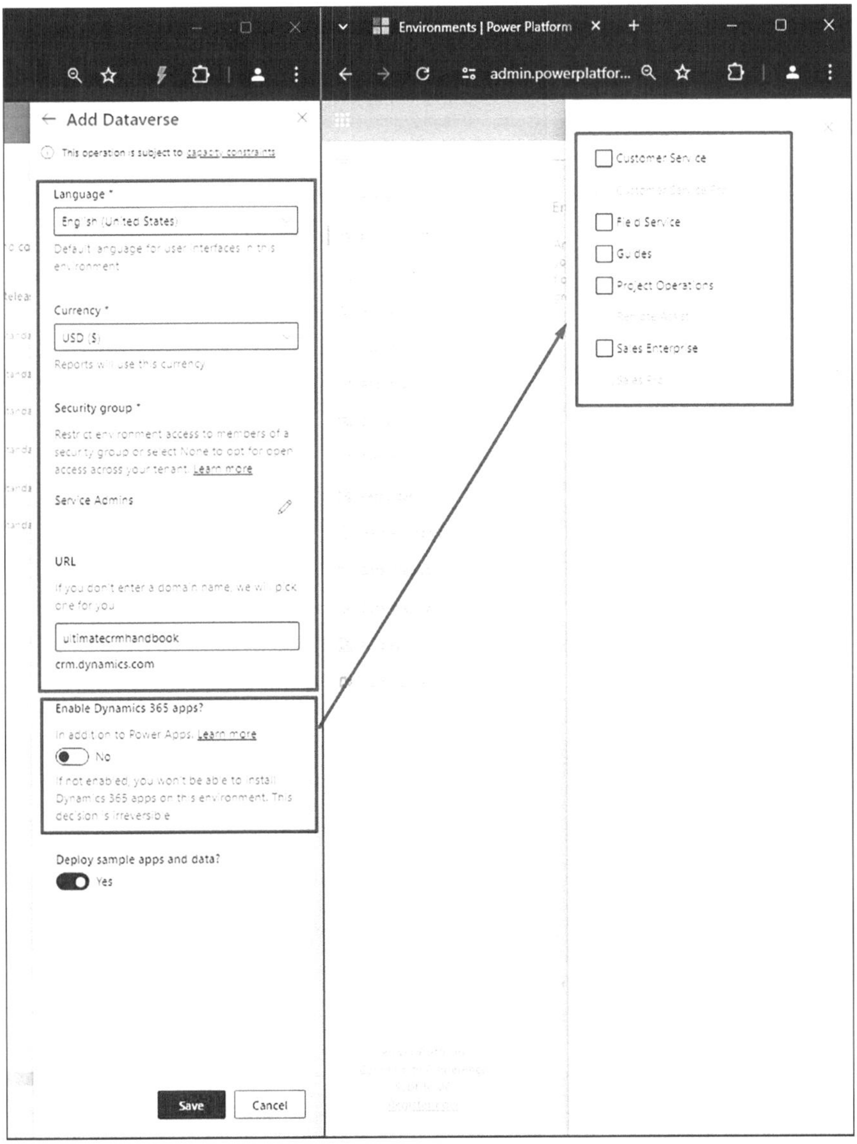

Figure 2.17: *Creating Environments in Power Platform Admin Center*

You can also install Dynamics 365 Applications after you have configured an environment.

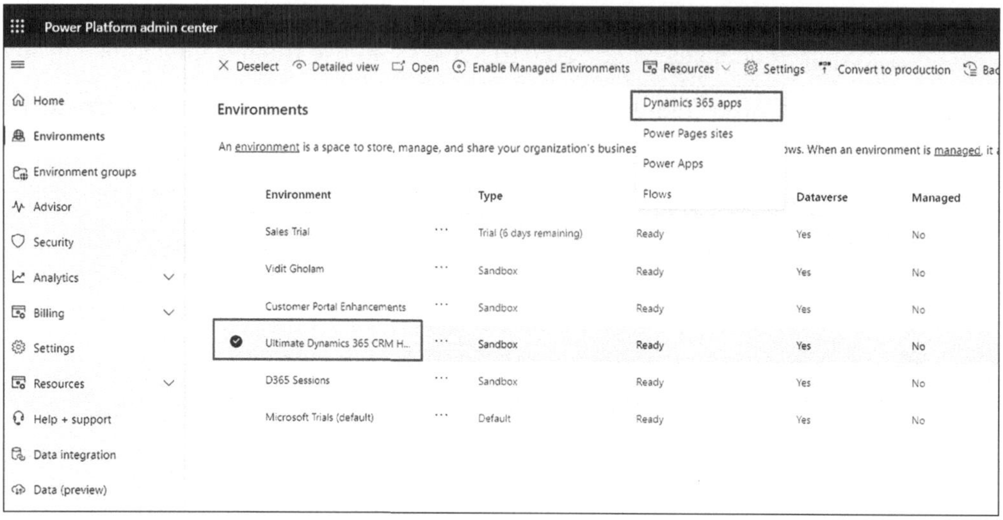

Figure 2.18: *Creating Environments in Power Platform Admin Center*

To install an application, select desired environment, then navigate to **`Resource`**> **`Dynamics 365 Apps`**. You will see all the applications you have installed, and can install the desired services, as shown in *Figures* 2.18 and 2.19.

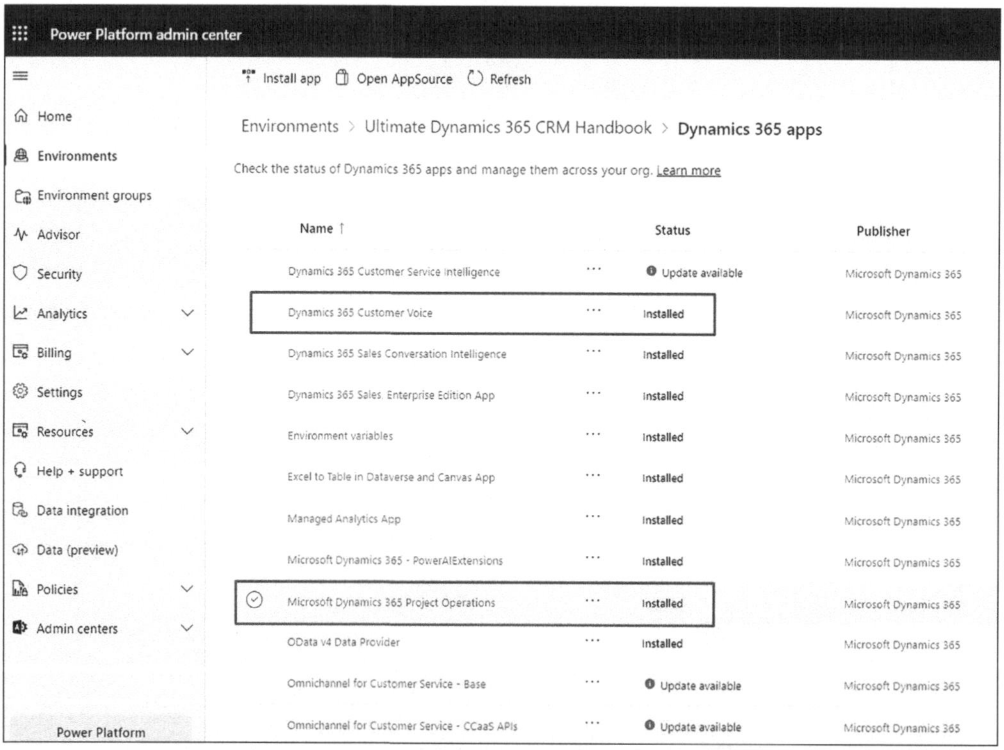

Figure 2.19: *Creating Environments in Power Platform Admin Center*

Users, Teams, Business Units, Security Roles, and Permissions

Now that we have created an environment, let us proceed to add users, creating teams and assign them appropriate security roles.

Users Set Up in Dynamics 365 CRM

Adding users to any environment is simple. To add a user, first select the environment you want to add the user to, then click **Settings** (see *Figure 2.20*).

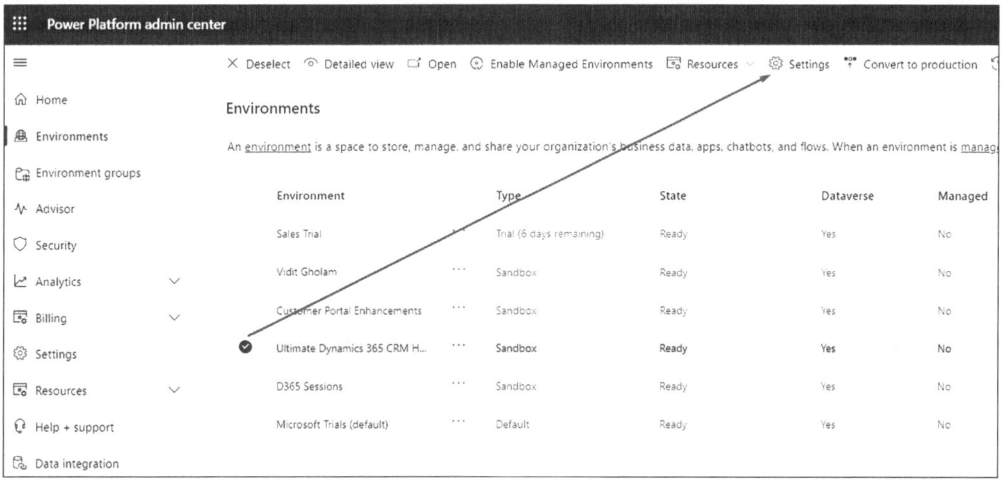

***Figure 2.20**: Environment Settings*

In the setting area under **Users + permissions**, you will see **Security roles** and **Users** (see *Figure 2.21*).

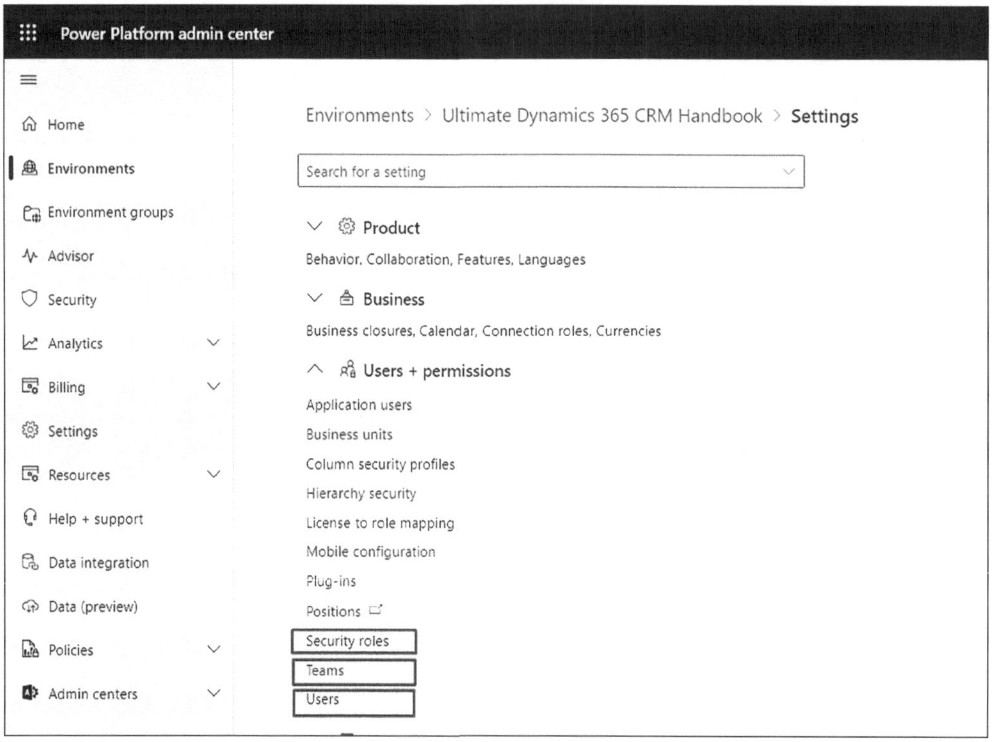

***Figure 2.21**: User Permissions Settings Area – step 1*

Click the "**`Users`**" option to view the list of all users already added to the environment. Click "**`Add user`**," then search for the user you want to add in the dialog box and click "**`Add`**." Remember, you need to first add the user in the **`Microsoft Admin Center`** and assign the appropriate license, as we discussed earlier in this chapter.

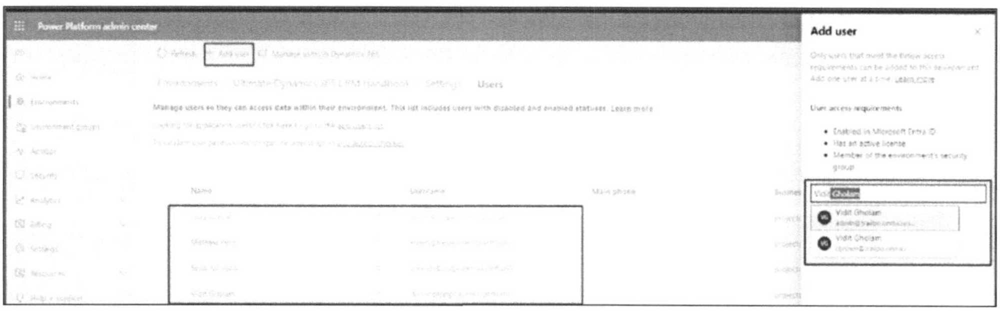

***Figure 2.22**: User Permissions Settings Area– step 2*

Teams Set Up in Dynamics 365 CRM

A team in Dynamics 365 is a group of users who can share records and collectively manage activities, facilitating collaborative work within the organization. Teams can be used to simplify security management and enhance teamwork by allowing role-based access to records and entities. Teams are of two types:

Owner Teams:

- **Ownership**: Owner teams can own records. The members of the team inherit the team's privileges for records owned by the team.
- **Security Roles**: You can assign security roles directly to the team, and all members of the team will inherit these roles.
- **Use Cases**: Ideal for scenarios where a group of user's needs to collectively own and manage records.

Access Teams:

- **Access**: Access teams do not own records but provide access to records. They are used to grant specific record-level permissions to users without assigning a security role.
- **Team Templates**: Use templates to define the access rights that the team will have on a particular record.
- **Use Cases**: Useful for scenarios where temporary access to specific records is needed, such as project-based work or task forces.

Microsoft Entra Group Teams:

- In Dynamics 365 CRM, Microsoft Entra group teams are another type of team that organizations can use to simplify access and collaboration.
- These teams are linked to Microsoft Entra ID (formerly Azure Active Directory) groups, allowing all group members to inherit the same security roles and permissions in CRM. This type of team is especially useful for managing dynamic or large groups, as membership updates in Entra automatically reflect in Dynamics 365. By using group teams, administrators can efficiently manage access and enhance collaboration across CRM features.
- For more information on Microsoft Entra Groups, please refer to the link provided in **Reference 21**.

To create a team, start by selecting an environment and clicking "**`Settings`**". Then, under "**`Users + Permissions`**", navigate to "**`Teams`**" as shown in *Figure* 2.23.

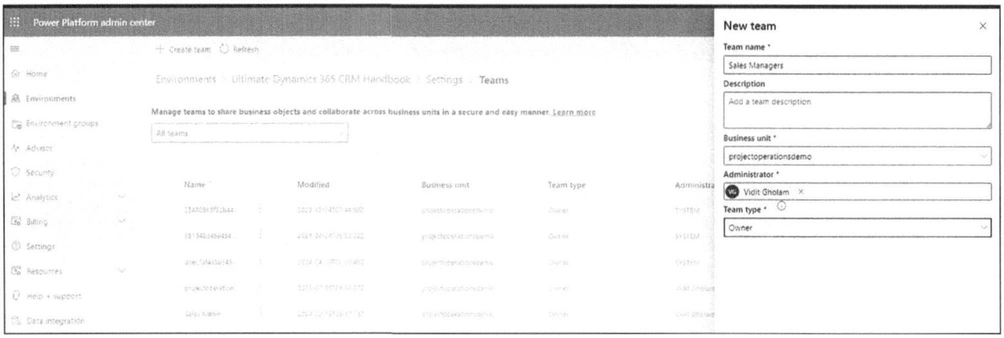

Figure 2.23: *Creating Teams in Dynamics 365 Environment*

Click the "**`Create Team`**" option, provide a suitable name for your team, specify the business unit, assign an administrator, and select the team type. Then, add members to the team and click "**`Save`**" to complete the setup, see *Figures* 2.23 and 2.24.

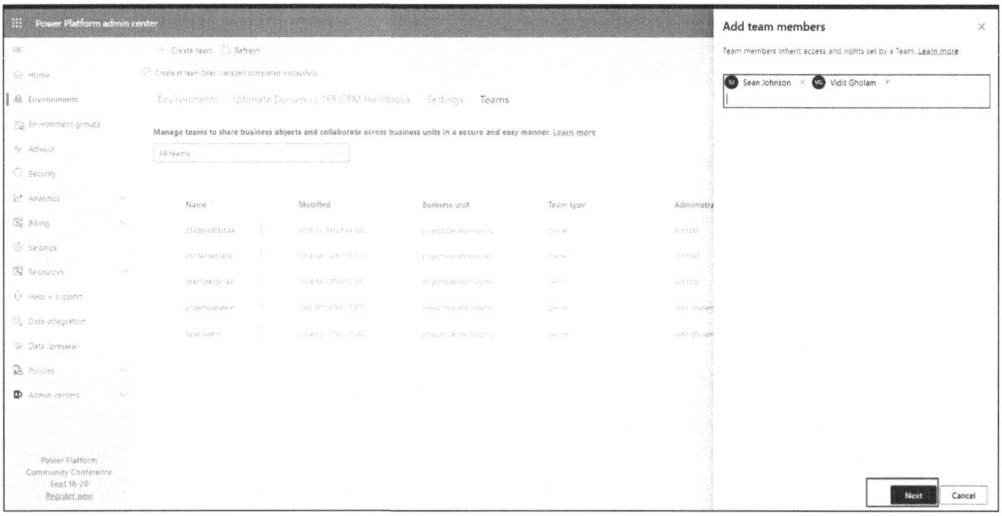

Figure 2.24: *Adding Team Members to the Team*

Let us now look into security roles and assign them to the users and teams.

Security Roles Set Up in Dynamics 365 CRM

Security roles are sets of privileges and permissions assigned to users to control their access to various parts of the Dynamics 365 environment. These roles help safeguard sensitive information and ensure users can only perform actions relevant to their responsibilities.

Security roles are a combination of two key components: Privileges and Access Levels.

- **Privileges**: Privileges define the type of actions a user can perform on entities (records) within Dynamics 365. Common privileges include Create, Read, Write, Delete, Append, Append To, Assign, and Share.

- **Access Levels**: Access levels determine the scope within which the user can perform their actions. These levels include:
    - **None**: No access to the record or function.
    - **User (Basic)**: Access to records owned by the user.
    - **Business Unit (Local)**: Access to records owned by the user's business unit.
    - **Parent (Deep)**: **Child Business Units**: Access to records owned by the user's business unit and its child units.
    - **Organization (Global)**: Access to all records within the organization.

Security roles can be categorized in two types: Standard Security Roles and Custom Security Roles.

Standard Security Roles

Dynamics 365 CRM comes with predefined security roles that cover common business scenarios related to each model driven apps. Examples include Salesperson, Customer Service Representative, System Administrator, and Marketing Manager. These roles can be assigned directly or customized to fit specific needs. Some examples of standard roles that are available out-of-the-box in the sales and customer service module are listed as follows:

Dynamics 365 Sales:

- Salesperson:
    - **Privileges**: Create, read, write, delete, and share records related to leads, opportunities, accounts, contacts, quotes, orders, and invoices.
    - **Access Levels**: Typically, access is scoped to user or business unit level.
- Sales Manager:
    - **Privileges**: Inherits all Salesperson privileges plus additional capabilities to manage sales teams, forecast sales, and analyze sales performance.
    - **Access Levels**: Higher than Salesperson, usually including business unit or parent: child business units.
- Vice President of Sales:
    - **Privileges**: Broad access to sales data and reports across the organization.
    - **Access Levels**: Organization-wide access to oversee the entire sales process.

Dynamics 365 Customer Service:

- Customer Service Representative:
  - **Privileges**: Create, read, write, and resolve cases, manage activities and knowledge articles.
  - **Access Levels**: Typically, user or business unit level.
- Customer Service Manager:
  - **Privileges**: Inherits Customer Service Representative privileges plus the ability to manage service queues, assign cases, and monitor service metrics.
  - **Access Levels**: Higher access, usually at the business unit level or parent: child business units.
- Knowledge Manager:
  - **Privileges**: Manage and publish knowledge articles, ensuring up-to-date information for service reps.
  - **Access Levels**: Usually scoped to the organization or business unit.

Custom Security Roles

Organizations can create custom security roles tailored to their unique requirements. This involves defining specific privileges and access levels for various entities and functions. Custom roles provide flexibility and granular control over user permissions.

You can customize security roles by either creating new ones or modifying existing standard roles to suit your needs. To begin, navigate to the security roles section as shown in *Figure* 2.22. Here, you will find a list of all existing and custom security roles. To create a new role, click the "`Create`" option and proceed with defining the security role. *(For more details on When roles is assigned to a Team option, refer to Reference* 6.)

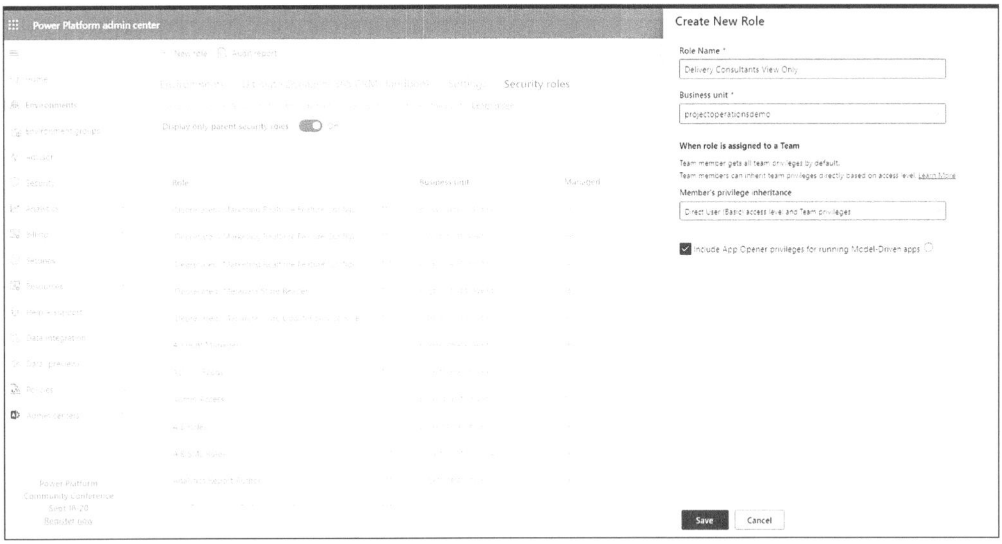

Figure 2.25: *Creating Security Role in Power Platform Admin Center*

After creating the role define privileges (**`Create`**, **`Read`**, **`Write`**, **`Delete`**, **`Append`**, **`Append To`**, **`Assign`**, **`Share`**) for core records such as accounts, contacts, leads, and opportunities.

Go through other tabs (for instance, Business Management, Service Management) to define additional privileges. For each privilege, set the appropriate access level: **`None`**, **`User`**, **`Business Unit`**, **`Parent: Child Business Units`**, or **`Organization`**.

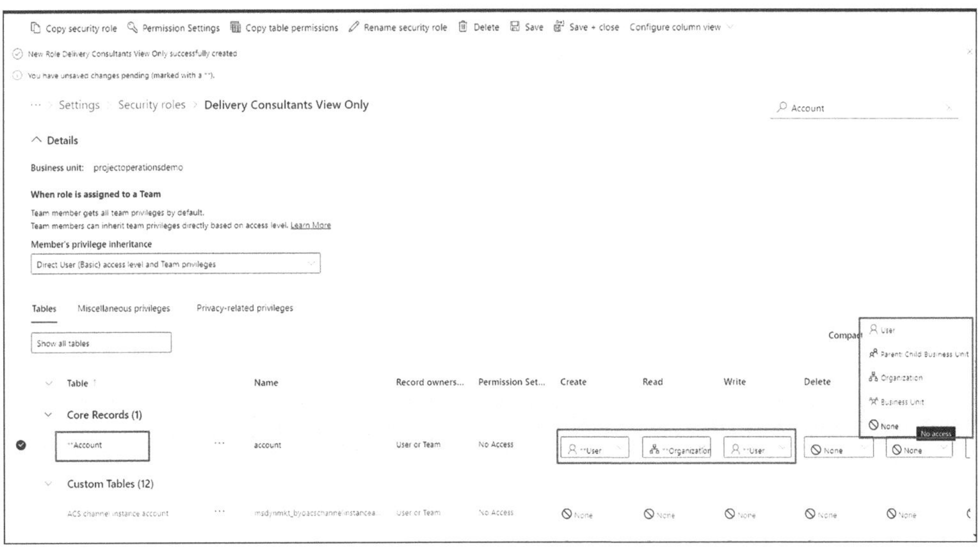

Figure 2.26: *Setting Privileges and Access Levels in Security Roles*

The final step is to assign security roles to users and teams. Navigate to the users and team's section, select the user or team to which you want to assign roles, click "**`Manage Security Roles`**," and proceed to assign the roles accordingly.

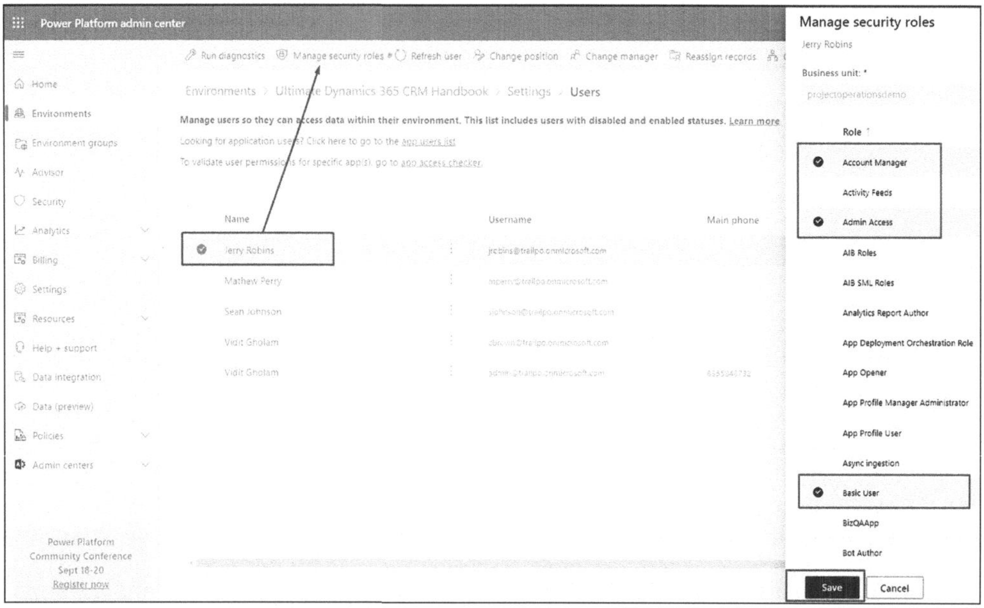

***Figure 2.27**: Assign Security Roles to Users*

Business Units in Dynamics 365 CRM

Business units in Dynamics 365 CRM are organizational structures used to manage and segregate data, security, and processes within an organization. They help define the hierarchy and scope of operations, allowing for effective management and control of different parts of the organization.

Let us take an example: Universal Technology Corporation is a multinational technology company that operates in multiple regions around the world, offering a range of products and services including hardware, software, and consulting services.

The structure of their business units can be as follows:

Parent Business Unit (BU):

Universal Technology Corporation: This is the root business unit representing the entire corporation.

- Regional BU:
  - **Americas**: This business unit oversees operations in North and South America.

  - **EMEA** (Europe, Middle East, and Africa): This business unit oversees operations in the EMEA region.
  - **APAC** (Asia-Pacific): This business unit oversees operations in the Asia-Pacific region.
- Country-Specific BU:
  - **USA**: Under the Americas business unit, managing operations in the United States.
  - **Canada**: Under the Americas business unit, managing operations in Canada.
  - **UK**: Under the EMEA business unit, managing operations in the United Kingdom.
  - **Germany**: Under the EMEA business unit, managing operations in Germany.
  - **Japan**: Under the APAC business unit, managing operations in Japan.
  - **Australia**: Under the APAC business unit, managing operations in Australia.
- Departmental BU:

  USA:

  - Sales USA: Manages sales operations in the USA.
  - Support USA: Manages customer support operations in the USA.

  UK:

  - Sales UK: Manages sales operations in the UK.
  - Support UK: Manages customer support operations in the UK.

When you set up any Dynamics 365 environment, the default business unit created is called the "`Root Business Unit`". This business unit is the top-level entity in the organizational hierarchy and cannot be deleted or disabled. All examples in this book are only with respect to a single business unit, that is the default business unit.

Note: *For more details on business units, refer to the links in References 7 and 8.*

Field Level Security in Dynamics 365 CRM

Field-level security in Dynamics 365 CRM enables organizations to control access to specific fields within entities based on user roles. This capability ensures that sensitive information, such as financial data or personal details, is only accessible to authorized individuals or teams. By defining field-level security profiles and permissions, administrators can restrict who can view or edit sensitive fields, maintaining data confidentiality and compliance with organizational policies and regulatory requirements. Field-level security enhances data protection without restricting access to entire records, thereby optimizing user productivity and safeguarding critical information within Dynamics 365 CRM.

We will explore this in detail in *Chapter 4, Customizing Your Dynamics 365 CRM*; see **Reference 19** for this chapter.

Setup Dynamics 365 Project Operations

Next, we will set up the newly created environment. Setting up a Dynamics 365 CRM environment involves initially configuring essentials, such as currency, organizational units, and roles necessary for application functionality. Subsequently, each application is customized to meet specific business needs, including setting up workflows, customizing forms, importing data, and implementing custom business logic through code. While detailed coverage of these aspects will be provided later in this chapter and upcoming ones, let us begin by exploring basic configurations essential for operating a Dynamics 365 Model-driven Application.

Let us take an example and set up a Project Operations environment. Before proceeding, it is recommended to review the Project Operations module, its features, and the Business Process Flow discussed in *Chapter 1, Introduction to Microsoft Dynamics 365 CRM*.

All the setup is with respect to the Project Operation Lite Deployment (*For more details on Project Operations deployments, refer to the link in Reference* 9).

Following is the checklist for the Project Operation Setup. Let us go through each of the items in detail:

1. Force Sync Users (Optional)
2. Set up Bookable Resources
    a. Create Work Hours Template
    b. Assign Work Hours Template to the Bookable Resource(s)
3. Set up Resource Categories (Roles)
4. Set up Transaction Categories (Expense Type) and Expense Categories
5. Set up Invoicing Frequency
6. Set up Price Lists
7. Set up Organization Units

1. **Force Sync Users (Optional)**

    This step is completely optional, Force Syncing essentially means adding users manually to the environment like we did in the user setup section of this chapter referring to *Figure* 2.22. If you have recently provisioned a new environment, it is essential to sync users to that environment. This step is necessary to ensure that the users are available when creating Bookable Resources in the subsequent step. Additionally, assign the appropriate security roles to these users as needed.

2. **Set Up Bookable Resources**

   In Dynamics 365 Project Operations, bookable resources refer to any entities (people, equipment, facilities) that can be scheduled or allocated to projects, tasks, or service activities. These resources are essential for planning and executing projects efficiently, ensuring that the right resources are available at the right time.

   a. Navigate to the **`Resource Group`** by accessing the **`Change Area`** on the site map of **`Project Operations`**.

   b. Within the **`Resource Group`**, select "**`Resources`**" and click "**`New`**" to proceed.

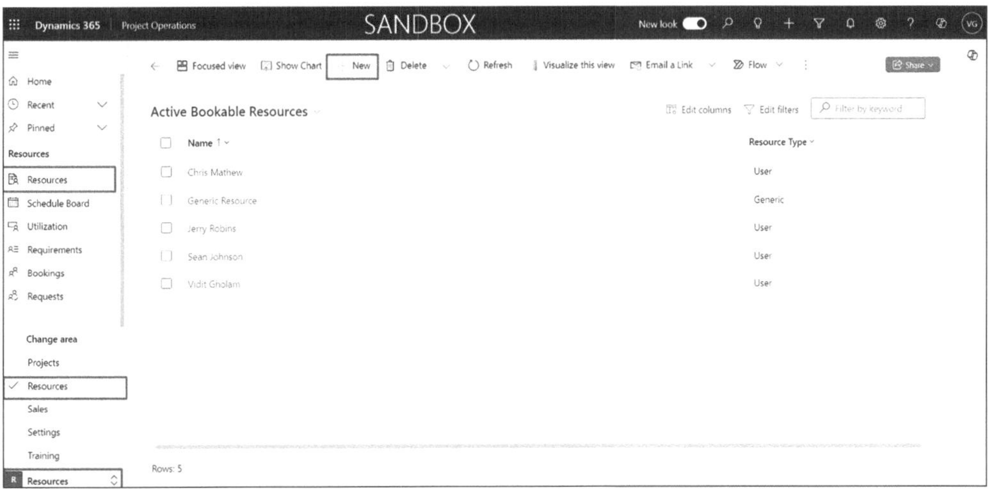

***Figure 2.28**: Creating Bookable Resources*

c. Enter the resource type as "**`User`**" for setting up user-bookable resources. Specify the Type of Worker (**`Employee`** or **`Contract Worker`**), set the time zone of the bookable resource, and click "**`Save`**". :

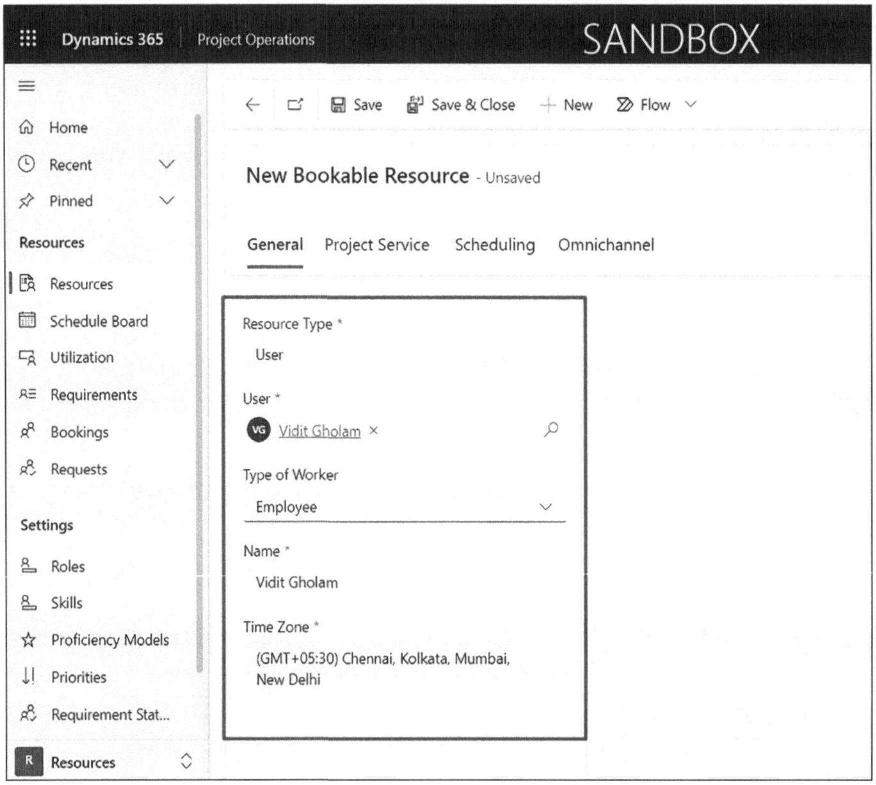

Figure 2.29: *Creating Bookable Resources*

d. Once the bookable resource is created, click "**Work Hours**" to set up the working hours. In the **Work Hours** tab, click "**New**" to add new work hours.

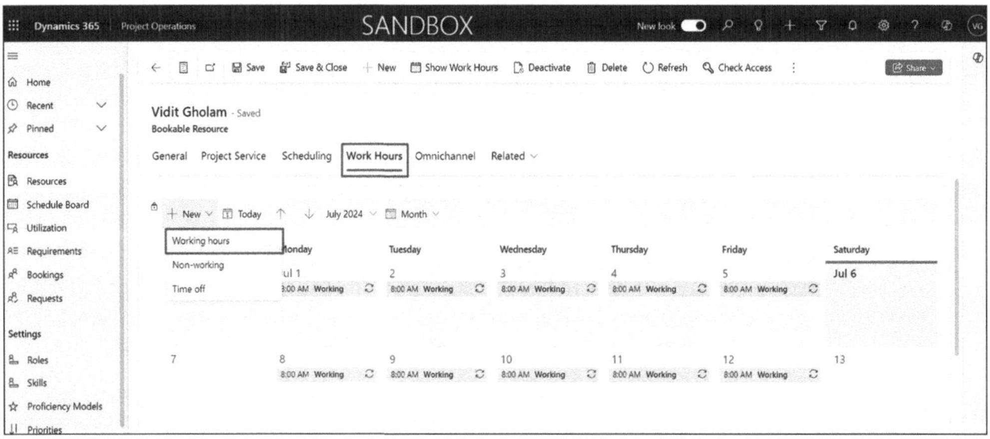

Figure 2.30: *Creating Work Hours for Bookable Resource*

e. Enter the details as shown in *Figure* 2.31 according to your requirements, then click "**Save**".

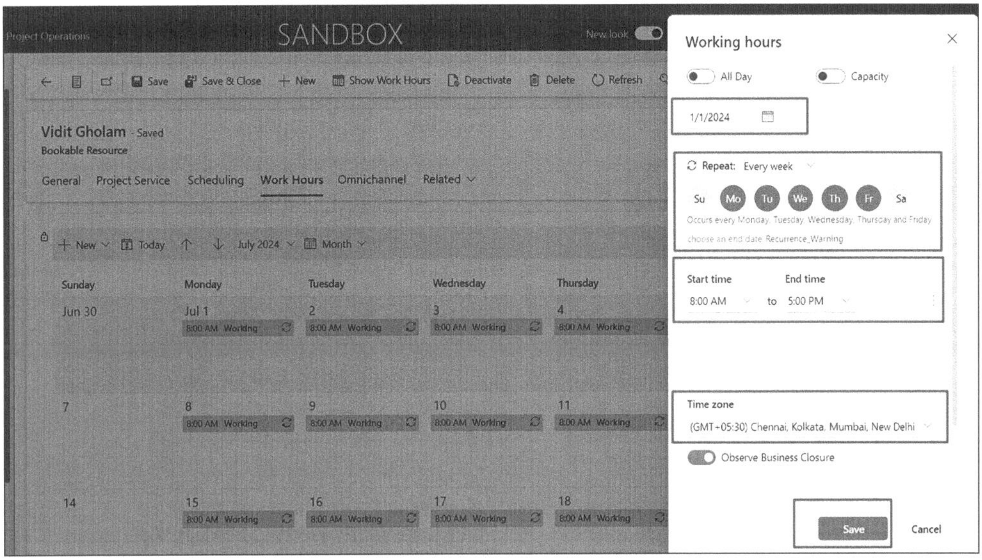

Figure 2.31: *Set Up Work Hours Parameters for The Bookable Resource*

f. If you have multiple resources with the same work hours, set up the work hours for a single resource first. Then, create a calendar template using these work hours. To create a calendar template, navigate to "`Settings`" from the Change Area on the site map and go to **`Calendar Templates`**. You can use this template to apply the same work hours to other resources.

g. Create a calendar template from the resource you have set up.

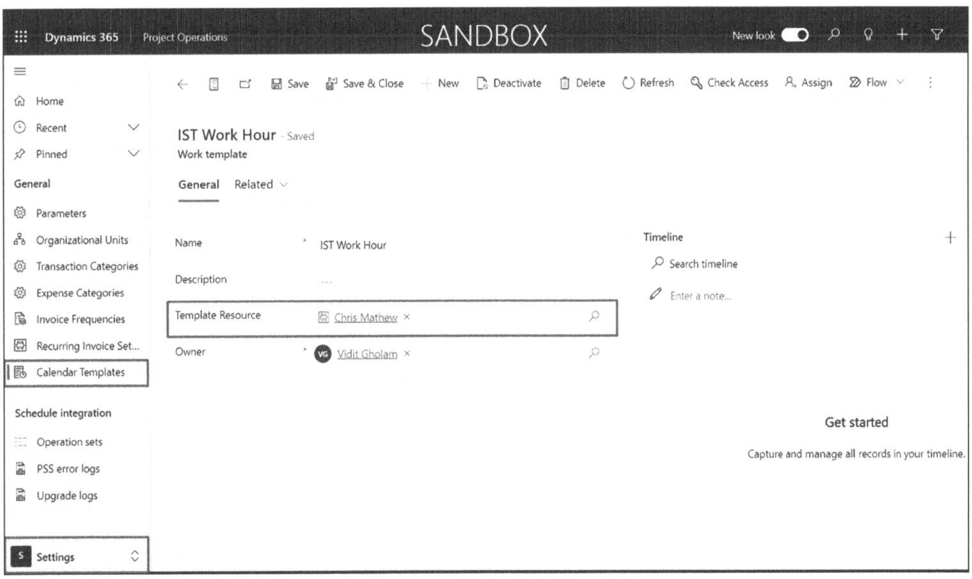

Figure 2.32: *Creating a Calendar Template*

h. Once you have created a calendar template, return to the Resources section. From the home screen, choose the resources for which you wish to set the work hours. Select the appropriate calendar template and click "**Apply**" to assign the template's work hours to the selected resources.

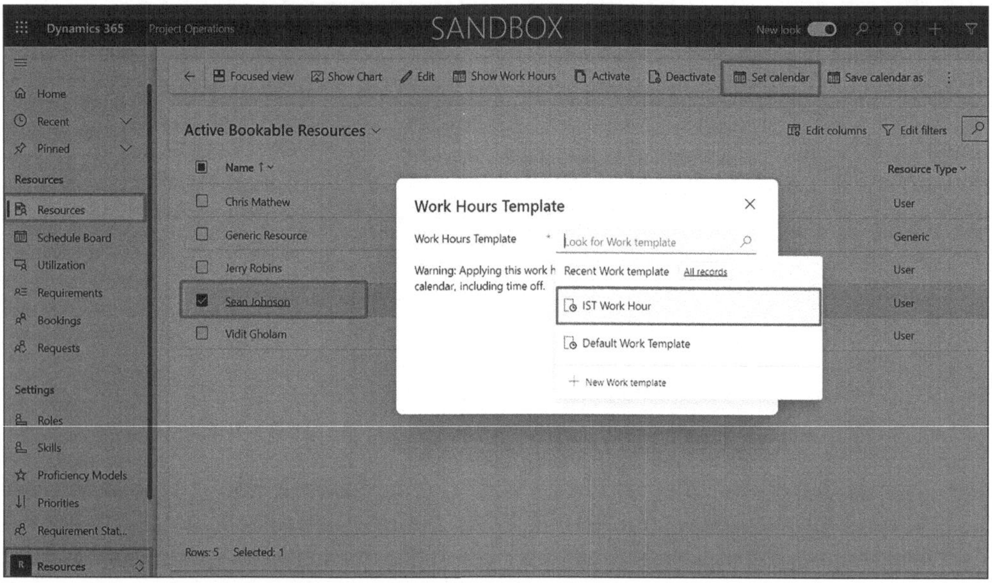

***Figure 2.33**: Applying Calendar Templates to Resources*

3. **Set Up Resource Categories (Roles)**

   In Project Operations, resource categories are called roles, they are classifications used to organize and manage resources based on their skills, roles, or types within projects. These categories help streamline resource allocation, scheduling, and cost management by categorizing resources into groups such as consultants, technicians, or specific skill sets like software developers or project managers. By defining resource categories, organizations can efficiently match the right resources to projects, optimize utilization, and ensure projects are staffed appropriately to meet client needs and project requirements.

   To create a role, navigate to the "**Resources**" section from the change area on the site. Under the "**Settings**" group, select "**Roles**" and click the "**New**" button to initiate the creation of a new role.

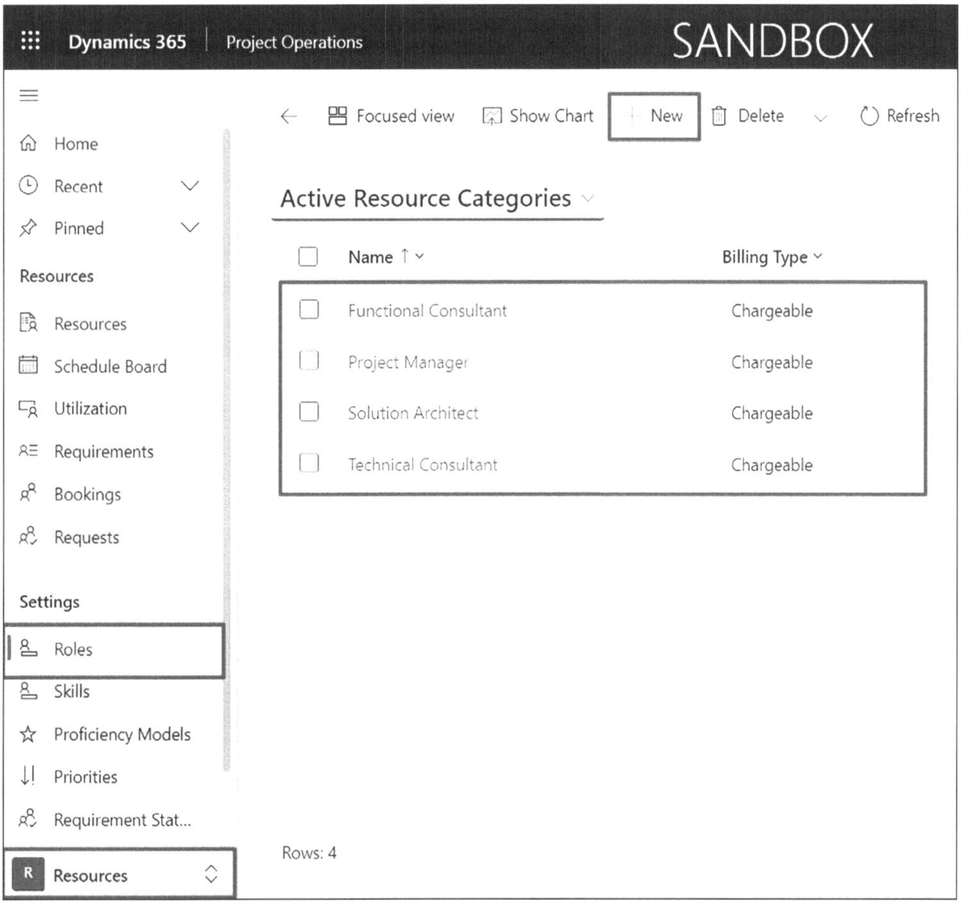

***Figure 2.34**: Creating Resource Categories in Project Operations*

Once you have created the role, you can enter some role parameters such as target utilization of the resource, and billing type. Let us examine these parameters in detail:

- **Target Utilization:** In Project Operations, target utilization refers to the percentage of time that a role or resource is expected to be actively engaged in billable or productive work within a specified period, typically measured over a week, month, or year. It serves as a benchmark or goal for how efficiently resources should be utilized on projects.
- **Billing Types**: In Project Operations, billing types such as "`chargeable`," "`non-chargeable`," and "`complementary`" categorize how resources' time and expenses are treated for billing purposes:
    - **Chargeable**: Time and expenses for these resources are billed directly to clients or projects, typically based on agreed-upon rates or pricing structures.
    - **Non-Chargeable**: These resources' time and expenses are not billed

to clients or projects. They may be used for internal tasks, training, or administrative purposes.

- **Complimentary**: Resources categorized as complimentary may provide services or products free of charge, often for promotional or goodwill purposes, without invoicing clients.

- **Skills and Professions:** In Project Operations, skills and professions refer to the specific capabilities and professional qualifications that individuals or teams possess, which are essential for carrying out tasks and responsibilities within projects. These attributes help define the expertise and capabilities needed to effectively execute project tasks and deliverables.
  - **Skills**: Skills in `Project Operations` denote the specific competencies and capabilities that individuals possess, such as technical skills (for instance, programming languages, software proficiency) or soft skills (for instance, communication, leadership).
  - **Professions**: Professions refer to the broader professional qualifications or roles individuals hold, such as Project Manager, Software Engineer, Consultant, or Specialist in a particular field (for example, Finance, Marketing).

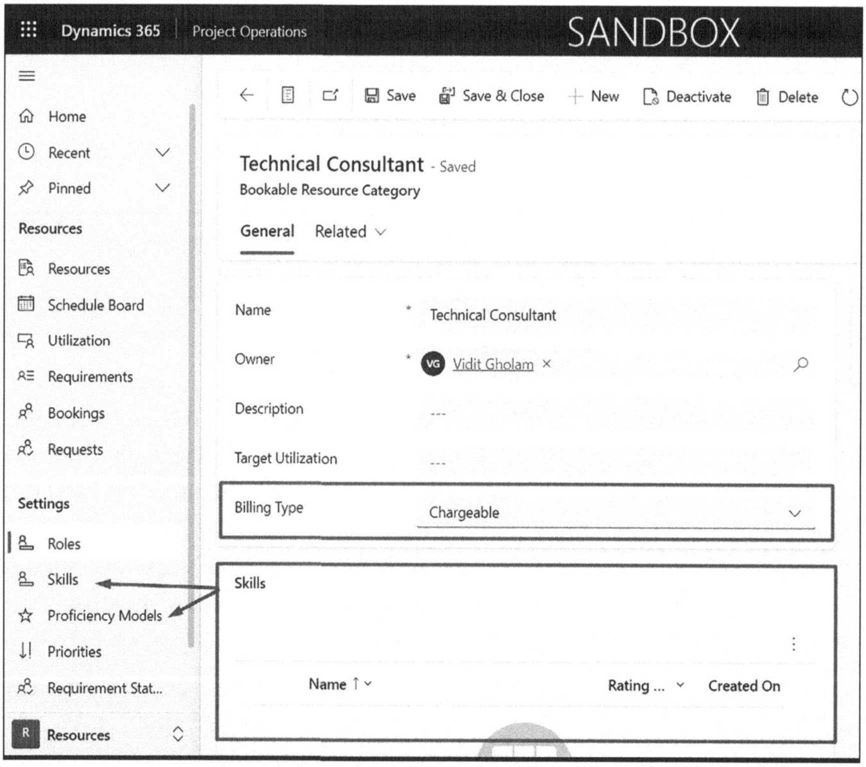

***Figure* 2.35**: *Resource Category Parameters*

4. **Set Up Transaction Categories (Expense Type) and Expense Categories**

   Transaction Categories: Transaction Categories classify various financial transactions within projects, such as invoices, payments, adjustments, and revenue recognition entries. They help track the flow of money and financial activities associated with project operations, providing a structured way to manage project finances.

   Expense Categories: Expense categories classify costs incurred during project execution, including materials, labor, subcontractor fees, travel expenses, and other project-related expenditures.

Relation Between Transaction and Expense Categories:

- Every transaction category can have many expense categories related to it.
- Transaction categories often generate corresponding expense entries when costs are incurred. For example, a purchase order transaction (transaction category) may lead to expenses categorized under "**`Materials`**" or "**`Services`**" (expense categories).
- Together, these categories provide a comprehensive view of project finances. Transaction categories track the movement of funds, while expense categories categorize and analyze where those funds are allocated.

  You can link one transaction category to one expense category to make expense tracking clearer on Project Estimates. For instance, a "**`Hotel Expense`**" transaction category can be linked to an expense category named "**`Hotel Expense`**." Alternatively, one transaction category can link to multiple expense categories. For example, a "**`Billable Expense`**" transaction category can cover various expenses such as airline tickets or hardware purchases.

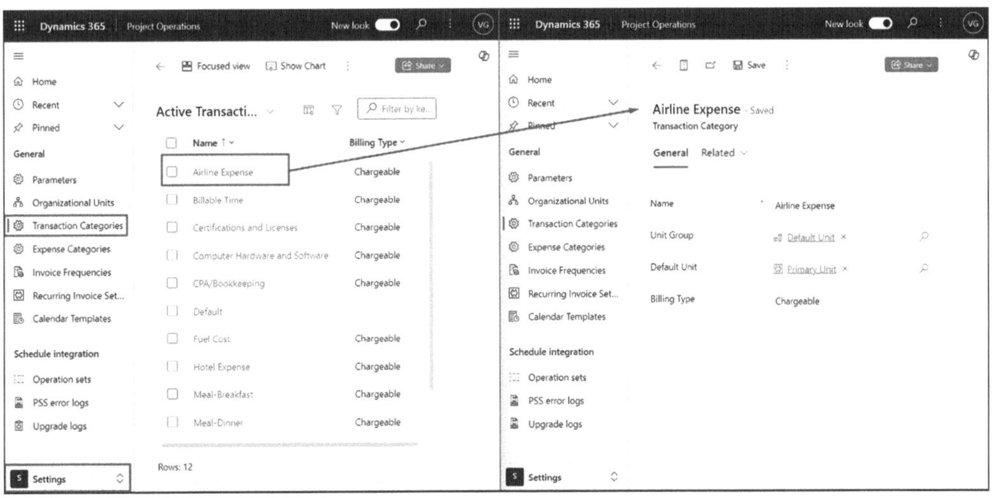

***Figure 2.36**: Setting Up Transaction Categories in Project Operations*

To create expense and transaction categories, go to the settings in the site map's change area. Under the **`General`** group, locate and create transaction categories first, followed by expense categories, as shown in *Figures* 2.36 and 2.37.

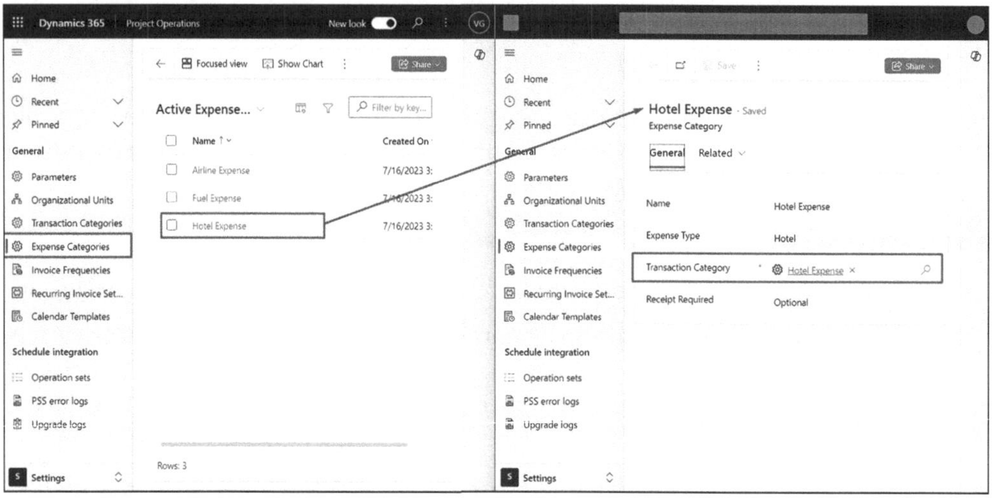

***Figure* 2.37**: *Setting Up Expense Categories in Project Operations*

5. **Set Up Invoice Frequency**

   Invoicing frequency refers to how often invoices are generated and sent to clients for services rendered or products delivered. This frequency is typically determined based on contractual agreements or project milestones.

   The choice of invoicing frequency depends on project dynamics, client preferences, and contractual terms, aiming to maintain cash flow, transparency, and adherence to financial agreements throughout the project lifecycle in Project Operations.

   To create invoicing frequencies, go to the settings in the site map's change area. Under the General group, locate Invoice Frequencies as shown in *Figure* 2.38. You can create a weekly, biweekly, or monthly invoicing frequency.

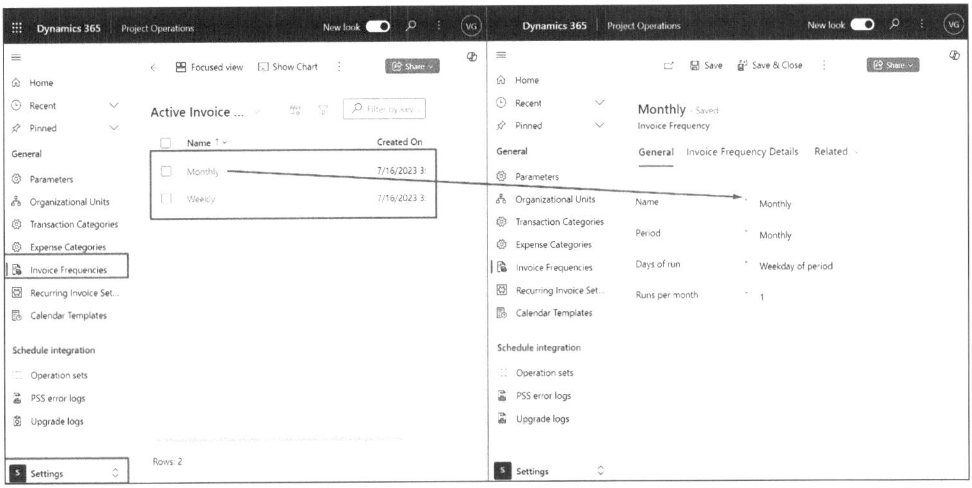

Figure 2.38: *Setting Up Invoice Frequency in Project Operation*

6. **Contracting Units**

   In **`Project Operations`**, contracting units are the organizational units responsible for managing contracts and project delivery. They play a key role in tracking the financial and operational aspects of projects, ensuring that resources, pricing, and billing are aligned with the organizational structure. By defining contracting units, organizations can streamline project workflows, maintain consistency in project execution, and ensure accurate financial reporting. Each contracting unit is associated with a cost price list, and opportunities, quotations, projects, sales orders, and pricelists are created within the respective organizational unit.

   To create invoicing frequencies, go to the settings in the site map's change area. Under the General group, locate Organization Units as shown in *Figure* 2.39. Associate the cost pricelist that we will be creating in the next step of the setup.

   (For more information on organization units, refer to link in Reference 10)

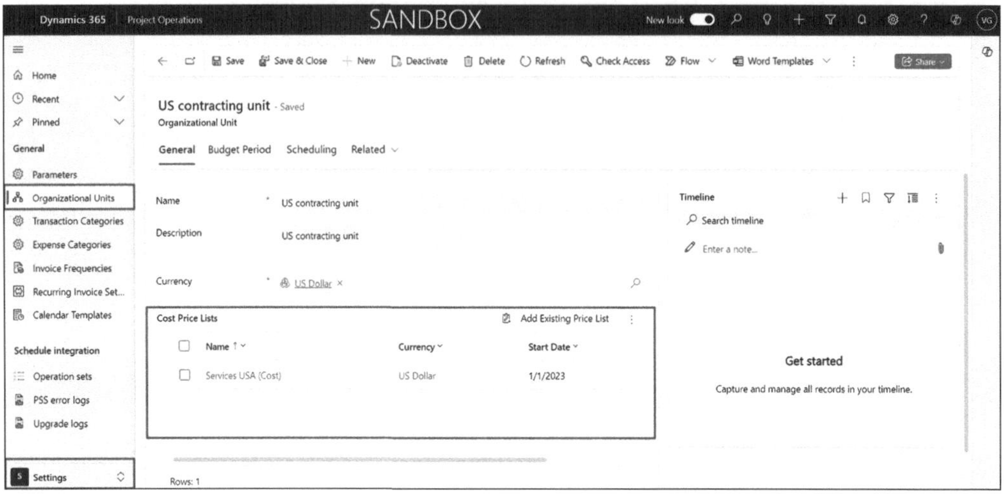

***Figure 2.39**: Set Up Organization Units in Project Operations*

7. **Set Up Price Lists**

   In **`Project Operations`**, price lists define the standardized rates or prices at which products and services are offered to clients or customers. They play a crucial role in managing pricing consistency across projects and help in quoting and invoicing processes.

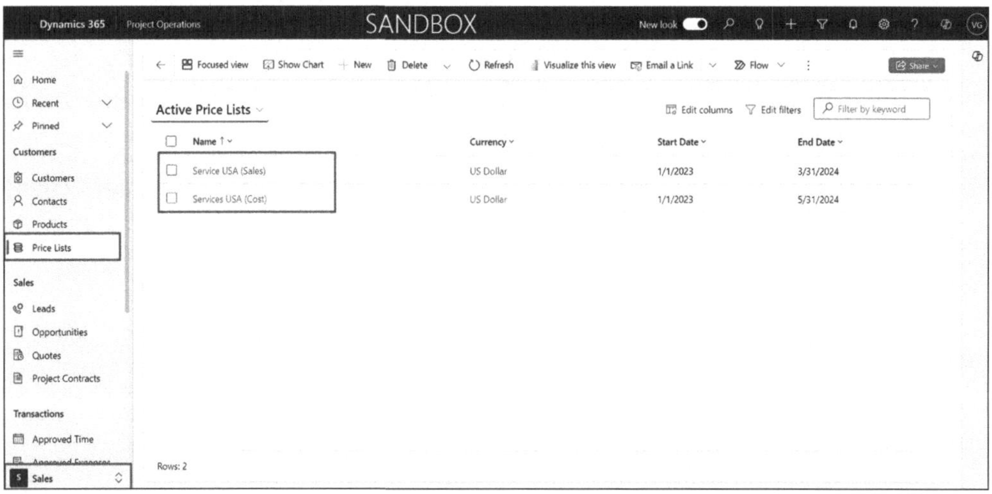

***Figure 2.40**: Pricelists in Project Operations*

Price lists in **`Project Operations`** typically include:

- **Cost Price Lists**: These lists specify the internal costs incurred by the organization for products or services. They help calculate the actual expenses associated with delivering goods or services within projects.

- **Sales Price Lists**: These lists determine the prices at which products or services are sold to clients or customers. They establish the rates charged to clients, ensuring profitability and covering costs while setting competitive prices in the market.

Price lists enable organizations to streamline pricing strategies, maintain financial control, and effectively manage profitability in their project operations.

To create pricelists, go to the sales from the site map's change area under the Customers group.

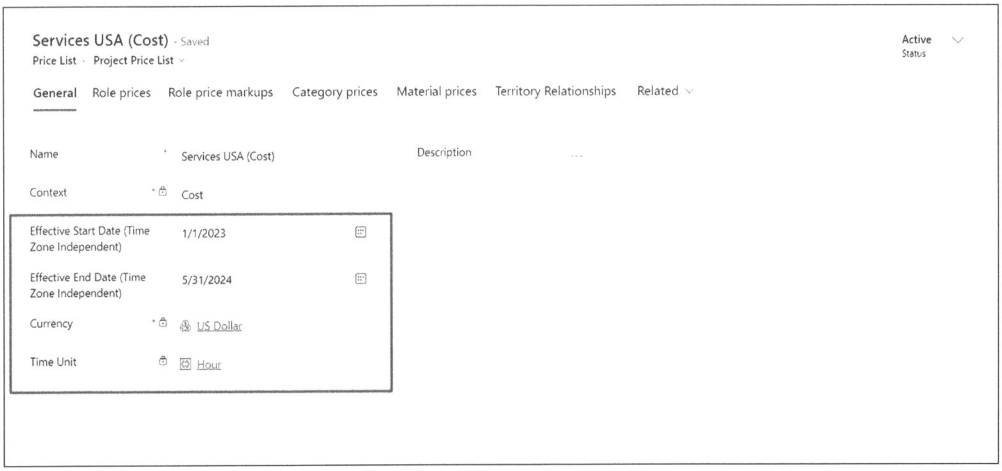

***Figure 2.41**: Cost Pricelists in Project Operations*

Each price list has a start and end date, making it valid only within that period. Prices are calculated based on the specified currency and time unit. Multiple price lists can be created to accommodate different customers and currencies.

Now, let us explore price dimensions of price lists:

- **Role Prices**: These define prices based on resource categories. In a cost price list, they represent internal costs for resources with specific roles. In a sales price list, they indicate the prices charged to customers for resources with those roles.

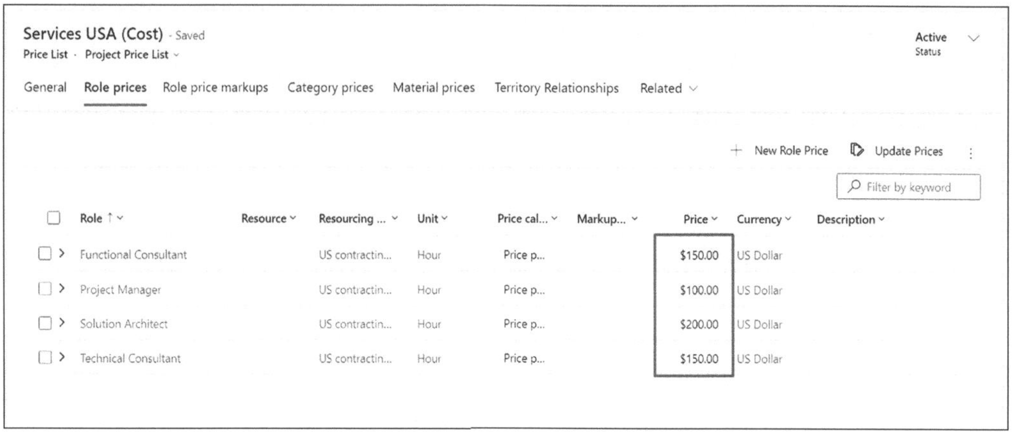

***Figure 2.42(a)**: Role Prices on a Cost Pricelists*

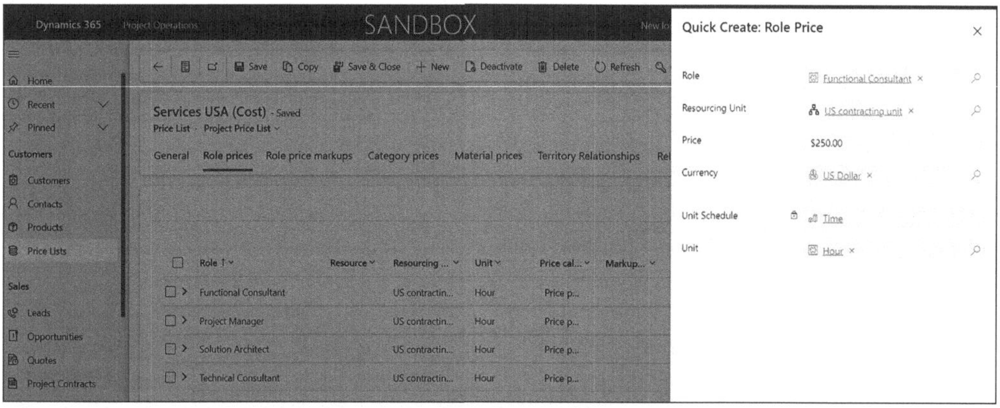

***Figure 2.42(b)**: Creating Role Prices on a Cost Pricelist*

- **Role Price Markups:** In Project Operations (PO), role price markups refer to adjustments made to base costs or sales prices based on the role assigned to resources. Here's how they work with examples for both cost and sales price lists:

  Cost Price List Example:

  - Base Cost: Assume the base cost of a service is $100.
  - Role Price Markup: For a specific role, like a Senior Consultant, you might apply a markup of 20%.
  - Calculation: Markup adjusts the cost to $100 + (20% of $100) = $120 for Senior Consultant services.

  Sales Price List Example:

  - Base Sales Price: Assume the base sales price of a product is $200.

- Role Price Markup: For a VIP Customer role, you might apply a discount of 10%.
- Calculation: Markup adjusts the sales price to \$200 - (10% of \$200) = \$180 for VIP Customers.

- **Category Prices:** Category prices are transaction categories added to your cost and sales price lists. They allow you to define prices for materials or expenses incurred on a project. Even if transactions are cost-to-cost, you must include transaction categories in your sales and cost price lists. All the transaction categories involved in the project must be added on both the cost and sales pricelists, without these categories, the actuals for your expense entries would always be zero.

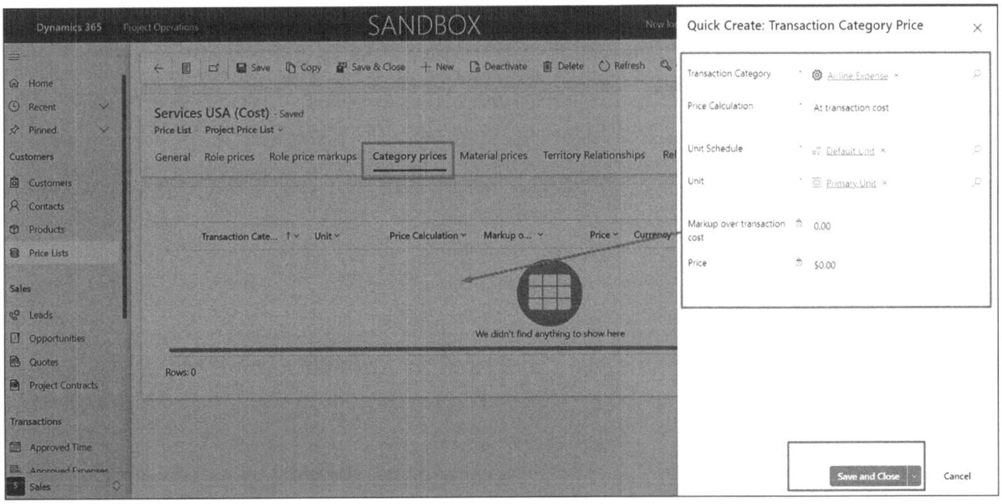

***Figure 2.43**: Category Prices in Pricelists*

With this, we have successfully completed the basic setup for **`Project Operations`**.

Setup Dynamics 365 Sales

The following resources provide a concise list of steps and references for setting up Sales, simplifying the process without overwhelming you with setup procedures only in this chapter.

1. Dynamics 365 Sales Overview: Reference 11.
2. Set up and configure Dynamics 365 Sales: Reference 12
3. Learn basics of Dynamics 365 Sales: Reference 13
4. Understanding the Sales Process: Reference 14

5. Set up product catalogue: Reference 15
6. Set up product families: Reference 16

You can use these references. Further resources are available on https://learn.microsoft.com/.

Data Management in Dynamics 365 (Exporting and Importing)

Data import and export are vital because they help businesses keep their information organized and up to date. Importing data lets you bring in new details smoothly, ensuring everything is current in your systems such as Dynamics 365. On the other hand, exporting data allows you to create reports, analyze trends, and make smart decisions based on the information you have. These tools make it easier to manage your data effectively and use it to improve how you work day-to-day.

Let us look at how we can export and import data from a Dynamics 365 CRM environment.

Importing Data

In Dynamics 365 CRM, importing data is simple using tools such as Excel Online and Excel templates. Excel Online allows direct import from spreadsheets into Dynamics 365, with easy field mapping for data consistency.

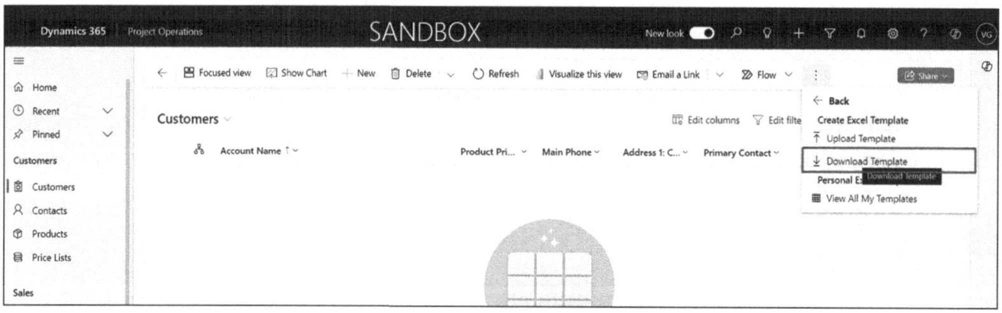

Figure 2.44: *Importing Option Using Excel Template*

Excel templates provided by Dynamics 365 ensure data formats correctly, making it efficient to integrate customer records, sales data, and other vital information into your system.

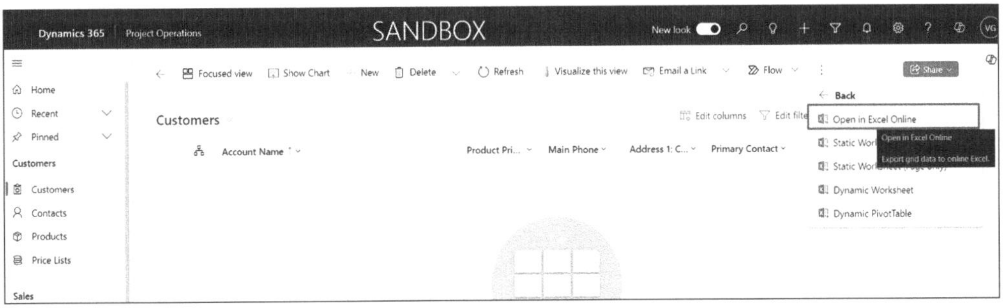

Figure 2.45: *Importing Option Using Excel Online*

So, when do you opt for Excel Online versus an Excel template?

Consider this scenario:

1. **Importing Using an Excel Template:**

   When onboarding a customer from their old system to Dynamics 365 CRM, you can offer them an Excel template already filled with essential fields such as Account Name, Phone Number, Website, and Address. This method streamlines data collection, making it simple for them to input required details. Subsequently, you can smoothly import the provided data into Dynamics 365 CRM.

   Detailed steps to import data from an excel template are provided in **References 17 and 18**.

2. **Importing Using Excel Online:**

   In the same example, if there are discrepancies or incorrect data in a set of records, you can query and update these records quickly using Excel Online.

   To update records using Excel Online, follow these steps:

   a. Navigate to the entity where you need to import your records. Choose an appropriate view or customize the view by adding fields using the edit column option. Then, click "**`Open in Excel Online`**" as shown in *Figure 2.46*.

   b. Filter the records you want to edit using the filtering options available in the view or by editing filters.

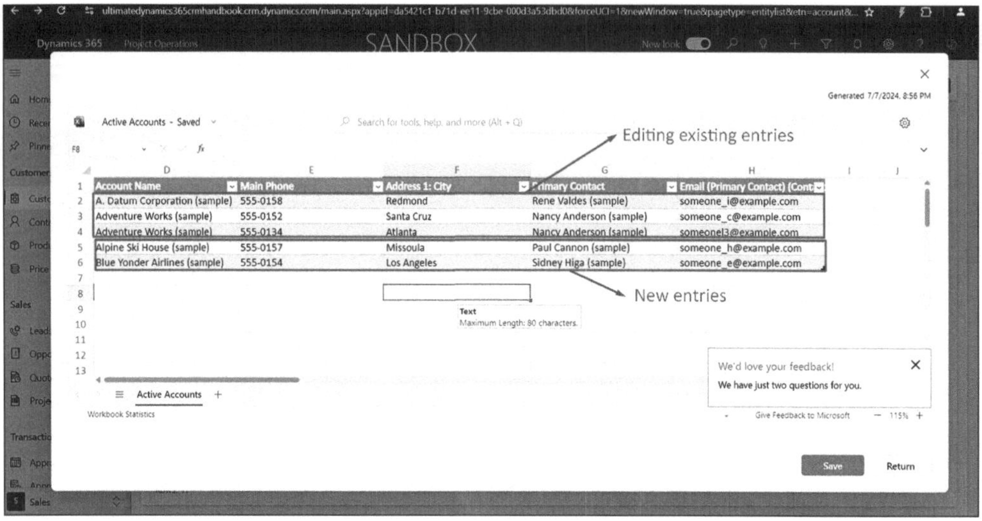

***Figure 2.46**: Importing Records Using Excel Online*

c. Make the necessary edits to the records. You can also add new records and then import them.

d. Monitor the process and review any failures that occur.

Exporting Data

Exporting data from Dynamics 365 CRM is a straightforward process that allows you to extract information from various entities such as Accounts and Contacts. By selecting "**`Export to Excel`**" or "**`Export to CSV`**," you can quickly download the data in your preferred format, facilitating reporting, analysis, and external use of CRM data.

Follow these steps to export data from Dynamics 365 CRM:

1. Navigate to the entity (such as, Accounts, Contacts) whose data you want to export.

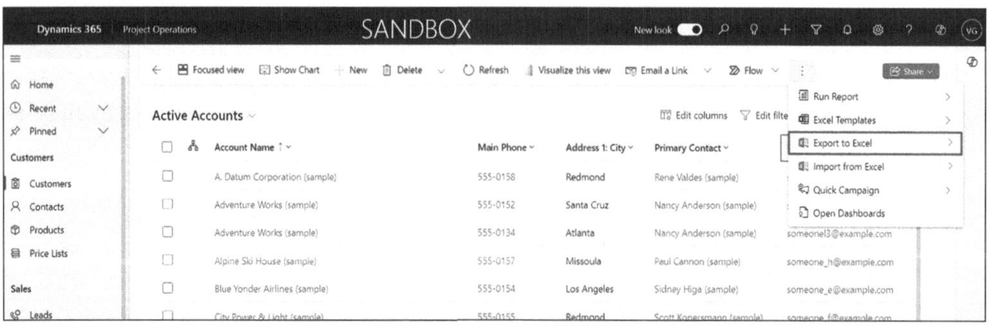

***Figure 2.47**: Exporting Data Using Excel*

2. Select "**`Export to Excel`**" or "**`Export to CSV`**" based on your preference.
3. Choose your export options, such as data format and including related records if needed.

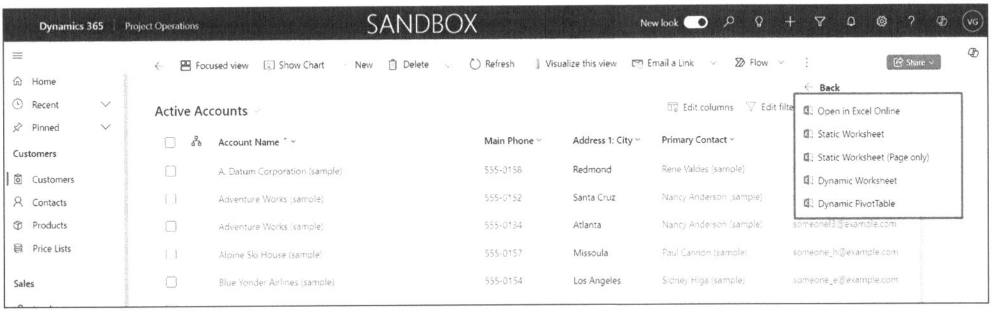

***Figure 2.48**: Data Export Options Using Excel*

4. Confirm and download the exported file to your local system.

For more information on exporting data, you can refer to the link in **Reference 19**.

Conclusion

In this chapter, we have covered some crucial elements to help you get started with Dynamics 365. We began with creating user accounts and understanding licensing. We also discussed security roles, including field security profiles, to protect sensitive data and provide customized access. Using practical examples, we walked through setting up Dynamics 365 environments for Project Operations and Sales, showcasing how to tailor configurations to your needs. Finally, we detailed strategies for exporting and importing data. Now, we are ready to move on to the next chapter, where we will explore how to use these configurations and what a sales cycle looks like in Dynamics 365.

References

1. Microsoft 365 Business Signup page: https://www.microsoft.com/microsoft-365/business/compare-all-microsoft-365-business-products
2. Dynamics 365 Sales licensing details 2024: Sales Pricing | Microsoft Dynamics 365
3. Dynamics 365 Team Member License FAQ: Dynamics 365 Team Members license overview and FAQ - Dynamics 365 | Microsoft Learn
4. Product Licensing Dynamics 365: Dynamics 365 Licensing
5. Product Pricing Dynamics 365: Product Pricing

6. Team Member's Privilege inheritance: https://learn.microsoft.com/en-us/power-platform/admin/security-roles-privileges#team-members-privilege-inheritance
7. Understanding Business Units (Blog by Carl de Souza): https://carldesouza.com/dynamics-365-business-units-teams-and-security-in-depth/
8. Creating Business Units in Dynamics 365: https://learn.microsoft.com/en-us/power-platform/admin/create-edit-business-units
9. Project Operation Deployments: https://learn.microsoft.com/en-us/dynamics365/project-operations/environment/determine-deployment-type#deployment-types
10. Organization units: https://learn.microsoft.com/en-us/dynamics365/project-operations/sales/orgunits
11. Dynamics 365 Sales Overview: https://learn.microsoft.com/en-us/dynamics365/sales/overview
12. Setup and configure Dynamics 365 Sales: https://learn.microsoft.com/en-us/training/modules/configure-dynamics-365-sales/
13. Learn basics of Dynamics 365 Sales: https://learn.microsoft.com/en-us/dynamics365/sales/user-guide-learn-basics
14. Understanding sales process: https://learn.microsoft.com/en-us/dynamics365/sales/nurture-sales-from-lead-order-sales
15. Setup Product Catalogue: https://learn.microsoft.com/en-us/dynamics365/sales/set-up-product-catalog-walkthrough
16. Set up product families: https://learn.microsoft.com/en-us/dynamics365/sales/create-product-family
17. Import Data using Excel Templates: https://learn.microsoft.com/en-us/power-apps/user/import-data?context=%2Fdynamics365%2Fcontext%2Fsales-context
18. Importing and Exporting Data: https://learn.microsoft.com/en-us/dynamics365/customerengagement/on-premises/basics/import-export-data?view=op-9-1
19. Field-Level-Security: https://learn.microsoft.com/en-us/dynamics365/customerengagement/on-premises/admin/field-level-security?view=op-9-1
20. Download Licensing Guide: https://download.microsoft.com/documents/en-us/dynamics365/pricing/Dynamics%20365%20Licensing%20Guide.pdf
21. Setup Teams in Dynamics 365 CRM: https://learn.microsoft.com/en-us/power-platform/admin/manage-group-teams

CHAPTER 3
Sales to Billing Cycle in Microsoft Dynamics 365 CRM

Introduction

In this chapter, we will examine the sales-to-billing process in Dynamics 365 CRM. We will begin by learning how to manage leads and opportunities, create and track quotes, and keep an eye on project profitability. We will also cover how to handle contracts, manage projects, allocate resources, and track time and expenses efficiently. Furthermore, we will explore the sales dashboards and demonstrate how to use Power BI to generate insightful reports. By the end of this chapter, you will have a solid understanding of managing the entire sales-to-billing cycle in Dynamics 365 CRM, preparing you for successful daily operations. Before proceeding, please note that this chapter assumes the Sales and Project Operations apps are installed and configured in your Dynamics 365 environment. If these steps have not yet been completed, refer to the setup instructions in the previous chapter.

Structure

In this chapter, we will discuss the following topics:

- Leads and Opportunities in Dynamics 365 CRM
    - Sales Cycle
    - Sales Dashboards in Dynamics 365 CRM
- Quotations in Dynamics 365 CRM
    - Quote Lines in Dynamics 365 CRM
    - Time and Material, and Fixed Price Contracting
    - Quotations Profitability

- Project Contracts/Sales Orders in Dynamics 365 CRM
- Managing Projects in Dynamics 365 CRM
- Resource Allocations, Expense, and Time Entries
- Creating Proforma Invoices in Dynamics 365 CRM
    - Invoice Reporting
- Reporting
    - Project Reporting
    - Contract Consumption Reporting

Leads and Opportunities in Dynamics 365 CRM

In Dynamics 365 CRM, leads represent potential customers or sales prospects who have shown interest in your product or service. These leads are often the starting point of your sales process. When a lead is qualified, it can be converted into an opportunity, which is a more concrete sales prospect with a higher likelihood of resulting in a sale.

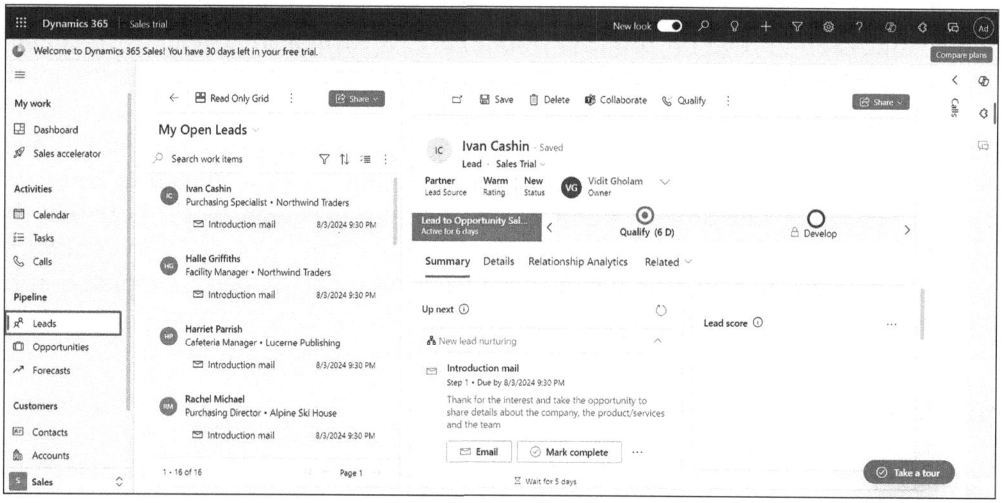

Figure 3.1: *Leads in Dynamics 365 CRM*

`Opportunities` allow you to track the sales process more closely, manage customer interactions, and forecast potential revenue. By effectively managing leads and opportunities, you can streamline your sales pipeline and increase your chances of closing deals.

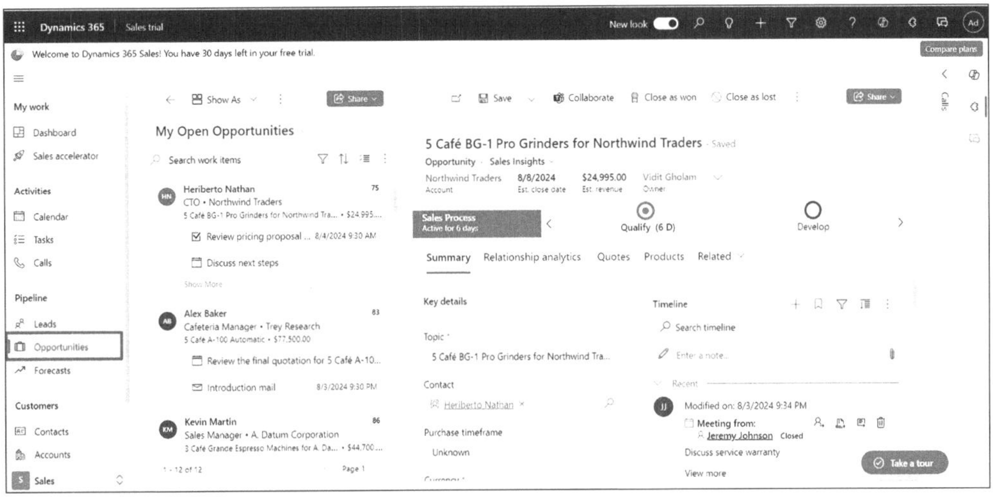

Figure 3.2: *Opportunity in Dynamics 365 CRM*

Sales Cycle

As discussed in *Chapter 1, Introduction to Microsoft Dynamics 365 CRM*, the sales process flow (also known as the sales cycle) begins with creating a lead. We will briefly revisit this process here (see *Figure 1.8(a)*). Once the lead is qualified, it turns into an opportunity, and Dynamics 365 Sales automatically transfers the lead's details to account and contact records.

The sales team then prepares and submits quotations linked to the opportunity. If a quotation is accepted, it is marked as "**won**," and the opportunity follows suit. If rejected, it is recorded as a lost opportunity, offering insights for future strategies.

Once a deal is closed, orders are created from the accepted quotations, leading to the delivery of products or services and the generation of invoices. Dynamics 365 Sales centralizes this process, helping manage customer interactions and sales activities efficiently.

Generating Leads

The question is how to generate and integrate leads into Dynamics 365. This can differ depending on your business. For example, a car rental company might consider the drivers renting their cars as leads, while a service company might capture website inquiries as leads. Larger companies with dedicated sales teams may import or create leads directly in the system. Here are some commonly used lead generation tools and methods to consider:

- **WordPress Website Integration**: If you have a WordPress website, you can create custom forms using plugins such as Gravity Forms or Contact Form

7. These forms can be integrated with Dynamics 365 CRM, allowing leads generated from website visitors to be automatically captured and stored within the CRM. Every inquiry or sign-up can be tracked and managed effectively.

- **LinkedIn Sales Navigator:** LinkedIn Sales Navigator is a powerful tool for finding and connecting with potential leads. By integrating Sales Navigator with Dynamics 365 CRM, you can directly import leads from LinkedIn into your CRM system.
- **Email Marketing Campaigns:** Tools such as Mailchimp or Dynamics 365 Customer Insights – Journey allow you to run targeted email campaigns. Leads generated through these campaigns can be automatically captured and synced with your CRM, linking email interactions to corresponding customer records.
- **Webinars and Online Events:** Hosting webinars or online events is another effective way to generate leads. Platforms such as Zoom or GoToWebinar can be integrated with Dynamics 365 CRM, so participants' details are automatically added as leads. You can follow up with interested participants and nurture them through your sales process.

Other Lead Generation Tools: Tools such as Leadfeeder or HubSpot can track visitors on your website, identify them, and automatically create leads in Dynamics 365 CRM. These tools help you capture leads that might otherwise go unnoticed, giving your sales team more opportunities to engage with potential customers.

Let us take a closer look at the Sales-to-Billing cycle and how you can generate reports and dashboards at various stages of the process.

Use Case

Consider this scenario: VVG Constructions, a company using Dynamics 365 Sales, wants to integrate their system with Dynamics 365 Business Central. They contact you via a web inquiry on your company website. You are a part of XYZ Consulting, a Microsoft Partner that uses Dynamics 365 Project Operations to manage sales and projects internally. Let us walk through the sales-to-billing cycle for this inquiry, from creating a lead, converting it into an opportunity, to proposing a quote based on the provided estimates, creating a project contract, managing the project with expense and time entries, and ultimately invoicing and billing the customer.

Resources (Roles) involved [SP (Sales Price), CP (Cost Price)]

1. Project Manager: SP =$100, CP = $50.
2. Sr. Solution Architect: SP = $400, CP = $200.
3. Sr. Technology Consultant: SP = $200, CP = $100.

The Project estimates and timeline:

Tasks	Estimates	Resources	Timeline
Requirement gathering	30 hours	Project Manager	1st Aug - 7th Aug 2024
Integration architecture	50 hours	Sr. Solution Architect	10st Aug -20th Aug 2024
Integration development	90 hours	Sr. Technology Consultant	20th Aug -22nd Sept 2024
Integration master data setup	5 hours	Sr. Technology Consultant	22nd Sept -26th Sept 2024
Documentation	5 hours	Sr. Technology Consultant	1st Aug -30th Sept 2024
Go-live	10 hours	Project Manager	26th Sept -30th Sept 2024
Total	190 hours		
Expenses			
Airline Ticket	4 tickets	Project Manager	1st Aug - 20th Aug 2024
Hotel Stay	20 days	Project Manager	

Table 3.1: *Sample Project Estimates and Timelines*

As shown in the business process flow, we begin with creating a lead in Dynamics 365 CRM. Leads in dynamics 365 CRM are of two types; item-based and work-based.

- **Item-Based**: An item-based lead refers to a potential customer interested in a specific product or service. The focus is on a tangible item or offering that the lead is considering purchasing. For example, in retail, a lead expressing interest in a particular product, such as a smartphone or a piece of furniture, would be considered item-based. The sales process involves understanding the lead's specific needs related to that item and guiding them toward making a purchase.
- **Work-Based:** A work-based lead, on the other hand, involves a potential customer interested in a service or a project rather than a physical product. This type of lead is common in industries such as consulting, construction, or professional services, where the lead is looking for expertise or work to be done. For example, a lead seeking help with a marketing campaign, or a construction project would be considered work-based. The sales process here focuses on understanding the scope of work, the customer's goals, and how the service can meet those needs.

Since our example involves a service or project, we will focus on creating a work-based lead, which will guide us through a service or project-based sales-to-billing cycle.

1. Create a work-based lead with lead source "**Web**" for the services inquiry by CTO Tony Stark of VVG Consulting.

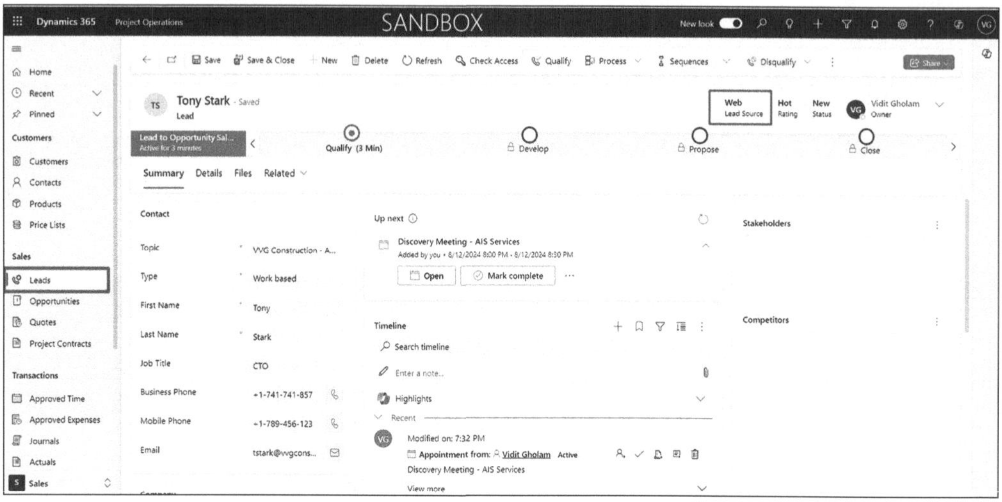

Figure 3.3(a): *Creating a Lead for the Web Inquiry*

2. At the **`Qualify`** stage of the business process flow, key details about the lead are gathered, and discovery meetings are scheduled. Once sufficient information is collected and assessed, the lead is qualified.

Figure 3.3(b): *Qualifying the Lead*

3. Once the lead is qualified, an opportunity is created, and the business process flow transitions from the **`Qualify`** stage to the **`Develop`** stage.

4. Since we did not associate any existing **`Contact`** or **`Account`** with the lead record, a new contact record and account record are automatically created

and linked to the **Opportunity**. You can customize this setting to either enable or disable the automatic creation of records.

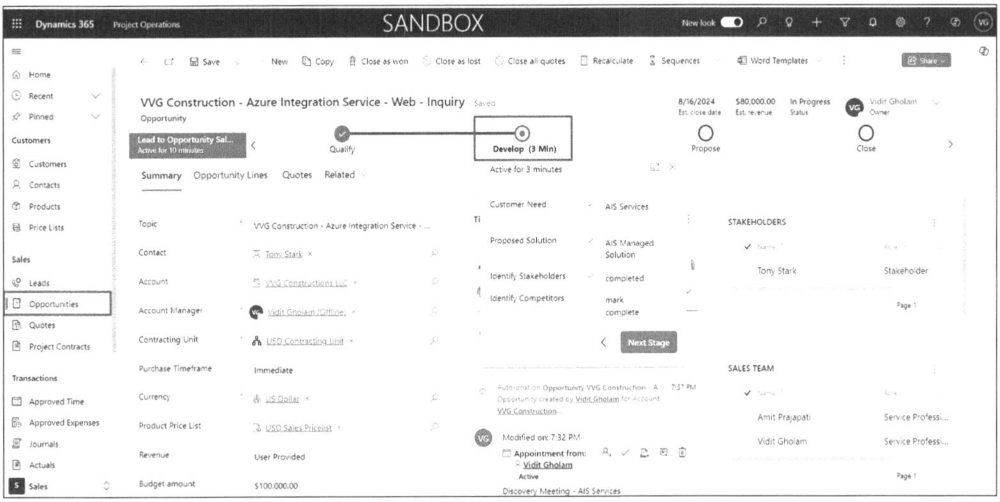

Figure 3.3(c): *Opportunity Created for the Qualified Lead*

5. Details such as **Estimated Close Dates**, **Estimated Revenue**, and **Sales Pricelist** are added to the **Opportunity**, and the creation of a sales quote is initiated.

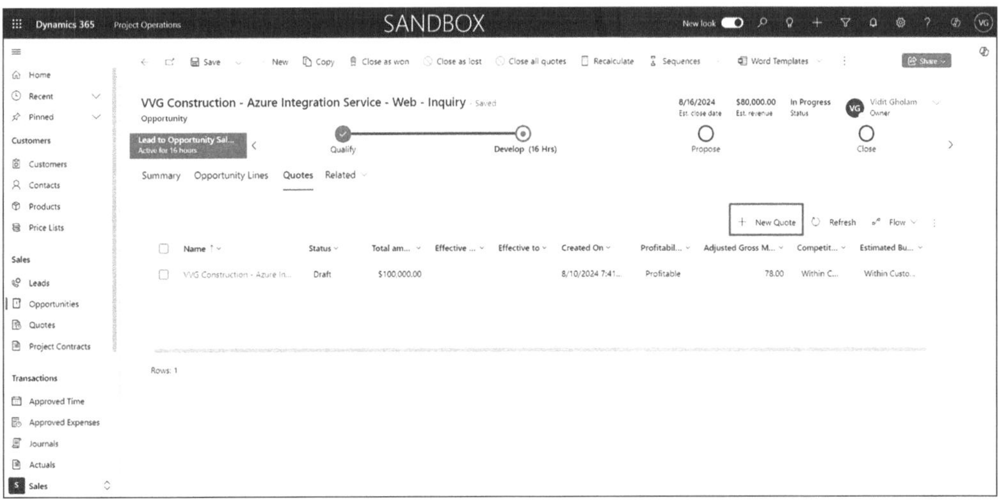

Figure 3.3(d): *Creating a Quote Against the Opportunity*

Now, before we explore the **Quotations**, let us look at the reports and dashboards that the **Sales** team can use to monitor **Opportunities** and **Leads**.

Sales Dashboards in Dynamics 365 CRM

Dashboards in Dynamics 365 CRM are visual displays that provide an at-a-glance view of key metrics and data related to your business processes. They help users track performance, monitor activities, and make informed decisions by bringing together different charts, lists, and other visual elements in one place.

Dynamics 365 CRM comes with several pre-built dashboards that provide insights into sales activities and performance. Here are a few:

- **Sales Activity Dashboard**: This dashboard focuses on day-to-day sales activities. It includes charts and lists that show open leads, opportunities, and activities such as calls, emails, and appointments. It is designed to help salespeople manage their daily tasks and stay on top of their pipeline.

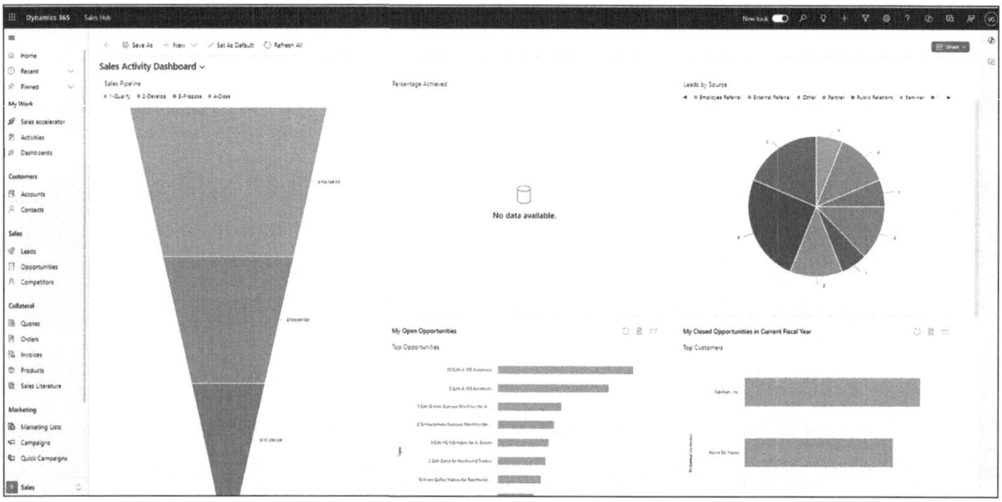

Figure 3.4: *Sales Activity Dashboard in Dynamics 365 CRM*

- **Sales Dashboard:** This is a broader overview of the sales pipeline. It shows key metrics such as open opportunities, pipeline revenue, and top accounts. This dashboard is useful for sales managers who want to track overall performance and identify trends.

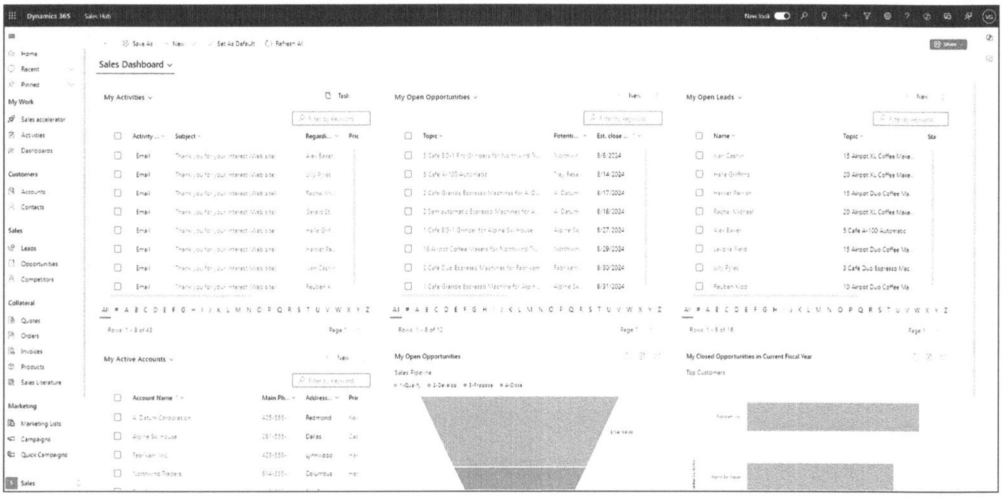

Figure 3.5: *Sales Dashboard in Dynamics 365 CRM*

- **Sales Activity Social Dashboard**: Dynamics 365 CRM integrates social media insights with traditional sales data. It lets you track sales activities alongside social engagement, helping you monitor customer interactions, track key sales metrics, and understand social media impact on your sales pipeline. This dashboard provides real-time insights into both sales and social performance, enabling more informed decisions and better customer engagement.

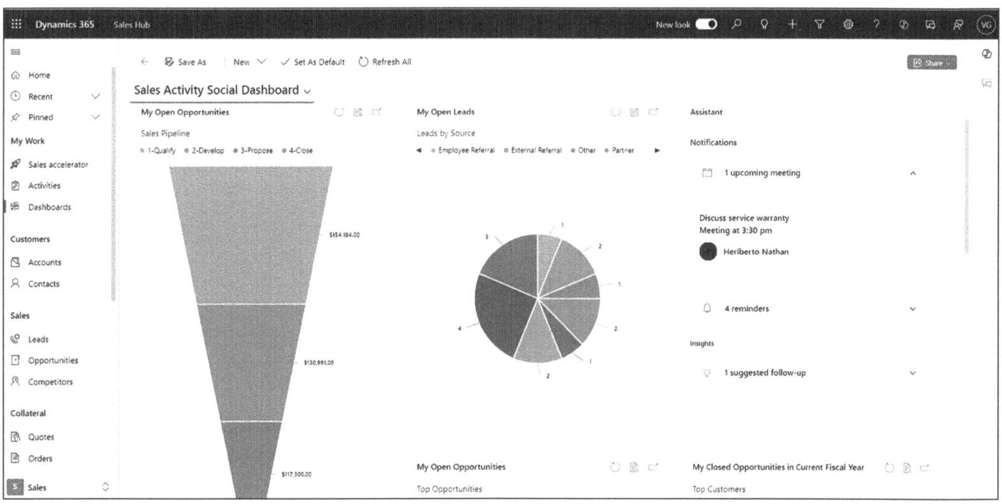

Figure 3.6: *Sales Activity Social Dashboard in Dynamics 365 CRM*

You can create or modify dashboards to fit your needs. Here are the steps:

1. Visit www.make.powerplatform.com, choose your environment, and create a **`New solution`**.

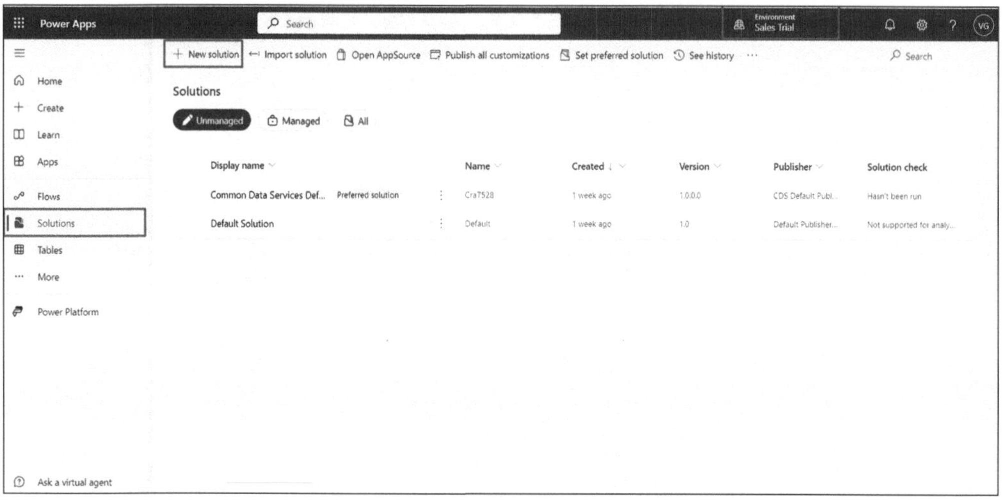

***Figure 3.7(a)**: Creating a Solution in Power Apps Studio*

2. Name the solution according to your needs and assign a **`Publisher`** to it.

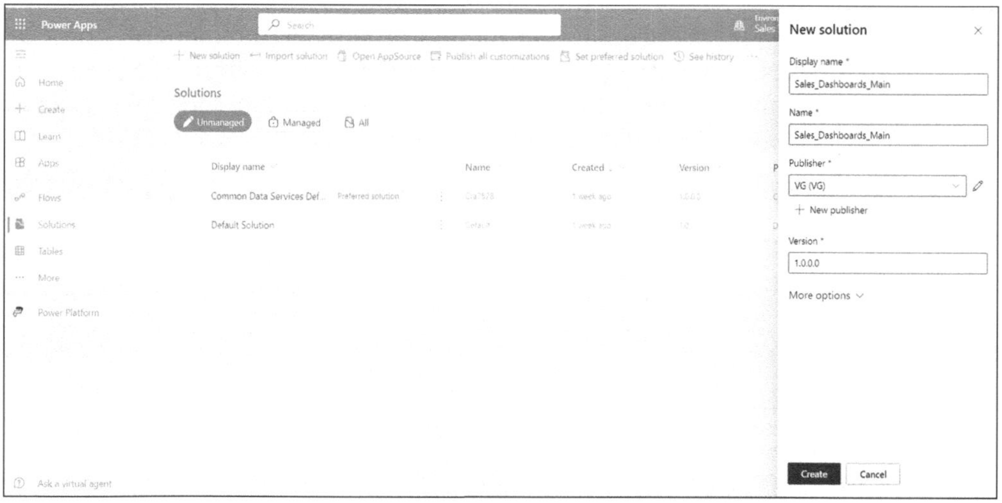

***Figure 3.7(b)**: Creating a Solution in Power Apps Studio*

3. Click the "**`New`**" button and select "**`Dashboards`**." You can choose from options like 2 columns or 4 columns, and you can also embed Power BI reports directly into your Dynamics 365 dashboard.

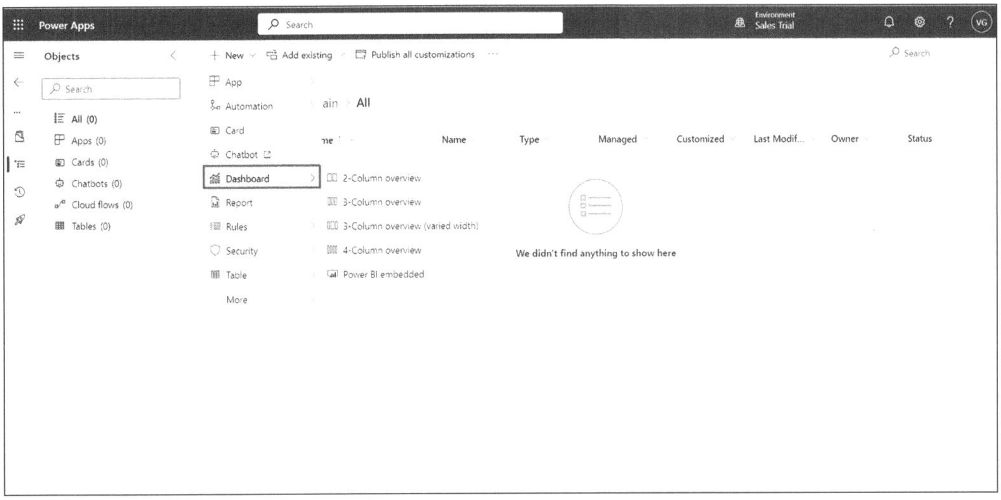

Figure 3.8: *Creating Dashboards in Dynamics 365 CRM*

4. In the Dashboard editor (see *Figure* 3.9), you can add various components such as **`Charts`**, **`Lists`** (Views), **`Web Resources`** (Custom HTML pages), and **`IFrames`**.

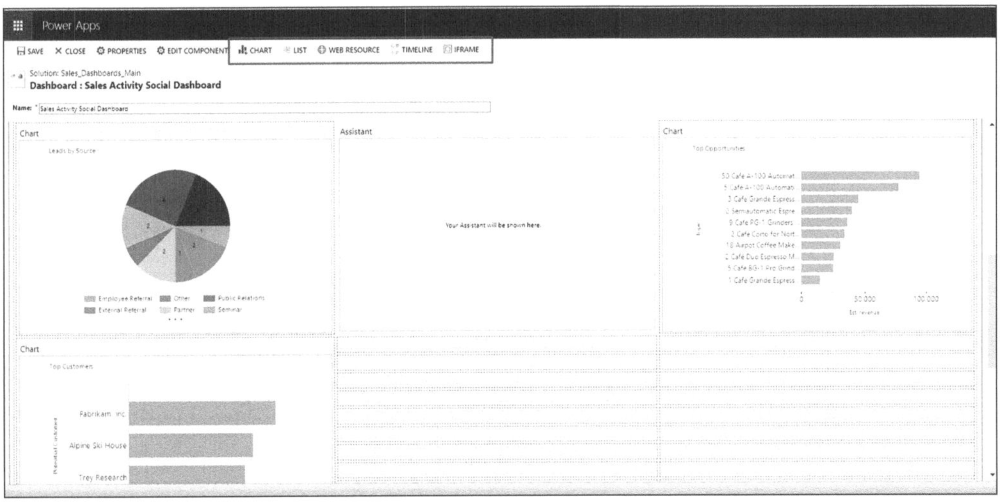

Figure 3.9: *Dynamics 365 CRM Dashboard Editor*

We will cover **`Lists`** (Views) and **`Web Resources`** in the next chapter. For now, let us focus on how to work with **`Charts`** and explore their details.

Charts

Creating a chart in Dynamics 365 CRM allows you to visually represent data, making it easier to analyze trends and patterns. Here is how to create a chart and some details about it:

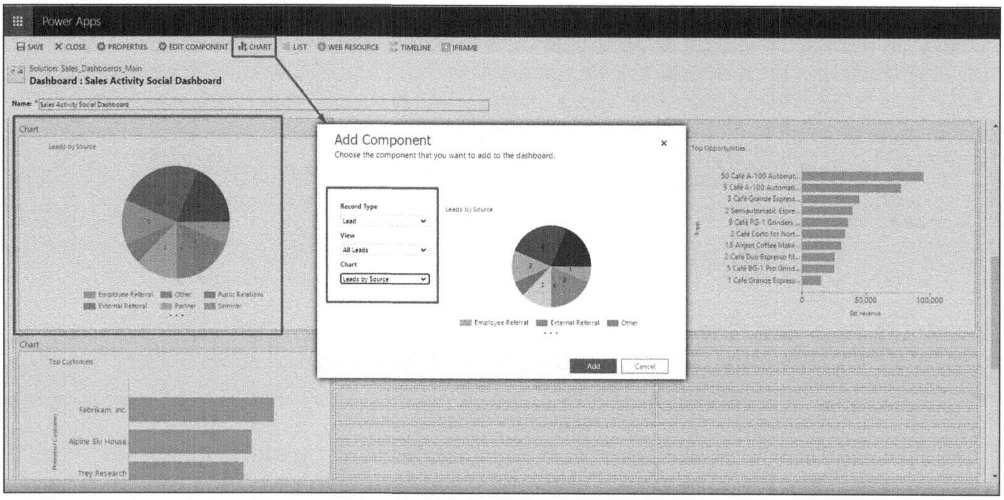

***Figure 3.10**: Chart*

To create a chart, follow the steps outlined:

1. **Navigate to the Entity**: Go to the entity (for example, **`Leads`**, **`Opportunities`**, **`Accounts`**) for which you want to create a chart.

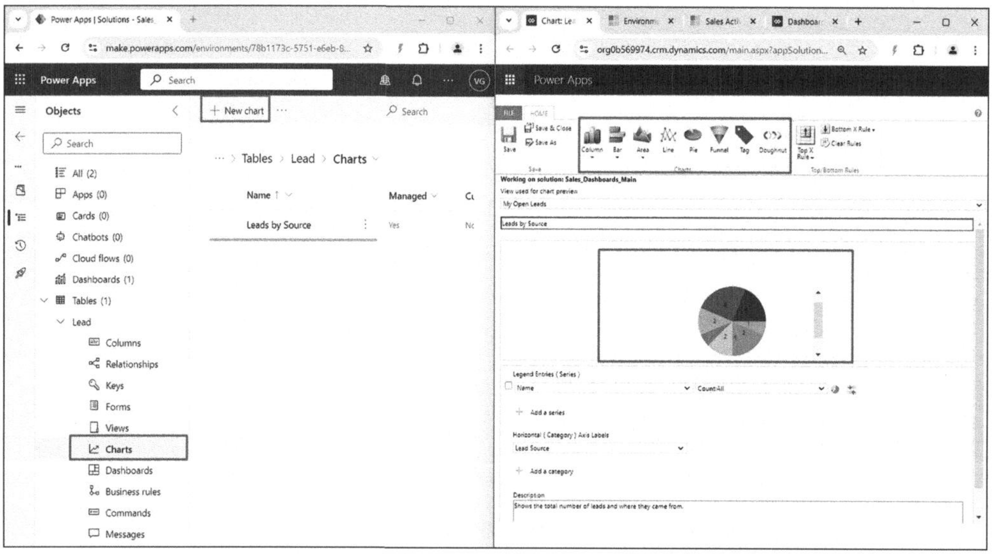

***Figure 3.11**: Creating a Chart in Dynamics 365 CRM*

2. **Click `Charts`**: In the top-right corner of the view, click the "**`Charts`**" pane.
3. **Select '`New Chart`'**: Click the "**`New Chart`**" button to start creating a new chart.
4. **Choose Chart Type:** Select the type of chart you want to create, such as bar, pie, line, or funnel chart.

5. **Set Data Fields:** Choose the fields you want to use for the chart's axes and series. For example, you might choose "**`Estimated Revenue`**" for the Y-axis and "**`Account Name`**" for the X-axis.
6. **Customize Appearance**: You can customize the appearance of the chart by setting colors, labels, and display options.
7. **Save the Chart:** Once you are satisfied with the settings, save the chart with an appropriate name.

Now that we have explored managing **`Leads`** and **`Opportunities`** and analyzing data with sales dashboards, let us move on to our use case and see how to manage Quotes in Dynamics 365 CRM.

For more details on **`Dashboards`** and **`Charts`**, refer to the link in **Reference 1**.

Quotations in Dynamics 365 CRM

In Dynamics 365 CRM, Quotes play a crucial role in formalizing sales proposals by detailing products or services, pricing, terms, and conditions. They can be linked to Opportunities and converted into Orders once approved, streamlining the sales process. Additionally, Dynamics 365 CRM allows for profitability analysis on quotes, helping you assess the potential profit margins and make informed decisions about pricing and sales strategies. This ensures accurate billing and provides valuable insights into your sales performance.

1. A newly created quote starts in the draft stage until it is activated. If the quote is generated from an opportunity, details such as the customer's **`Contracting Unit`**, **`Currency`**, and **`Product Pricelist`** are automatically filled in based on the opportunity.

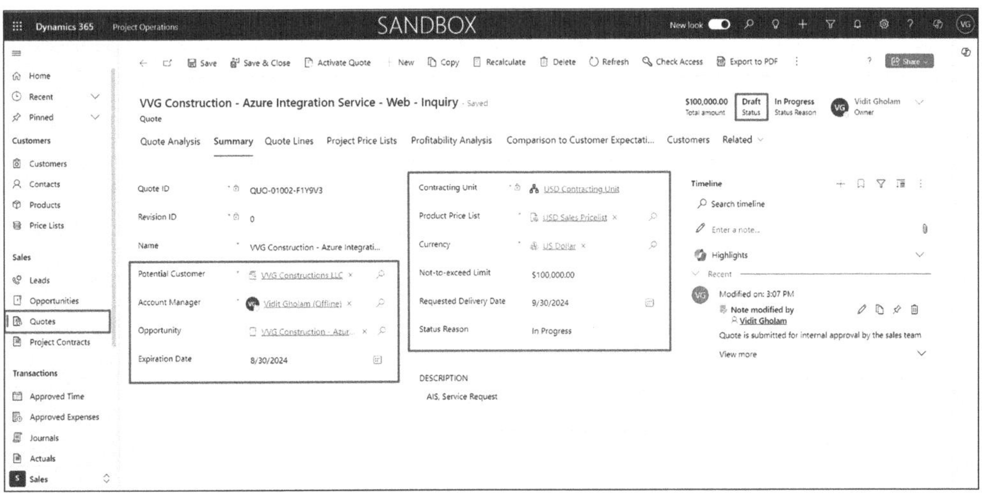

Figure 3.12: Quotation Record in Dynamics 365 CRM

2. The next step after creating a quote is to add the appropriate sales pricelist. Without this, the quote prices will remain empty or zero. After adding the pricelist, you should set the expiration date, not-to-exceed limit, and delivery date for the quote.

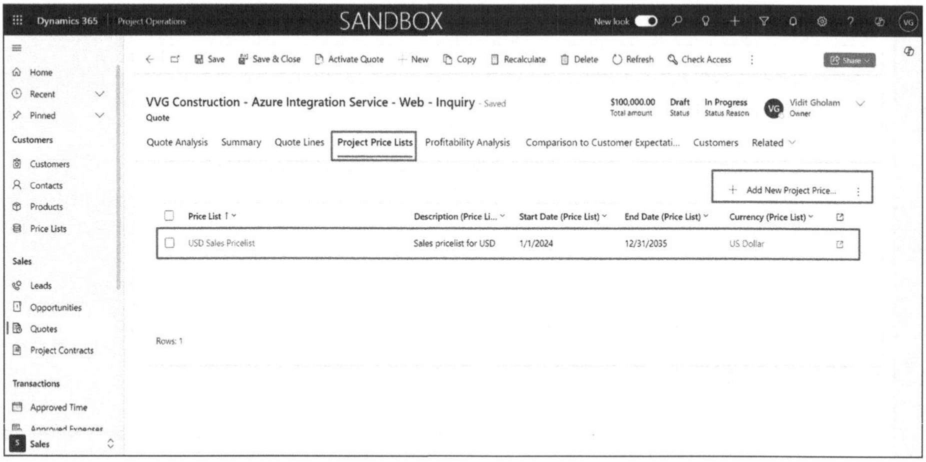

Figure 3.13: *Adding the Sales Pricelist to the Quote Record*

3. Next, you will need to add project-based or product-based quote lines to complete the quote setup.

Quote Lines in Dynamics 365 CRM

Quote lines on a quote depend on the type of quotation being made. If it is a product-based quote, the line will detail the products being sold. If it is a service-based quote, the line will outline the service being provided through a project. Quote lines are further classified into two types of lines: **`Project-Based`** and **`Product-Based`**.

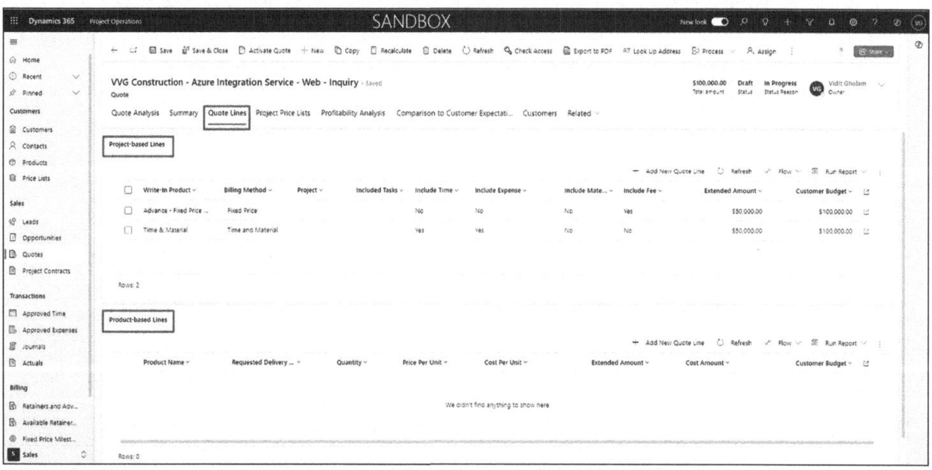

Figure 3.14: *Quote Lines in Dynamics 365 CRM*

- **Project-Based Lines:** Project-based lines are typically used for managing and tracking the progress and costs of projects. They are crucial for project management, ensuring that tasks are completed on time and within budget. Project-based lines are of two types: **`Fixed Price`** Lines, and **`Time & Material`** Lines.
    - **Fixed-Price Lines (FP):** Fixed-price lines in a quote refer to items or services offered at a predetermined price, regardless of the actual time or resources spent. This means the cost to the customer remains the same, regardless of any changes in the project scope or duration. Fixed-price lines are useful for projects where the scope is well-defined and unlikely to change, providing clarity and certainty for both the customer and the service provider.

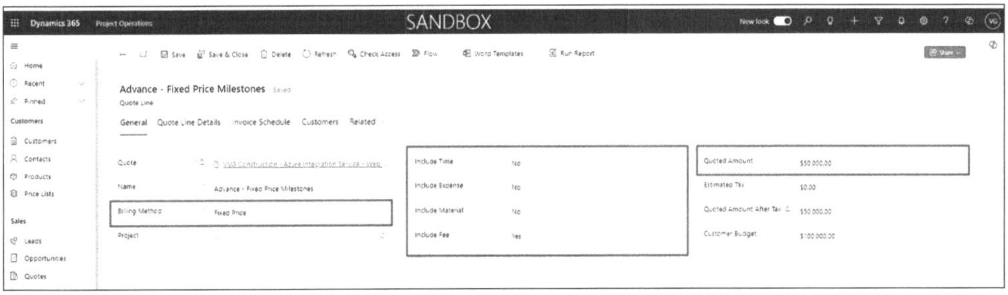

***Figure 3.15(a)**: Fixed Price Quote Lines*

Milestones: Every fixed-price line has milestones associated with it. In simpler terms, milestones are nothing but bills that should be generated on Project completion targets. For example, milestones could include "**`Requirement gathering`**" (from our estimate table), "**`Integration Architecture`**", and more.

Milestones are generated based on the defined invoicing frequency, the fixed price quoted amount, and the requested delivery date; they can also be generated manually.

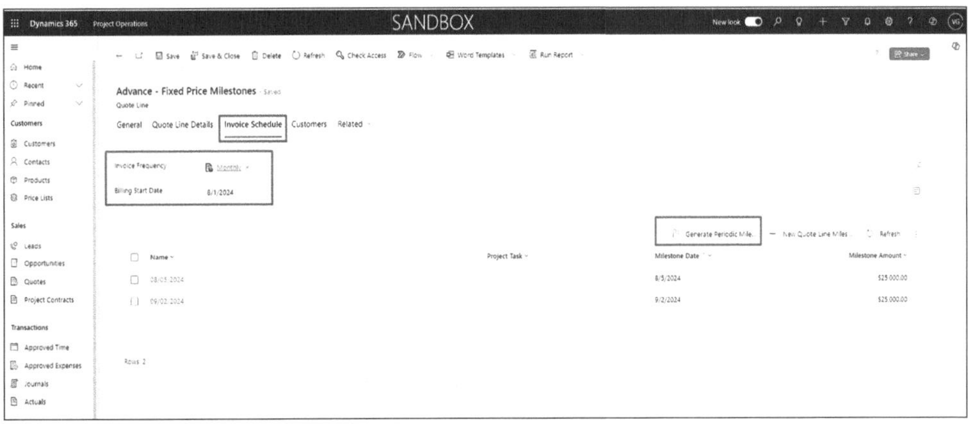

***Figure 3.15(b)**: Invoice Schedules (Milestones) on a Fixed Price Quote Line*

- **Time and Material Lines (TM):** Time and material lines, on the other hand, refer to items or services billed based on the actual time spent and materials used. This pricing model is flexible and adjusts according to the project's progress, making it suitable for projects with uncertain or evolving requirements. Customers are charged based on the actual effort and resources used, which can vary over the course of the project. Time and material lines, often referred to as labor lines, reflect costs based on labor, expenses, and materials. These estimates for labor, expenses, and materials are entered in the quote line details area for each Time and Material line.

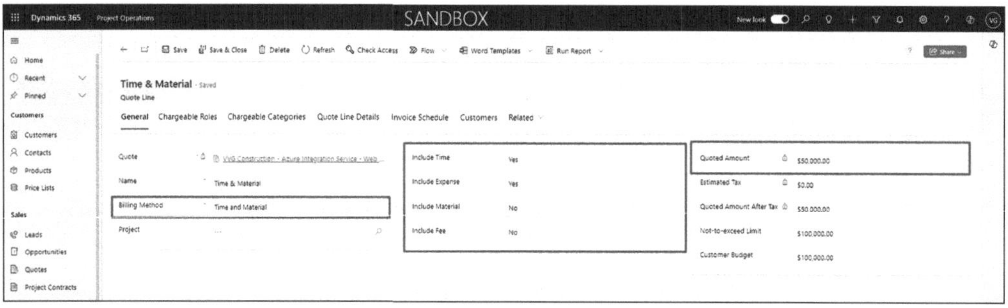

Figure 3.16(a): *Time and Material Quote Lines*

- **Quote Line Details:** Quote line details provide a detailed breakdown of the total estimated costs and sales prices. For time and material quote lines, these details include labor expenses and material cost estimates. The total sale price of the quote line detail is the quoted amount on the time and material quote line. These estimates are automatically calculated based on the sales price list in the quote and the cost price list attached to the contracting unit.

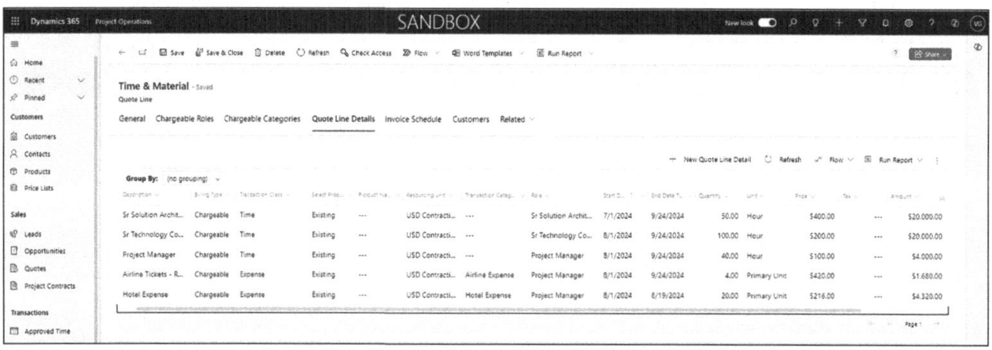

Figure 3.16(b): *Sales Quote Line Details on the Time and Material Quote Line*

For example, all the amounts shown in *Figure 3.16(b)* represent the sales prices being quoted to the customers. These prices are calculated based on the Sales Pricelist, as illustrated in *Figure 3.16(c)*, which was added to the quote.

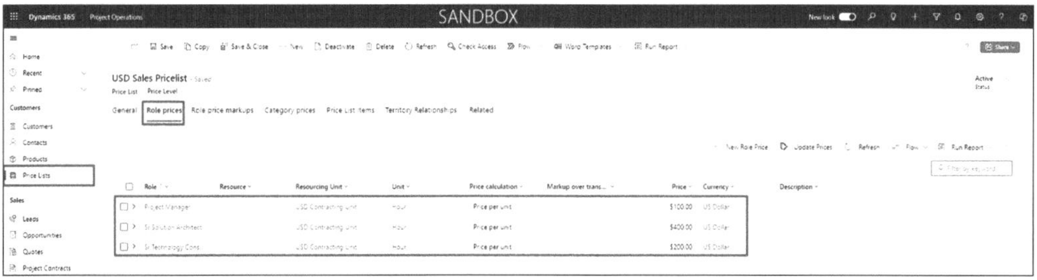

***Figure 3.16(c)**: Sales Pricelist*

Now, if you select any quote line detail, for example, the quote line detail for a Sr. Solution Architect, you will see an option to view the cost details of that line. By clicking it, you can access the cost details, showing how much the resource is costing you in this project.

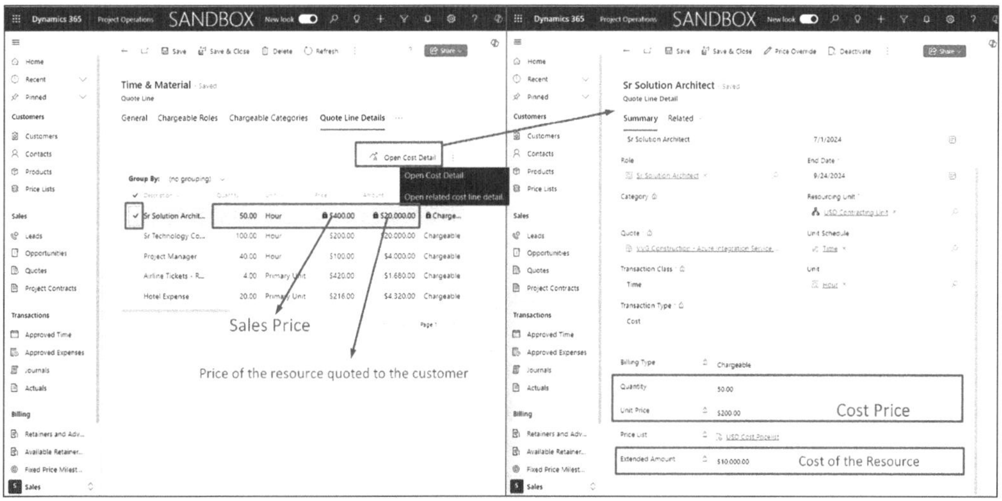

***Figure 3.16(d)**: Cost Quote Line Details on the Time and Material Quote Line*

This cost is derived from the cost pricelist attached to the contracting unit on the quote.

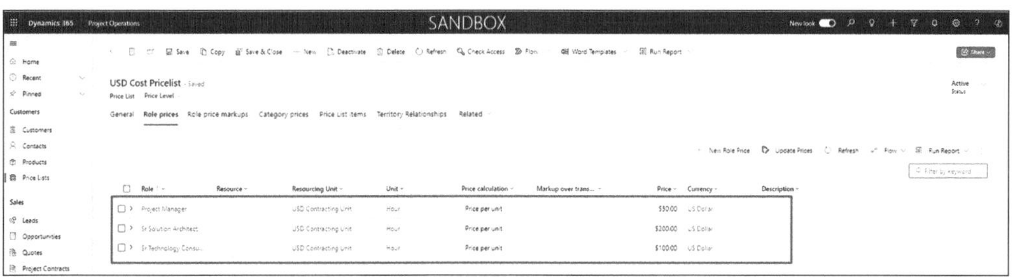

***Figure 3.16(e)**: Cost Pricelist*

- **Product-Based Lines:** Product-based lines are used for managing the sales and delivery of products or services associated with the project. They help in tracking inventory, sales, and ensuring that the project deliverables align with customer expectations, you can make a product-based line for an Existing product or a Write-in Products.
    - **Existing Products:** Existing products in Dynamics 365 CRM are pre-defined items listed in your product catalog. These products have set prices, descriptions, and other attributes that are used consistently across quotes and orders. Using existing products helps ensure consistency and accuracy in pricing and reduces manual entry errors.
    - **Write-in Products:** Write-in products are custom or non-standard items that are not listed in the existing product catalog. These products are added manually to quotes when you need to include items that are not part of your standard inventory. Write-in products allow for flexibility in creating quotes and accommodating unique customer needs or special requests.

  For more detailed information on product-based lines, see **Reference 2**.

Quote Profitability

The **`Quote Profitability Analysis`** tab in Dynamics 365 CRM is a feature that allows businesses to evaluate and understand the profitability of their quotes before they are finalized and sent to customers. This tab provides key insights into the financial aspects of the quote, helping sales teams and project managers make informed decisions.

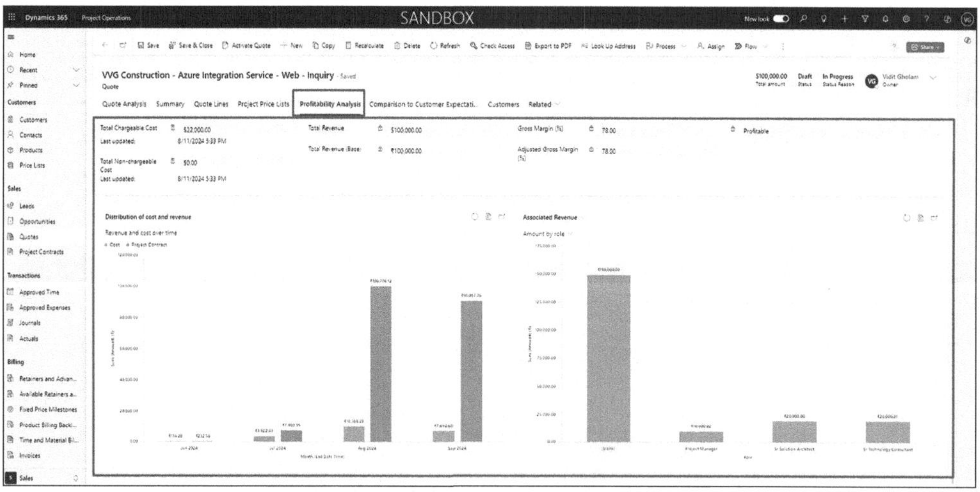

***Figure 3.17**: Profitability Analysis on Quote*

Key Features of the Quote Profitability:

- **Sales Price Overview:** This section displays the total sales price of the quote, which is the sum of all the sales prices for the products, services, or project tasks listed in the quote lines. It reflects the amount the customer will be charged.
- **Cost Price Overview:** Here, you can see the total cost price associated with the quote. This is the aggregate of all internal costs, such as labor, materials, and other expenses. These costs are derived from the Cost Pricelist attached to the contracting unit within the quote.
- **Gross Margin Calculation:** The gross margin is calculated as the difference between the total sales price and the total cost price. It is typically expressed as a percentage and provides a clear indicator of the profitability of the quote.

  For example, if the sales price is significantly higher than the cost price, the gross margin will be higher, indicating better profitability.
- **Margin Analysis by Line Item:** This section breaks down the profitability on a line-by-line basis. Each quote line's sales price and cost price are compared, and the margin for that specific line is calculated.

  This granular view helps identify which specific products, services, or project tasks are contributing most to the overall profitability and which might be less profitable or even at a loss.
- **Profitability Summary:** The profitability summary aggregates the total sales prices, cost prices, and gross margins into a concise overview, allowing decision-makers to quickly assess the financial viability of the quote.
- **Adjustments and Recommendations:** Based on the analysis, the system may provide recommendations for adjustments, such as revising sales prices, reconsidering cost estimates, or negotiating better rates with suppliers to improve profitability.

You can also create custom Power BI reports using the data available in the quote.

Finally, after completing the profitability analysis and preparing the quote for the customer, the quote is activated using the **`Activate Quote`** Ribbon Button, and a formal quotation is generated from the quote details. A Quote Document can be created by clicking a button with a little customization. We will explore how to do this in *Chapter 6, Document Management in Dynamics 365 CRM.*

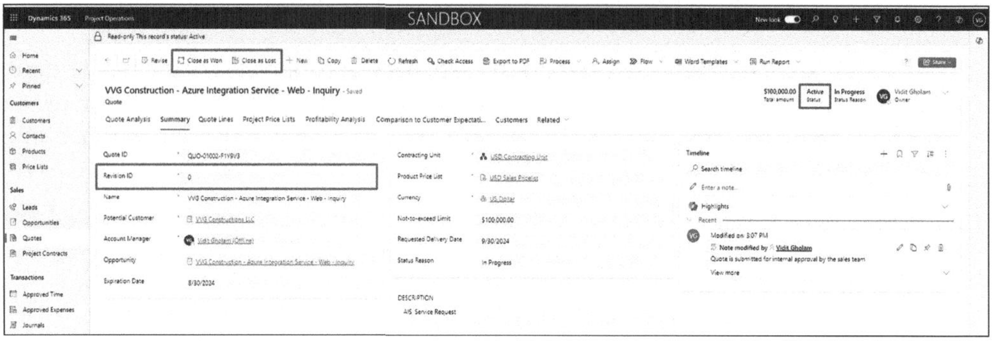

Figure 3.18: *Activated Quote*

Generating Automatic Quote using a **`Custom Ribbon`** button.

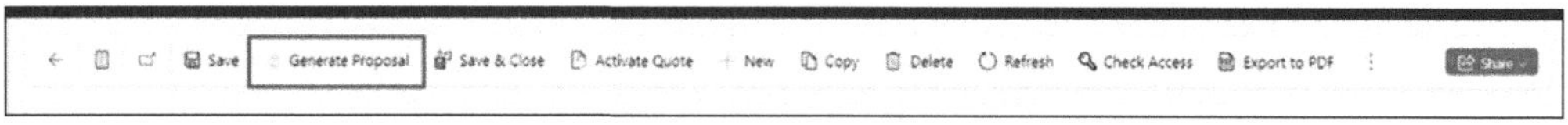

Figure 3.19: *General Proposal Button*

Quote summary document generated to be sent to the customer, it contains all the detailed estimates from the **`Quote Lines`**.

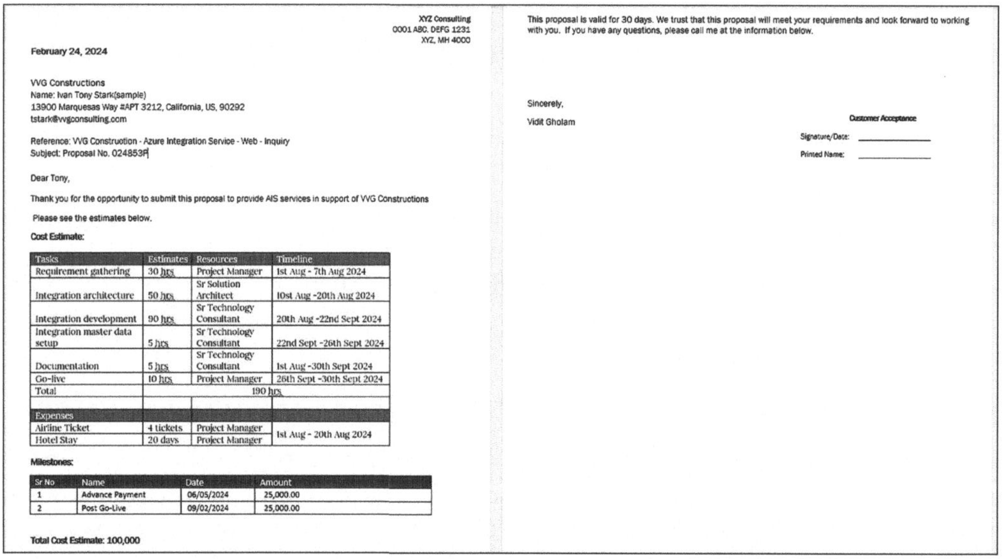

XYZ Consulting
0001 ABC. DEFG 1231
XYZ, MH 4000

February 24, 2024

VVG Constructions
Name: Ivan Tony Stark(sample)
13900 Marquesas Way #APT 3212, California, US, 90292
tstark@vvgconsulting.com

Reference: VVG Construction - Azure Integration Service - Web - Inquiry
Subject: Proposal No. 024853R

Dear Tony,

Thank you for the opportunity to submit this proposal to provide AIS services in support of VVG Constructions

Please see the estimates below.

Cost Estimate:

Tasks	Estimates	Resources	Timeline
Requirement gathering	30 hrs	Project Manager	1st Aug - 7th Aug 2024
Integration architecture	50 hrs	Sr Solution Architect	10st Aug -20th Aug 2024
Integration development	90 hrs	Sr Technology Consultant	20th Aug -22nd Sept 2024
Integration master data setup	5 hrs	Sr Technology Consultant	22nd Sept -26th Sept 2024
Documentation	5 hrs	Sr Technology Consultant	1st Aug -30th Sept 2024
Go-live	10 hrs	Project Manager	26th Sept -30th Sept 2024
Total	190 hrs		
Expenses			
Airline Ticket	4 tickets	Project Manager	1st Aug - 20th Aug 2024
Hotel Stay	20 days	Project Manager	

Milestones:

Sr No	Name	Date	Amount
1	Advance Payment	06/05/2024	25,000.00
2	Post Go-Live	09/02/2024	25,000.00

Total Cost Estimate: 100,000

This proposal is valid for 30 days. We trust that this proposal will meet your requirements and look forward to working with you. If you have any questions, please call me at the information below.

Sincerely,

Vidit Gholam

Customer Acceptance

Signature/Date: ____________

Printed Name: ____________

Figure 3.20: *Quotation to be sent to the Customer*

If the quote requires any corrections, you can revise it, and the **`Revision ID`** will be updated, with "**`0`**" indicating no revisions, as shown in *Figure* 3.18. If the quote is accepted by the customer, it is marked as "**`Closed as Won`**," and the associated opportunity is also closed as won, and vice versa.

1. Quote accepted by the customer quote is closed as won.

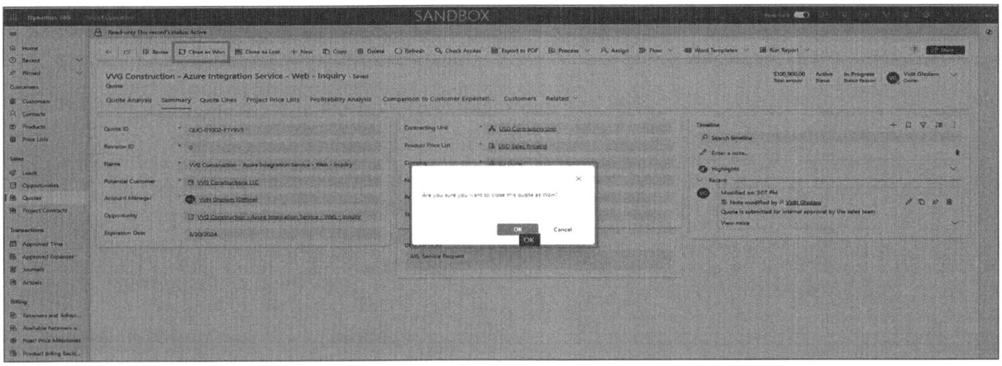

Figure 3.21: *Mark Quote as Won*

2. **`Opportunity`** related to the **`Quote`** is also marked as **`Won`**.

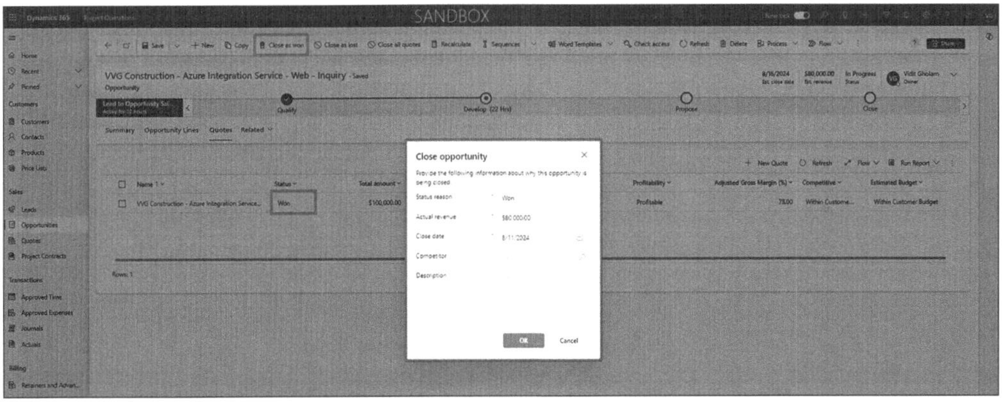

Figure 3.22: *Mark Opportunity as Won*

Project Contracts/Sales Orders in Dynamics 365 CRM

As soon as the quote is won a **`Project contract/Sales`** order gets created. All the details entered on the **`Quote`** are transferred to the **`Project Contracts`**.

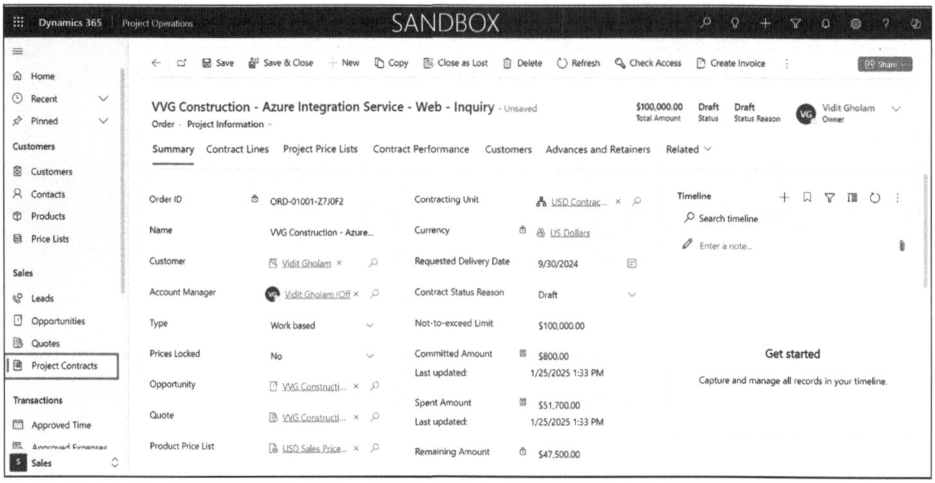

Figure 3.23: *Project Contract/Sales Order in Dynamics 365 CRM*

Quote lines become **`Project Contract`** lines, and similarly, Quote line details become **`Project Contract`** line details.

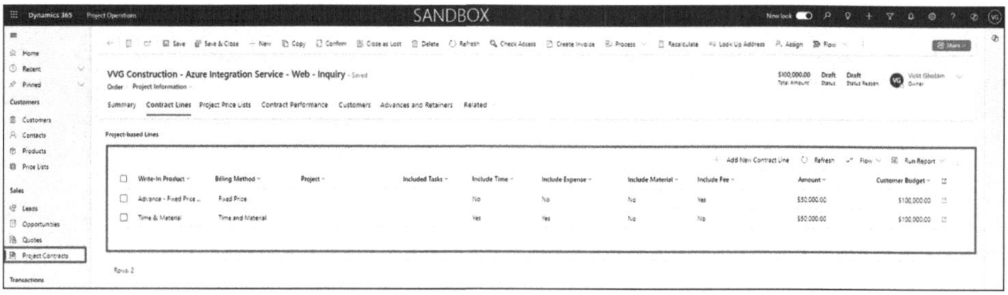

Figure 3.24: *Project Contract Lines in Dynamics 365 CRM*

The next step is to set up a project for the **`Project Contract`**, which includes adding team members, setting up project tasks, and allocating resources. We will create a project and assign it to each Contract line. It is important to remember that a single project can be assigned to two unique contract lines, as long as the contract line parameters—such as "**`include time`**," "**`expense`**," or "**`fee`**"—are not identical in both lines. Setup a Project and assign it to the **`Time and Material`** Contract Line.

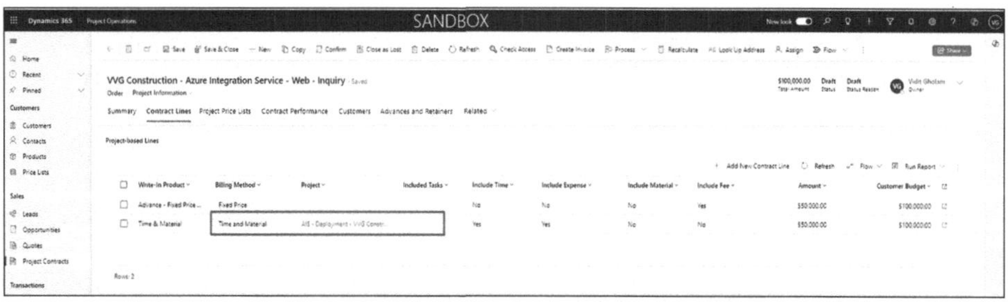

Figure 3.25: *Assign Project to the Contract line*

The milestones added against the **`Fixed Price Quote line`** are now converted into **`Project Contract`** line milestones. Additionally, an invoice status is available for each contract line milestone.

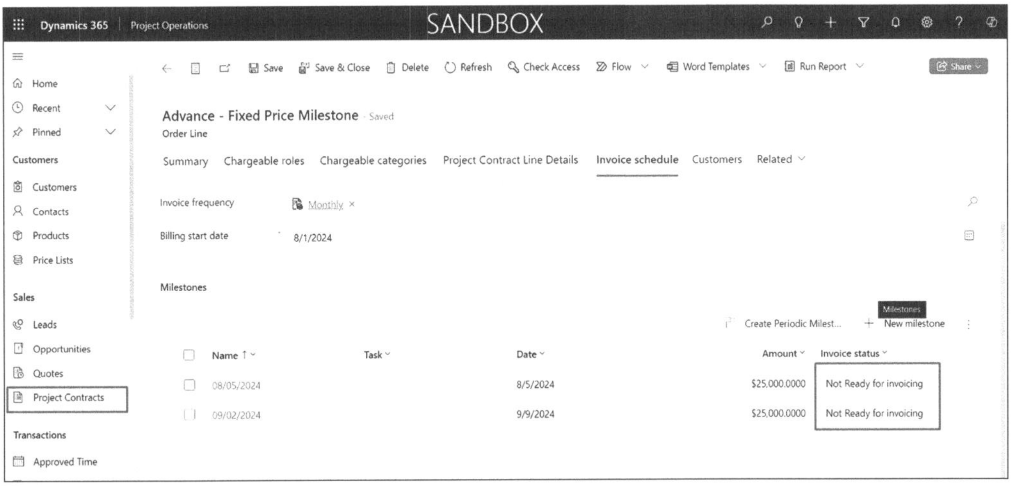

***Figure 3.26**: Project Contract Line Milestone*

Once the milestone is ready to be invoiced, you can update the invoice status to "**`Ready to Invoice`**." All milestones marked as "**`Ready to Invoice`**" will be included in the invoice if it is generated on or after the milestone date.

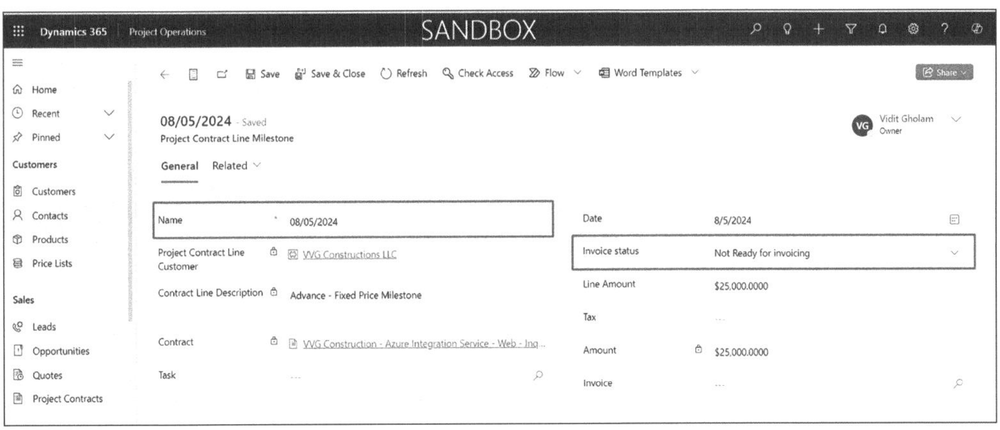

***Figure 3.27**: Marking Milestones Ready to Invoice*

Now, we have an invoice milestone ready to be invoiced, now let us look at the **`Project Setup`**.

Managing Projects in Dynamics 365 CRM

A Project is a structured and organized effort to achieve specific objectives within a defined timeframe and budget. It involves planning, executing, and managing tasks, resources, and budgets to deliver the desired outcomes efficiently.

Projects in Dynamics 365 are designed to help businesses align their operations by tracking progress, managing resources, and ensuring that project goals are met. The system supports various aspects of project management, including task allocation, time tracking, and financial management, providing a detailed solution for overseeing projects from initiation to completion.

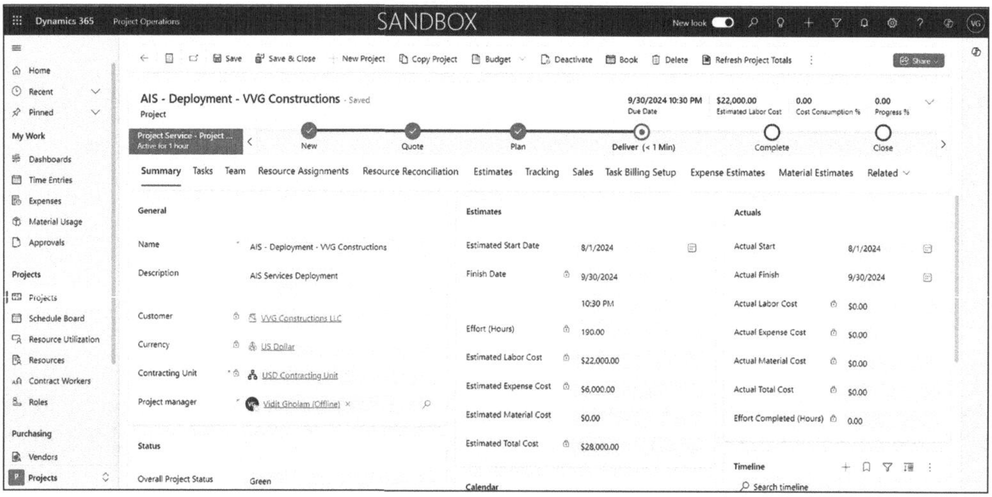

Figure 3.28: *Projects in Dynamics 365 CRM*

Figure 3.28 shows the **`AIS - Deployment - VVG Construction`**, we will be using this project to manage the **`Project Deployment`**.

Let us first begin with assigning **`Team Members`** to the team.

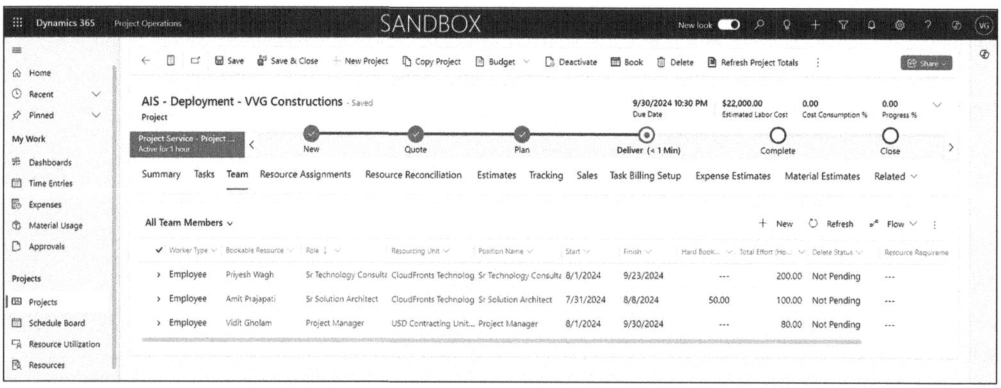

Figure 3.29: *Assigning Team Members to the Project*

1. To add team members to a project, go to the "**`Team Members`**" tab within the project.

2. Click "**`New`**" and enter the details as shown in *Figure* 3.30. Assign at least one resource as the project approver, ideally a resource with the **`Project Management`** role.

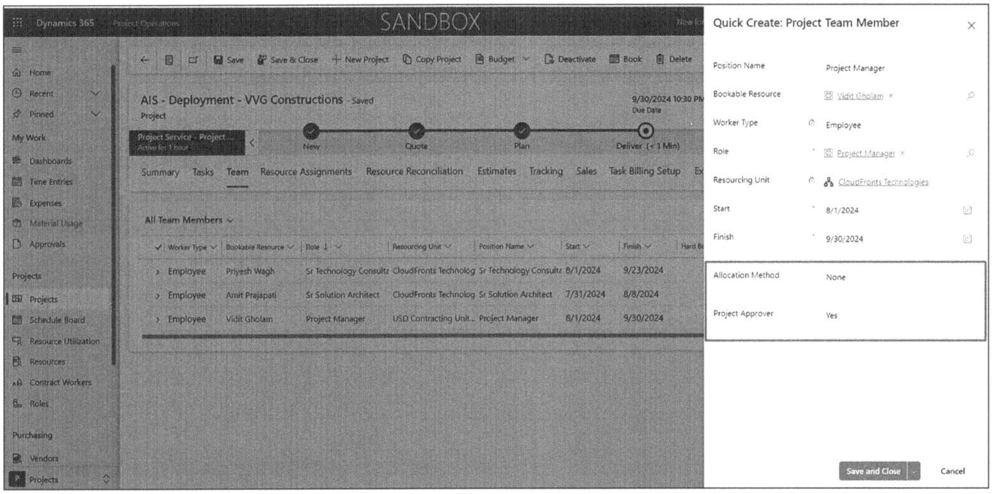

***Figure 3.30**: Creating a Project Team Member*

3. Next, create project **`Tasks`** and assign team members to these tasks according to the estimates provided in the quote.

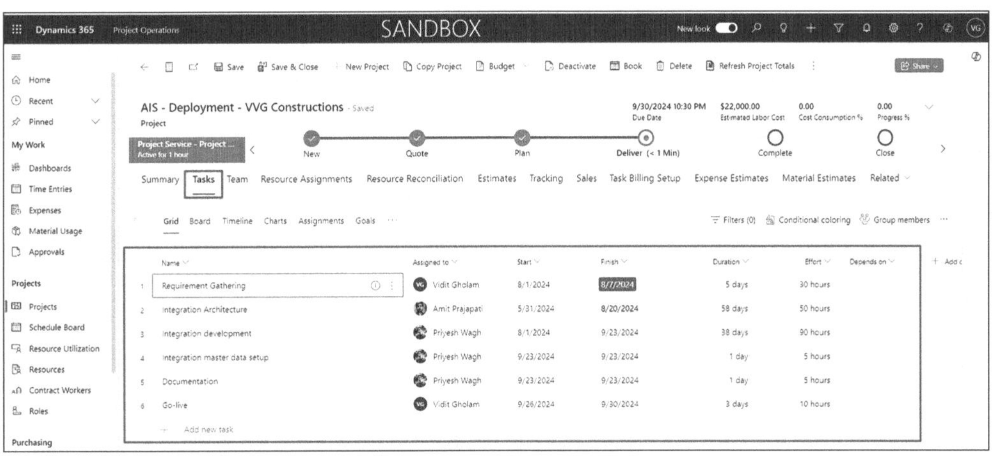

***Figure 3.31**: Creating Project Tasks as per the Estimates*

4. Since our deployment involves expenses, we will also include the expense estimates.

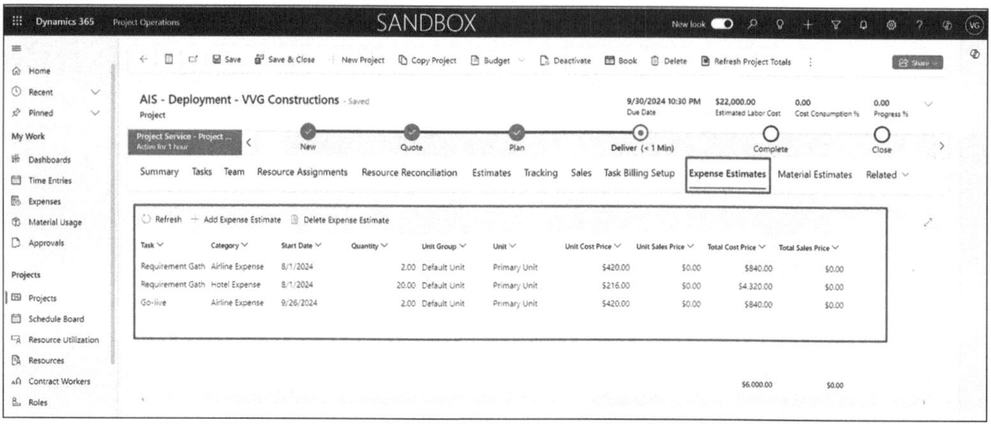

Figure 3.32: *Expense Estimates on the Project*

5. Once everything is set up, the estimated costs will automatically be updated in the summary tab under the estimate section of the project.
6. Additionally, notice that the business process flow is now at the delivery stage, indicating that the project has officially started. In IT terms, this means the project has kicked off.

Resource Allocations, Expense, and Time Entries

Once the project kicks off, Project Managers start assigning team members to the project. Time and expense entries are then submitted for approval to be approved by the Project Approvers.

Let us explore how this process unfolds.

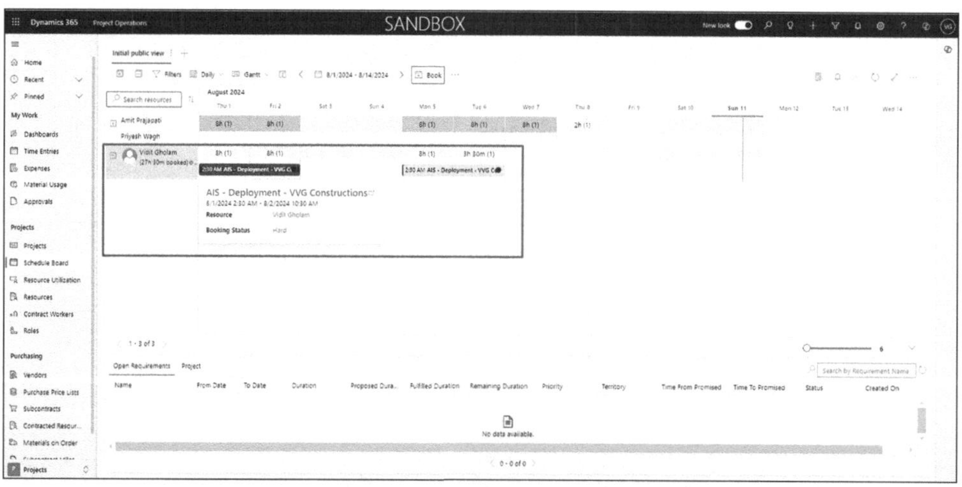

Figure 3.33(a): *Resource Allocation Using the Schedule Board*

To bill time for a project, the first step is to allocate resources to project tasks, allowing them to submit their time entries. This resource allocation is handled through the schedule board, as shown in *Figure 3.33(a)*.

1. To allocate a resource, click on the desired resource, choose the appropriate date range, and then click the **`'Book'`** button.
2. A booking window will open where you can select the project, resource, and the start and end times for the allocation.

   For example, for the Requirement Gathering task on our deployment, the Project Manager (**`Vidit Gholam`**) needs a 30-hour allocation from August 1 to August 7, 2024, as shown in *Figure 3.33(b)*.

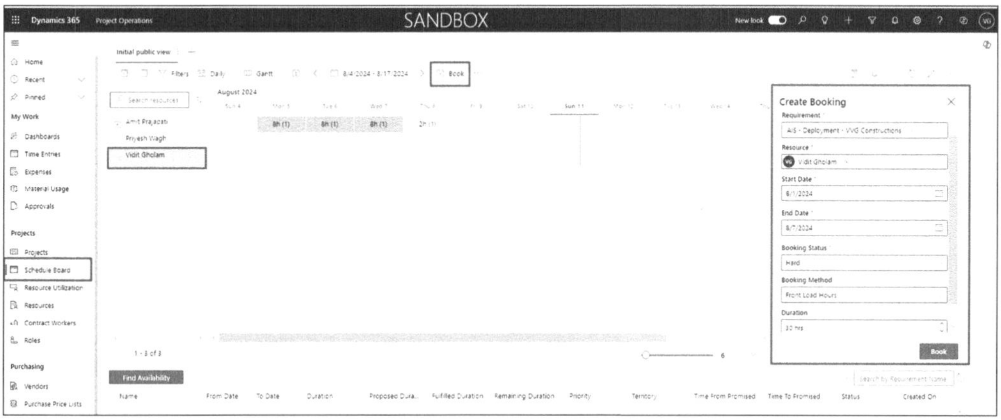

***Figure 3.33(b)**: Allocation a Resource Using the Schedule Board*

3. For this example, we have selected the booking status as hard and the booking methods as Front load hours.
4. You can select the booking status and booking as per your requirement. Details about each are provided here:

   a. Booking Status

      i. **Hard Booked**: Resources are confirmed and committed to the project. The time is guaranteed and cannot be easily changed or reallocated.

      ii. **Soft Booked**: Resources are tentatively reserved for the project but are not yet confirmed. There is flexibility to adjust or reassign these resources based on project needs.

      iii. **Proposed**: Resources have been suggested for the project, but the commitment is not yet firm. It is more of a preliminary allocation that requires confirmation.

b. Booking Methods

   i. **Full Capacity**: Resources are booked based on their total available hours. The scheduling assumes the resource will be fully utilized during the allocated time.

   ii. **Front Load Hours**: Scheduling method where the hours are concentrated at the beginning of the project or task. This approach helps in managing workloads and can be useful for tasks that need early completion.

   iii. **Percentage Capacity**: Resources are allocated a percentage of their total available capacity. For example, if a resource is 50% booked, they are only scheduled for half their available hours.

   iv. **Remaining Capacity**: This method books resources based on the hours remaining in their schedule after accounting for existing commitments. It ensures that resources are not overbooked.

   v. **Evenly Distributed Hours**: Hours are distributed evenly across the available time period. This method helps in balancing the workload and avoiding peaks in resource allocation.

Now that the resource is booked, let us move on to how resources will submit their time entries, and how this time gets approved and billed against the project.

Time and Expense Entries

When managing a project in Dynamics 365 Project Operations, tracking time and expenses is essential. Time entries let you capture the hours your team spends on specific tasks, which is key for keeping billing accurate and tracking the project's progress. Expense entries, on the other hand, log costs related to the project, such as travel or accommodation. Both time and expense entries go through an approval process before they are linked to the project and billed to the client, ensuring everything stays on track.

Time Entry

There are two ways for resources to bill their time: they can either create a time entry manually or simply import the time allocated to them on the schedule board.

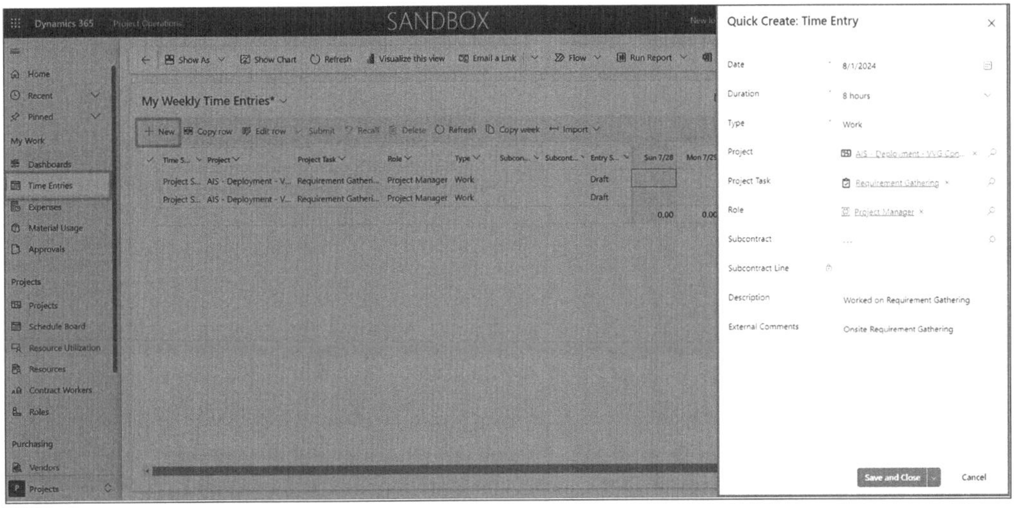

***Figure 3.34(a)**: Manual Time Entry in Dynamics 365 Project Operations*

To create a time entry, follow these steps:

1. Click **New** to create a new time entry.
2. A new time entry form will open.
3. **Date**: Select the date for which you are logging time.
4. **Project**: Choose the project you are working on.
5. **Task**: Select the specific task or work package you worked on.
6. **Duration**: Enter the number of hours worked.
7. **Description**: Provide a brief description of the work done during this time.

To import time entries:

1. Click the "**Import**" button, which allows you to pull in the time that has already been allocated to you on the schedule board.

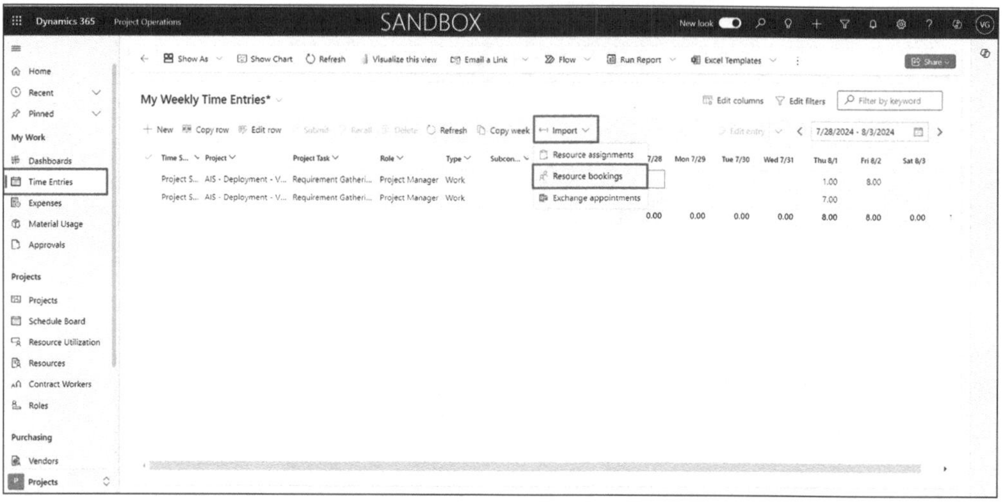

Figure 3.34(b): *Time Entries in Dynamics 365 Project Operations*

2. Select the specific date range for which you want to import time entries. The system will display all tasks assigned to you during this period.

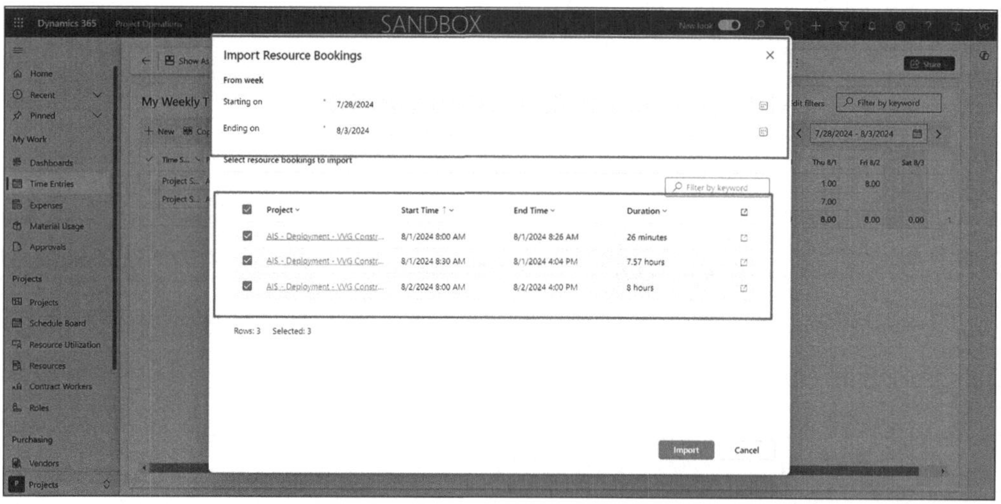

Figure 3.34(c): *Importing Time Entries in Dynamics 365 Project Operations*

3. Review the list of tasks and select the ones you want to import as time entries and click the import button.

4. All the created and imported time entries will be in the draft stage, using the submit button.

5. Review the details. Make any necessary adjustments, then select and submit the time entry for approval.

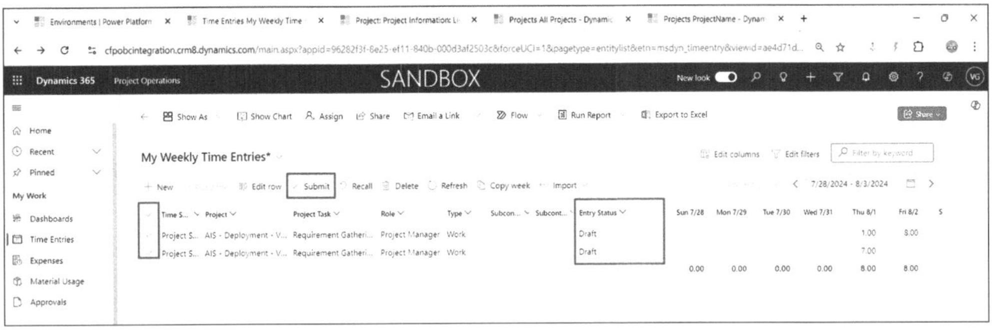

Figure 3.34(d): *Submitting Time Entries for Approval*

6. Submitted time entries are sent to the project managers for approval.

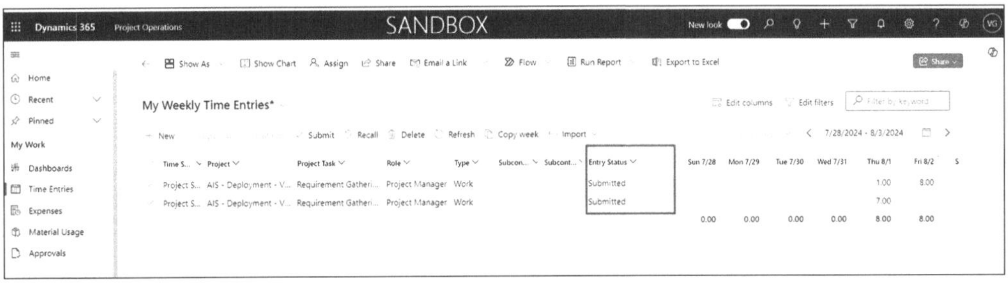

Figure 3.34(e): *Submitted Time Entries for Approval*

Time Approval

All submitted time entries will appear in the Approvals section of the site map, ready for review by the Project Approver. In this example, the Project Manager serves as the Project Approver. As shown in *Figure* 3.30, the Project Manager role is highlighted as the Project Approver. This setup ensures that the correct person reviews and approves the time entries for each project. Project Approvers will only see time entries that are associated with their respective projects. A custom power automate email or Teams notification can be created to notify project approvers once time entries are submitted for approval by the resources. We will learn how to create this notification in the upcoming chapters.

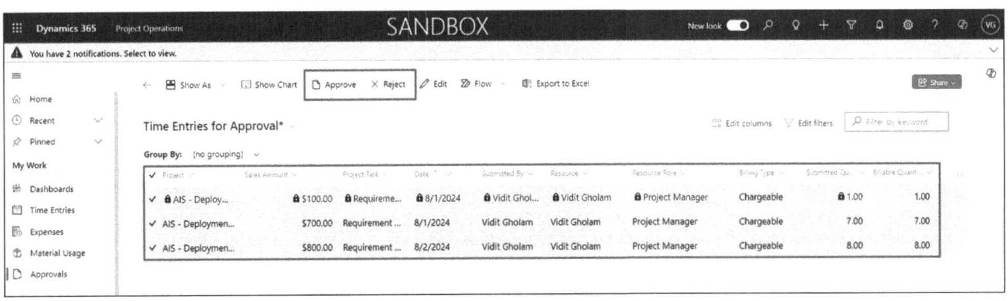

Figure 3.35: *Time Entry Approvals in Project Dynamics 365 Operations*

Project Approvers can reject incorrect time submitted by the resource.

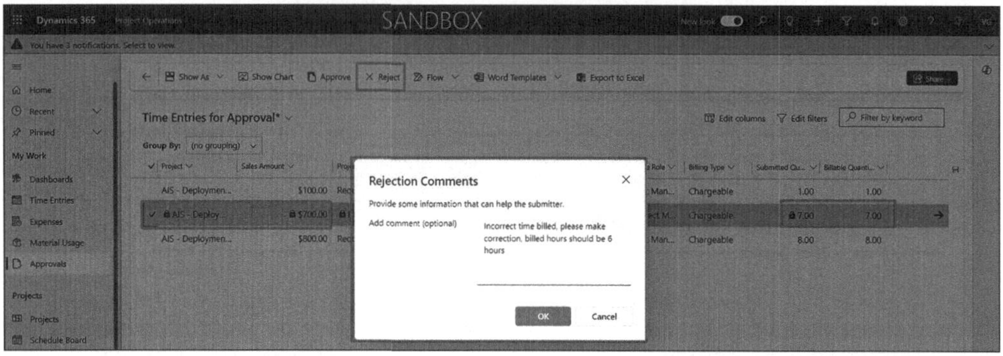

Figure 3.36: *Rejecting Time Entry submitted for Approval*

Approved time entries will be marked as "**`Approved`**" in the Time Entry section, while rejected entries will be labeled as "**`Returned`**" or "**`Rejected`**." Rejected entries are sent back to the draft state, allowing the resources to make necessary corrections before resubmitting.

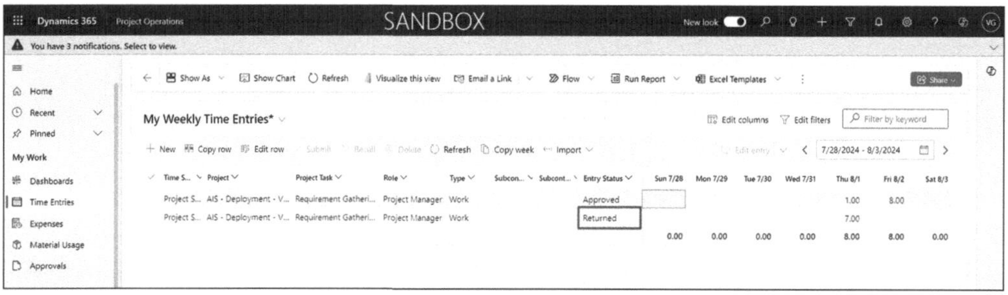

Figure 3.37: *Approved and Returned Time Entry*

If a time entry is approved but needs changes, the resource can recall the entry.

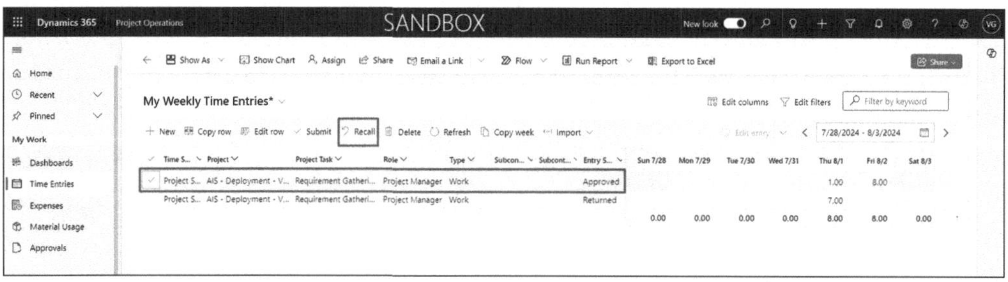

Figure 3.38(a): *Recall Approved Time Entry in Dynamics 365 Project Operations*

Once recalled, the time entry will be sent back to the Project Approver for approval.

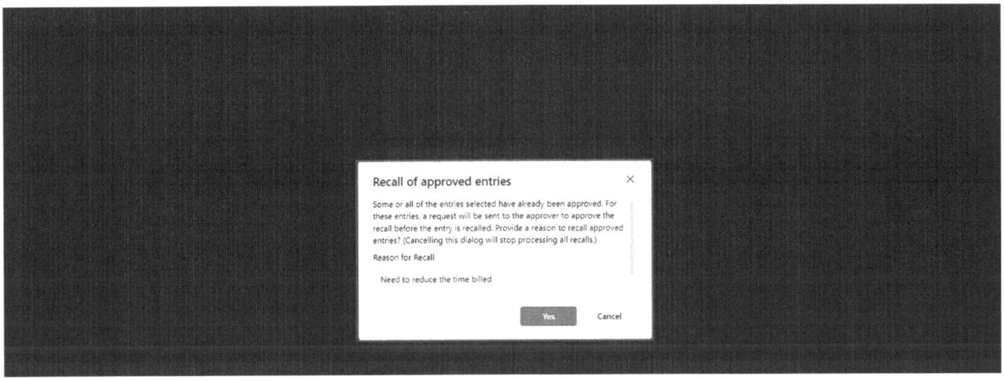

Figure 3.38(b): *Recall Approved Time Entry in Dynamics 365 Project Operations*

The status of all recalled time entries will be displayed as "**`Recall Requested`**."

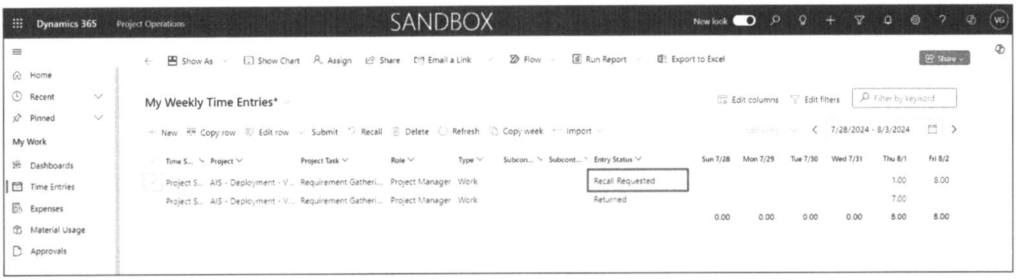

Figure 3.38(c): *Recalled Time Entry in Dynamics 365 Project Operations*

All recall requests will appear in the **`Approvals`** section under the "**`Recalled Request for Approvals`**" view.

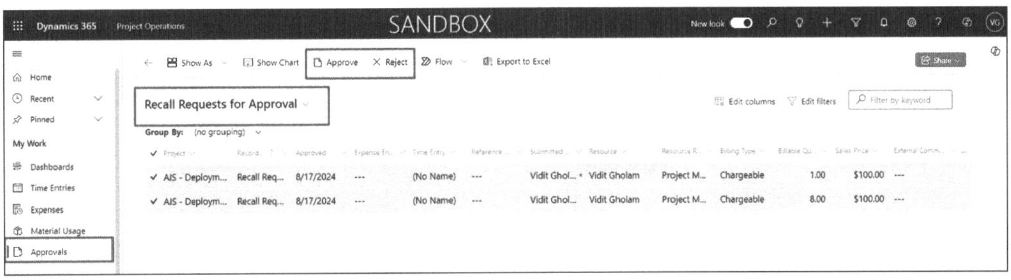

Figure 3.38(d): *Recall Request in Approvals*

Approved recall requests will show up with a time entry status of "**`Returned`**," while rejected recall requests will revert to the "**`Approved`**" stage in the **`Time Entry`** section.

Expense Entry

When you are managing expenses in Dynamics 365 Project Operations, it is important to track every project-related cost accurately, whether it is for travel, accommodation, or other reimbursable items. Let us explore the process of entering an expense to ensure everything is properly recorded.

1. Start by clicking "**`New Expense`**" to create a new entry.
2. Fill in the necessary details, such as the expense category, date, and amount. If you have receipts or other documentation, you can attach them here.
3. Link the expense to a specific project task or activity to make sure it is correctly tracked.
4. Choose the relevant project and task from the dropdown menus provided.

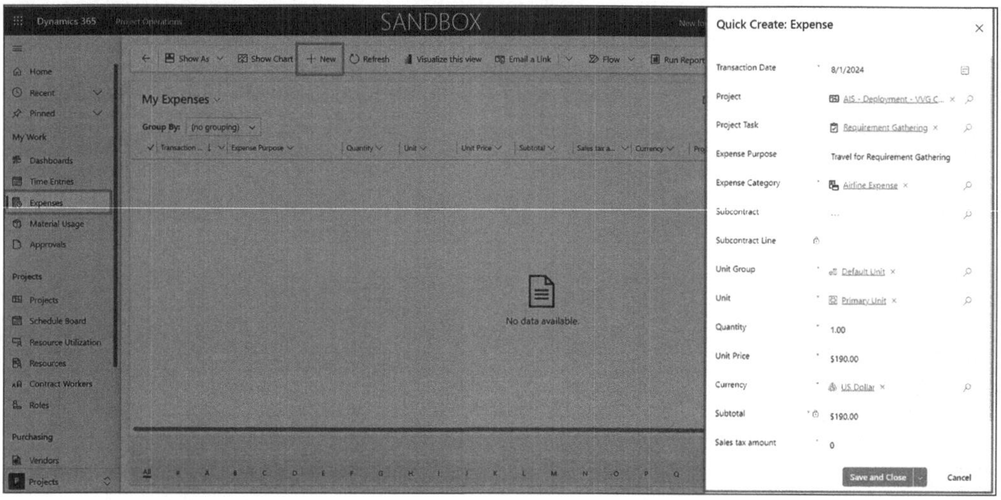

Figure 3.39(a): *Creating Expense Entries in Project Operations*

5. Once all the details are entered, submit the expense for approval.

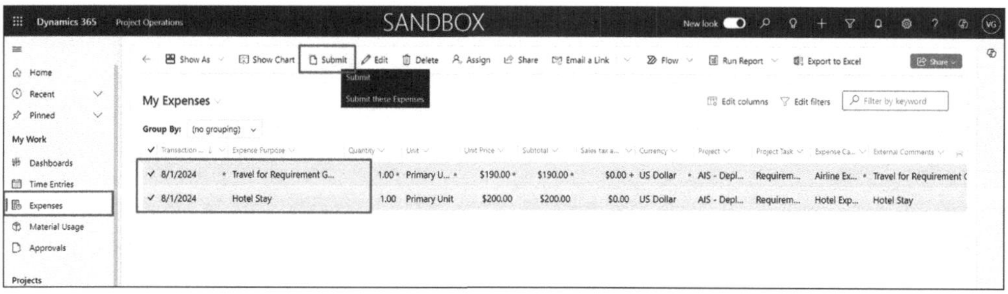

Figure 3.39(b): *Submitting Expense Entries for Approval*

6. The expense entry will then go through the same approval workflow as time entries.
7. After submission, the expense will appear in the Project Approver's queue for review.

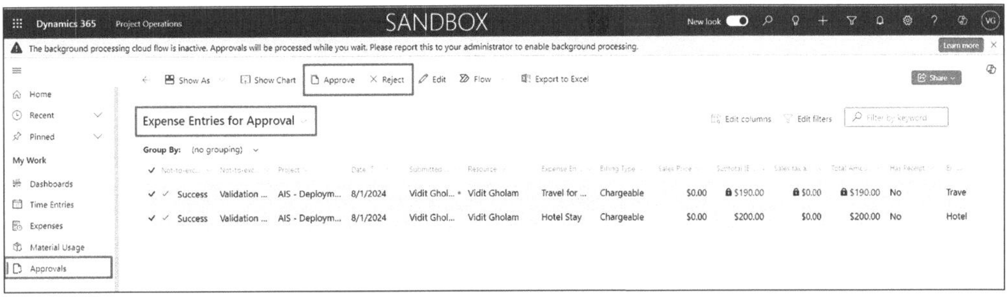

***Figure 3.39(c)**: Expense Entry Approvals*

8. Once approved, the expense will be recorded against the project, and the status will be updated accordingly.

After submitting and approving the time and expense entries, the sales and cost actuals for these entries are created. Now, let us look at how to create a **`Proforma`** invoice.

Creating Proforma Invoices in Dynamics 365 CRM

In Dynamics 365 Project Operations, a Proforma Invoice is a preliminary invoice that provides a detailed estimate of the costs and charges for a project before the final invoice is issued. It is used to review and confirm the billing details with the client, giving them an overview of the expected charges based on the time, expenses, and milestones that have been recorded.

Now for all approved time and expense entries, the system automatically creates actuals, which then reside in the **`Time and Material Billing Backlog`** within the **`Sales Area`** under **`Billing`** on the site map. This backlog collects the billable time and expenses from all projects, awaiting the accounting team to mark them as ready for invoicing.

Some of you might be wondering: What exactly are actuals?

In Dynamics 365 Project Operations, "**`actuals`**" refer to the recorded financial impact of the work completed, and expenses incurred on a project. When time and expense entries are submitted and approved, the system generates actuals to reflect the cost and revenue associated with those entries. Similarly, for fixed fee milestones, actuals are created once the milestone is reached, showing the revenue earned for that phase of the project. These actuals provide a clear picture of the project's financial status, helping to track profitability and manage billing accurately.

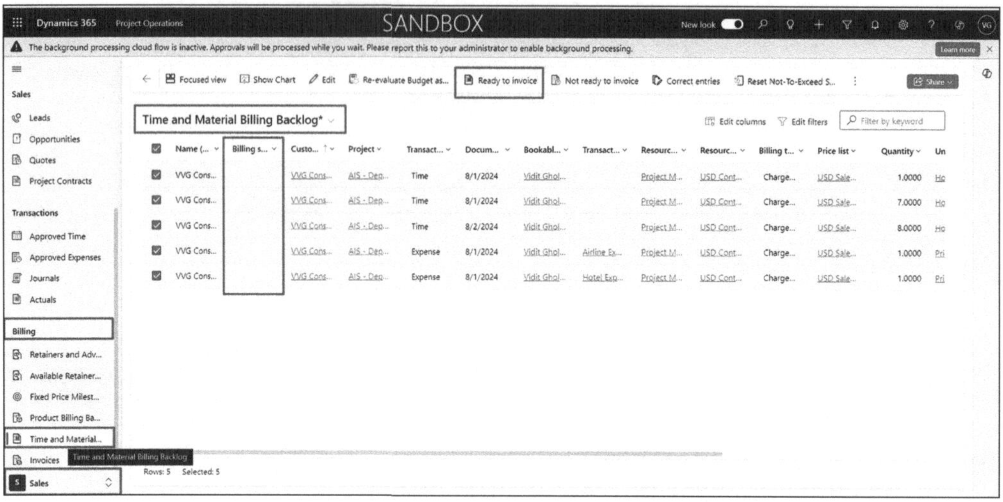

Figure 3.40(a): *Expense Time and Expense Entry Actuals in Billing Backlog*

You can also view and manage cost and sales actuals directly from the project, including marking them as ready to invoice. To filter for actuals ready to invoice, set the **`Transaction Type`** to "**`Unbilled Sales`**", the **`Adjustment Status`** to "**`Does not contain data`**," and the **`Billing Status`** to "**`Empty`**".

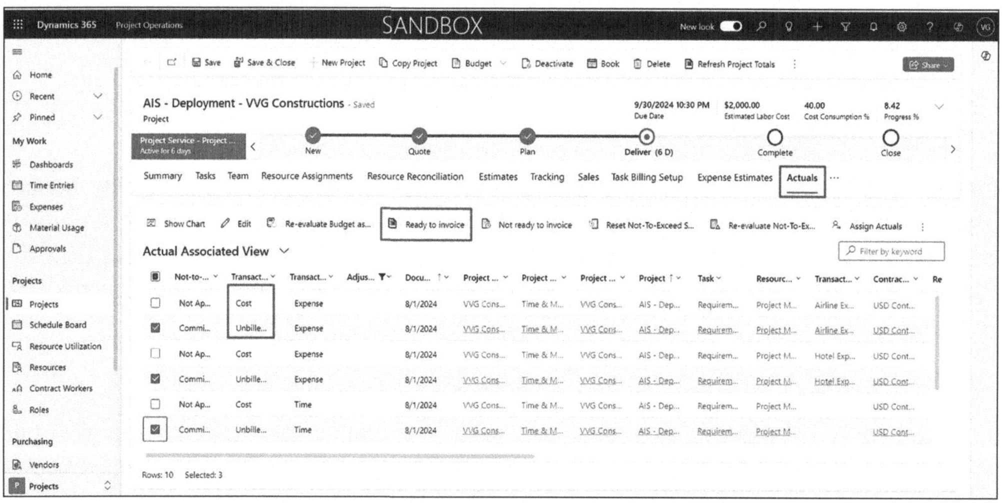

Figure 3.40(b): *Actuals Related to Projects in Project Operations*

These actuals help in determining project costs and profitability, also can be used with a Power BI report, to can gain deeper insights. Additionally, since these actuals are associated with the project contract (order), which can help assess contract consumption and profitability.

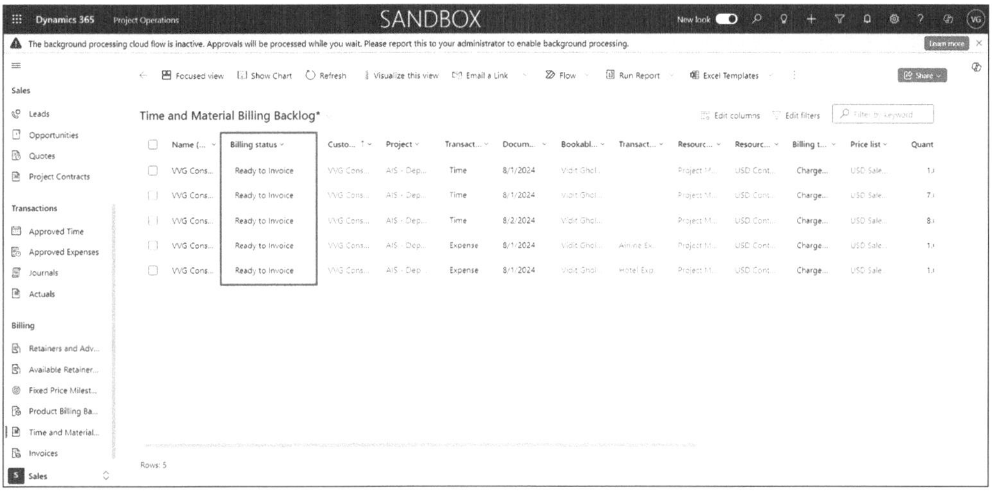

Figure 3.40(c): *Actuals Ready to Invoice in Time and Material Billing Back Log*

Once actuals are marked as ready to invoice, their billing status is updated to "**Ready to Invoice**." Now that we have a milestone and a set of time and expense entries marked as ready to invoice, let us move on to creating an invoice for these project actuals.

To create an invoice, go to the project contract (order) and click "**Create Invoice**." If there are any ready-to-invoice actuals, the system will automatically generate an invoice for those items.

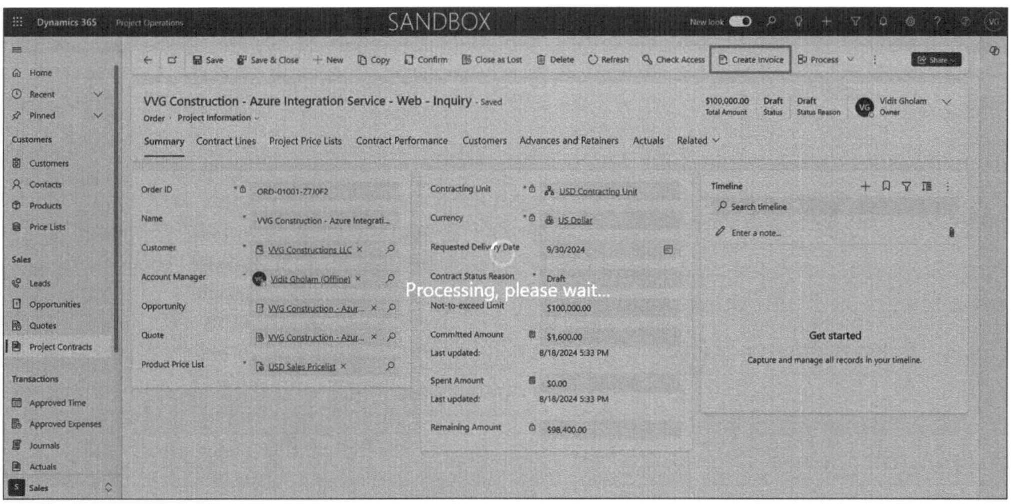

Figure 3.41: *Creating Proforma Invoice from the Project Contract*

The proforma invoice includes two types of lines: one for the fixed price milestone amount and another for billed time and expenses related to the time and material line.

***Figure 3.42**: Proforma Invoice in Project Operations*

If a contract includes both fixed price and time and material lines, and if actuals for any of these lines are not ready to be billed, the proforma invoice will create a line with zero amount for those contract lines.

Invoice also stores information such as payment terms, billing due date, customer billing address, and associated invoice line details. This data can be used to draw useful reports, including:

- Revenue Forecasting Report (Accrued Income)
- AR-Aging Reports
- Profitability Report
- Customer Billing Summary Report

Invoice Reporting

Since a proforma invoice is essentially a preliminary bill, it is important for both management and potentially your customers to review it carefully.

Generating a detailed invoice document or report that outlines all the billed items can be very helpful in this process. You can open each invoice line to view the specifics of what's being billed, providing clarity and ensuring everything is accurate before finalizing the invoice.

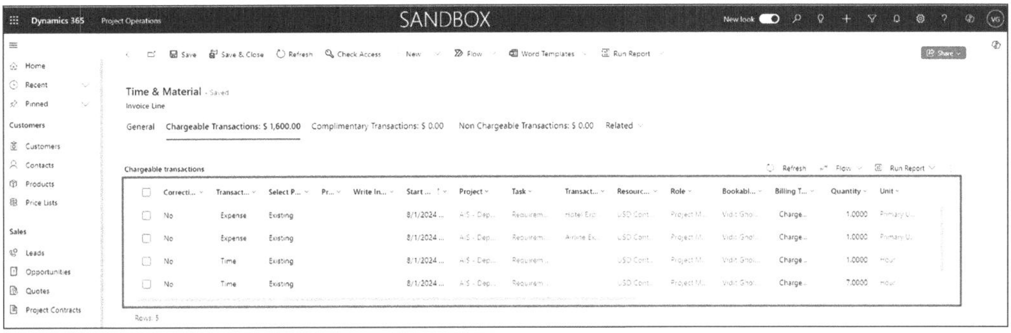

Figure 3.43: *Invoice Line Details for Time and Material Invoice Line*

These invoice line details can be used to generate an invoice report document, which you can automatically create by simply clicking a button, as shown in *Figure* 3.44. We will cover the development area of this process in more detail in *Chapter* 6, *Document Management in Dynamics 365 CRM.*

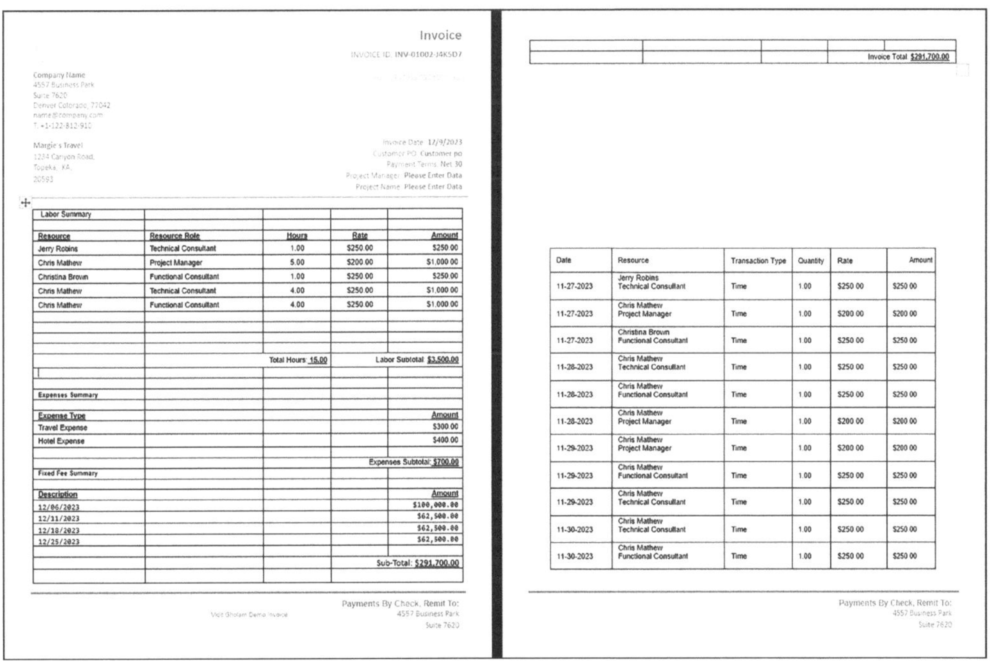

Figure 3.44: *Invoice Report Document Generated from the Invoice*

Once the invoice is reviewed, you can confirm it and send the final version to the customer.

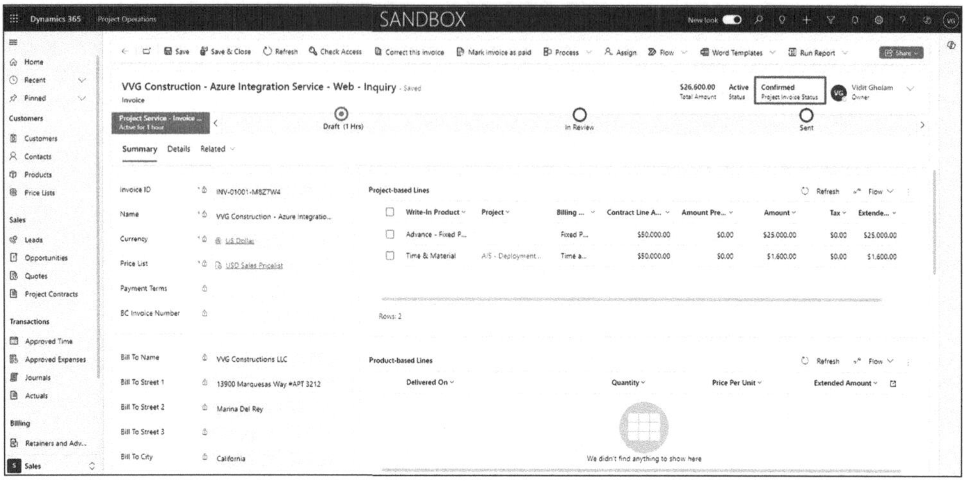

Figure 3.45: *Confirmed Invoice in Project Operations*

At this stage, many organizations choose to integrate these proforma invoices with financial systems such as Dynamics 365 Business Central, D365 Finance and Operations, QuickBooks, or Zoho Books. After payment is received, the invoice is marked as paid.

Figure 3.46: *Marking Invoice as Paid in Project Operations*

Once the invoice is marked as paid, its status changes to **"Invoice Paid**," and the invoice becomes read-only.

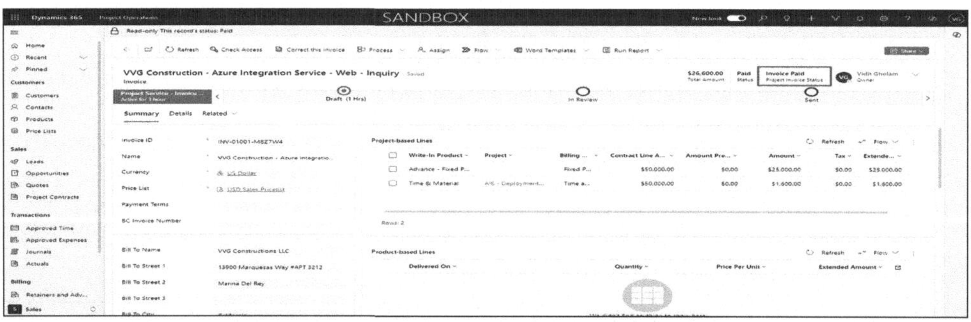

Figure 3.47: Paid Invoice in Project Operations

With the invoice processed and payment received, we have completed the sales-to-billing cycle. This structured approach ensures that each step from initial sale to final billing is handled efficiently, keeping your projects well-managed and financially on track.

Reporting

Before we wrap up this chapter, let us explore a bonus section on the types of Power BI and SSRS reports you can create for Project and Contract Management. These reports provide valuable insights to help manage your projects and contracts effectively.

- **Project Status Report:** Track the overall health of your projects with visual indicators of progress, milestones, and key performance metrics. This report helps in understanding whether projects are on schedule, within budget, and meeting objectives.

  An example of the project status report is the following SSRS report. This report is generated using Project Tasks and Actuals Billed against the projects, which can also be shared with customer as a weekly status update.

AIS - Deployment - VVG Constructions

Percentage Complete 100% | **Remaining Hours** 0 Hrs. | **Actual Hours** 625 Hrs.

Project Name	Task Number	Task Name	Start Date	End Date	Status	Actual Hours	Budget Hours	Progress
AIS - Deployment - VVG Constructions	1	Code Upgradation	22-11-2021	29-04-2022	Active	300.00	300.00	100%
	2	Data Upgradation	17-01-2022	03-06-2022	Active	99.50	100.00	99.5%
	3	Testing	20-12-2021	08-04-2022	Active	40.00	40.00	100%
	4	Changing endpoints in Integration	21-03-2022	18-04-2022	Active	20.00	20.00	100%
	5	Power BI Report Changes	04-04-2022	22-04-2022	Active	26.00	26.00	100%
	6	UAT	21-03-2022	03-06-2022	Active	40.50	40.00	101.25%
	7	Documentation	28-03-2022	06-05-2022	Active	24.00	24.00	100%
	8	Project Management	16-11-2021	15-03-2022	Active	75.00	75.00	100%

Figure 3.48: *Project Status Report*
This report is inspired and referenced from www.cloudfronts.com

- **Contract Performance Report**: Monitor the performance of various contracts by comparing budgeted versus actual costs, tracking contract milestones, and analyzing financial performance. This report helps ensure that contracts are managed effectively, and any deviations are addressed promptly.

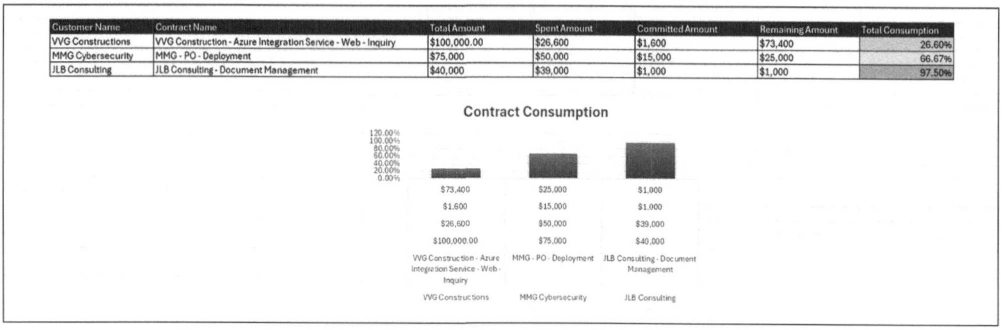

Customer Name	Contract Name	Total Amount	Spent Amount	Committed Amount	Remaining Amount	Total Consumption
VVG Constructions	VVG Construction - Azure Integration Service - Web - Inquiry	$100,000.00	$26,600	$1,600	$73,400	26.60%
MMG Cybersecurity	MMG - PO - Deployment	$75,000	$50,000	$15,000	$25,000	66.67%
JLB Consulting	JLB Consulting - Document Management	$40,000	$39,000	$1,000	$1,000	97.50%

Figure 3.49: *Contract Consumption Report*
This report is inspired and referenced from www.cloudfronts.com

All the data needed for the consumption report is readily available on the project contract. You can refer to *Figure* 3.50 for a visual representation of where this information can be accessed.

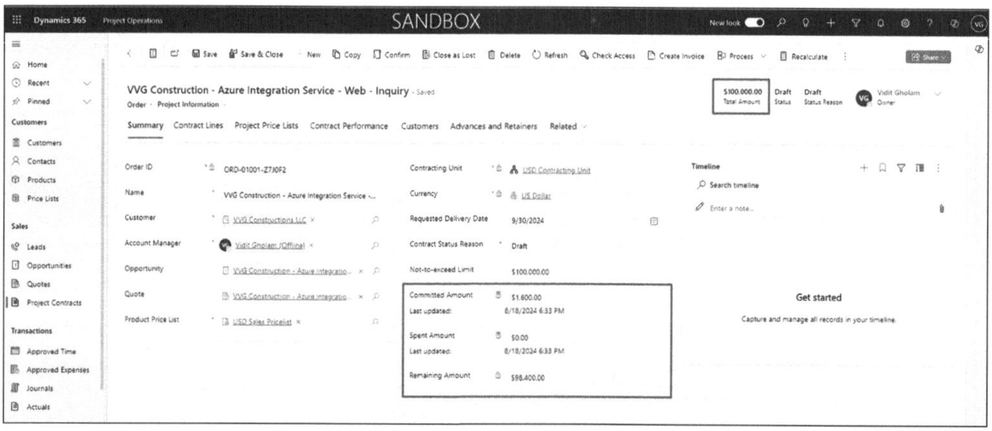

Figure 3.50: *Contract Consumption Report Data Points*

- **Resources Allocation Report:** The Resource Allocation Report provides a detailed view of how resources are assigned to various project tasks and milestones. It highlights the distribution of workload among team members, allowing managers to track resource utilization and adjust assignments as needed. The following report shows how many hours a resource is allocated per week. Data for this report is fetched from **`Bookable Resource`** bookings.

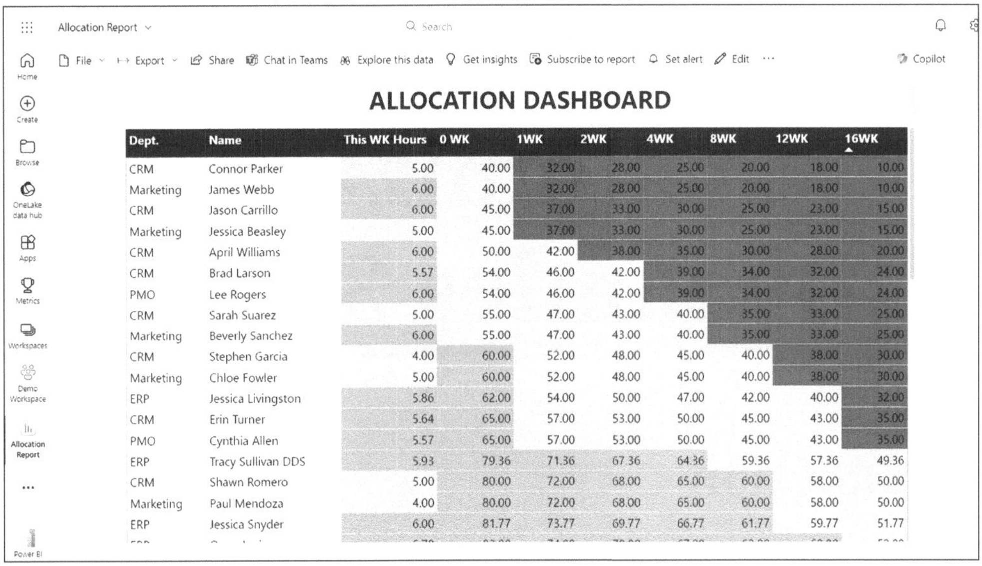

Dept.	Name	This WK Hours	0 WK	1WK	2WK	4WK	8WK	12WK	16WK
CRM	Connor Parker	5.00	40.00	32.00	28.00	25.00	20.00	18.00	10.00
Marketing	James Webb	6.00	40.00	32.00	28.00	25.00	20.00	18.00	10.00
CRM	Jason Carrillo	6.00	45.00	37.00	33.00	30.00	25.00	23.00	15.00
Marketing	Jessica Beasley	5.00	45.00	37.00	33.00	30.00	25.00	23.00	15.00
CRM	April Williams	6.00	50.00	42.00	38.00	35.00	30.00	28.00	20.00
CRM	Brad Larson	5.57	54.00	46.00	42.00	39.00	34.00	32.00	24.00
PMO	Lee Rogers	6.00	54.00	46.00	42.00	39.00	34.00	32.00	24.00
CRM	Sarah Suarez	5.00	55.00	47.00	43.00	40.00	35.00	33.00	25.00
Marketing	Beverly Sanchez	6.00	55.00	47.00	43.00	40.00	35.00	33.00	25.00
CRM	Stephen Garcia	4.00	60.00	52.00	48.00	45.00	40.00	38.00	30.00
Marketing	Chloe Fowler	5.00	60.00	52.00	48.00	45.00	40.00	38.00	30.00
ERP	Jessica Livingston	5.86	62.00	54.00	50.00	47.00	42.00	40.00	32.00
CRM	Erin Turner	5.64	65.00	57.00	53.00	50.00	45.00	43.00	35.00
PMO	Cynthia Allen	5.57	65.00	57.00	53.00	50.00	45.00	43.00	35.00
ERP	Tracy Sullivan DDS	5.93	79.36	71.36	67.36	64.36	59.36	57.36	49.36
CRM	Shawn Romero	5.00	80.00	72.00	68.00	65.00	60.00	58.00	50.00
Marketing	Paul Mendoza	4.00	80.00	72.00	68.00	65.00	60.00	58.00	50.00
ERP	Jessica Snyder	6.00	81.77	73.77	69.77	66.77	61.77	59.77	51.77

Figure 3.51: *Resource Allocation Report. This report is inspired and referenced from www.cloudfronts.com*

Conclusion

In this chapter, we covered the intricacies of the Sales-to-Billing Cycle in Microsoft Dynamics 365 CRM, including managing Leads and Opportunities, utilizing Sales Dashboards, and handling Quotations. We also explored Project Contracts and Sales Orders, resource allocations, time and expense entries, and the creation of Proforma Invoices. Additionally, we discussed various reporting options such as Project Reporting and Contract Consumption Reporting.

In the next chapter, we will delve into the world of C# Plugins, focusing on customizing Entities, Fields, Forms, and Views within Dynamics 365 CRM. We will also explore the use of JavaScript Web Resources and the application of Business Rules and Workflows. This will provide you with deeper insights and practical skills to further enhance your Dynamics 365 CRM implementation.

References

1. Dashboards and Charts in Dynamics 365: https://learn.microsoft.com/en-us/dynamics365/customerengagement/on-premises/basics/start-your-day-dashboard-chart?view=op-9-1
2. Product based Quote lines: https://learn.microsoft.com/en-us/dynamics365/project-operations/psa/product-based-quote-lines
3. CloudFronts Blogs: https://www.cloudfronts.com/blog/
4. Microsoft Documentation: https://learn.microsoft.com/en-us/

CHAPTER 4
Customizing Your Dynamics 365 CRM

Introduction

As we have seen in previous chapters, Dynamics 365 CRM has a robust set of pre-existing entities (or tables), such as Accounts and Contacts, that come with built-in forms, fields, and views. These are used across different model-driven apps such as Project Operations and Sales. For example, the Account Table includes Columns such as Name, Website, Phone, and Address, along with various forms such as the Accounts Form, tailored for different purposes within these apps.

These pre-configured forms, fields, and views are known as out-of-the-box (OOB) customizations and are part of managed solutions created by Microsoft. If you need functionalities beyond what is provided out-of-the-box, Dynamics 365 CRM offers the flexibility to tailor the system to your specific needs. This means you can create custom tables, forms, columns, and views, or modify existing ones. For instance, if you require a custom auto-numbering format for accounts, such as "ACC-FEB2024-001," or if you want to generate a view for accounts created in the first financial quarter of a specific year, customization is the way to go.

In this chapter, we will explore how you can customize Dynamics 365 CRM to fit your business needs. We will walk through the different ways you can adjust entities (tables), fields (attributes), forms, and views to better suit your needs. We will also introduce you to using C# Plug-ins, which allow you to add custom logic to your CRM for enhanced functionality. Additionally, we will discuss how JavaScript web resources can bring more interactivity to your forms and fields, making them more responsive. Finally, we will cover business rules and workflows, as well as tools that help you automate processes and apply business logic without the need for coding. By the end of this chapter, you will have a clear understanding of how to make Dynamics 365 CRM work best for your business.

Note: *In Dynamics 365 CRM, tables, columns, and rows were previously known as entities, fields, and records. This book will use these terms interchangeably to ensure clarity for all readers.*

Structure

In this chapter, we will discuss the following topics:

- Customizing Entities (Tables), Fields (Columns), Forms, and Views in Dynamics 365 CRM
- Introduction to C# Plug-ins in Dynamics 365 CRM
- Using JavaScript's Web resources in Dynamics 365 CRM
- Business Rules in Dynamics 365 CRM
- Workflows in Dynamics 365 CRM
    - Actions, Custom Actions, and Custom APIs in Dynamics 365 CRM

Customizing Entities (Tables), Fields (Columns), Forms, and Views in Dynamics 365 CRM

Before we start customizing, there are a few important things to keep in mind. Customizations are developed in an unmanaged solution within a development environment. Once they are fine-tuned and tested, these customizations can be deployed to the production environment using a managed solution. Now you might wonder what solutions are and what are managed and unmanaged solutions in Dynamics 365. Solutions in Dynamics 365 CRM are essentially packages that contain all your customizations and configurations, making it easier to manage and deploy changes across different environments. They act as containers for components such as entities (tables), fields (attributes), forms, views, Plug-ins, workflows, and business rules, helping you keep everything organized.

There are two types of solutions in Dynamics 365: Managed and Unmanaged.

- **Managed Solutions** are typically used in production environments and are locked down to prevent further modifications. This makes them ideal for distributing finished products or customizations, as they can be easily installed or uninstalled without affecting the underlying system. Managed solutions ensure that your changes are controlled and protected, which is especially important in stable environments. *Figure* 4.1 shows the managed solution that got deployed in the environment for the Dynamics 365 `Project Operations` App.

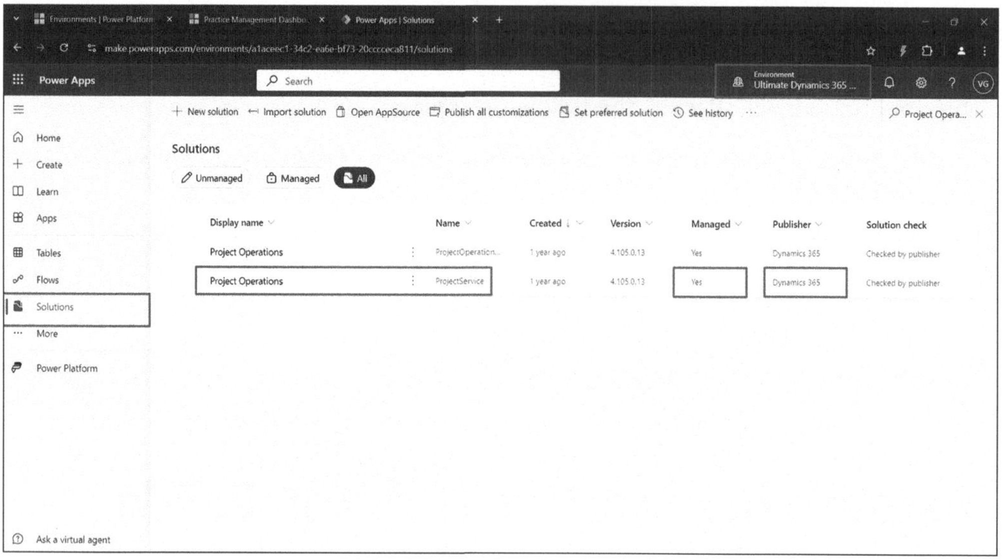

Figure 4.1: *Project Operations Managed Solution*

- **Unmanaged Solutions** are primarily used during the development phase. They allow you to freely edit and customize components, offering flexibility during the building and testing process.

However, they do not provide the same level of protection as managed solutions, meaning that changes are permanent once deployed. It is common practice to convert an unmanaged solution into a managed one when moving to a production environment. *Figure* 4.2 shows an unmanaged solution created to customize the Accounts entity.

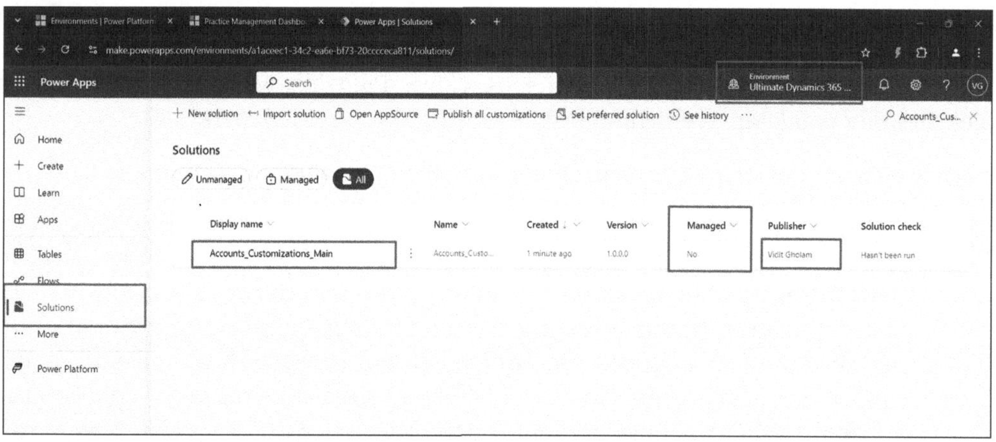

Figure 4.2: *Unmanaged Solution Created for Customizing Accounts Entity in Dynamics 365 CRM*

We will be using these concepts for effectively managing customizations in Dynamics 365 and ensuring that the changes are applied consistently across different environments.

With that let us begin customizing!

Entities (Tables)

Entities in Dynamics 365 are essentially the digital tables that store data in the system. Think of them as the building blocks of your CRM where each entity represents a specific type of data, such as accounts, contacts, leads, or opportunities. Each entity has fields (or attributes) that define the kind of data it can hold.

For example, an "**`Account`**" entity might have fields for the account name, address, phone number, and so on. Entities can be customized to include additional fields, forms, and views, allowing you to tailor Dynamics 365 to meet your specific business needs.

Here are the primary types:

- **Standard Entities**: These are the out-of-the-box (OOB) entities provided by Dynamics 365, such as Accounts, Contacts, and Opportunities. You can customize these entities by adding fields, forms, or views to meet specific requirements.
- **Activity Entities:** These entities are used to track interactions or actions within Dynamics 365, such as emails, phone calls, appointments, tasks, and custom activities. Activities are often related to other entities such as Accounts or Contacts.

Figure 4.3 illustrates Standard and Activity Entities, along with both Out-of-the-Box (OOB) and Custom Forms and Fields.

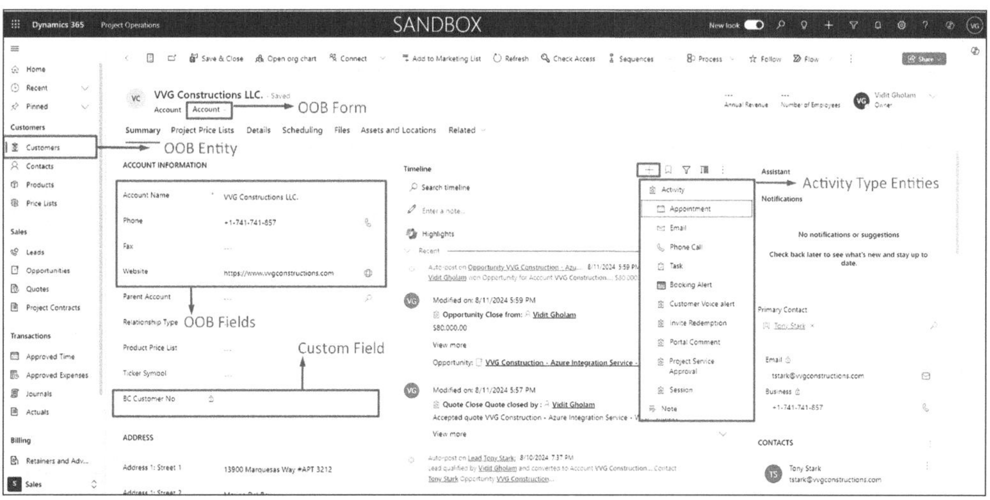

***Figure 4.3**: Standard, Activity Entities along with OOB and Custom Fields and Forms*

- **Custom Entities**: These are entities you create to address specific business needs that are not covered by the standard entities. For example, you might create a custom entity to track a unique business process or data set.

Figure 4.4 shows custom **`Zip Code`**, **`Country Code`**, and **`Error Logging`** entities that have been created as per business needs.

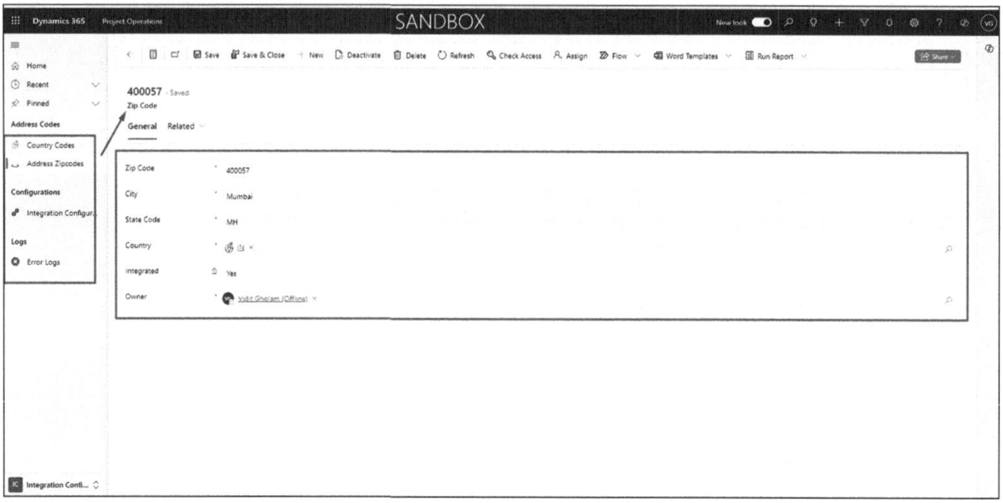

Figure 4.4*: Custom Entities in Dynamics 365 CRM*

- **Virtual Entities:** These entities allow you to integrate external data sources into Dynamics 365 without storing the data in the CRM database. The data remains in the external system but is accessible within Dynamics 365 as if it were a standard entity. For more details on virtual entities, refer to the link in **Reference 1**.

Fields (Columns)

Every entity in Dynamics 365 comprises a set of fields that define the data stored within that entity. Fields are the building blocks of an entity, capturing specific pieces of information such as names, dates, and other attributes relevant to the entity. For example, an "**`Account`**" entity might have fields such as "**`Account Name`**," "**`Website`**," "**`Phone Number`**," and "**`Address`**."

In Dynamics 365, fields are categorized into various types, each serving different purposes:

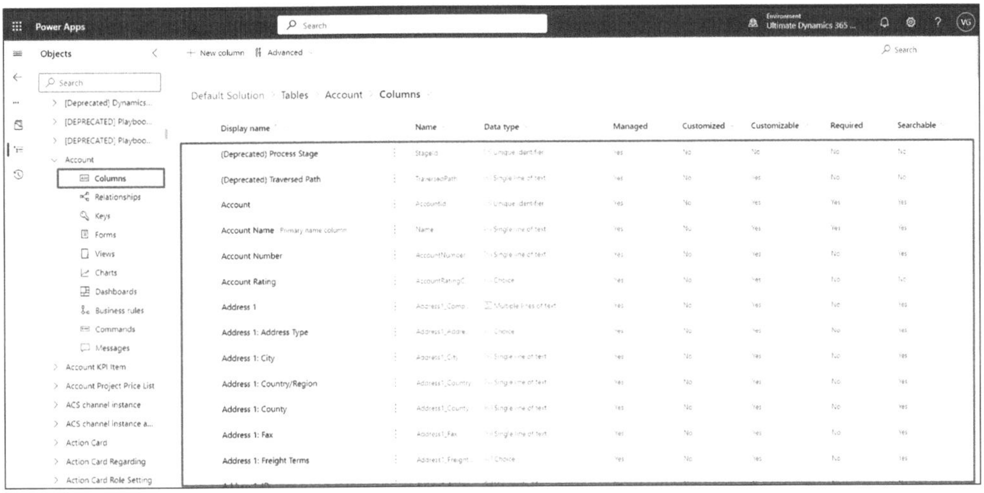

***Figure 4.5**: Fields in Dynamics 365 CRM Entities*

- **Single Line of Text (Text Columns):** Captures plain text data, such as names or descriptions. This field can be configured in different formats to suit the specific needs of your entity. Some common formats for a single line of text fields include:
    - **Text**: Used for simple text entries such as names or descriptions.
    - **Email**: Specifically formatted to capture and validate email addresses.
    - **Phone**: Designed to store phone numbers, often with validation.
    - **URL**: Used for web addresses, such as a company website.

  Refer to the link in **Reference 4** for more detailed information on Text Columns.
- **Option Set (Choice):** Provides a dropdown list of predefined options that users can select from. Refer to the link in Reference 5 for more detailed information on Choice Columns.
- **Two Options (Yes/No):** A simple field that allows for a binary choice, such as Yes/No or True/False.
- **Whole Number**: Stores integer values, suitable for counts or other numerical data without decimals.
- **Decimal Number:** Captures numbers with decimal points, allowing for more precision. Refer to the link in Reference 6 for more detailed information on Number Columns.
- **Currency:** Specifically designed for financial data, storing amounts in a currency format. Refer to the link in Reference 7 for more detailed information on Currency Columns.
- **Date and Time:** Records dates and times, which can be essential for tracking events or deadlines.

- **Lookup:** Creates a relationship between entities, allowing users to select a record from another entity as a value in this field. For example, the account entity has a 1:N relations with the contact entity through the "Primary Contact" lookup field. Refer to the link in Reference 8 for more detailed information on Number Columns.
- **Multi-Select Option Set (Multi-Choice):** Similar to an Option Set but allows multiple selections.

One of the most important fields in any entity is the Primary Key field. This field uniquely identifies each record within the entity. In Dynamics 365, the primary key is typically an auto-generated field, such as "`Account ID`" or "`Contact ID`," which ensures that each record can be distinctly referenced.

Forms

Every entity in Dynamics 365 CRM includes a set of forms that users interact with to view, create, or update records. Forms are essential for presenting data in a structured and user-friendly manner. Dynamics 365 CRM offers different types of forms, each serving specific purposes:

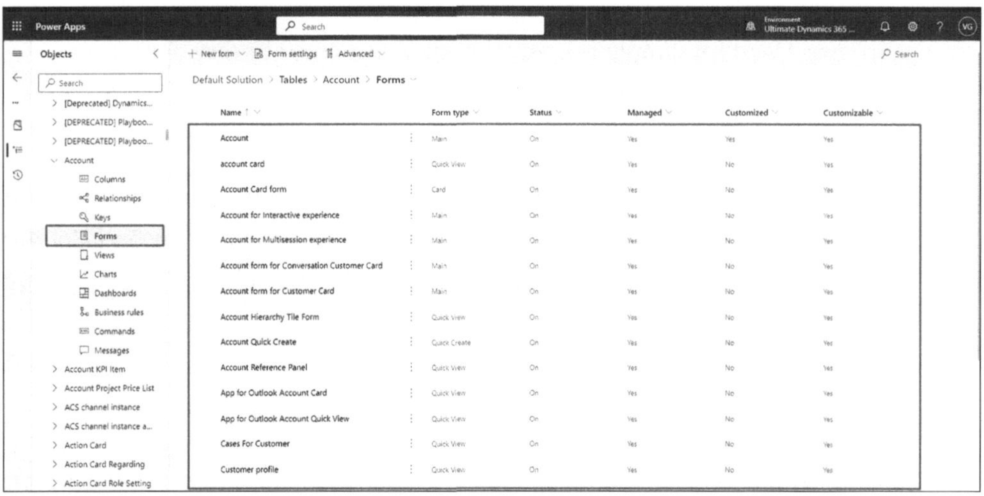

***Figure 4.6**: Forms in Dynamics 365 CRM Entities*

- **Main Forms**: The primary forms used in model-driven apps. They are versatile and provide the most detailed view of records. Users typically interact with these forms when working on desktop or tablet devices.
- **Quick Create Forms**: These forms allow users to quickly add records with minimal fields. They are useful for speeding up data entry tasks, especially when the user needs to create records on the fly without filling out extensive details.

- **Quick View Forms**: These forms provide a compact view of related entity data within another form. For example, if you are viewing a contact record, a quick view form might display related account information.
- **Card Forms**: These forms are mainly used for mobile devices, card forms present records in a compact, card-like format, making them ideal for use on smartphones.

Views

Similar to fields and forms, views are another essential component in Dynamics 365 CRM that helps users interact with data in a meaningful way. Every entity in Dynamics 365 comes with a set of views that display records in a structured format, allowing users to easily access and manage the information they need. Views are essentially predefined queries that pull specific data from the entity and display it in a list or grid format. There are several types of views available:

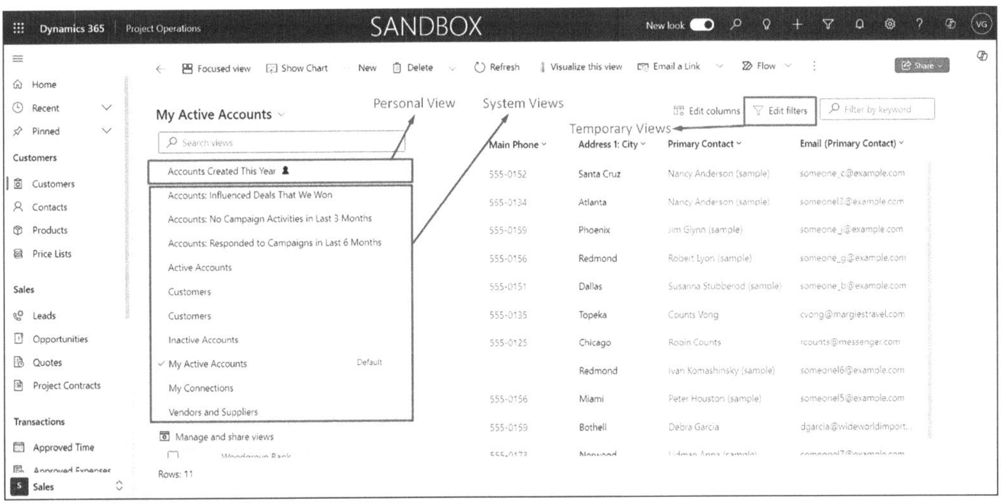

Figure 4.7: *Views in Dynamics 365 CRM Entities*

- **System Views:** These are default views provided by Dynamics 365 and are available to all users. Examples include "`Active Accounts`" or "`All Opportunities`."
- **Public Views:** Created by users or administrators, these views are available to everyone in the organization. They are helpful when a specific subset of data needs to be shared across teams.
- **Personal Views:** These are custom views that an individual user can create for their use. Personal views help users focus on the data that is most relevant to their role without affecting others' views.

Users can customize their views in Dynamics 365 CRM by using the **`Edit Filter`** or **`Edit Columns`** options highlighted in *Figure* 4.7. This allows them to modify the filters and columns displayed in a list view to suit their specific needs. Once these changes are made, the customized view can be saved as a private or personal view, also known as a temporary view. This view is accessible only to the user who created it, enabling personalized data visualization without affecting the default or shared views in the system.

- **Associated Views:** These views are displayed when you look at related records from within a parent record. For example, when viewing an account, you might see an associated view of all related contacts.
- **Quick Find Views:** Used when performing a search in Dynamics 365, these views define the fields that are searched and displayed in the results.
- **Lookup Views:** These are used when you look up a record from another entity, displaying a list of potential records to select from.
- **Advanced Find Views:** These allow users to create complex queries with multiple conditions to filter records according to specific criteria.

You can also filter through entity records by creating temporary views or adding columns to existing views. Use the "**`Edit Filter`**" and "**`Edit Column`**" options, as shown in *Figure* 4.7, to customize your view.

Creating and Customizing Entities, Attributes, Forms, and Views

Customizing Entities, Attributes, Forms, and Views begins from the Power Apps Maker Portal (make.powerapps.com).

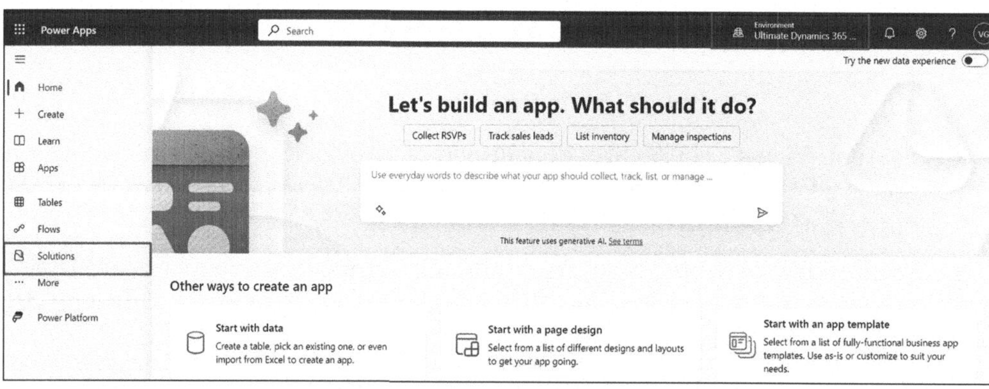

***Figure* 4.8**: *Power Apps Maker Portal*

1. In the power apps make a portal, we first begin creating with creating an unmanaged solution. Make sure to add a publisher to your solution:

Publisher: In Dynamics 365 CRM, publishers are used to identify the creator of a solution. When you create a solution, you associate it with a publisher, which serves as a unique identifier for the origin of customizations. The publisher's details, such as its prefix, are used to differentiate custom elements such as tables, fields, and other components within the solution. The publisher also defines a prefix (for example, "**new_**") that is automatically added to the names of components (such as custom fields, forms, and views) within the solution. This helps ensure that customizations are uniquely identifiable and do not conflict with other customizations in the system.

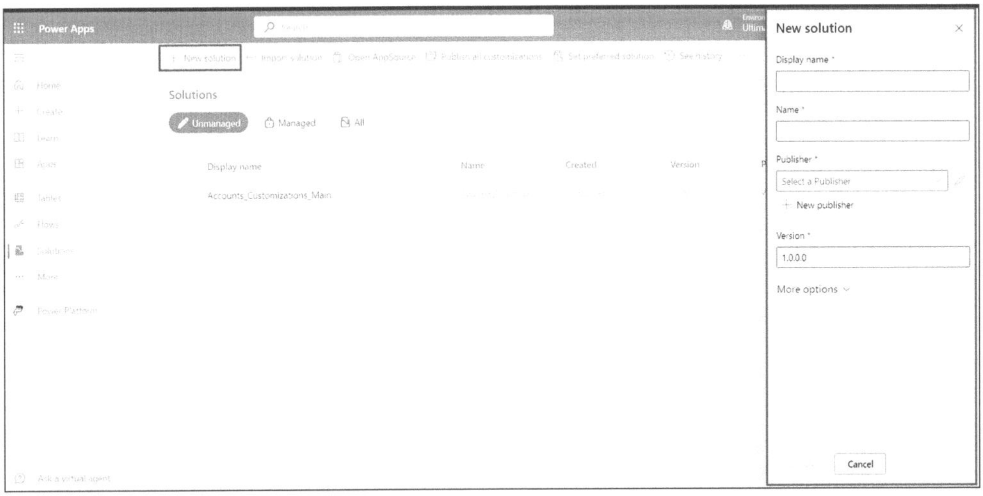

Figure 4.9: *Creating Solution in Power Apps Maker Portal*

2. The next step is to add components to your solution. These can include a **Power Automate Flow**, a new or existing **Entity**, or a Model-Driven App.

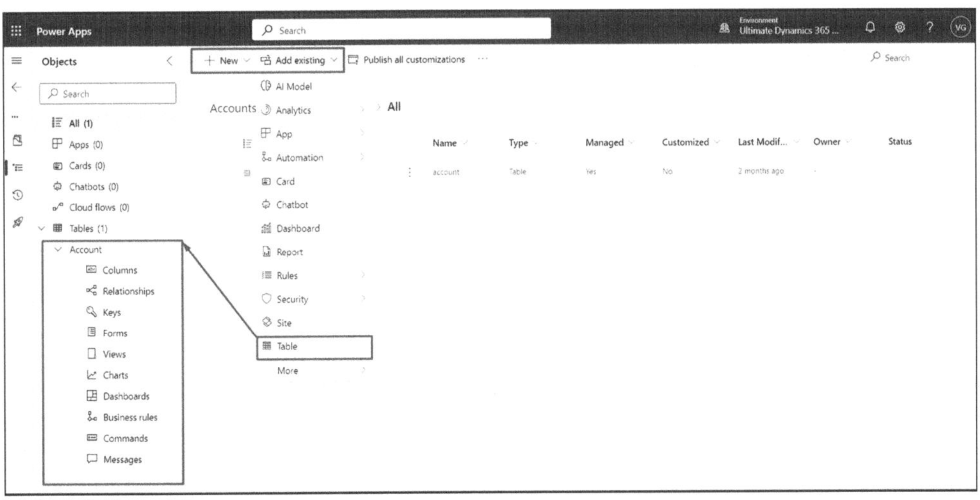

Figure 4.10: *Adding Entities to the Solution*

3. Now you can begin editing or adding forms, fields, views, and various other components to your **`Entity`**. You can add new **`columns`**, and edit existing columns, forms, views, and so on.

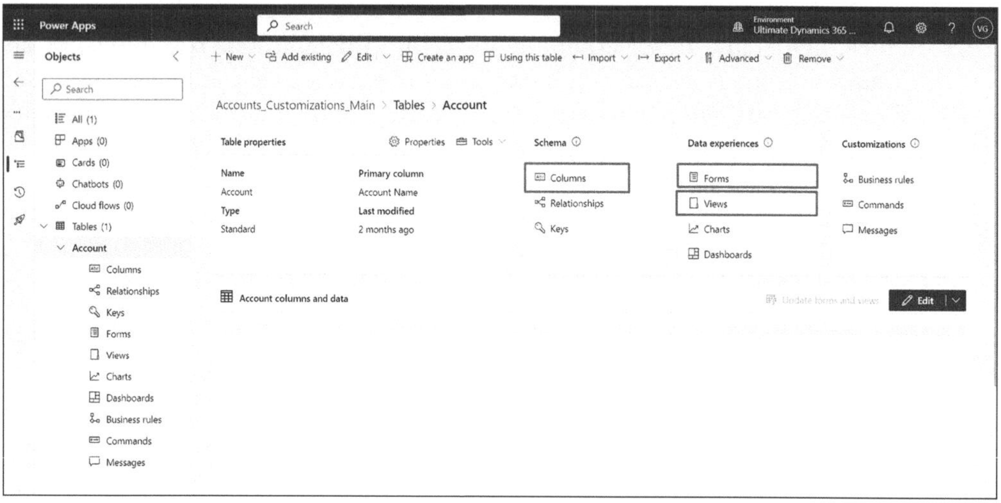

***Figure 4.11**: Components of the Dynamics 365 CRM Entities*

4. *Figure* 4.12 shows an example of a Two option field that is added to the account's entity, in the solution we just created.

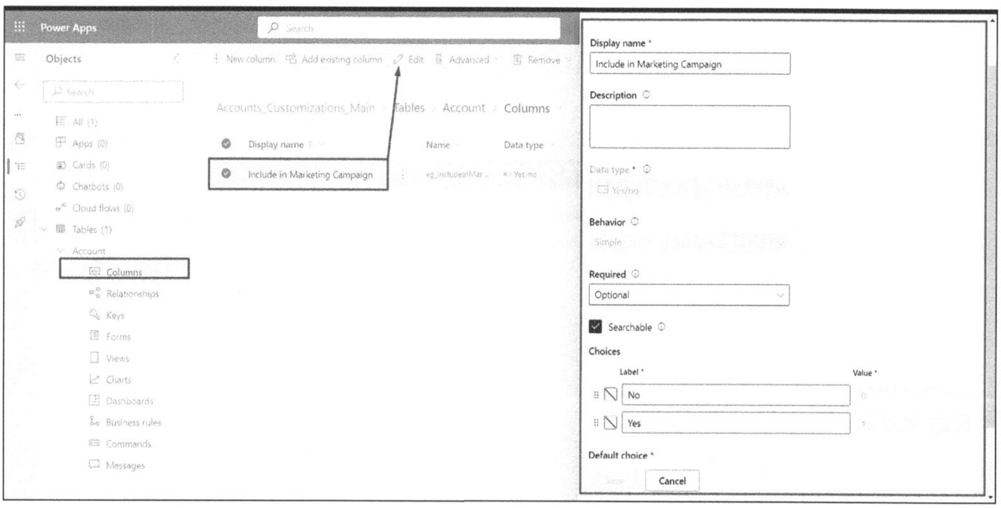

***Figure 4.12**: Creating/ Editing Components of the Entity in the Solution*

Now that we have gone through creating and customizing entities, attributes, forms, and views, you have seen how easy it is to shape Dynamics 365 to fit your business needs. These customizations set the foundation for a more personalized experience within the system.

Next, we will be looking at C# Plug-ins in Dynamics 365 CRM, where we will go through how to extend the system even further by adding your own custom logic with C#.

Introduction to C# Plug-ins in Dynamics 365 CRM

Plug-ins in Dynamics 365 CRM are a way to extend and modify the standard behavior of the system by injecting custom business logic. Essentially, a Plug-in is a piece of C# code that is triggered by specific events within the system, such as when a record is created, updated, or deleted. Plug-ins are always executed on the server side, meaning they run in the background (often referred to as the "*back-end*").

When developing a Plug-in, you need to inform Dynamics 365 when and where the Plug-in should run. This is done through a process called Plug-in registration, where you define the specific action (referred to as a Plug-in "*message*") that will trigger the Plug-in. This setup allows you to automate processes, validate data, or perform other custom operations when certain conditions are met within the CRM platform.

Some scenarios where you would write a Plug-in are as follows:

- You want to execute some business logic such as updating certain fields of a record or updating related records, and more when you create or update a CRM record.
- You want to call an external web service on certain events such as saving or updating a record.
- You want to automate processes such as sending e-mails to your customers on certain events in CRM.
- You want custom auto numbering to Quotations, Invoices, and so on.

Types of Plug-ins

There are two main types of Plug-ins in Dynamics 365 CRM, each serving different purposes based on when and how they are triggered:

- **Synchronous Plug-ins:** These Plug-ins run immediately succeeding the triggering event (such as creating, updating, or deleting a record) and are part of the main execution pipeline. Since they are executed in real-time, users have to wait for the Plug-in to complete its task prior to continuing. Synchronous Plug-ins are often used for scenarios where instant feedback or validation is needed.
- **Asynchronous Plug-ins:** These Plug-ins are executed in the background succeeding the event has occurred. They do not block the user from continuing their work, as they are queued and processed later by the system.

Asynchronous Plug-ins are ideal for operations that are not time-sensitive, such as sending notifications or integrating with external systems.

Both types of Plug-ins are used depending on the need, whether it is real-time processing or background automation.

Plug-in Messages

Messages are events that trigger the execution of a Plug-in or business logic. For instance, you can register a Plug-in to activate/trigger when a new Contact record is created, using the "**`Create Message`**" for the Contact entity.

For default, out-of-the-box entities, there are over 100 supported messages. Some apply to all entities, while others are specific to certain ones. You can find the full list of supported messages in an Excel file included in the SDK: **`SDK\Message-entity support for plug-ins.xlsx`**.

For custom entities, the supported messages vary depending on whether the entity is user-owned or organization-owned, as listed in the following table:

Message Name	**Ownership Type**
`Assign`	User-owned entities only
`Create`	User-owned and organization-owned entities
`Delete`	User-owned and organization-owned entities
`GrantAccess`	User-owned entities only
`ModifyAccess`	User-owned entities only
`Retrieve`	User-owned and organization-owned entities
`RetrieveMultiple`	User-owned and organization-owned entities
`RetrievePrincipalAccess`	User-owned entities only
`RetrieveSharedPrincipalsAndAccess`	User-owned entities only
`RevokeAccess`	User-owned entities only
`SetState`	User-owned and organization-owned entities
`SetStateDynamicEntity`	User-owned and organization-owned entities
`Update`	User-owned and organization-owned entities

Table 4.1: *Plug-in Messages for Custom Entities*
(Table is referenced from learn.microsoft.com)

In Dynamics 365 CRM, the ownership of an entity determines how records in that entity are managed and secured. There are two primary types of ownership: User-Owned and Organization-Owned.

User-Owned Entities:

- Records in user-owned entities are associated with specific users or teams.
- Access to these records is managed through security roles and the concept of ownership, meaning only the owner or users with the appropriate permissions can view, edit, or share these records.
- Examples of user-owned entities include Accounts, Contacts, and Opportunities.

Organization-Owned Entities:

- Records in organization-owned entities do not have individual owners. Instead, they are shared across the organization, and access is determined by broader organizational permissions rather than individual ownership.
- These entities are commonly used for data that is shared across teams, such as system configurations or business units.
- Examples include entities such as Products or Currencies.

For more information on Plug-in messages, refer to Reference 3.

Event Framework and Event Execution Pipeline

Now that we understand the messages on which we can register our custom Plug-in code, it is essential to learn how these messages and the Plug-in execute. The Event Framework and the Event Execution Pipeline in Dynamics 365 CRM provide a structured way to implement custom business logic through Plug-ins, by defining specific event stages and managing when and how Plug-ins are executed.

Event Framework: The Event Framework in Dynamics 365 CRM is a system that controls how custom actions (called Plug-ins) run when some operation happens on the records, such as creating, updating, or deleting them. It lets developers set up Plug-ins that can react to these actions, ensuring that they run at the right time.

Here is how it works:

1. The framework listens for important actions, such as creating or updating a record.
2. When one of these actions occurs, it checks if any Plug-ins are registered to respond.
3. It makes sure those Plug-ins run in the correct order and at the right stage, whether preceding or succeeding the main operation.

4. This setup helps automate tasks and keeps everything running smoothly.

Event Execution Pipeline: The Event Execution Pipeline is the process that handles these Plug-ins when events happen. It has several stages, each serving a different purpose and timing. This way, developers can ensure that their custom actions happen just when they should, keeping everything efficient and organized. The four stages in the event execution pipeline are as follows:

- **Pre-Validation**
    - This stage occurs preceding the main system operation and outside the database transaction. It is ideal for performing validations and can cancel the main operation if validation fails. To stop the operation, you can throw an **`InvalidPlug-inExecutionException`**, providing a message to the user explaining the cause of the failure. Since this stage runs before the system checks security roles and permissions, validations happen regardless of user privileges.
    - **Example**: You might use Pre-Validation to check if the required fields, such as "**`Phone Number`**," follow a specific format prior to proceeding to save the record. If the number is invalid, the operation is stopped with an error message.
- **Pre-Operation**
    - This stage also occurs before the main system operation but is part of the database transaction. Any unhandled exceptions at this stage will cause the entire transaction to roll back, including the main operation. This stage is ideal for making field modifications to the entity object before it is committed to the database. However, canceling the system operation at this stage or later can lead to performance penalties due to transaction rollbacks.
    - **Example**: You could use Pre-Operation to format a phone number prior to saving it. If the phone number entered by the user lacks spaces or hyphens, the Plug-in could automatically correct it at this stage.
- **Main-Operation**
    - This stage includes the core system operation itself and is part of the database transaction. It is reserved for internal use by the system. Custom code should generally not be added to this stage unless working with custom APIs or virtual data providers.
    - **Example**: This stage is automatically used when the system executes its primary operations, such as creating or updating records. Typically, no custom Plug-in code runs here unless you are building a custom API.
- **Post-Operation**
    - This stage occurs succeeding the main system operation but is still within

the database transaction. Any unhandled exceptions in Post-Operation will roll back the transaction, including the main operation. It is suitable for modifying message properties returned to the caller or triggering actions based on the successful completion of the main operation. However, modifying the entity object itself at this stage is discouraged, as it may trigger a new update event and restart the entire pipeline, leading to performance issues.

  - **Example**: After a record is successfully created, you might use Post-Operation to send a confirmation email or trigger an external service. This stage also allows for asynchronous processing, where the custom code runs succeeding the main system operation completes without affecting the database transaction.

In summary,

- **Pre-Validation**: Ideal for validation checks and early exits.
- **Pre-Operation**: Best for modifying entity fields prior to saving.
- **Main-Operation**: Used internally by the system; avoid adding custom code here.
- **Post-Operation**: Useful for actions succeeding the main system operation, including asynchronous tasks.

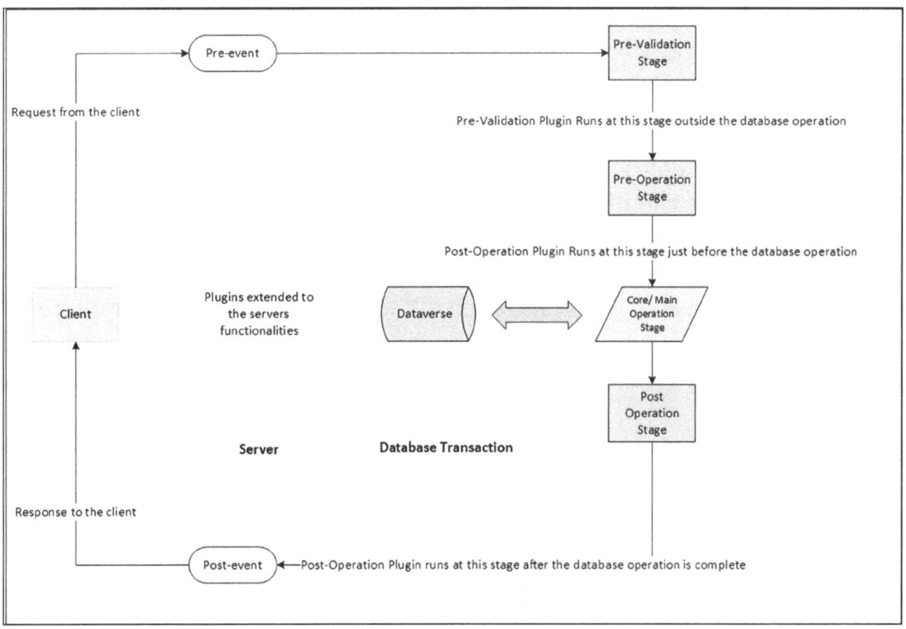

Figure 4.13: *Event Framework in Dynamics 365 CRM*

Figure 4.13 shows an overview of the execution of a client request in the event execution pipeline.

Plug-in Images

Plug-ins in Dynamics 365 CRM allow you to register images for the steps of a Plug-in assembly. Images serve as snapshots of the record currently being processed, either preceding or succeeding a database action is performed. Essentially, they reflect the state of the record as it exists in the Dataverse.

There are two types of images supported: Pre-Image and Post-Image.

A **Pre-Image** provides the state of the record as stored in the dataverse database prior to the database action on the table (Create, Update, Delete) being executed. In contrast, a **Post-Image** returns the state of the record after the database action has been completed.

Let us try to understand how images are utilized in business logic.

In Dynamics 365 CRM, you can run business logic during the creation, update, or deletion of any entity records. Each operation provides a context for the entity within the Plug-in, reflecting the state of the entity record in the Dataverse. For example, when a record is created, all its attributes are available in the Plug-in context, serving as a snapshot or image of the entity.

When you create a record and a Plug-in is registered on the creation event, you gain access to the complete entity context, meaning you get access to the data in all the attributes of the entity. Conversely, if you trigger a Plug-in to update a specific attribute, you will only receive the value of that attribute, while all other attributes will show as null in the context, even if they contain data. This situation raises the question of how to access those values, and this is where Plug-in images become useful.

Example: Consider a scenario where you are deleting duplicate contact records from CRM. You need to copy the phone number from the duplicate contact to the original contact if the phone number in the original contact is different. To accomplish this, you would register a post-operation Plug-in for the deletion of a contact and add a pre-image to the delete step. This approach allows you to access the complete context or image of the deleted contact within your Plug-in after the record is removed. You can then compare the phone numbers and update the original contact as needed.

Creating a Plug-in

Now that we know a lot about Plug-ins, let us begin with creating a Plug-in.

Step 1: Create a Class Library Project

Plug-ins are typically written in C# using Visual Studio as the Integrated Development Environment (IDE).

a. Start by creating a new Class Library project in Visual Studio. This project will contain your Plug-in code.

i. Open Visual Studio.

ii. Select "**`Create a new project`**."

iii.Choose "**`Class Library (.NET Framework)`**" as the project type and click "**`Next`**."

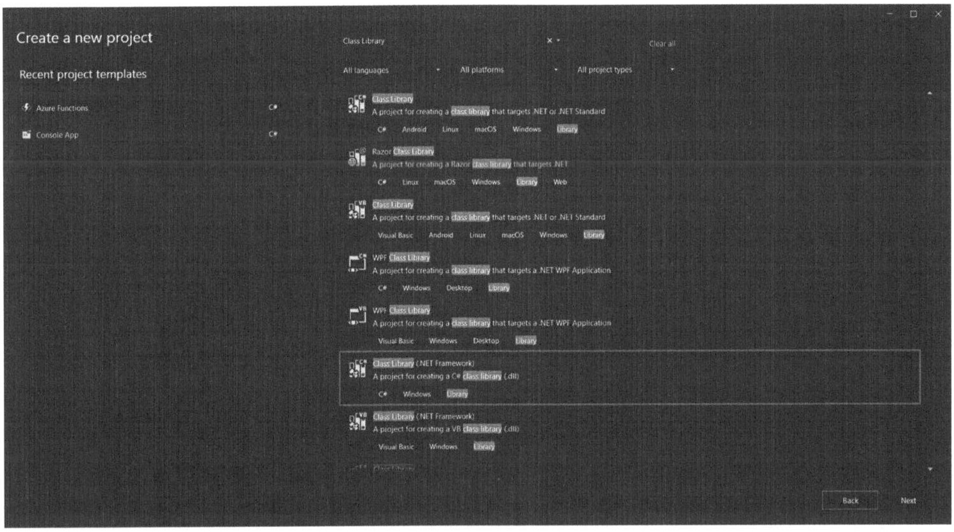

***Figure 4.14(a)**: Creating a Plug-in Project in Visual Studio*

b. Name your project (for example, "**`MyPlug-in`**") and select the appropriate .NET Framework version. Use .NET Framework 4.6.2 (usually 4.6.2 or higher for Dynamics 365). Dynamics 365 Online supports these versions, and it is recommended to use 4.6.2 or higher for compatibility and long-term support.

***Figure 4.14(b)**: Creating a Plug-in Project in Visual Studio*

c. After the project is set up, we will begin adding the Dynamics 365 SDKs.

Step 2: Add References

Your Plug-in will require certain assemblies to interact with Dynamics 365.

Required Assemblies: **`Microsoft.Crm.Sdk.CoreAssemblies`**

The **`Microsoft.Crm.Sdk.CoreAssemblies`** package contains core assemblies that provide the essential functionality for interacting with Dynamics 365 CRM and Power Platform services. Specifically, these assemblies include APIs, classes, and methods that enable developers to work with entities, messages, and services within the Dynamics 365 platform.

1. Right-click on "**`References`**" in your project in Solution Explorer.

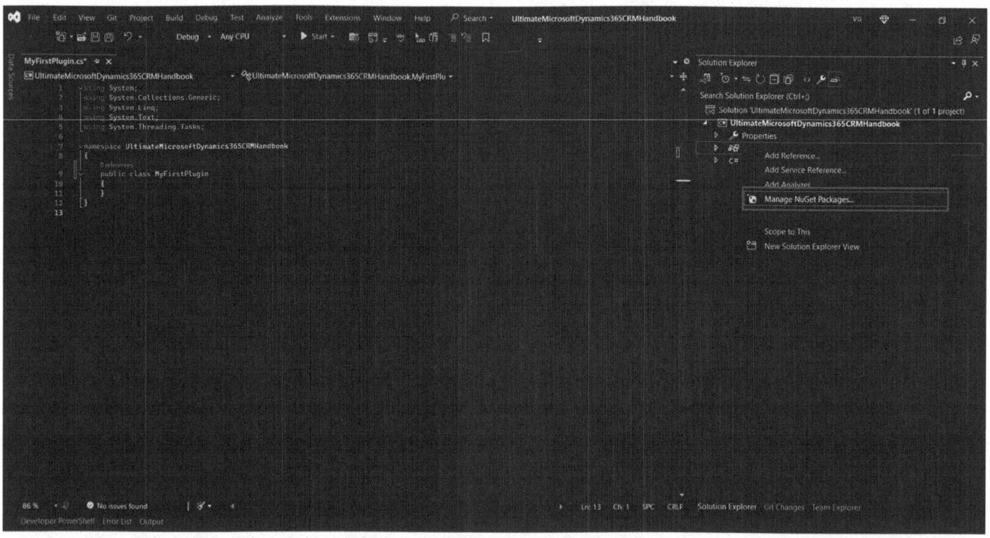

Figure 4.15(a): *Adding Dynamics 365 CRM Assembly References to the Project*

2. Click "**`Add Reference`**" and browse to locate the required assemblies, which you can download from the NuGet Package Manager or the SDK folder.

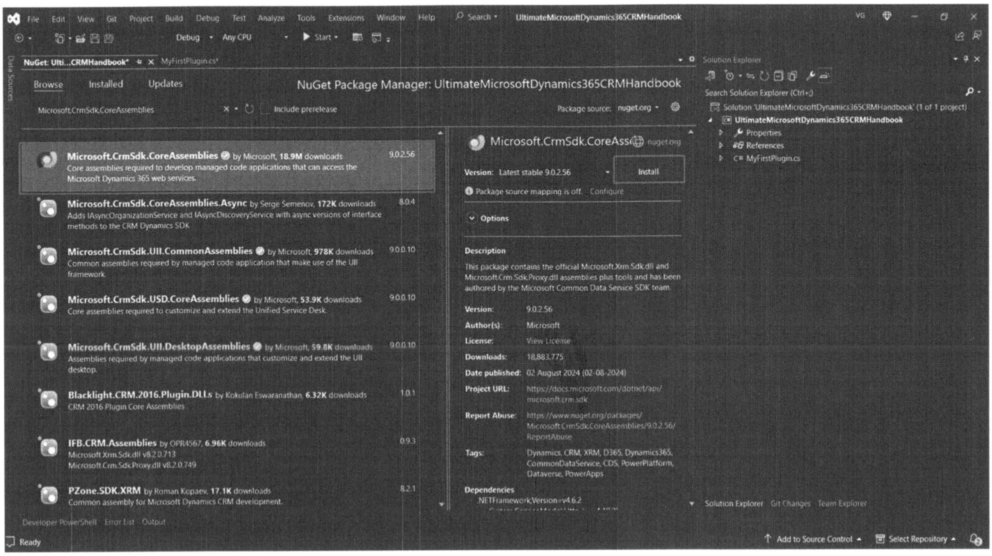

Figure 4.15(b): Adding Dynamics 365 CRM Assembly References to the Project

Step 3: Implement the `IPlugin` Interface

All Plug-ins in Dynamics 365 must implement the **`IPlugin`** interface.

1. Rename the class file that was created by default with the project and implement the IPlugin interface.
2. Override the Execute method, which will contain the main logic for your Plug-in. (Visual Studio will auto-suggest overriding the execute method) as shown in the following code block:

```
public class MyFirstPlugin : IPlugin
    {
        public void Execute(IServiceProvider serviceProvider)
        {
            try
            {
                //Your Custom Logic
            }
            catch (Exception)
            {
                throw new NotImplementedException();
            }


        }
    }
```

The following figure illustrates the implementation of the IPlugin interface:

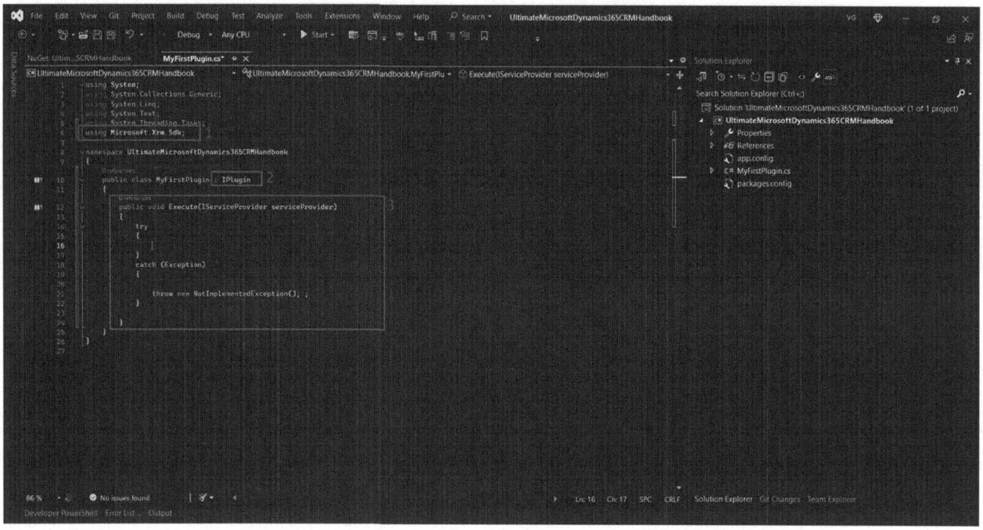

Figure 4.16: *Implementing the IPlugin Interface*

Step 4: Accessing the `IServiceProvider` and the `IOrganizationService`

We have learned Plug-ins in Dynamics 365 implement the IPlugin interface. The Execute method in the interface provides access to the **`IServiceProvider`**, which is a container of several key services required to execute the Plug-in's logic.

Figure 4.17(a) shows the context, the service, and the tracing service in a single generic method used for every Plugin. The **`IServiceProvider`** allows you to access essential services such as **`IPluginExecutionContext`**, **`IOrganizationServiceFactory`**, and **`ITracingService`**.

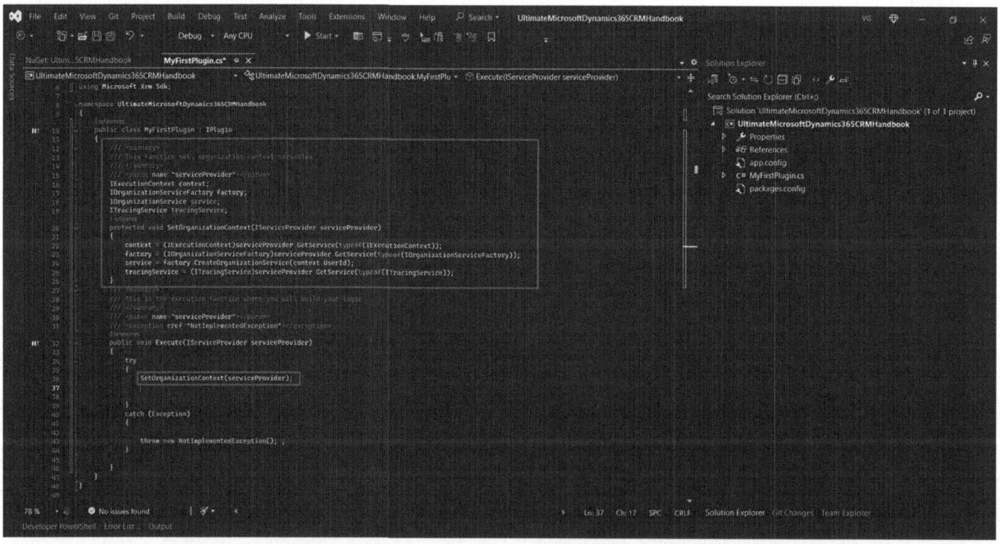

Figure 4.17(a): *Accessing Services in Dynamics 365 CRM Plug-in*

- **`IServiceProvider`**: The **`IServiceProvider`** parameter in the Execute method provides access to various services required for the Plug-in's operation. The **`IServiceProvider`** contains the following services:
  - **`IPluginExecutionContext`**: Provides information about the current operation and entity data. (This gives the **context** shown in *Figure 4.17(a)* line number 22).
  - **`IOrganizationServiceFactory`**: Used to create instances of the organization service. (This gives the **`service`** shown in *Figure 4.17(a)* line number 24).
  - **`ITracingService`**: Helps log messages for debugging. (This gives the **`tracingService`** shown in *Figure 4.17(a)* line 25).
- **`IPluginExecutionContext`:** The **`IPluginExecutionContext`** is a key part of your Plug-in that provides information about what is happening when your code runs. Think of it as a detailed report about the current situation when your Plug-in is triggered. It tells you important things, such as:
  - **`UserId`**: This is the ID of the user who triggered the Plug-in. It ensures your Plug-in acts with that user's permissions, keeping everything secure and in line with what they can do.
  - **`MessageName`**: This tells you what action started the Plug-in, such as creating, updating, or deleting a record. It helps you understand what is happening.
  - **`InputParameters`**: This includes all the data your Plug-in needs to do its job. For instance, if someone is creating a new contact, these parameters will hold all the details about that contact.
  - **`OutputParameters`**: This is where you can specify any data you want to send back once your Plug-in has finished running.
  - **`EntityName`**: This tells you what type of record the Plug-in is working on—such as a contact, account, or any other entity.
  - **Pre- and Post-Images**: These snapshots show the record's state before and after the operation. They are super handy for comparing changes.
  - **Stage**: This indicates when your Plug-in runs—whether it is before or after the main action takes place, such as Pre-Operation, Post-Operation, and so on. It helps you know exactly when your code is executing in the process.
- **`IOrganizationServiceFactory`:**

  The **`IOrganizationServiceFactory`** is similar to a tool that helps your Plug-in connect to the Dynamics 365 system on behalf of a specific user.
  - When a Plug-in runs, it does so as if it is acting on behalf of the user who triggered the action (such as creating or updating a record). The

CreateOrganizationService method allows the Plug-in to create a connection to the system under that user's permissions.

- This way, the Plug-in can perform tasks (such as updating records) as though the users themselves are doing it.
- In simple terms, the **IOrganizationServiceFactory** makes sure the Plug-in is working with the right permissions, similar to the user who caused it to run.
- When you call **CreateOrganizationService(context.UserId)** from the **IOrganizationServiceFactory**, it creates a **service** called **IOrganizationService** that runs under the context of the current user.
- This **service** allows you to interact directly with Dynamics 365 data and perform actions, as illustrated in *Figure 4.17(b)*, which demonstrates how some of the Database operations are carried out using the **IOrganizationService** (Service).

Note: *Dynamics 365 CRM also allows for impersonation, which means that a plugin can run under a different user's context, rather than the context of the triggering user.*

Impersonation is useful in scenarios where the plugin needs to perform actions on behalf of another user, such as a system administrator or a user with higher privileges. This is done by passing the desired user's ID (instead of **context.UserId**) *to* **CreateOrganizationService**. *This allows the plugin to perform operations as if it were that user, thus providing a way to execute logic with different permissions or access rights.*

By using impersonation, plugins can be used to handle specific scenarios that require elevated permissions or different user contexts, which can be particularly useful for managing security and access control in custom business logic.

```
//Create am entity record in CRM
Entity newAccount = new Entity("account");
newAccount["name"] = "New Account";
Guid accountId = service.Create(newAccount);


// Update am entity record in CRM
Entity accountToUpdate = new Entity("account", accountId);
accountToUpdate["name"] = "Updated Account Name";
service.Update(accountToUpdate);

//Retrive an entity record from CRM
Entity account = service.Retrieve("account", accountId, new ColumnSet("name", "telephone1"));

//Delete an entity record from CRM
service.Delete("account", accountId);

// Retrive multiple record from CRM
QueryExpression query = new QueryExpression("account");
query.ColumnSet = new ColumnSet("name");
EntityCollection results = service.RetrieveMultiple(query);
```

Figure 4.17(b): *Using IOrganizationService to Perform Database Operations*

- **Create**: Adds a new record to the system.
- **Retrieve**: Fetches an existing record based on its ID.

- `Update`: Modifies an existing record.
- `Delete`: Removes a record from the system.
- `RetrieveMultiple`: Fetches multiple records based on a query.
- `Execute`: Executes a message request (such as workflows, custom actions, and so on).

- **`ITracingService`**: The **`ITracingService`** allows you to log messages during the execution of your Plug-in. This is incredibly useful for debugging and understanding the flow of your code. By using this service, you can capture key information about what your Plug-in is doing at any given moment. Think of it as a diary or a logbook that you can write in while your Plug-in is executing. Some code examples are as follows:

```
tracingService.Trace("The contact name is: {0}", contact.Name);
tracingService.Trace("This is a trace message indicating that the
Plug-in has started.");
```

For more details on how to view trace logs and use the tracing service, please refer to the link in **Reference 9**.

Step 5: Access Entity Data from Input Parameters and Images

The **`InputParameters`** collection that we get from the **`IPluginExecutionContext`** (context) contains data related to the event that triggered the Plug-in. For instance, in a create operation, you can access the entity being created thus this entity will be called a Target Entity. Similarly, the target entity is obtained from the **`PreEntityImage`** and **`PostEntityImage`** collection.

Figure 4.18 shows a generic method to get the target entity from the input parameters, Pre-Images, and Post Images.

***Figure 4.18**: Access Entity Data from Input Parameters and Images*

The **`GetTargetEntity`** method retrieves the target entity being processed in a Dynamics 365 Plug-in based on the operation type (**`create`**, **`update`**, or **`delete`**).

- **Create Operation**: If the current operation is a creation event, it checks if the "**`Target`**" parameter is present in the input parameters and assigns it to the **`targetEntity`**.
- **Update Operation**: For updates, it checks if a "**`PostEntityImage`**" exists in the context and if the operation is within a specified depth (less than 3 to avoid loop a of updates). If so, it assigns this image to the **`targetEntity`**.
- **Delete Operation**: For deletions, it checks if a "**`PreEntityImage`**" exists in the context and assigns it to the **`targetEntity`**.

Finally, the method returns the appropriate **`targetEntity`** based on the operation being executed. This allows the Plug-in to work with the correct entity data regardless of the operation type.

Also, The **`context.Depth`** property in *Figure* 4.18 represents the depth of the current plugin execution in the execution pipeline. In Dynamics 365, plugins can be triggered multiple times in a single operation, especially if multiple steps are configured for the same message. The Depth property indicates how deep the current plugin step is within the pipeline.

For example:

- A depth of 1 indicates that the plugin is executing as the first step in the pipeline.
- Higher values (for example, 2, 3) represent deeper steps, such as those triggered by other plugins or post-operation events.

In most cases, developers do not need to directly interact with the Depth property, but it can be useful for debugging or when managing complex workflows with multiple plugin steps. You can choose to remove this reference from the screenshot if it is not needed.

Step 6: Implement Your Business Logic

Inside the Execute method, implement the specific logic that you want your Plug-in to perform, using the retrieved entity and services. *Figure* 4.19 shows the business logic for validating the phone number entered during account creation. This Plug-in is registered to run in the pre-operation stage when an account is created. If the phone number is invalid, it triggers an exception alert for the user.

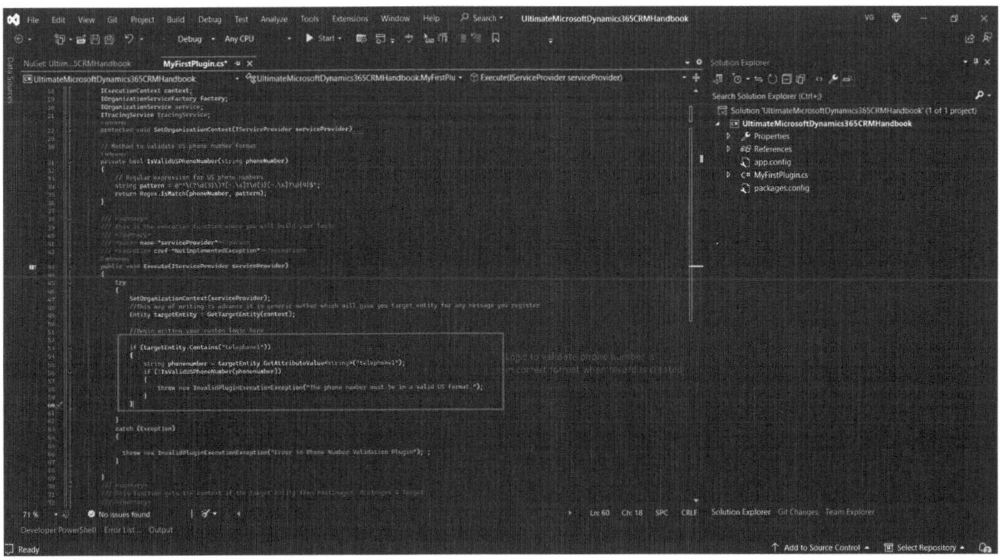

Figure 4.19: *Adding Business Logic in the Execute Function of the Plug-in*

Step 7: Build the Plug-in

Build the Plug-in and make sure there are no logical or compilation errors. To build the Plug-in, you can right-click on the project and build it.

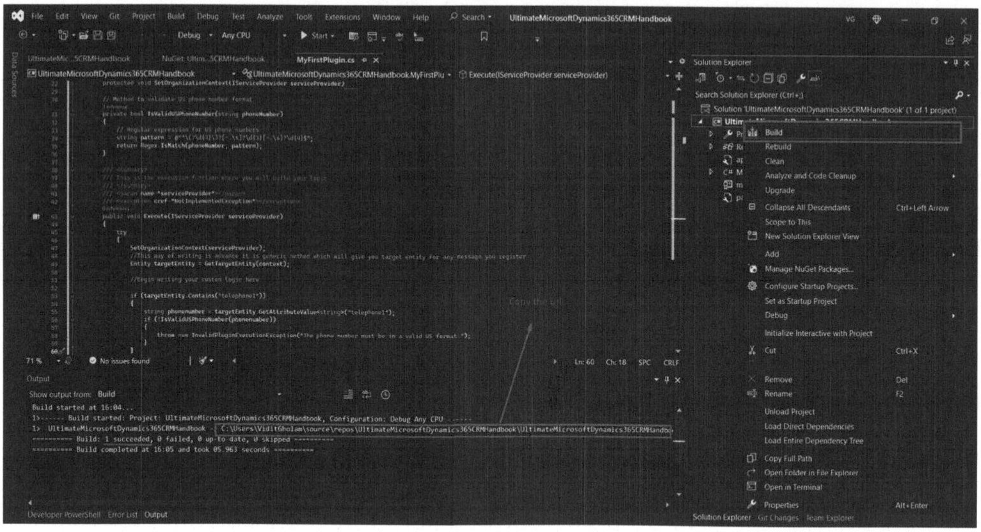

Figure 4.20: *Building Plug-in in Visual Studio*

After your build is successful, make sure to copy the DLL link as highlighted in *Figure* 4.20.

Step 8: Sign the Plug-in

Signing ensures that the Plug-in's code has not been tampered with since it was compiled. It provides a way to verify the integrity of the code. To sign a Plug-in, right-click on the project and select **`Properties`**.

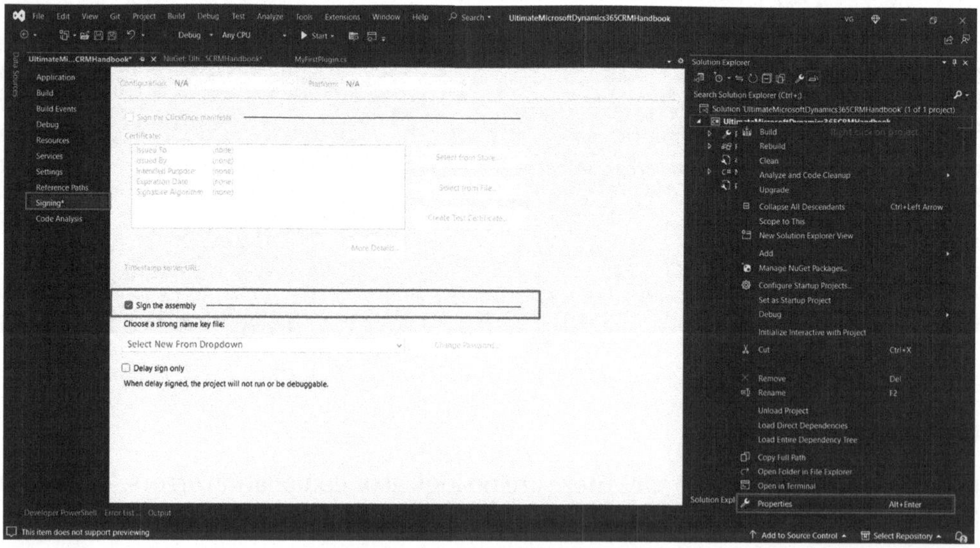

Figure 4.21(a): *Signing a Plug-in*

Under the **`Signing`** tab, check the option to sign the assembly. Next, click "**`Choose a strong name key file`**" and select "**`New`**."

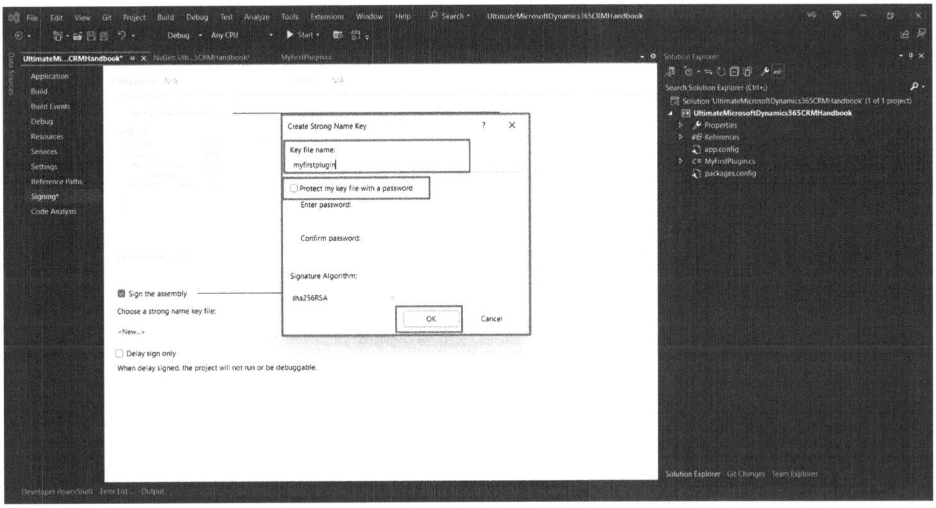

Figure 4.21(b): *Signing a Plug-in*

Create a key and click **OK**, this key will be added to your project. You can rebuild the project, making it ready for registration.

Step 9: Register Plug-in

To register a plugin, you will need the **Plug-in Registration Tool**. You can download it using the link in **Reference 3** or simply search for it in your browser. Once you have downloaded the tool, open it by clicking on **PluginRegistration.exe**

1. Create a connection to your instance as shown in *Figure 4.22(a)*.

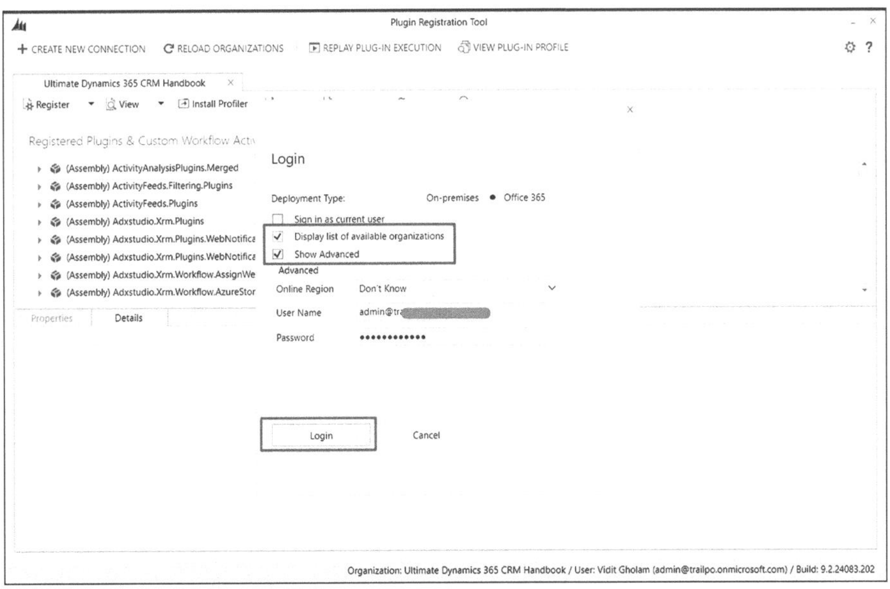

Figure 4.22(a): *Connecting to an Instance in the Plugin Registration Tool*

2. Choose your environment from the list of available environments in your instance, as shown in *Figure 4.22(b)*:

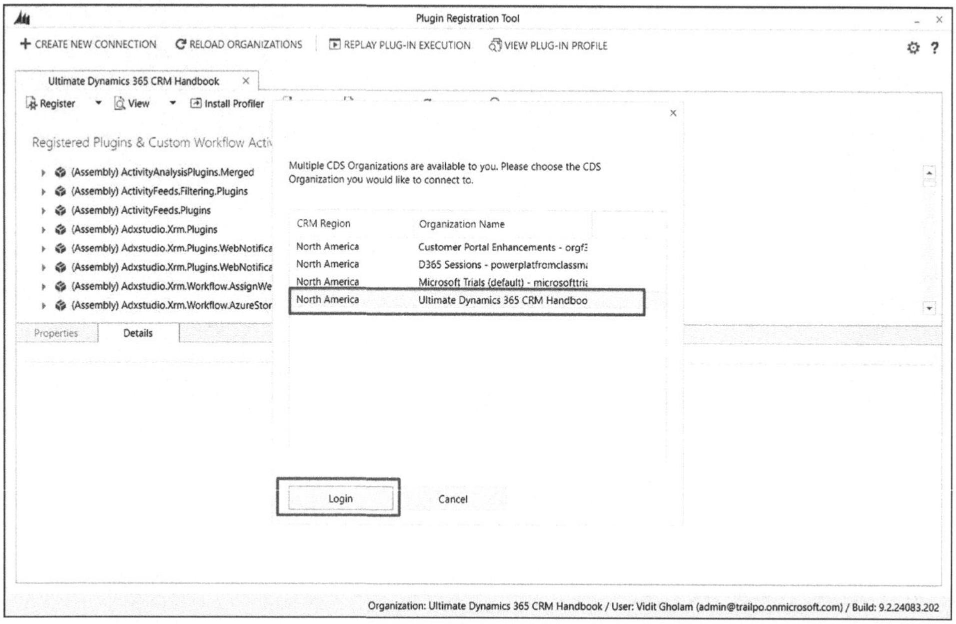

Figure 4.22(b): *Select an Environment in the Plugin Registration Tool*

3. Set up a new assembly in the registration tool as shown in *Figure 4.22(c)*:

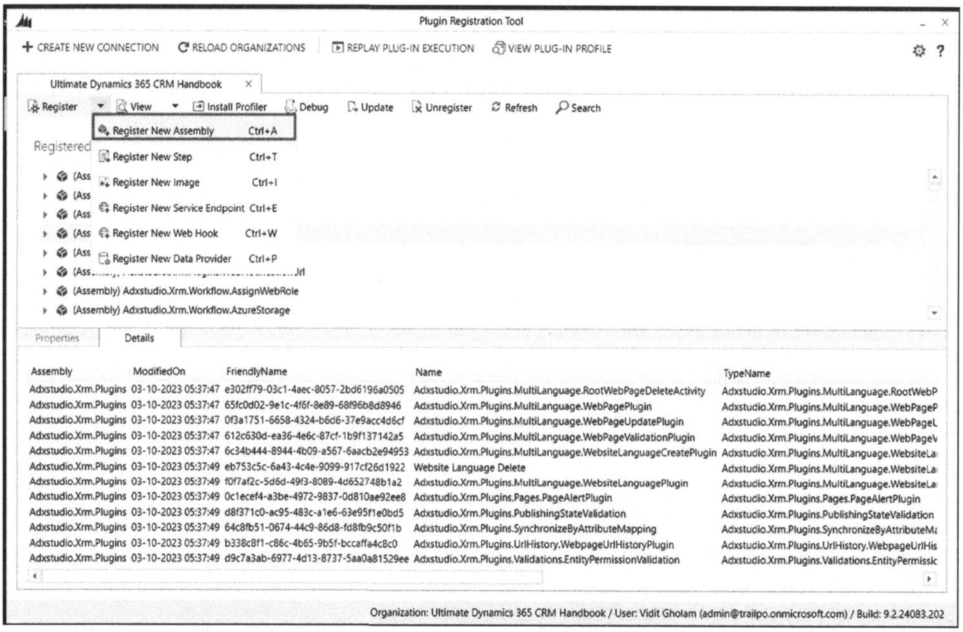

Figure 4.22(c): *Creating an Assembly in the Plugin Registration Tool*

4. Load the DLL of your plugin project (which you copied subsequent to building it) by clicking on "**`Load Assembly`**," then select "**`Register Selected Plugin`**" as shown in *Figure 4.22(d)*:

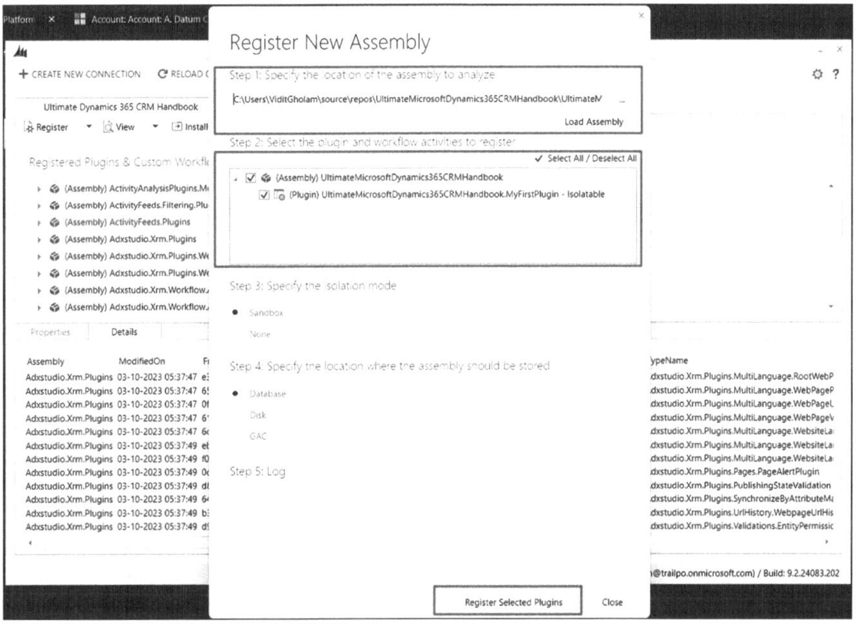

Figure 4.22(d): *Registering an Assembly in the Plugin Registration Tool*

5. Once the plugin assembly is registered, add a new step to it as shown in *Figure 4.22(e)*:

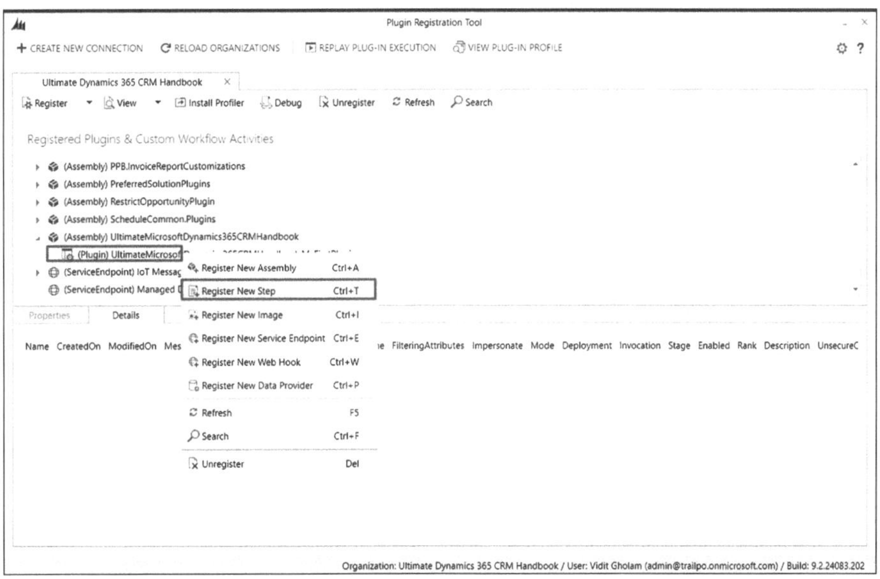

Figure 4.22(e): *Registering Plug-in Using the Plugin Registration Tool*

6. Since our plugin logic executes when an account is created, register the step for the account creation event to run in the pre-operation context as an admin user, as shown in *Figure 4.22(f)*:

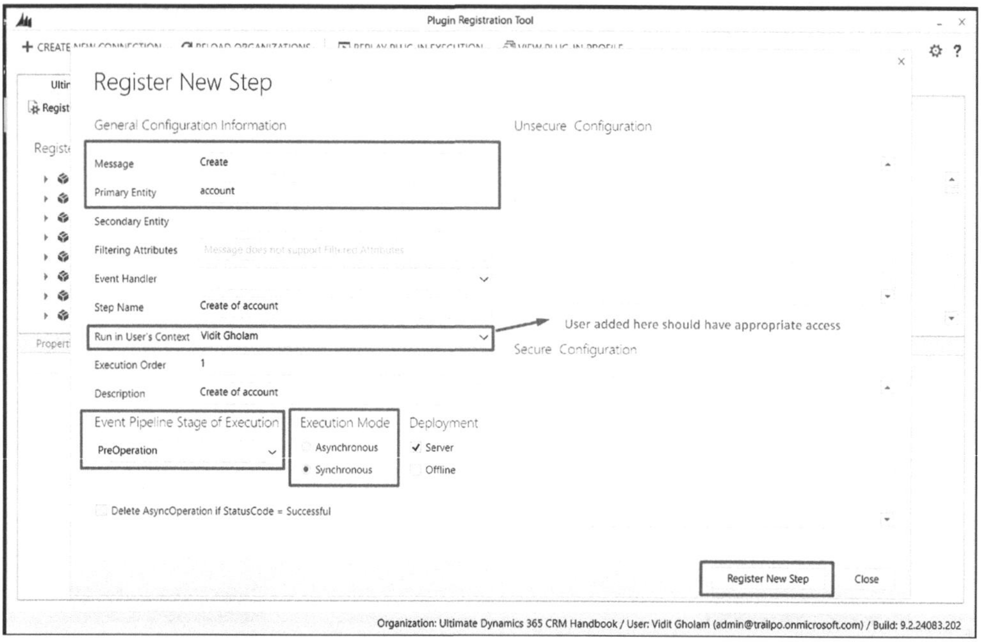

Figure 4.22(f): *Registering Plug-in Using the Plugin Registration Tool*

7. The plugin is now successfully registered and ready for testing. *Figure 4.22(g)* displays the exception triggered due to an incorrect phone number preceding the record saved.

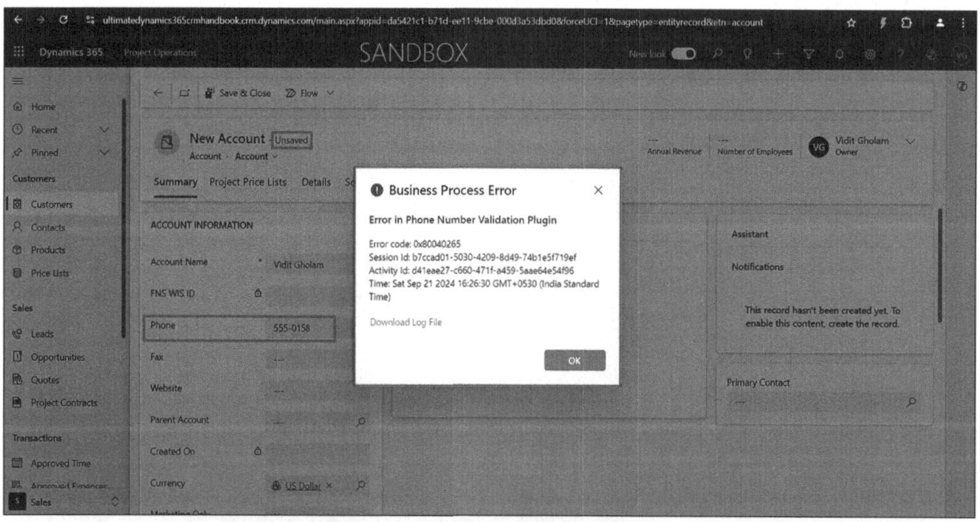

Figure 4.22(g): *Testing the Plugin*

Step 10: Registering Images on the Plugin Steps

To register an image over a plugin step, right-click on the step and click **`Register New Image`**, as shown in *Figure 4.22(h)*:

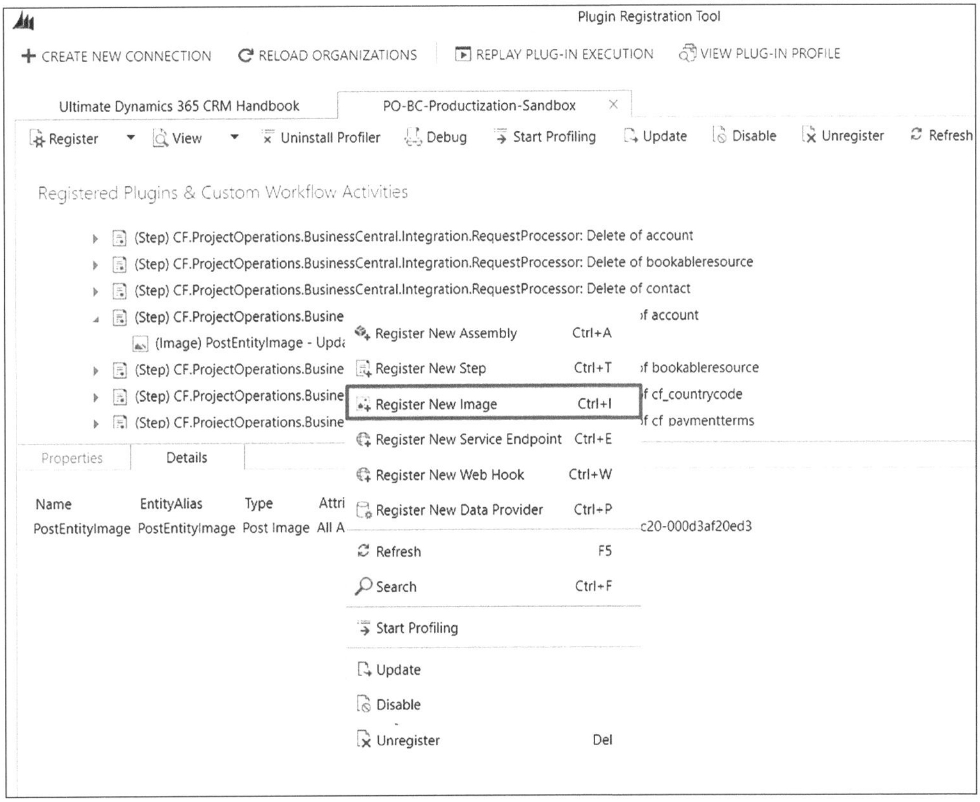

Figure 4.22(h): *Registering Images in the Plugin Registration Tool*

Select the **`Image Type`** and **`Parameters`** or Attributes that the Image will store, and then click update image, as shown in *Figure 4.22(i)*:

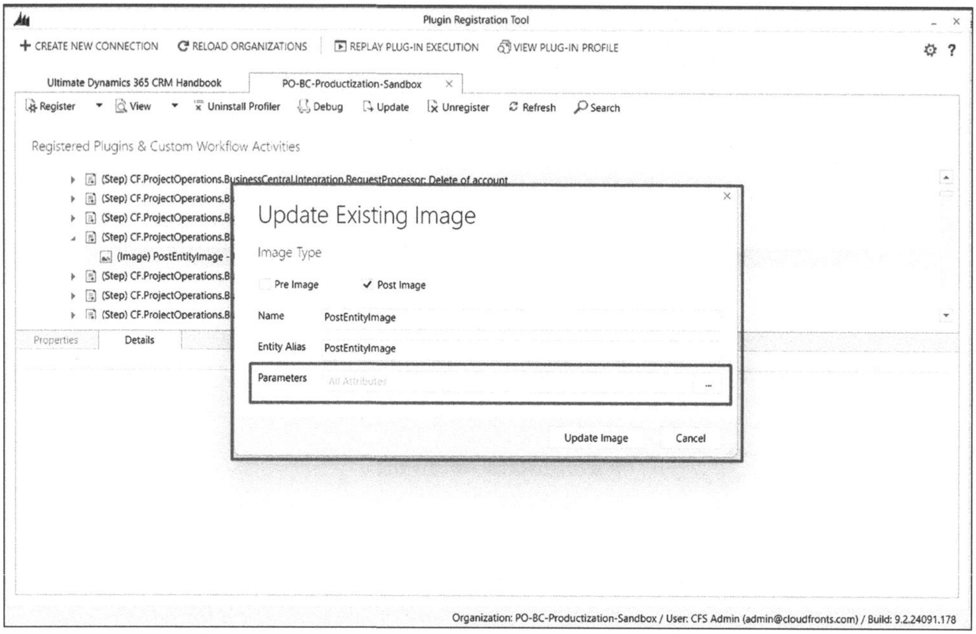

***Figure 4.22(i)**: Registering Images in the Plugin Registration Tool*

As an additional note, the platform has also introduced some new messages, **`CreateMultiple`** and **`UpdateMultiple`**, which allow for the creation or updating of multiple records in a single operation. These batch operations are useful especially when dealing with large datasets. **`CreateMultiple`** enables the creation of several records simultaneously, while **`UpdateMultiple`** allows for updating multiple records at once. These features are particularly useful for scenarios such as data imports, migrations, or bulk updates. For more details, refer to the link in **Reference 10**.

With this, we have successfully created and executed custom business logic through a C# plugin in Dynamics 365 CRM. For a more detailed tutorial on plugins, you can refer to the link in **Reference 11**. For details on how to debug a plugin, please check the link in **Reference 12**.

Using JavaScript's Web Resources in Dynamics 365 CRM

Web resources in Dynamics 365, such as JavaScript, HTML, CSS, or images, enhance the user interface by adding custom logic and making the app more interactive. JavaScript web resources are often used to control form behavior, performing tasks such as validation or triggering actions based on user input. Unlike backend business logic managed through plugins, JavaScript enables client-side logic, allowing you to manipulate data and respond to user interactions directly on the form. These web resources can be triggered when a form loads or when users interact with specific fields.

JavaScript is typically used in form events such as:

1. **`OnLoad`**: When the form loads.
2. **`OnSave`**: When the form is saved.
3. **`OnChange`**: When the value of a specific field changes.

To use JavaScript in Dynamics 365, you must first create and register your web resource, and then associate it with a form event.

Let us walk through the steps to register a JS file to a form.

1. Create a Web Resource:
   a. Go to make.powerapps.com and navigate to your solution. (Make sure the correct environment is selected)

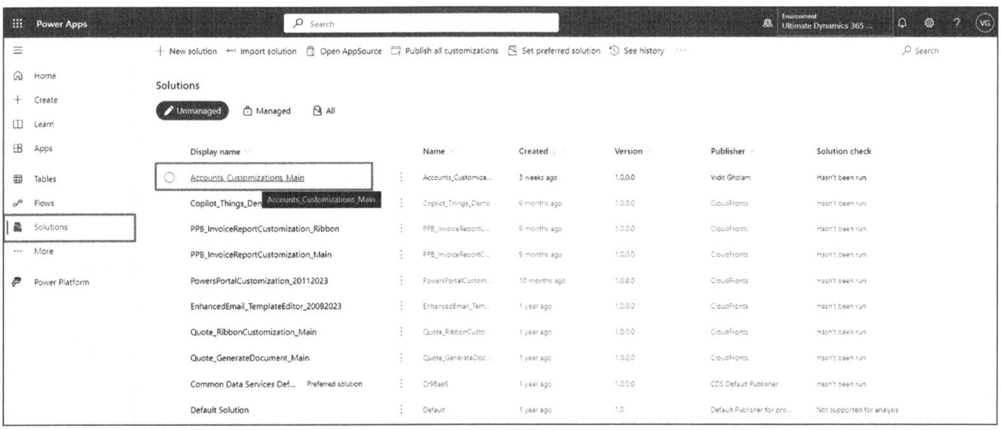

Figure 4.23(a): *Navigating to Solution in Power Apps Studio*

   b. Click on **`Add New`** and select **`Web resource`**.

Figure 4.23(b): *Creating a Web Resource in the Solution*

c. Keep your JavaScript code ready.

   i. The main component that runs JavaScript in Dynamics 365 forms is the **`formContext`**, which represents the form's data and structure. The **`executionContext`** is automatically passed to your JavaScript code when a form event occurs, such as **`OnLoad`** or **`OnChange`**.

```
var validatePhoneNumber = {
    readAccountForm: function(executionContext){
        var formContext = executionContext.getFormContext();
        var telephoneVal = formContext.getAttribute("telephone1").getValue();
        var name = formContext.getAttribute("name").getValue();
        console.log(name);
        console.log(telephoneVal);
        if(telephoneVal.length !=10){
            var alertStrings = { confirmButtonLabel: "Ok", text: name +"\n"+"Make sure your phone number is 10 digits", title: "Please Verify" };
            var alertOptions = { height: 120, width: 260 };
            Xrm.Navigation.openAlertDialog(alertStrings, alertOptions);
        }
        else{
            var alertStrings = { confirmButtonLabel: "Ok", text: name +"\n"+"Phone Number Verifed : "+telephoneVal, title: "Please Verify" };
            var alertOptions = { height: 120, width: 260 };
            Xrm.Navigation.openAlertDialog(alertStrings, alertOptions);
        }
    }
}
```

Figure 4.23(c)*: JavaScript code for Validating Phone Numbers on Accounts Form*

   ii. The **`executionContext`** gives you access to the current event's context. By calling **`executionContext.getFormContext()`**, you can retrieve the **`formContext`**. This object allows you to interact with the form's fields, controls, and properties. For example, you can use **`formContext`** to get or set values in fields, manipulate form elements, or trigger alerts based on field data.

d. Provide a unique name (for example, **`validatePhoneNumber.js`**), set the type to JavaScript (JS), and upload your JS file.

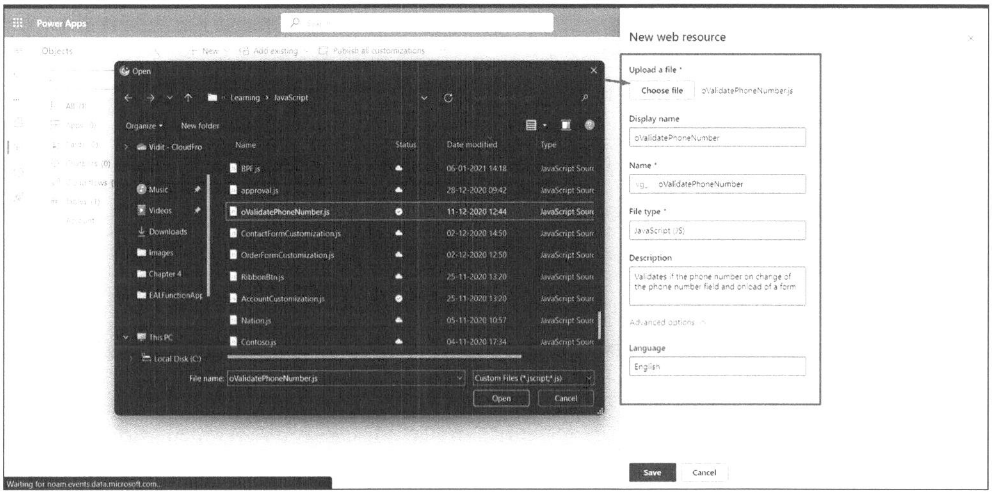

***Figure 4.23(d)**: Registering JavaScript Web resource*

  e. Do not forget to add a description so other users or developers can easily understand its purpose.

2. Add the JavaScript to a Form:

  a. Open the Account entity form where you want this logic to run.

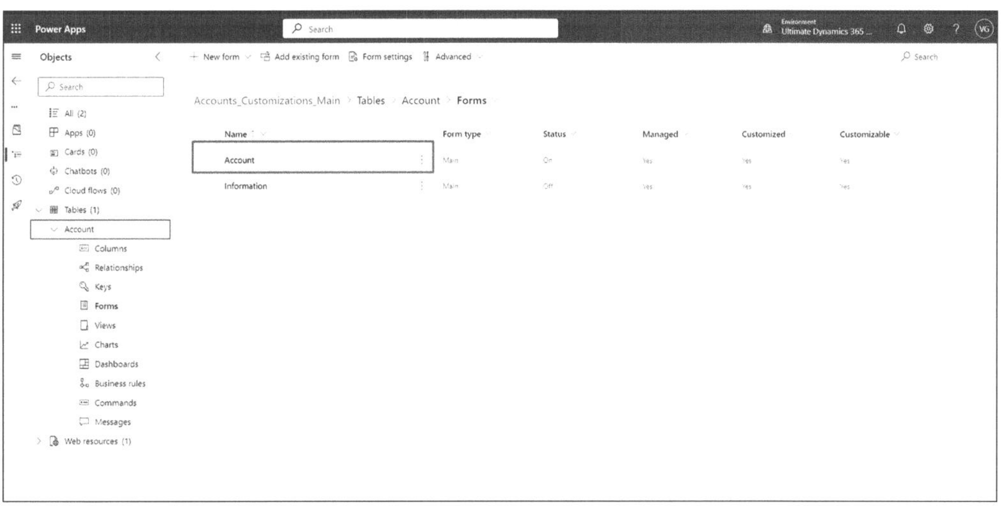

***Figure 4.23(e)**: Selecting Entity Form to Register the JavaScript*

  b. In the Form Editor, open Form Properties.

  c. The Form Properties will be displayed in the right-hand side corner of the window, click on events.

  d. To call your JavaScript function, you need to register it to a specific event.

For instance, if you want to validate the phone number when the form loads or when the phone number field is updated, you will register your JavaScript function on the **OnLoad** and **OnChange** events. The following is a list of form events triggers in Dynamics 365 CRM when a specific user action occurs:

- **OnLoad**: Fired when the form is first loaded.
- **OnSave**: Fired when the form is saved.
- **OnChange**: Triggered when the value of a field changes.
- **OnRecordSelect**: Occurs when a user selects a record in a quick view or **subgrid**.

e. Now to register the JavaScript, go to the Event section and select the events you want to link to the script. There are only two options available: **OnSave** and **OnLoad**. In this example, we will associate the script with the **OnLoad** event.

f. In the **Event** selection under **OnLoad** section, add a new **Event Handlers**.

g. This will open the event configuration pop up window.

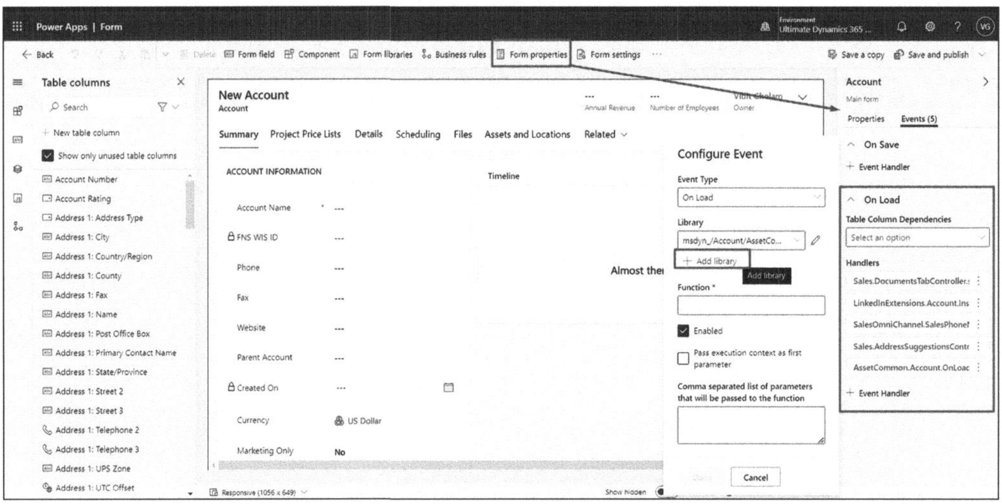

***Figure 4.23(f)**: Adding Event Handler for the OnLoad Event*

h. Add the JavaScript web resource we registered as a library in the library section of the event configuration pop-up window.

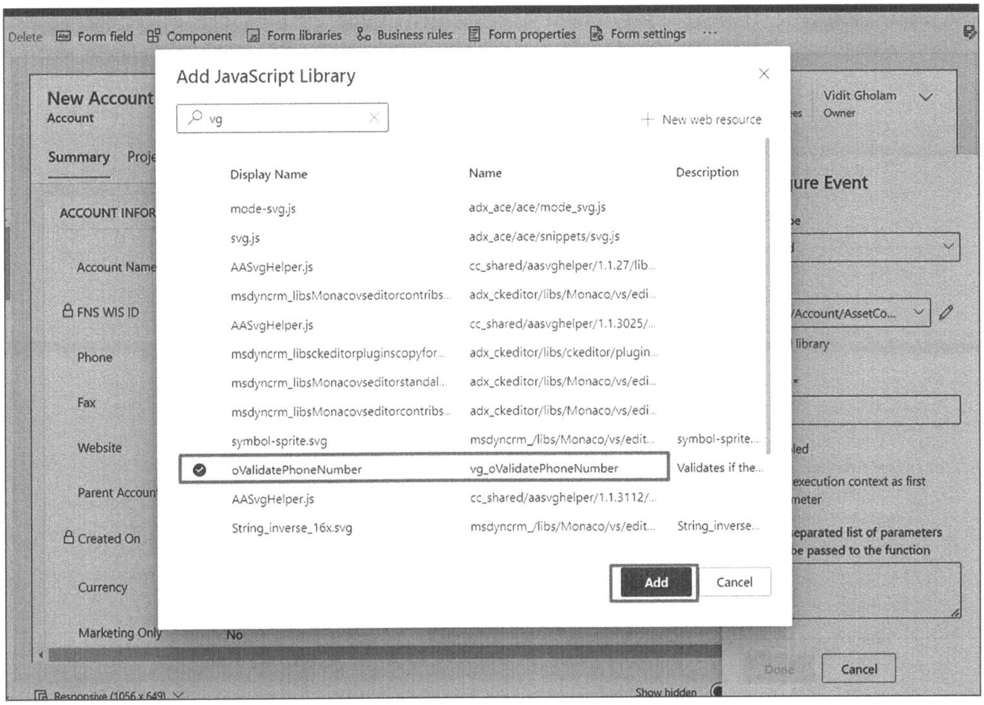

Figure 4.23(g): *Adding JavaScript Web Resource in the Form Properties Libraries*

i. Select the added JavaScript library and enter the function name: **`validatePhoneNumber.readAccountForm`**.

j. Enable the script and pass the execution context to the script.

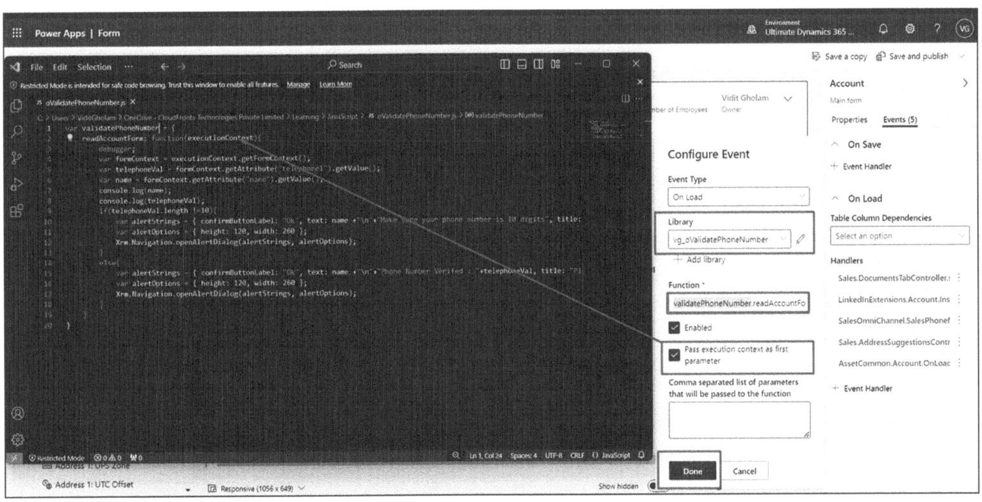

Figure 4.23(h): *Registering the JavaScript OnLoad of the Entity Form*

k. To register the JavaScript for the **`OnChange`** event, select the field that you want to use to trigger the script. You will then see an option to register the script for the **OnChange** event of that field. Follow the steps outlined previously to complete the process.

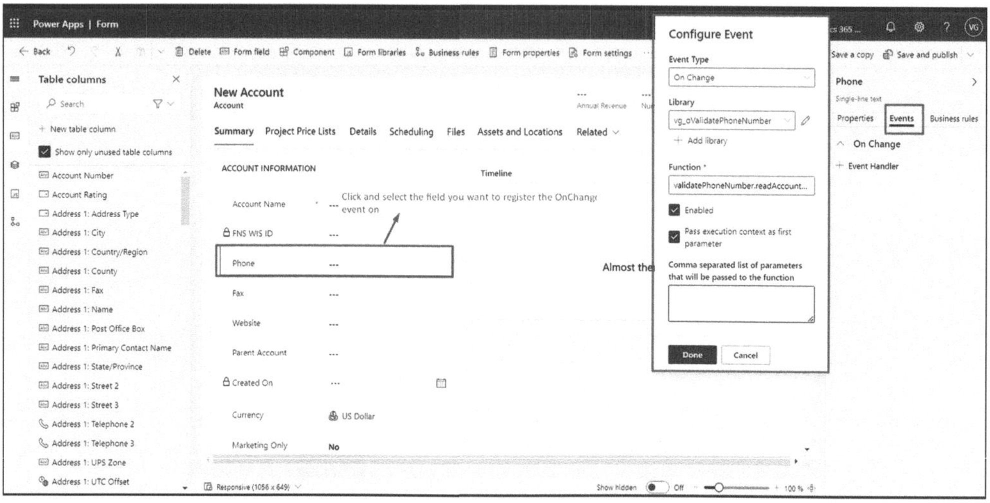

***Figure 4.23(i)**: Registering the JavaScript OnChange of an Entity Field*

l. The last step is to **Save** and **publish** the changes. Now reload the form and test the script.

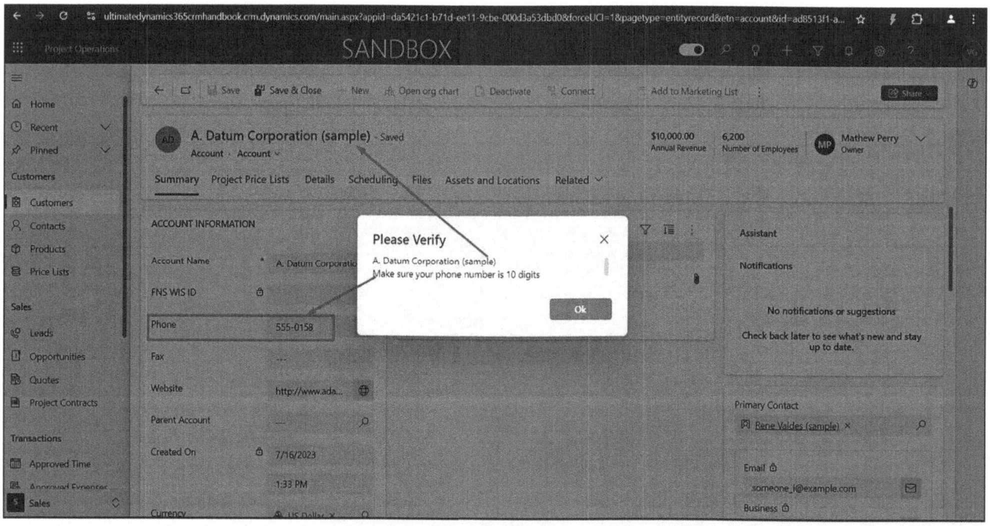

***Figure 4.23(j)**: Output of the JavaScript OnLoad of the Accounts Form*

Now that we have explored how JavaScript can be used to enhance functionality in Dynamics 365 with custom logic, let us turn our attention to Business Rules. Business Rules provide a no-code alternative for automating simple processes within the system. They allow non-developers to apply logic, such as showing or hiding fields, enabling or disabling fields, or setting values, all through a user-friendly interface.

Business Rules in Dynamics 365 CRM

Business Rules are a feature in Dynamics 365 that allows you to apply logic and automation without needing to write code. They enable you to perform common actions, such as setting field values, showing or hiding fields, enabling or disabling fields, validating data, and more, using a user-friendly interface.

Business Rules are great for simple logic and field-level actions that do not require advanced scripting. They are also helpful because they can run on both the client-side (in forms) and server-side, making them a flexible solution.

Similar to JavaScript, Business Rules are also associated with entity forms in Dynamics 365. To understand how they work, let us walk through the process of creating a Business Rule using a simple example.

In this case, we will create a Business Rule that automatically makes the "**`Address 1: State/Province`**", "**`Address 1: Country/Region`**", and "**`Address 1: ZIP/Postal Code`**" fields required if the "**`Address 1: City`**" field contains data, as shown in *Figure 4.24(a)*:

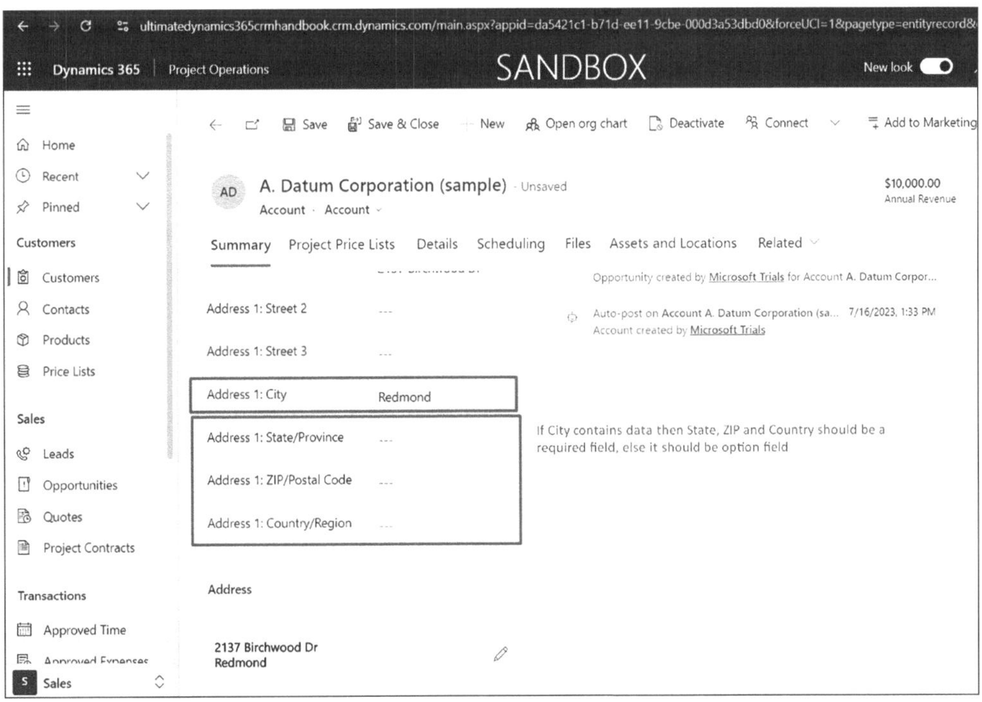

***Figure 4.24(a)**: Applying Business Rules Logic to Fields in CRM Entity*

Creating a Business Rule

Let us take a look at the step-by-step process for creating a business rule:

1. Similar to JavaScript, you create a **Business Rule** within a solution and apply it to a specific entity.

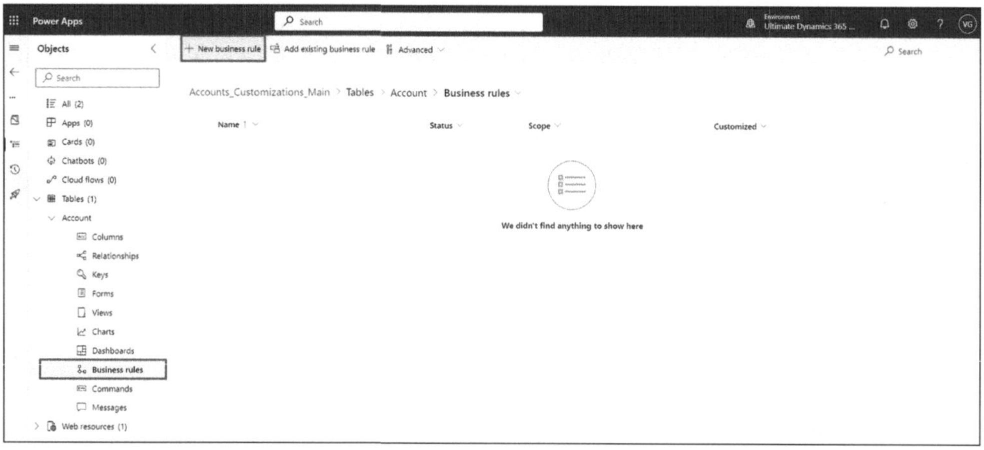

Figure 4.24(b): *Creating Business Rules in a Dynamics 365 CRM Entity*

2. The **Business Rule** interface in Dynamics 365 is easy to use, allowing you to create and manage rules without any coding. It has a drag-and-drop design that lets you build conditions and actions visually.

3. Every **Business Rule** is made up of components, such as a condition component, a component to hide a field, or a component to mark a field as required. These components are essentially pre-built code blocks that you can use to design business logic. Each component has properties, such as which entity it applies to, what rule it should execute, and on which field the action should be performed.

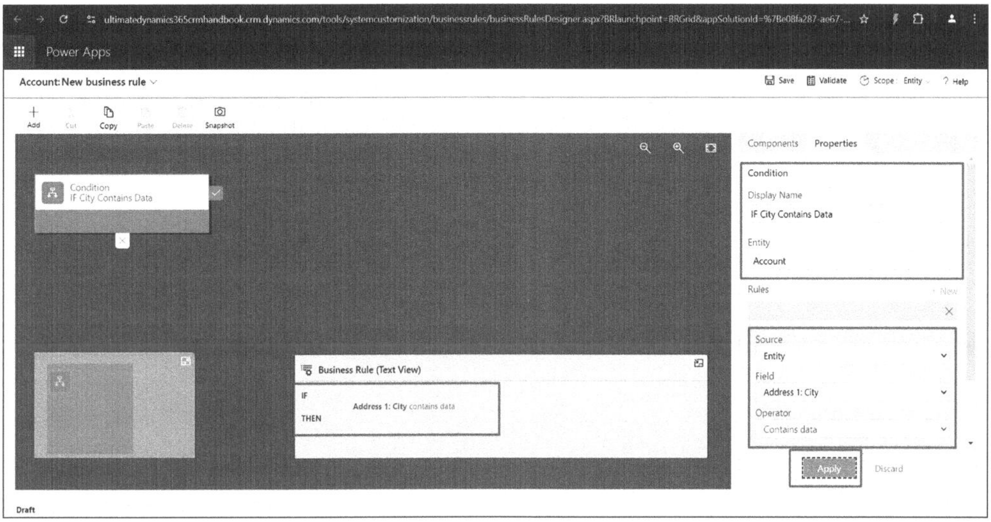

***Figure 4.24(c)**: Setting Condition Component and Defining its Properties in Business Rule*

4. *Figure* 4.24(c) shows a condition component added to check if the **`Address 1: City`** field on the account contains data.

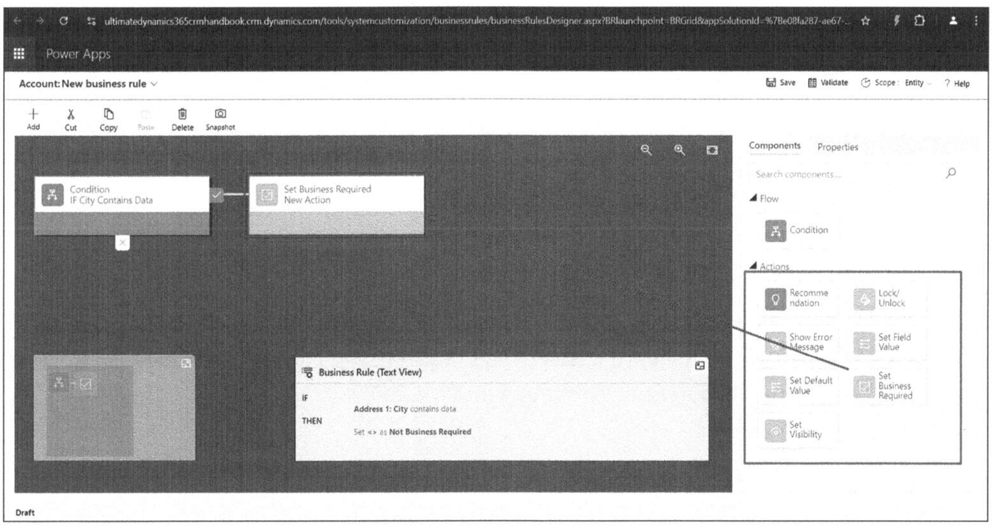

***Figure 4.24(d)**: Set of Available Components in Business Rule*

5. *Figure* 4.24(d) shows a set of available components in a **`Business Rule`**. To add a component, simply drag and drop it into the appropriate condition branch. In this example, since the condition checks if the **`City`** field contains data, the "**`Set Business Required`**" component is added to make certain fields required.

6. Once the business logic is configured, give the **`Business Rule`** a name, then

save and validate the rule to ensure it works as expected, as shown in *Figure 4.24(e)*:

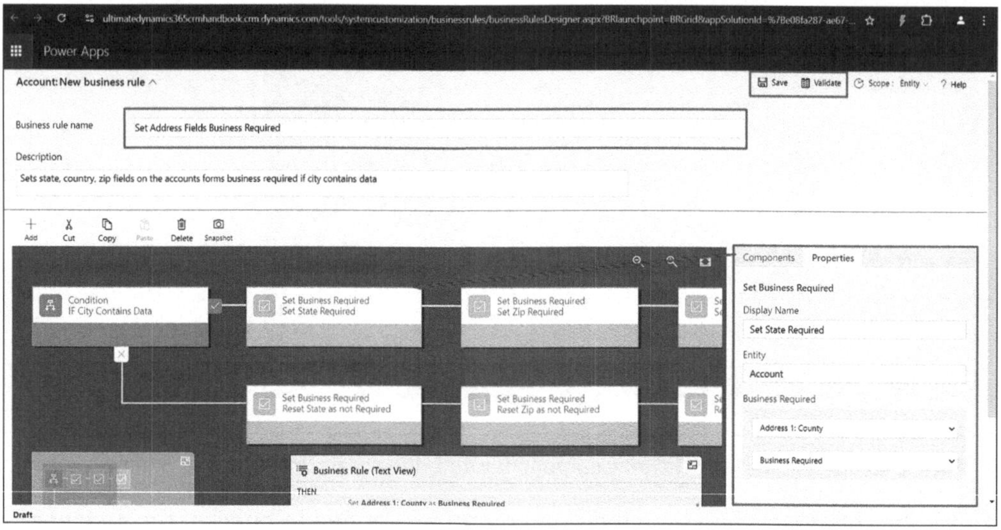

Figure 4.24(e): *Saving and Validating the Business Rule*

7. *Figure* 4.24(e) also shows the **`Scope`** property of the **`Business Rule`**, the Scope of a Business Rule defines where the rule applies within Dynamics 365 CRM. It determines whether the rule is applied at the Entity level or Form level. When set to Entity, the rule applies to all forms of the entity, ensuring consistency across the system. When set to Form, the rule only applies to a specific form, allowing for more targeted behaviors based on the form's requirements. This flexibility helps customize business logic to meet different user or process needs.

8. To make sure a **`Business Rule`** runs on the form, you need to activate it. You can activate or deactivate a **`Business Rule`** using the **`Activate`** or **`Deactivate`** button in the ribbon, as shown in *Figure 4.24(f)*:

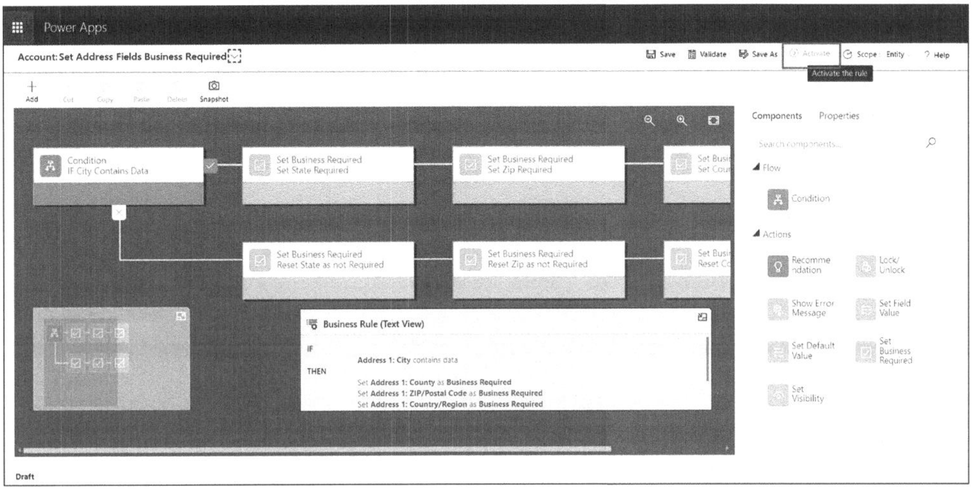

Figure 4.24(f): *Activating a Business Rule*

9. You can see all the business rules running on your entity form by clicking on the Business rule button on the ribbon of the form editor. You can add or remove business rules from the form. You can run a **`Business Rule`** for one form and not for others within the same entity.

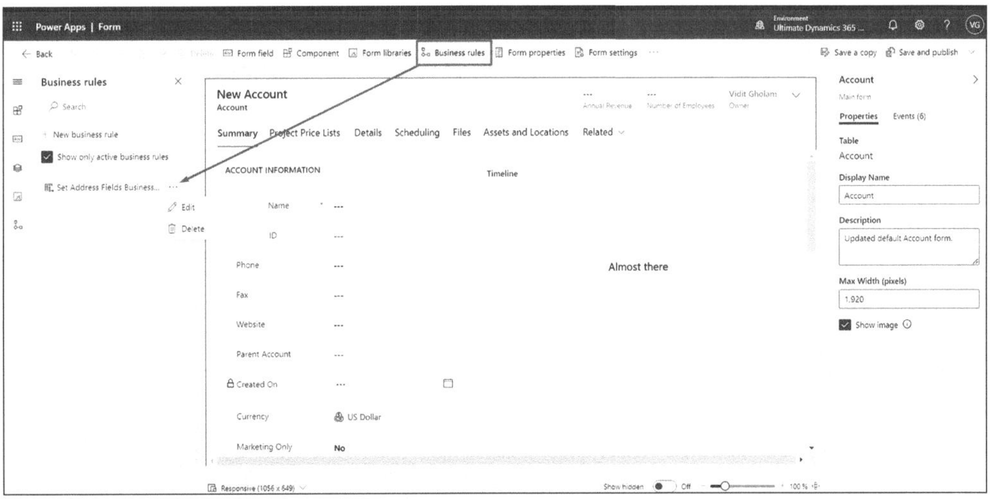

Figure 4.24(g): *Accessing Business Rules from the Form Editor*

10. The final step is to save and publish the solution. Subsequent to that, you can test the Business Rule on the entity form to ensure it works as intended.

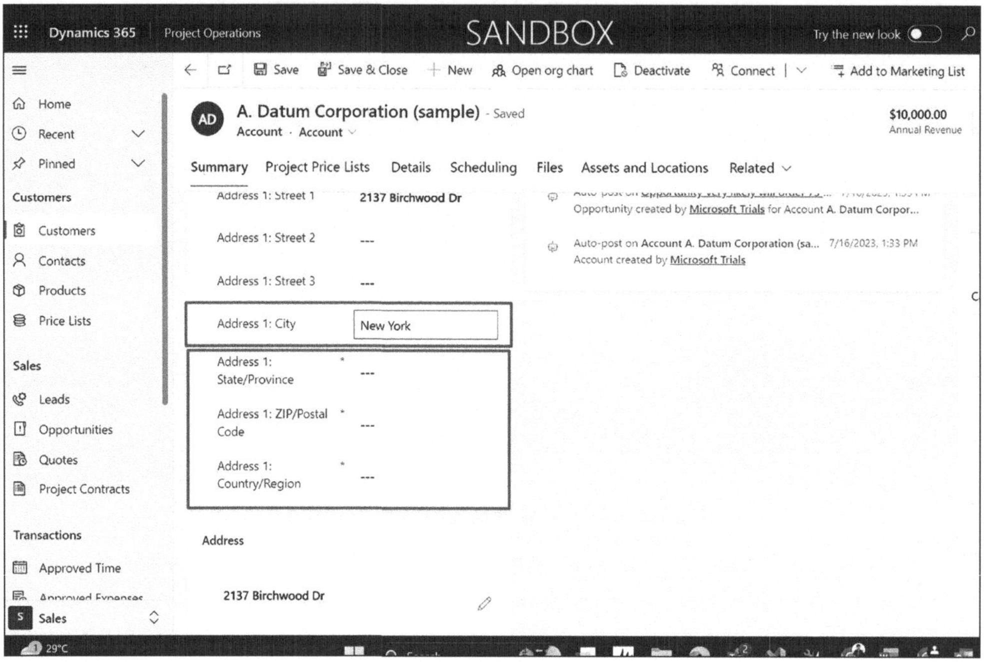

Figure 4.24(h): *Testing the Business Rule on the Entity Form*

Figure 4.24(h) illustrates the functionality of the **`Business Rule:`** when the **`City`** field contains data, the **`State`**, **`ZIP Code`**, and **`Country`** fields are marked as required (indicated by the asterisk *).

Workflows in Dynamics 365 CRM

Workflows in Dynamics 365 CRM are automated processes that help simplify business tasks. They let users set up a series of steps that run automatically when certain events happen, such as creating or updating a record. Common uses include sending notifications, updating records, and creating tasks.

However, Microsoft is slowly moving away (Deprecating) from traditional workflows in Favor of Power Automate (formerly Microsoft Flow), which offers more flexibility and features for automation. Power Automate allows for better integration with other services and has a more user-friendly design for creating complex workflows.

In *Chapter 5, Working with Microsoft Power Platform*, we will be learning about Power Automate and how it can enhance your automation processes.

You can refer to the link in **Reference 13** for detailed information on Workflows in Dynamics 365 CRM.

Actions, Custom Actions, and Custom APIs in Dynamics 365 CRM

Let us take a look at the actions, custom actions, and custom APIs in Dynamics 365 CRM in brief:

- **Actions** in Dynamics 365 CRM are custom operations that execute specific business logic. They allow users to define reusable processes that can be triggered manually or from workflows, providing a higher degree of customization compared to traditional workflows.
- **Custom Actions** take this further, enabling users to create operations that can be invoked from various areas within the system, such as other workflows or plugins for more advanced needs.
- **Custom APIs** allow developers to expose business logic to external systems, making it possible to integrate Dynamics 365 CRM with other applications. These capabilities, along with the Web API, provide powerful tools for building tailored solutions and enhancing system functionality.

In simpler terms, Actions and Custom Actions are used to create custom processes that can be triggered to perform tasks, such as sending an email or updating a record, without needing to manually intervene. These are great for automating repetitive tasks that follow a specific pattern, whereas a Custom API allows you to define your own custom operations and integrate them into the platform, making it easy to extend functionality. If you want to work with the system's data through code, Web API provides a way to interact with Dynamics 365 CRM using web standards. It is a flexible way to access and manipulate data programmatically.

You can refer to the link in **Reference 14** for detailed information on Actions and Web APIs in Dynamics 365 CRM.

Conclusion

In this chapter, we explored various ways to customize Dynamics 365 CRM, including working with entities, fields, forms, and views. We also introduced C# plug-ins and JavaScript web resources, which allow for added functionality and business logic. Additionally, we covered the importance of business rules and workflows in automating processes within the system.

In the next chapter, we will focus on using Microsoft Power Automate in Dynamics 365 CRM, covering topics such as triggers and actions, notifications through Teams and Outlook, and performing CRUD operations on Dataverse tables. We will also introduce Microsoft Power Apps and Microsoft Power Pages, expanding your toolkit for enhancing business processes.

References

1. Virtual Entities in Dynamics 365 CRM: https://learn.microsoft.com/en-us/dynamics365/customerengagement/on-premises/customize/create-edit-virtual-entities?view=op-9-1
2. Supported messages and entities for plug-ins: https://learn.microsoft.com/en-us/dynamics365/customerengagement/on-premises/developer/supported-messages-entities-Plug-in?view=op-9-1
3. Plugin Registration Tool - https://www.nuget.org/packages/Microsoft.CrmSdk.XrmTooling.PluginRegistrationTool/
4. Text Columns: https://learn.microsoft.com/en-us/power-apps/maker/data-platform/types-of-fields?utm_source=chatgpt.com#text-columns
5. Choices: https://learn.microsoft.com/en-us/power-apps/maker/data-platform/types-of-fields?utm_source=chatgpt.com#choices
6. Using the right type of number: https://learn.microsoft.com/en-us/power-apps/maker/data-platform/types-of-fields?utm_source=chatgpt.com#using-the-right-type-of-number
7. Using Currency Columns: https://learn.microsoft.com/en-us/power-apps/maker/data-platform/types-of-fields?utm_source=chatgpt.com#using-currency-columns
8. Different types of lookups: https://learn.microsoft.com/en-us/power-apps/maker/data-platform/types-of-fields?utm_source=chatgpt.com#different-types-of-lookups
9. View trace logs: https://learn.microsoft.com/en-us/power-apps/developer/data-platform/tutorial-write-plug-in#view-trace-logs
10. Write plug-ins for CreateMultiple and UpdateMultiple: https://learn.microsoft.com/en-us/power-apps/developer/data-platform/write-plugin-multiple-operation?tabs=single
11. Tutorial: Write and register a plug-in - https://learn.microsoft.com/en-us/power-apps/developer/data-platform/tutorial-write-plug-in
12. Tutorial: Debug a plug-in - https://learn.microsoft.com/en-us/power-apps/developer/data-platform/tutorial-debug-plug-in?tabs=prt
13. Workflows in Dynamics 365 CRM - https://learn.microsoft.com/en-us/dynamics365/customerengagement/on-premises/customize/workflow-processes?view=op-9-1
14. Using Web API Actions in Dynamics 365 CRM: https://learn.microsoft.com/en-us/power-apps/developer/data-platform/webapi/use-web-api-actions
15. Client Scripting Model: https://learn.microsoft.com/en-us/power-apps/developer/model-driven-apps/clientapi/understand-clientapi-object-model

Chapter 5
Working with Microsoft Power Platform

Introduction

In the previous chapter, we explored various ways to customize Dynamics 365 CRM, including working with entities, fields, forms, views, C# plug-ins, and JavaScript web resources. We also discussed how business rules and workflows help automate processes in the system. Now, we will look into some low-code customizations using the Microsoft Power Platform. We will begin with Microsoft Power Automate, where you will learn how to automate tasks with triggers, actions, and notifications through Teams and Outlook. We will also cover how to perform CRUD operations on Dataverse tables.

Afterward, we will introduce Microsoft Power Apps, which allows you to build custom apps with minimal coding, and Microsoft Power Pages, which lets you create external-facing websites that connect directly to your data. By the end of this chapter, you will see how these low-code tools can further align your processes and expand the capabilities of Dynamics 365 CRM.

Structure

In this chapter, we will discuss the following topics:

- Using Microsoft Power Automate in Dynamics 365 CRM
    - Power Automate Maker Studio
    - Creating a Power Automate Flow
    - Triggers and Actions in Power Automate
    - CRUD Operations on Dataverse Tables Using Power Automate

  - Teams and Outlook Notifications Using Power Automate
- Introduction to Microsoft Power Apps

Using Microsoft Power Automate in Dynamics 365 CRM

Microsoft Power Automate is a low-code platform designed to help users automate workflows and processes without needing to write extensive code. In Dynamics 365 CRM, Power Automate allows you to simplify routine tasks and connect with other applications to handle daily operations more efficiently.

In Power Automate, there are two types of flows, cloud flows and desktop flows.

- **Desktop Flows** enable the automation of tasks on your local machine. These flows can be triggered manually or automatically and allow automation of desktop applications, such as Excel, web browsers, and other legacy systems.
- **Cloud Flows** are used to automate tasks in the Microsoft cloud, and this chapter will focus on cloud flows, which are most relevant to Dynamics 365 CRM users.

Users can create automated cloud flows, referred to as "*flows*," that trigger specific actions when certain conditions are met. For example, you can automatically send notifications, update records, or integrate with tools such as Microsoft Teams, Outlook, and Dataverse. Power Automate makes it easier for users to set up these workflows by offering a user-friendly interface, allowing both technical and non-technical users to build and manage automation with ease.

Power Automate Maker Studio

Power Automate flows, also known as Cloud Flows, are created and managed using the Power Automate Maker Studio. You can access the Maker Studio by visiting https://make.powerautomate.com. Each Dynamics 365 environment has its own set of Cloud Flows. Similar to other customizations, these flows can be moved (exported and imported) between environments.

The following are some of the most used components in the Power Automate Maker Studio:

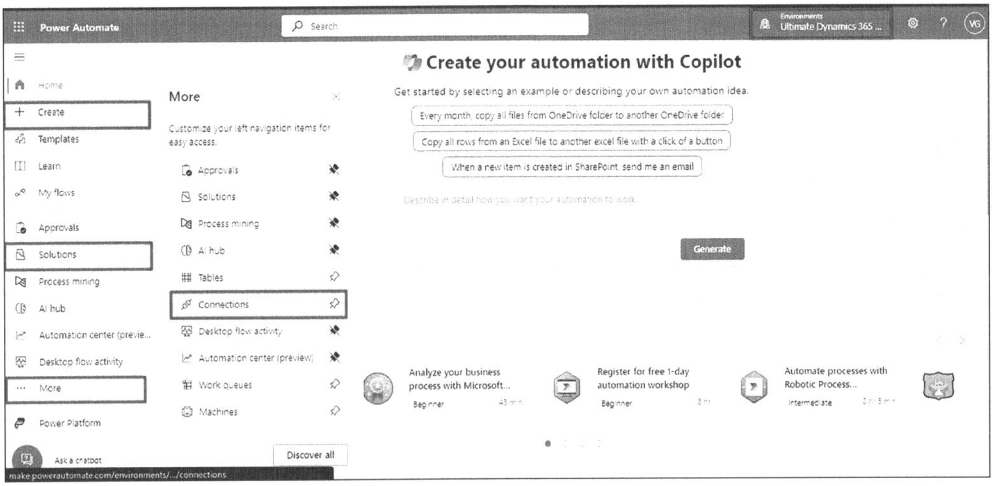

Figure 5.1: *Power Automate Maker Studio*

Connections

Here is a brief overview of connections, one of the most used components in the Power Automate Maker Studio:

- In Power Automate, flows can perform database-level operations similar to plugins, but they always run asynchronously.
- As we learned in the previous chapter, when registering a plugin with the Plugin Registration Tool, you must specify the user context in which the plugin will run, including the permissions of the calling user.
- Similarly, Power Automate flows operate within the context of the signed-in user. Each trigger prompts the user to sign in or automatically creates a connection reference linked to that user's identity.
- For instance, if a user named Vidit Gholam is using a Dataverse trigger, the flow will execute based on Vidit's permissions. If Vidit then sends an email using the Outlook "`Send Email`" action in Power Automate, the email will appear to be sent by Vidit Gholam. All these connections associated with the triggers and actions are known as connection references and are managed in the Connections section of Power Automate Maker Studio.

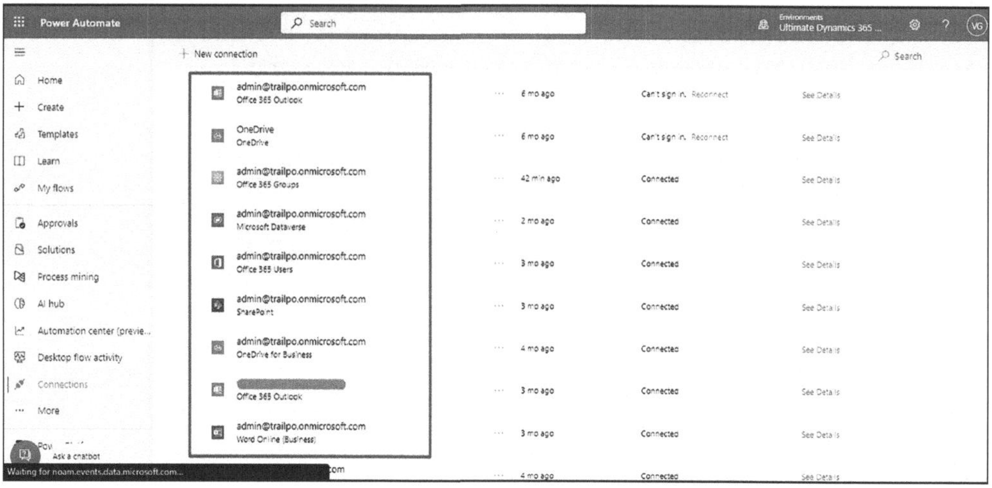

Figure 5.2: *Connection References in Power Automate Studio*

My Flows

Every flow has an owner, and you can share your flows with others, allowing for collaboration and teamwork. Similarly, you can access flows that have been shared with you. All flows that you create, as well as those shared with you, will be displayed in the "`My Flows`" section of the **`Power Automate Maker Portal`**.

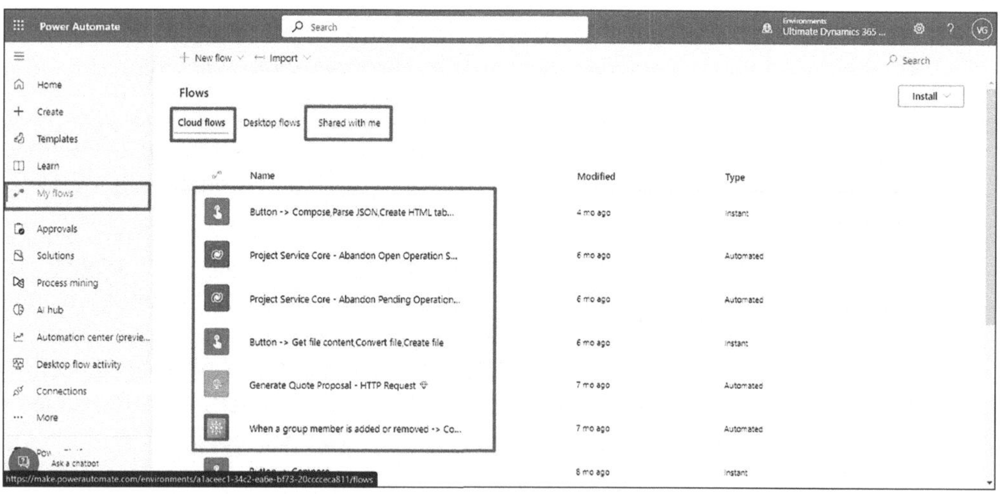

Figure 5.3(a): *My Flows Section in Power Automate Maker Portal*

Solutions

The concept of solutions in Power Automate is similar to that in Dynamics 365 CRM. In fact, this is the same Solution section from the Power Apps Studio.

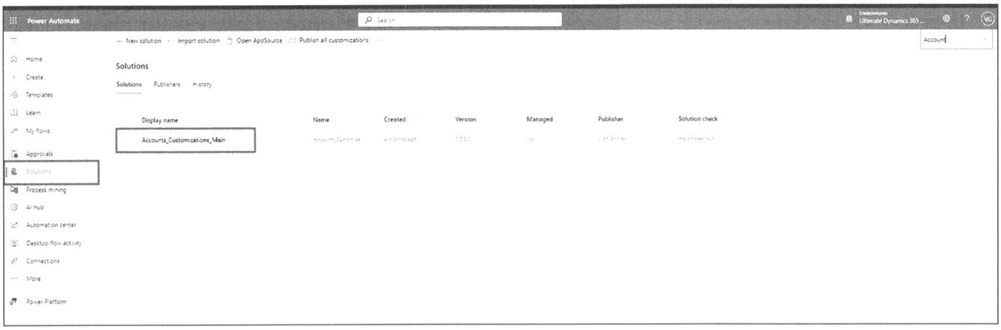

Figure 5.3(b): *Solutions in Power Automate Studio*

It is recommended to create Power Automate flows within a solution because it simplifies the exporting process.

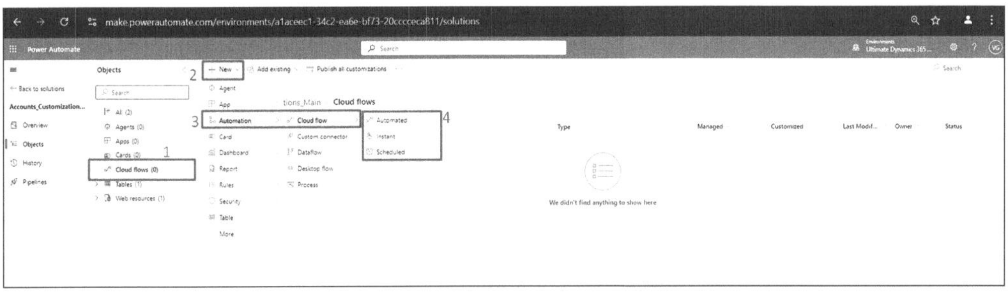

Figure 5.3(c): *Creating a Power Automate Flow in a Solution*

When a Power Automate flow is created inside a solution, all its dependencies, particularly connection references are automatically included. For beginners, exporting and importing flows outside a solution can be tedious, as many times a flow may export successfully but encounter numerous dependency errors during import, preventing it from being imported. Therefore, it is advisable to create all flows within a solution to avoid these issues.

Creating a Power Automate Flow

To create a Power Automate Flow in Dynamics 365 CRM, follow these steps:

1. **Sign in to Power Automate:** Go to `make.powerautomate.com` and sign in using your Microsoft account.
2. **Choose a Flow Type:** Click on "`New Flow`" to create a new flow. If you have an existing solution or if you are creating it inside a solution, then under the Cloud Flows section in the solution click "`New`" and select the type of flow you want to build as shown in *Figures* 5.3(*b*) and 5.3(*c*). For example, you can choose an automated flow, which runs when a specific event (trigger) occurs, or an instant flow, which you manually start.

3. **Select a Trigger:** The first step is to define a trigger. This could be anything from receiving an email, a new record being added to Dynamics 365 CRM, or a specific time and date. The trigger starts the flow whenever the defined event happens.

4. **Add Actions:** Once you have set up the trigger, you will need to add actions. These are the steps Power Automate performs in response to the trigger. For example, if a new customer is added in Dynamics 365, an action could be sending a welcome email through Outlook or updating a record in Dataverse. You can add multiple actions to handle different tasks as part of the same flow.

Triggers and Actions in Power Automate

Power Automate is essentially a flow of steps, where one action triggers another, allowing you to automate tasks efficiently. When creating a flow, you start by defining a "`trigger`," which is the event that initiates the automation. Succeeding that, you specify one or more "`actions`," which are the tasks you want Power Automate to perform in response to the trigger.

Note: *Dynamics 365 CRM offers two interfaces for creating Power Automate flows: the classic designer and the new designer. In this section, we will use the new designer, as it simplifies the explanation of certain concepts. However, later in this book, we will explore Power Automate examples using the classic designer as well. It is important to note that while the interface differs, the core functionality of Power Automate remains unchanged.*

Triggers

Triggers are the starting point of a flow. They define the event that kicks off the automation process. Examples of triggers include:

- When a new record is created in Dynamics 365 CRM.
- When an email arrives in your Outlook inbox.
- When a specific time and date is reached, such as the start of a business day.

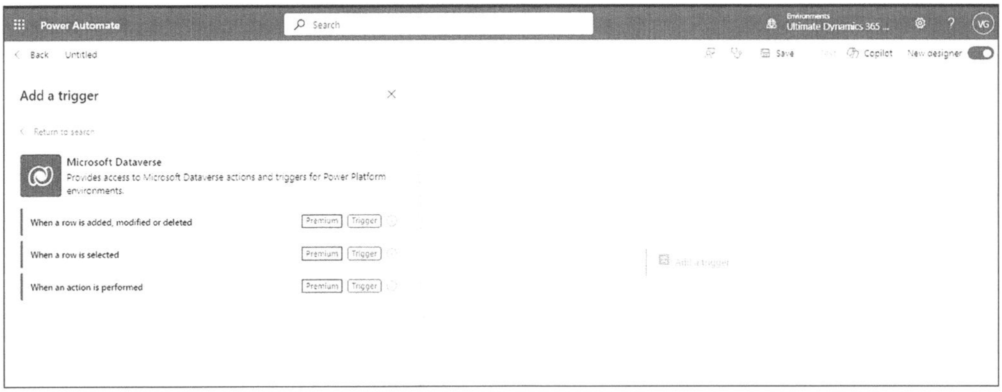

Figure 5.4(a): *Microsoft Dataverse Power Automate Triggers*

Figure 5.4(*a*) displays the available Power Automate triggers for Dataverse tables (also known as Dynamics 365 CRM tables). In Power Automate, a table is referred to as a "**`row`**," and the attributes of the table are called "**`columns`**." As shown in the figure, there are three trigger conditions for initiating a Power Automate flow based on any Dataverse row:

1. When a row is added, modified, or deleted: This trigger allows the Power Automate flow to run whenever a new record is created, deleted, or updated in any Dynamics 365 Model-Driven App.

Figure 5.4(b): *Details of the Dataverse Trigger*

2. *Figure* 5.4(*b*) illustrates the details that the user must specify in the trigger condition. According to the figure, the flow will run when an Account record is created (added) or updated (modified).

Actions

Actions are the tasks Power Automate performs in response to the trigger.

These could include:

- Sending an email to a contact via Outlook.
- Creating or updating a record in a Dynamics 365 table.
- Posting a message in a Microsoft Teams channel to notify team members.

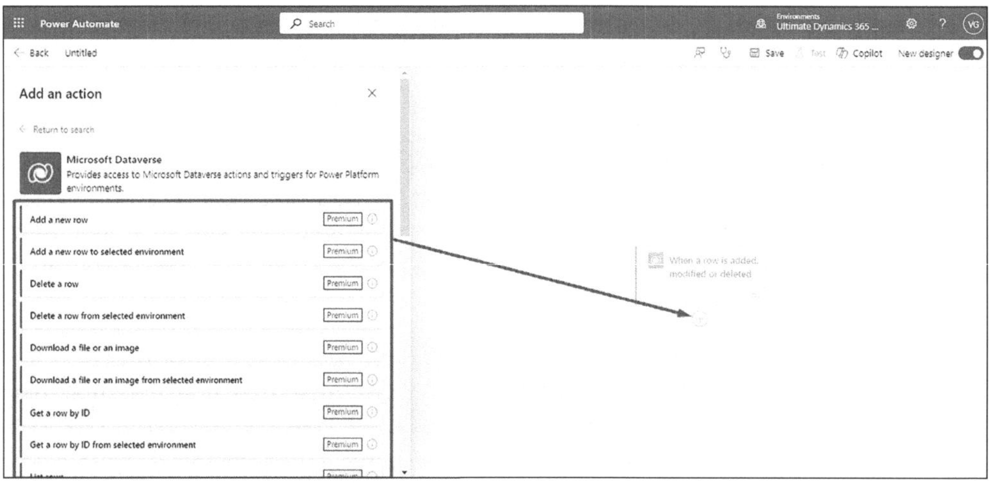

Figure 5.4(c): *Microsoft Dataverse Power Automate Actions*

Figure 5.4(c) shows all the available Dataverse Power Automate Actions. The following is a list of some of the actions:

1. **Add a New Row**: This action will add a new record when the flow triggers.
2. **Similarly, Get Row by ID**: This will get the records details, and all the attributes of the selected row.

Most actions in Power Automate require inputs from previous actions or the trigger itself. For example, as shown in *Figure* 5.4(*d*), subsequent to the trigger "`When a row is added, modified, or deleted,`" we use the "`Get a row by ID`" action. In this action, we need to provide inputs such as the table (Accounts) and the primary key (Row ID), which is obtained from the triggering event.

Every trigger and action in Power Automate produces an output when it runs. Power Automate allows you to dynamically pull inputs from previous steps, whether they are actions or triggers. These inputs can then be used to execute the next step in the flow.

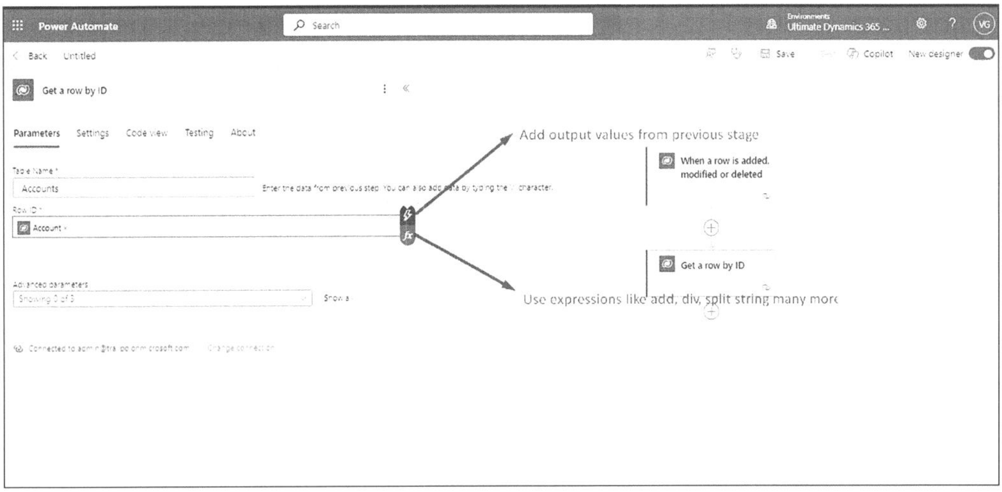

Figure 5.4(d): *Details of the Dataverse Action*

As shown in *Figures* 5.4(*d*) and 5.4(*e*), we use the dynamic input option to retrieve the Account's primary key, which is provided by the trigger condition. Using this primary key, we can fetch all the details of that specific account.

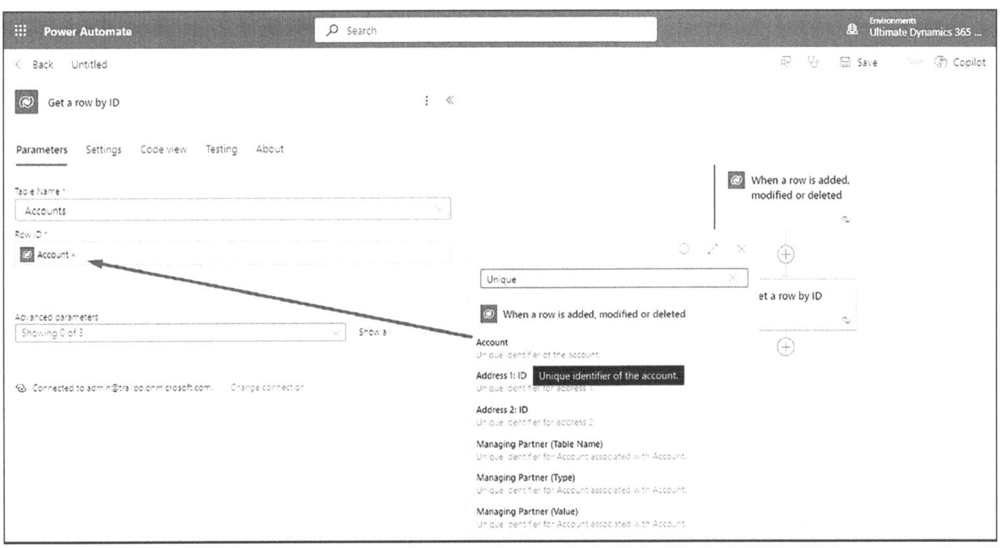

Figure 5.4(e): *Using Trigger's Outputs into the Actions*

Types of Triggers in Power Automate

Microsoft Power Automate offers three main types of flows, each designed for specific scenarios. Understanding these flow types can help you choose the right one for your automation needs.

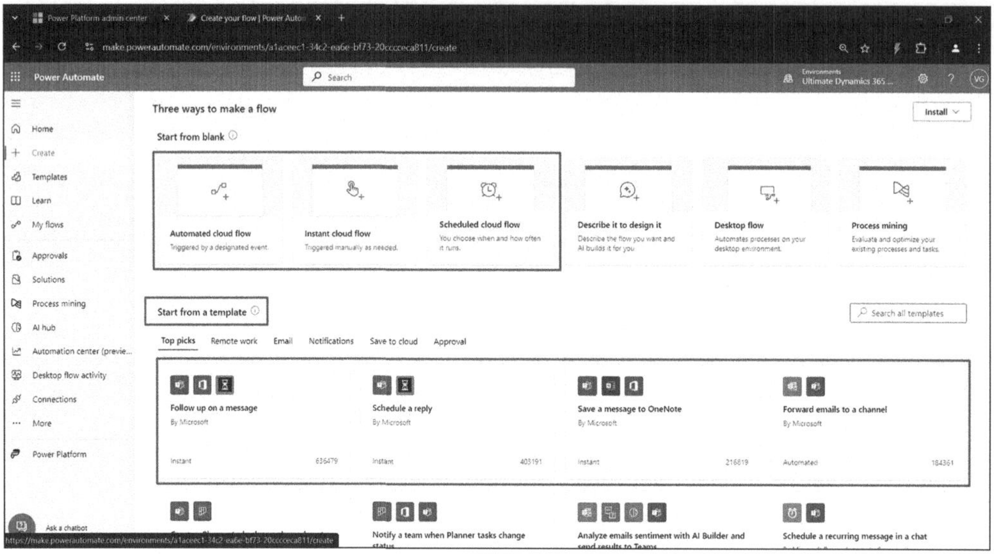

Figure 5.5(a): *Types of Power Automate Triggers*

- **Automated Cloud Flow:** An Automated Cloud Flow is triggered automatically based on a specified event. This type of flow runs without any user intervention once the trigger condition is met. Common use cases include:

  Sending notifications when a new record is created in Dynamics 365 CRM:

  - Automatically updating records when related data changes.
  - Integrating with other applications to perform actions based on incoming data.

  To create an Automated Cloud Flow, you define a trigger (such as receiving an email or a record update) and specify the actions that should follow when that trigger occurs.

- **Instant Flow:** An Instant Flow is designed for situations where you want to manually trigger the flow at your convenience. This type of flow is often initiated by a button press or a specific user action. Examples include:
  - Manually sending a report via email with a single click.
  - Creating a task in a project management tool when you need it.
  - Starting a process in Dynamics 365 CRM directly from a mobile app or a dashboard.

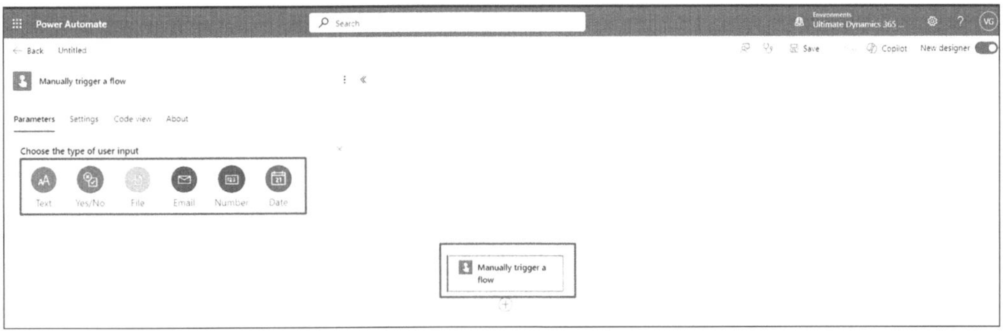

Figure 5.5(b): *Manually Triggered Flow*

To create an Instant Flow, you set up a button in the Power Automate app or embed it in a Microsoft Teams channel, allowing users to initiate the flow whenever needed.

- **Scheduled Cloud Flow:** A Scheduled Cloud Flow runs at predefined intervals, allowing you to automate tasks that need to be performed regularly. This type of flow is useful for routine operations. Examples include:
    - Sending weekly status reports to your team.
    - Performing data backups at the end of each day.
    - Collecting and aggregating data from various sources on a daily or weekly basis.

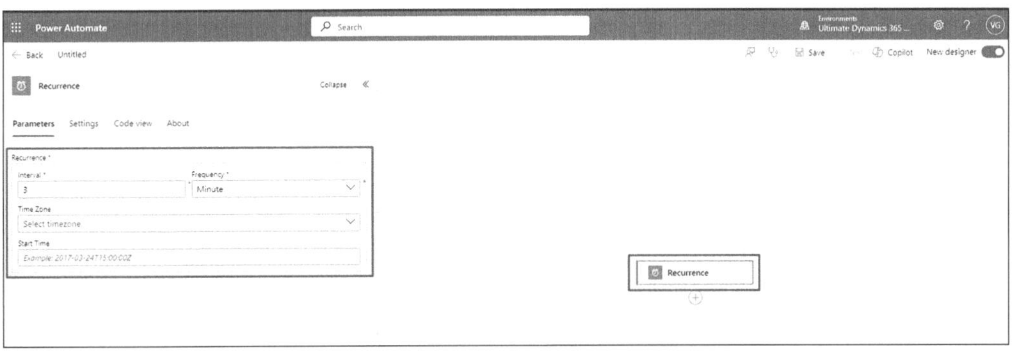

Figure 5.5(c): *Scheduled Power Automate Flow*

To create a Scheduled Cloud Flow, you specify the frequency (for example, daily, weekly) and the actions that should occur during each execution.

CRUD Operations on Dataverse Tables in Power Automate

In Power Automate, Create, Read, Update, and Delete (CRUD) operations on Dataverse tables allow users to manage and interact with data stored in the Dataverse (formerly known as the Common Data Service). These actions enable you to automate tasks such as adding new records, retrieving data, updating existing records, or deleting data from your Dataverse tables within a flow.

Create

The create operation allows you to add new rows (records) to a Dataverse table.

- **Action**: Add a new row, this action inserts a new record into the specified Dataverse table. You will need to specify the table name and provide values for the required fields. Example: Creating a new account, contact, or custom entity record.

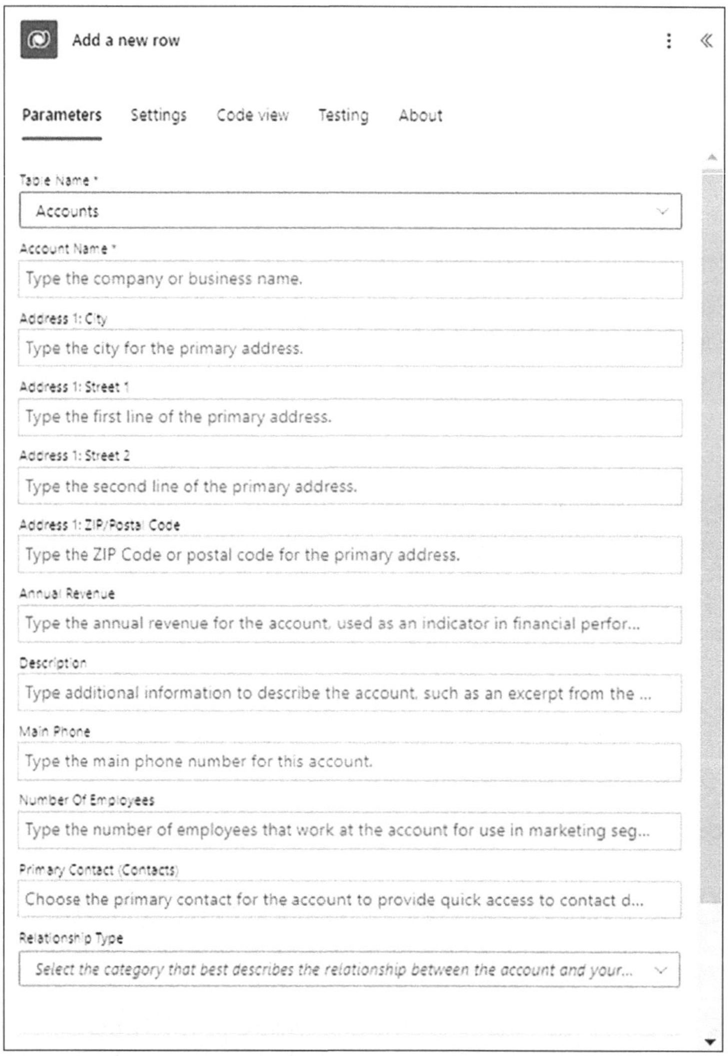

Figure 5.6(a): *Add a New Row Power Automate Action*

Read (Retrieve)

The read operation is used to fetch data from Dataverse tables. There are multiple ways to retrieve data depending on your needs.

- **Action**: Get a row by ID, this action retrieves a single row from a table based on the Unique Identifier (GUID). It is useful when you know the exact record you need to retrieve. This action is displayed in *Figure 5.4(d)*.
- **Action**: List rows, this action retrieves multiple records from a Dataverse table. You can apply filters, select specific columns, and even limit the number of rows retrieved.

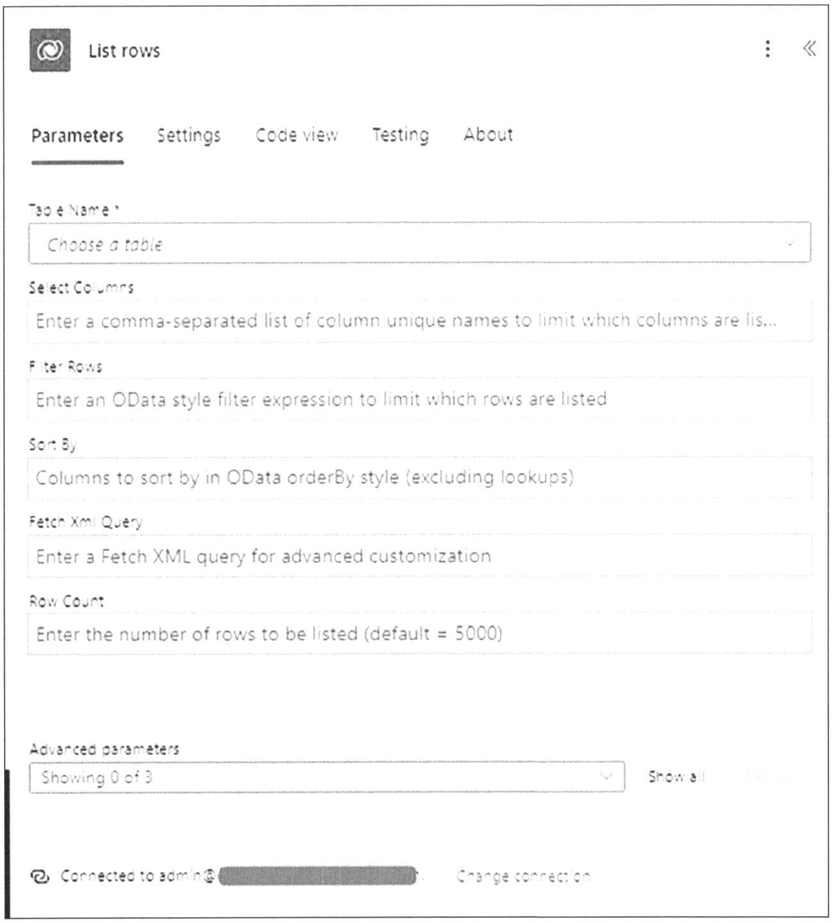

Figure 5.6(b): *List Rows Power Automate Action*

The "**`List rows`**" action in Power Automate is used to retrieve multiple rows of data from a Dataverse table.

Here are the properties of the "**`List rows`**" action, along with examples for each:

Select Columns

This property allows you to specify which columns to retrieve from the source. By default, it retrieves all columns, but using this option can improve performance by limiting the retrieved data to only what is necessary.

Example: If you have a SharePoint list with columns such as "`Title`," "`Created`," "`Assigned To`," and "`Priority`," you can specify to retrieve only the "`Title`" and "`Priority`" columns by using the Select Columns property.

Syntax - Select Columns: Title, Priority

This would only fetch data from the "`Title`" and "`Priority`" columns, ignoring other columns.

Filter Rows

This property lets you apply a filter to retrieve only the rows that match specific criteria. It uses OData syntax to define the conditions.

Example: Imagine you have a SharePoint list with columns such as "`Status`" and "`Priority`." You want to filter the rows where "`Status`" is "`In Progress`" and "`Priority`" is "`High`."

Syntax - Filter Rows: Status eq 'In Progress' and Priority eq 'High'

This query will return only rows where the "`Status`" is "`In Progress`" and the "`Priority`" is "`High`."

Sort By

This property allows you to sort the returned rows by one or more columns in either ascending or descending order.

Example: You might want to retrieve rows from a Dataverse table and sort them by the "`Created`" column in descending order (newest records first).

Syntax - `Sort By: Created desc`

This would sort the rows by the "`Created`" date in descending order, showing the newest records first.

Fetch XML Query

FetchXML is a powerful query language used with Dataverse (formerly CDS). You can use it to write custom queries that filter, sort, and retrieve data with advanced conditions.

Example: Let us say you want to retrieve records from the "`Accounts`" table in

Dataverse where the "**Revenue**" is greater than $1,000,000, and you want to sort them by "**Revenue**."

Syntax - Fetch XML Query:

```
<fetch>
  <entity name="account">
    <attribute name="name"/>
    <attribute name="revenue"/>
    <filter>
      <condition attribute="revenue" operator="gt" value="1000000"/>
    </filter>
    <order attribute="revenue" descending="true"/>
  </entity>
</fetch>
```

This query will return "**Accounts**" where the "**Revenue**" is greater than $1,000,000, sorted by "**Revenue**" in descending order.

Row Count

This property specifies how many rows should be returned. It allows you to limit the number of records fetched.

Example: You may want to retrieve only the first 10 rows of data from a SharePoint list, even if there are more records available.

Syntax - `Row Count: 10`

This will return only the first 10 rows based on your sorting and filtering conditions.

Update

The update operation modifies existing records in the Dataverse.

- **Action**: Update a row, this action updates specific fields in an existing row of a Dataverse table. You will need the record ID and the table name, along with the fields you want to update. For example, updating an account's contact details or modifying a case's status. This action is displayed in *Figure* 5.6(c).

Delete

The delete operation removes records from a Dataverse table.

- **Action**: Delete a row, this action deletes a specific record from a Dataverse table. You must provide the table name and the Unique Identifier (GUID) of the row you want to delete. For instance, deleting an obsolete account or removing test data from the system.

Figure 5.6(c): *Delete a Row Power Automate Action*

Teams and Outlook Notifications Using Power Automate

Let us go through an example to better understand how Power Automate flows work. In this example, we will create a Power Automate flow that triggers when a new account is created. The flow will generate a custom account number using Power Automate expressions, update the account with this new number, and send both a Teams and email notification to the relevant team.

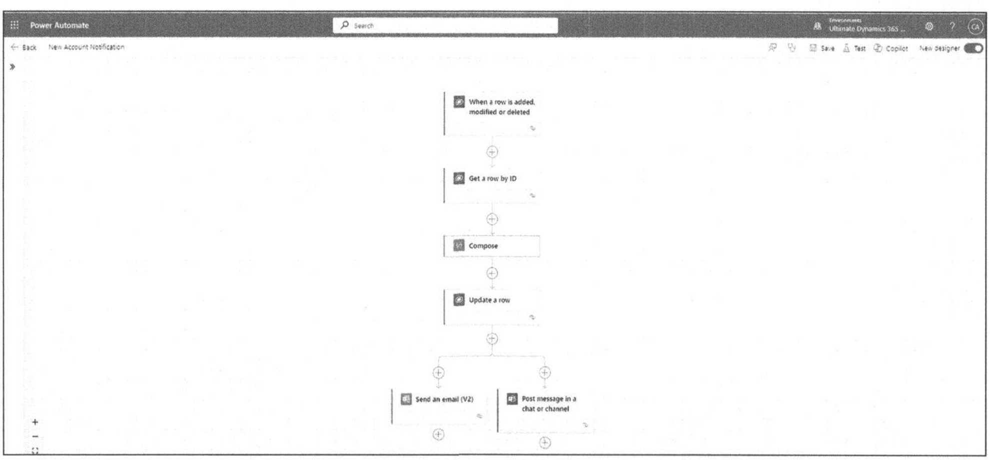

Figure 5.7(a): *Power Automate Flow to Send Email and Teams Notification when a New Account is Created*

Figure 5.7(a) shows the complete Power Automate Flow for our use case. Let us break down each component of the flow:

1. **Trigger:** This flow is an Automated Cloud Flow. Since we are working with a Dataverse table and want to send a notification when a new record is created in the Accounts table, we use the "**`When a row is added, modified, or deleted`**" trigger.
2. **Retrieve Account Data:** The next step is to retrieve the full details of the account using the "Get a row by ID" action. This step is optional but recommended. Instead of relying on trigger outputs, retrieving the row provides flexibility–if the trigger is changed or removed, the output values linked to the trigger will also be removed, causing issues throughout the flow. By retrieving the row early, only the outputs from this step will need adjustment if the trigger changes, rather than disrupting the entire flow.
3. **Create Account Number:** To create an Account Number, we use a Power Automate expression that concatenates the prefix "**`ACC`**" and a random 6-digit number using the rand function. This expression is added in a "**`Compose`**" action from Data Operations, though it could also be inserted directly into the "**`Update a row`**" action. We use "**`Compose`**" here to make the expression visible and easy to reference.

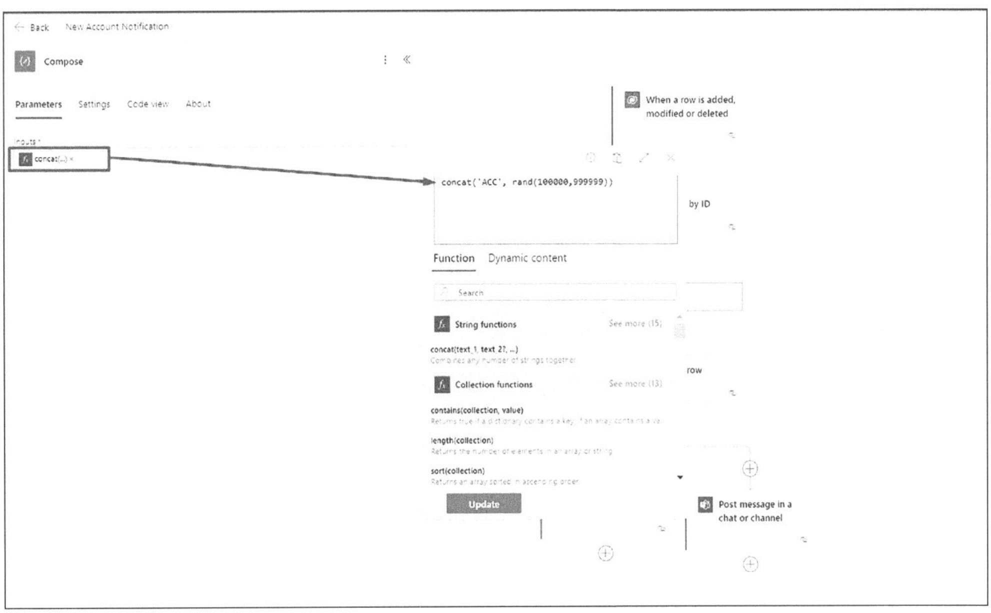

Figure 5.7(b): *Expression to Create Account Number in Compose Action*

4. **Update Account:** The newly created account is updated with the generated **`Account Number`** using the "**`Update a row`**" Dataverse action.

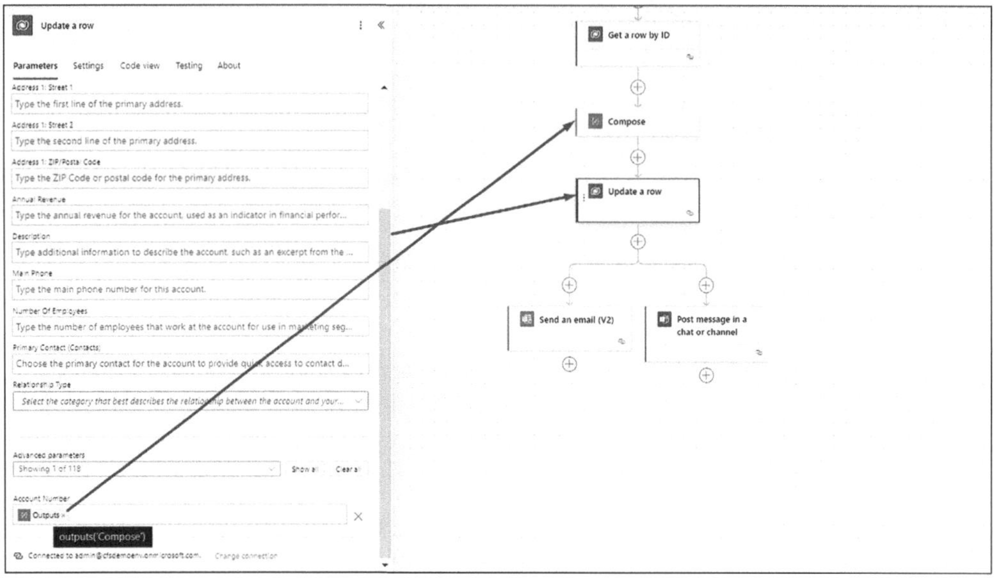

Figure 5.7(c): *Updating the Account Number on the Account*

5. **Send Email Notification:** We then send an email notification using the Outlook "`Send an email (V2)`" action. The body of the email is built using the outputs from previous steps in the flow.

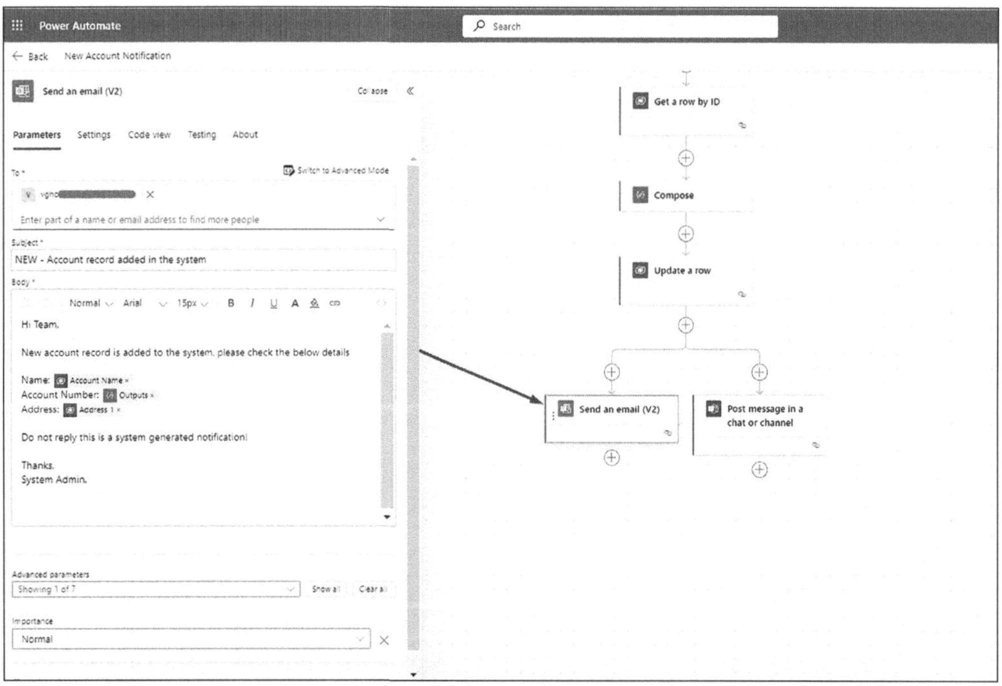

Figure 5.7(d): *Sending an Outlook Email Notification Using Power Automate*

6. **Send Teams Notification:** Simultaneously, we send a Teams notification using the "**`Post message in a chat or channel`**" action. Similar to the email, the message content is generated based on outputs from earlier steps.

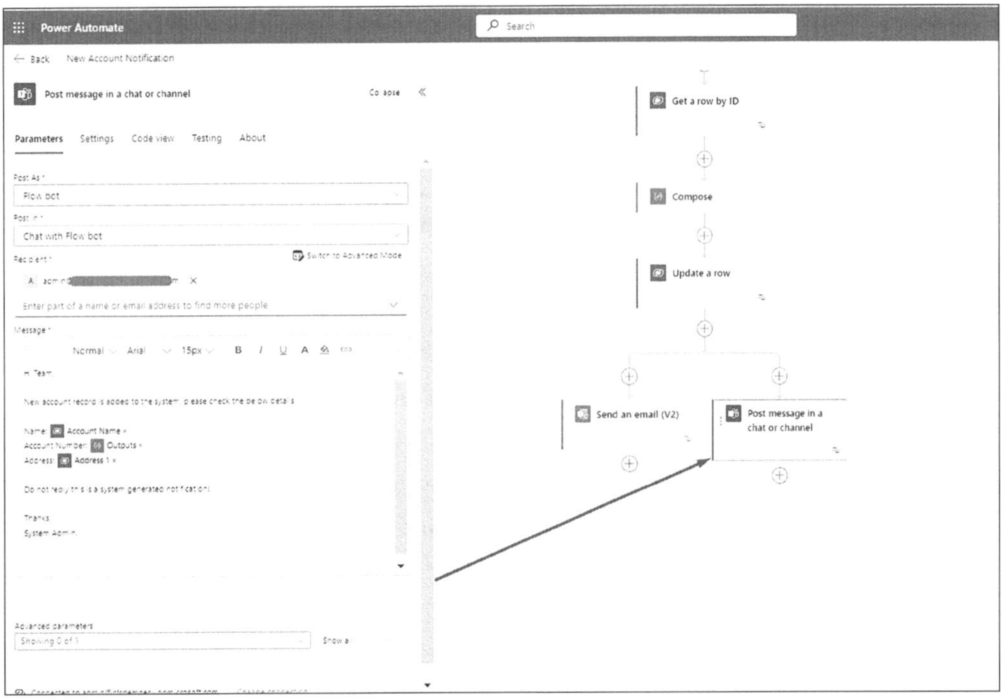

Figure 5.7(e): *Sending a Teams Notification Using Power Automate*

7. Email notification sent by the Power Automate flow.

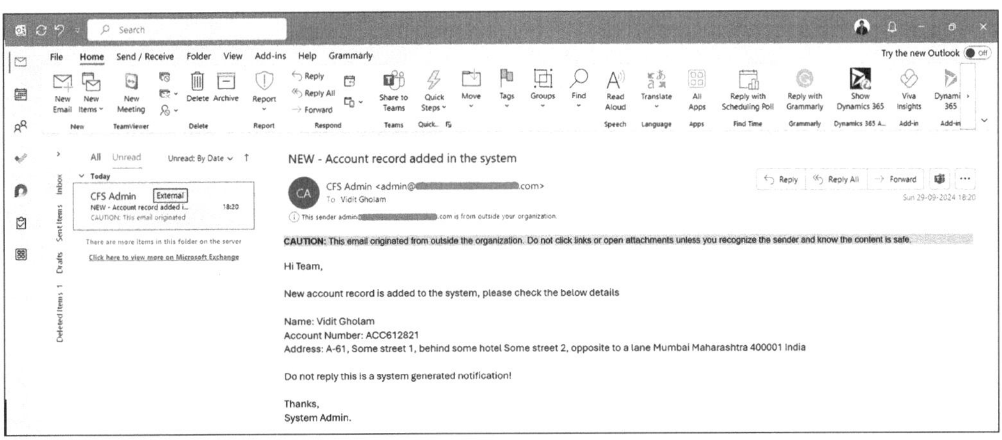

Figure 5.7(f): *Outlook Notification*

8. Teams notification sent by the Power Automate flow.

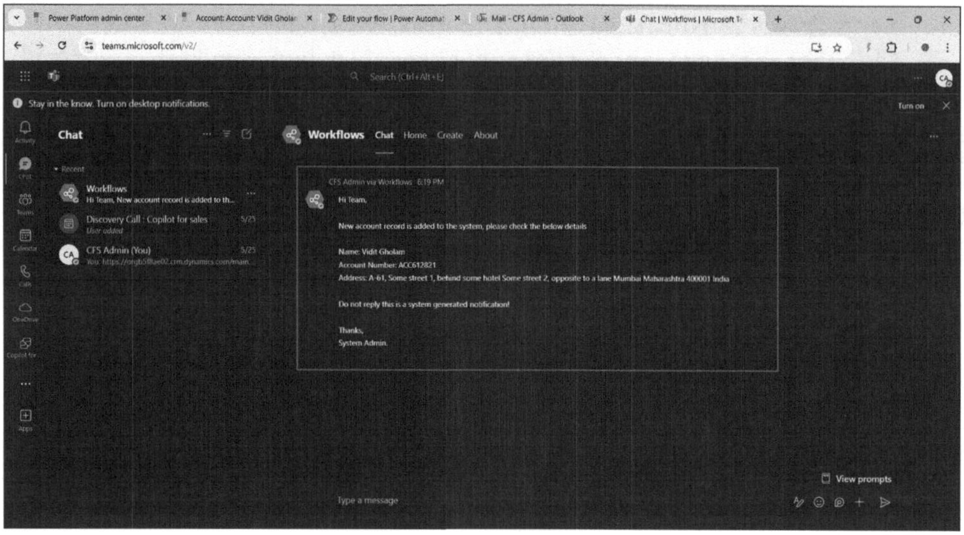

Figure 5.7(g): *Teams Notification*

Now that we have successfully created a Power Automate flow, let us look at how we can monitor its performance and review the key information available, such as the run history, connections, and other important details that help ensure the flow is running smoothly.

Power Automate Flow Information Screen

When you open a flow in the Power Automate Maker Portal, you are presented with a detailed overview of the flow, showing important information, such as run history, connections, and other insights. This screen helps you monitor, manage, and troubleshoot your flows.

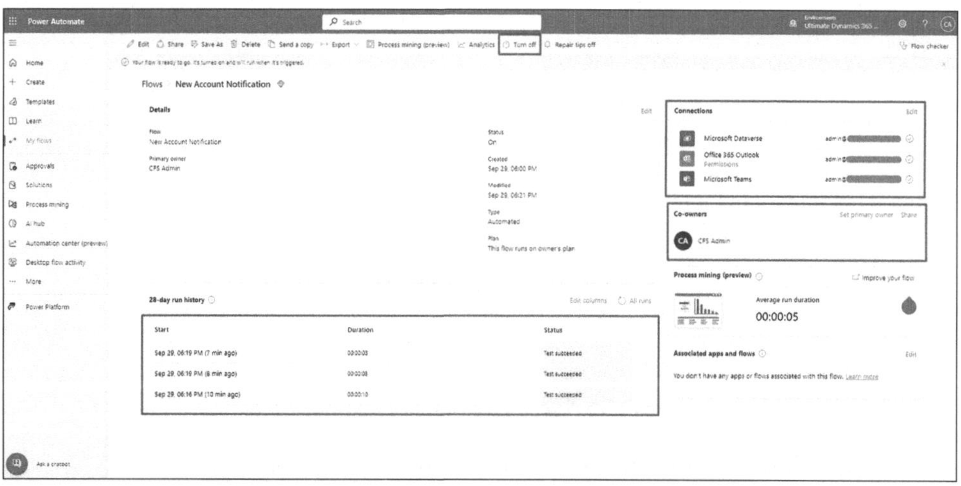

Figure 5.8: *Power Automate Flow Information Screen*

Here are the key sections of the Power Automate Flow Information Screen:

- **Run History:** This section displays a list of all past executions (runs) of the flow. You can view when each run occurred, the status (**`Success`**, **`Failed`**, or **`Running`**), and how long the flow took to execute. By clicking on any run, you can access detailed logs and step-by-step breakdowns, which help in troubleshooting failed or problematic runs.
- **Connections:** Under this section, you can see the connections (also known as connection references) that the flow uses for its triggers and actions. For example, if your flow interacts with Dataverse, Outlook, or Teams, you will see the associated connections here. You can also manage these connections, including refreshing or editing them if authentication issues arise.
- **Owners:** This section shows the owners of the flow, which includes the creator and any users with whom the flow has been shared. You can manage ownership by adding or removing collaborators, allowing others to modify or maintain the flow.
- **Flow Checker:** The Flow Checker is a built-in tool that scans your flow for potential issues, such as configuration errors, missing connections, or best practice recommendations. This feature helps you ensure that your flow is well-configured and runs smoothly.
- **Analytics:** Here, you can find insights into how frequently your flow is running and its success rate over time. The analytics dashboard provides a graphical view of the flow's performance, helping you track usage trends and identify any persistent issues.
- **Edit/Details Tab:** From the information screen, you can switch to the "**`Edit`**" tab to make changes to the flow. The "**`Details`**" tab typically contains metadata about the flow, such as its description, creation date, and the environment in which it resides.
- **Turn Off:** The **`Turn OFF`** button in Power Automate allows you to temporarily disable a flow without deleting it. When a flow is turned off (you can turn it on again), it no longer responds to triggers or executes any actions, but all its configurations and settings remain intact. This feature is particularly useful for pausing workflows during updates, maintenance, or troubleshooting. You can easily reactivate the flow by turning it back on when needed.

Introduction to Microsoft Power Apps

Canvas Power Apps are a versatile feature of Microsoft Power Apps that enable users to create highly customized applications with a focus on design and user experience. Unlike model-driven apps, which rely on the underlying data structure, Canvas Apps give users complete control over the layout, appearance, and functionality of the app. Users can start with a blank canvas and design their app using a drag-and-drop interface, making it easy to incorporate various controls, such as text boxes, buttons, and images.

Canvas Apps can connect to a wide range of data sources, including Microsoft Dataverse, SharePoint, Excel, and more. This flexibility allows businesses to create tailored applications that meet their specific needs, whether for data entry, reporting, or other business processes. The ability to customize both the user interface and the data integration makes Canvas Power Apps a powerful tool for organizations looking to improve efficiency and solve unique challenges.

While we will not dive deeply into Canvas Power Apps in this chapter, as it could easily fill an entire book on its own, here are some excellent resources to help you learn more about them:

- **Reference 4**: Get started with Power Apps canvas apps.
- **Reference 5**: Create a canvas app in Power Apps.
- **Reference 6**: Microsoft Power Apps documentation.
- **Reference 7**: Create a Canvas Power App.

Conclusion

In this chapter, we explored the powerful capabilities of Microsoft Power Automate within Dynamics 365 CRM. We began by understanding the fundamentals of triggers and actions, which enable us to automate workflows effortlessly. We then learned how to send notifications through Teams and Outlook and covered CRUD operations on Dataverse tables. We also introduced Microsoft Power Apps, highlighting how they allow users to create customized applications tailored to their unique business needs. Finally, we touched on Microsoft Power Pages, setting the stage for further exploration in future chapters.

As we move forward, we will focus on integrating Dynamics 365 CRM with SharePoint Online, exploring how to manage Word templates and generate important documents such as quotes and invoices. This will further enhance your ability to create efficient processes within your organization.

References

1. Power Automate Training: https://learn.microsoft.com/en-us/training/modules/get-started-flows/
2. Get started with Power Automate: https://learn.microsoft.com/en-us/power-automate/getting-started

3. Get started with triggers in Power Automate: https://learn.microsoft.com/en-us/power-automate/triggers-introduction?tabs=classic-designer
4. Get started with Power Apps canvas apps: https://learn.microsoft.com/en-us/training/modules/get-started-with-powerapps/
5. Create a canvas app in Power Apps: https://learn.microsoft.com/en-us/training/paths/create-powerapps/
6. Microsoft Power Apps documentation: https://learn.microsoft.com/en-us/power-apps/
7. Create a Canvas Power App: https://learn.microsoft.com/en-us/power-apps/maker/canvas-apps/

CHAPTER 6
Document Management in Dynamics 365 CRM

Introduction

In the previous chapter, we explored how the Microsoft Power Platform enhances the Dynamics 365 CRM experience with automation, app development, and external website integration. Now, we will shift our focus to the document management features within Dynamics 365 CRM, which play a crucial role in organizing and handling important business documents.

In this chapter, you will learn how to integrate Dynamics 365 CRM with SharePoint Online for seamless document storage, manage Word templates for standardized document creation, and generate essential business documents such as quotes and invoices directly within the system. By the end of this chapter, you will have a solid understanding of how to streamline your document processes and efficiently utilize Dynamics 365 CRM's document management tools.

Structure

In this chapter, we will discuss the following topics:

- Integrating Dynamics 365 CRM with SharePoint Online
- Managing Word Templates in 365 CRM
- Generating Quotation Documents Using Power Automate
- Generating Invoice Documents Using Power Automate

Integrating Dynamics 365 CRM with SharePoint Online

Document management is an essential part of any CRM system, as businesses need a reliable way to store documents such as quotations, invoices, and project requirements. While Dynamics 365 CRM includes built-in file storage, its capacity is limited. Many organizations using Dynamics 365 CRM often have Microsoft 365 (M365) licenses, which include tools such as Microsoft Teams, Outlook, and SharePoint Online. Unlike CRM's file storage, SharePoint Online is designed for larger and more flexible document storage. Dynamics 365 CRM offers an out-of-the-box integration with SharePoint, allowing businesses to manage documents more efficiently. With this integration, you can leverage the storage capacity of SharePoint while still maintaining a strong connection between your CRM records and related documents, such as quotes, invoices, or contracts. Instead of relying on CRM's limited storage, you can use SharePoint's document management features within the Dynamics 365 interface.

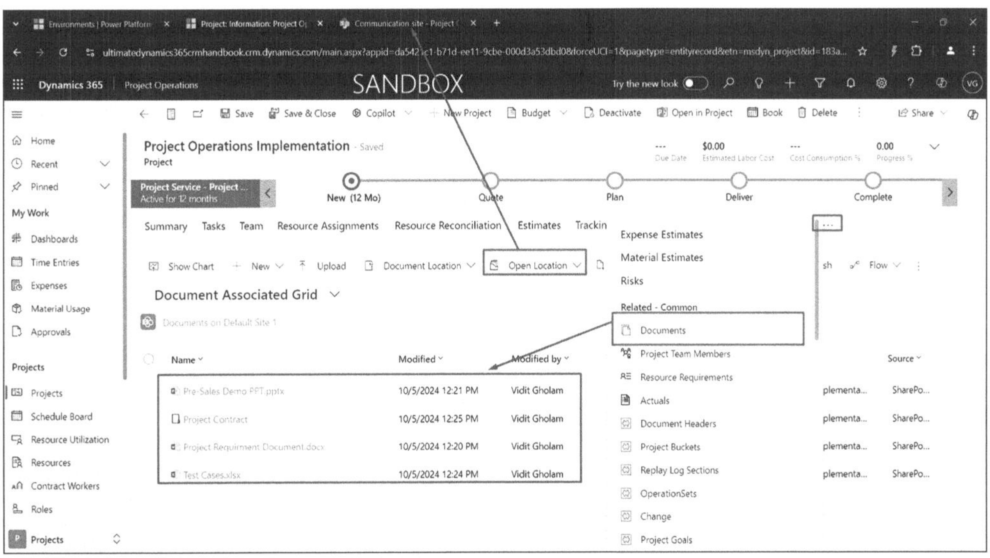

Figure 6.1: *Document Section of a Dynamics 365 CRM Project Record*

Figure 6.1 illustrates the document section of a project record in Dynamics 365 CRM. As shown, all project-related documents can be created, added, or updated directly from the Project Record. This section represents a SharePoint document library automatically created for the Projects entity on the communication site integrated with Dynamics 365 CRM.

You can navigate to the SharePoint document library using the Open Location option highlighted in *Figure* 6.1.

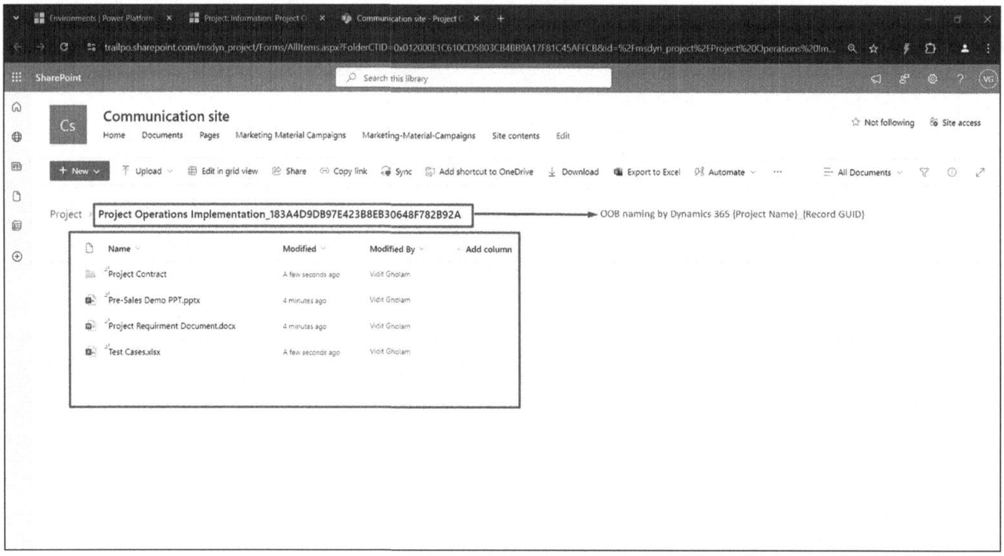

Figure 6.2: *SharePoint Document Library for Project Entity*

Figure 6.2 shows the document library in SharePoint for the Projects entity. When you navigate to the Documents tab on any project form in Dynamics 365 CRM, this library gets automatically created in the background. For every record, a folder with the naming convention **`{Record Name}_{Record GUID}`** is created in the document library. The document library name matches the entity name, which in this case, is "**`Projects`**." This allows each project record to have its own dedicated folder for document management within SharePoint.

Setting Up Integration: Linking SharePoint to a Dynamics 365 CRM Entity

The first step to integrate a SharePoint site into Dynamics 365 is to create a dedicated site for the Dynamics 365 environment. (While you can also use an existing site, it is recommended to create a new, dedicated site for better organization and management.)

Creating a SharePoint Site

In your SharePoint Online environment, create a dedicated site for each of your Dynamics 365 environments (for example, Production, Sandbox). Each environment should have its own separate SharePoint site to keep documents organized and clearly separated. These sites will serve as the document storage location for the CRM entities related to each environment, ensuring that the documents are stored in the appropriate context, whether it is for production use or testing in a sandbox environment.

To create a site, navigate to the SharePoint home page and select **`Create Site`**.

1. You can navigate to SharePoint directly from Dynamics 365, as shown in *Figure 6.3(a)*.

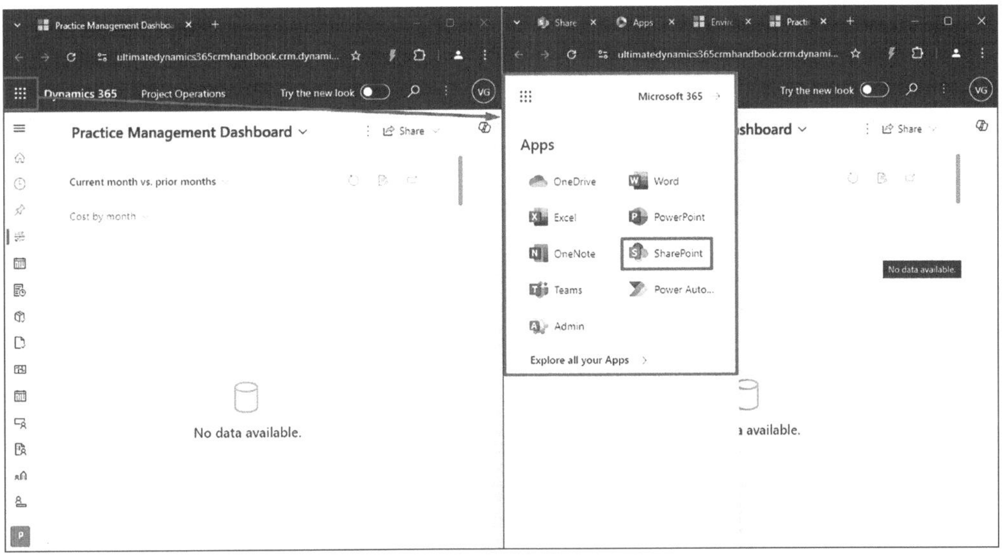

Figure 6.3(a): *Directing to SharePoint via Dynamics 365 CRM*

2. Alternatively, you can access SharePoint by visiting the link https://www.office.com/apps/, as shown in *Figure 6.3(b)*.

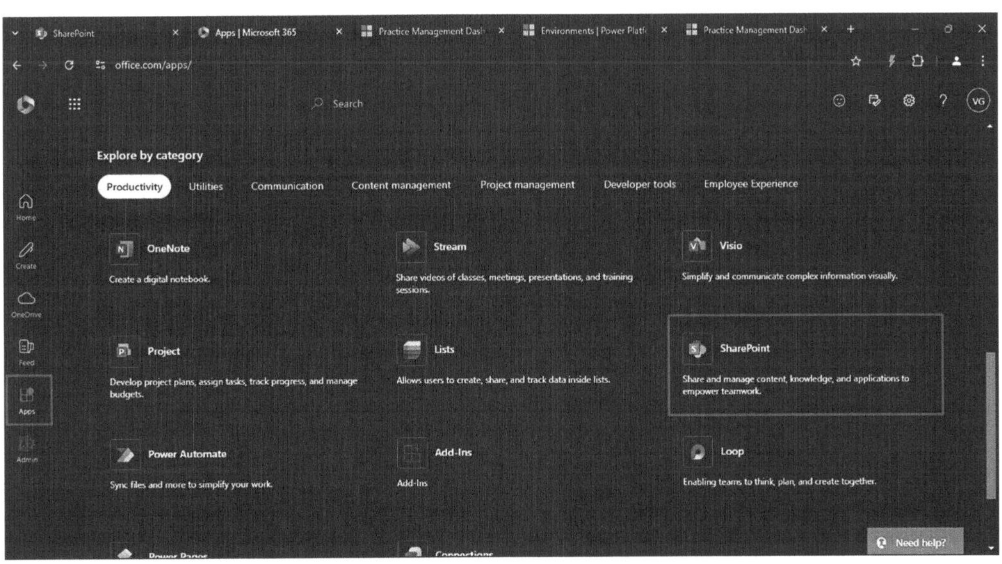

Figure 6.3(b): *Accessing SharePoint via office.com*

3. Choose a Team Site if you plan to collaborate on documents or a **`Communication`** Site for more broadcast-orientated content.

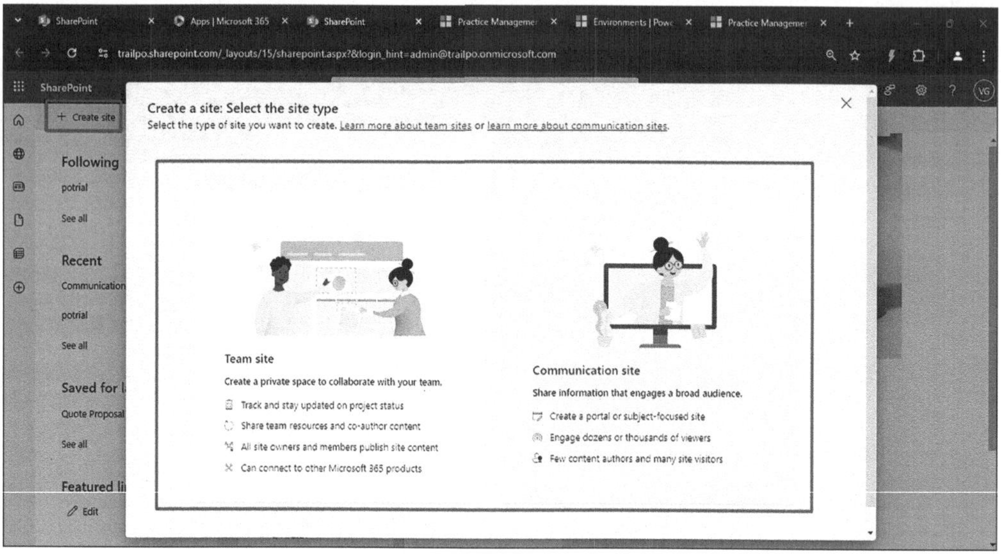

***Figure 6.3(c)**: Creating a SharePoint Site for Dynamics 365 CRM*

4. Copy the URL of the SharePoint site you just created and save it for later steps. You will need this URL when configuring the integration between Dynamics 365 CRM and SharePoint to ensure that documents are stored in the correct location.

Enabling Server-Based SharePoint Integration in Dynamics 365

To enable server-based SharePoint integration, follow these steps:

1. Navigate to **`Power Platform Admin Center`**:

    a. Select your environment in the **`Power Platform admin center`** and go to Settings. Under Integrations, select **`Document Management Settings`**. This will redirect you to the settings area.

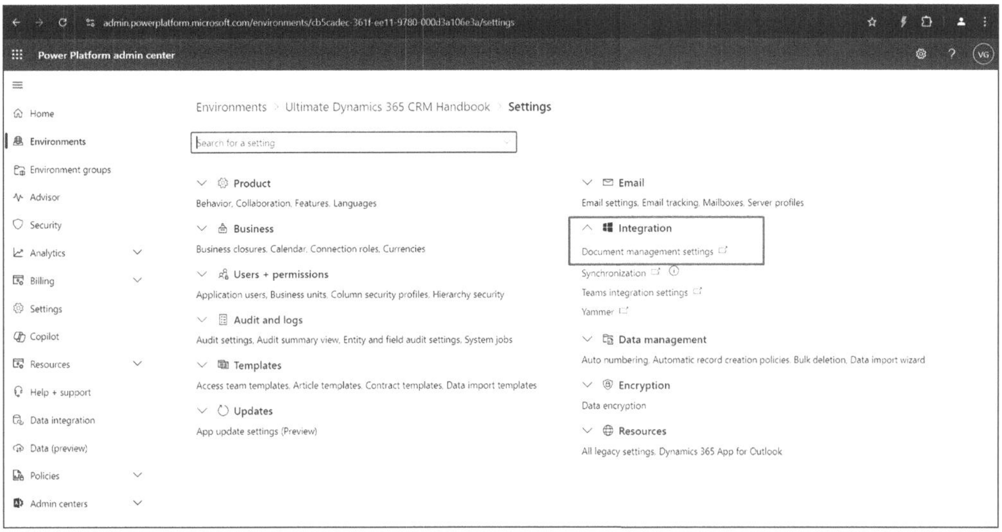

***Figure 6.4(a)**: Document Management Settings in Power Platform Admin Center*

2. **Enable Server-Based SharePoint Integration**:

    a. If you have not linked any SharePoint site with the environment, you will see the **`Enable Server-Based SharePoint Integration`** option.

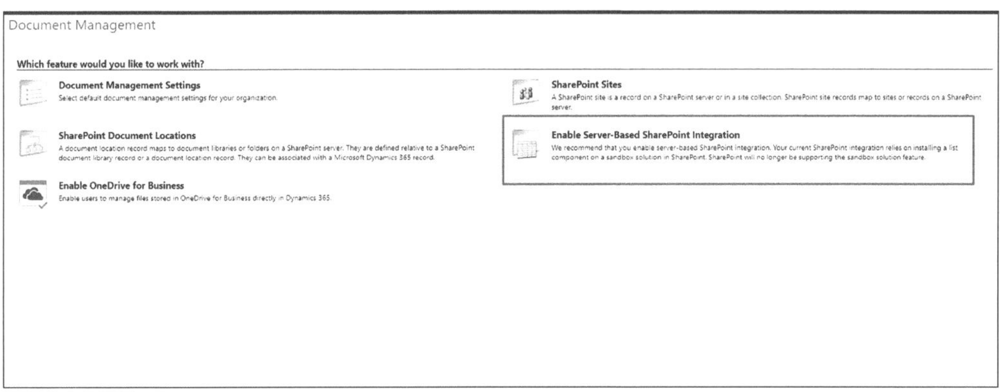

***Figure 6.4(b)**: Enable Server-Based SharePoint Integration option*

3. Click on **`Enable Server-Based SharePoint Integration`** and proceed to the next steps.

4. This is a three-step Deployment Process:

    a. Select **`Online`** under the **`Define Deployment`** step and click **`Next`**.

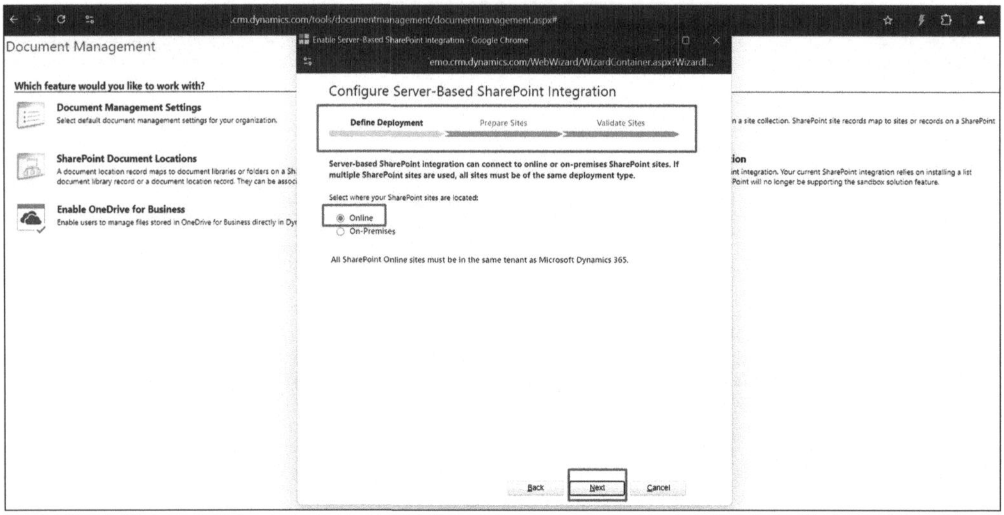

Figure 6.4(c): *Define Deployment stage of SharePoint Sync*

b. In the **`Prepare Site`** step, enter the URL of the SharePoint site you created earlier and click **`Next`**.

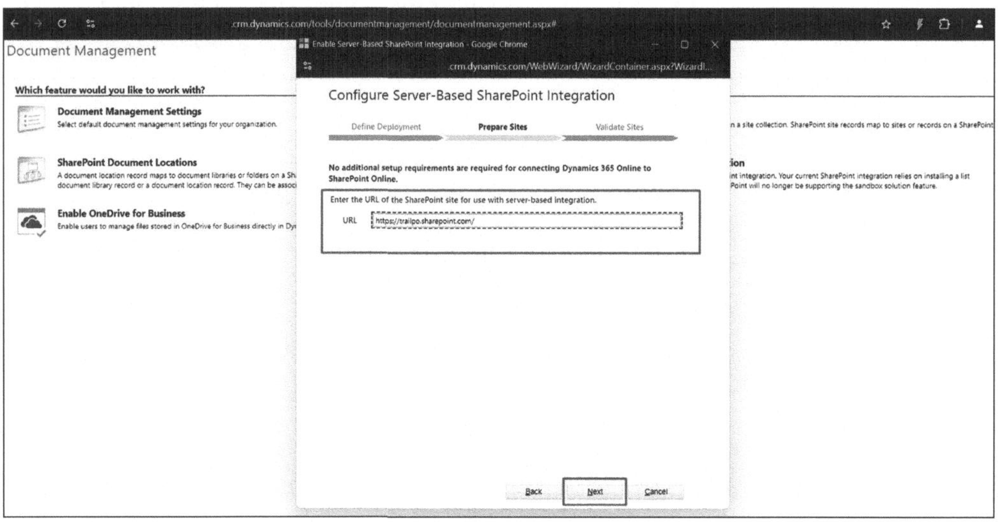

Figure 6.4(d): *Prepare site stage of SharePoint Sync*

c. **Validation and Completion**: The service will validate the SharePoint site. Once validation is successful, click **`Finish`**. It may take a few minutes for the integration to complete.

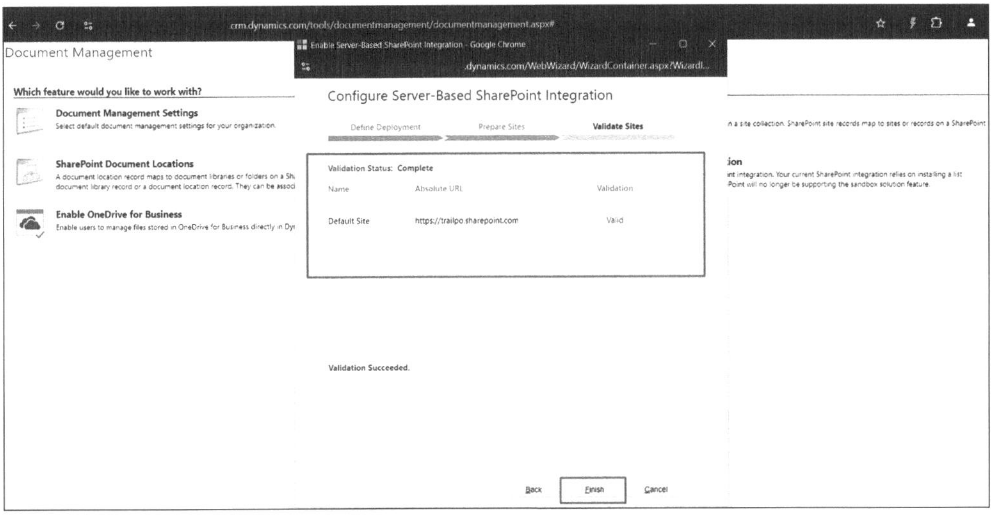

***Figure 6.4(e)**: Validate site stage of SharePoint Sync*

Setting Up Document Management for Entities

After integration, you need to enable document locations for the required CRM entities. By default, document locations are created for some out-of-the-box (OOB) entities. For custom entities or additional ones, you need to enable this manually.

1. In the same **`Document Management Settings`** area, select **`Document Management Settings`**:

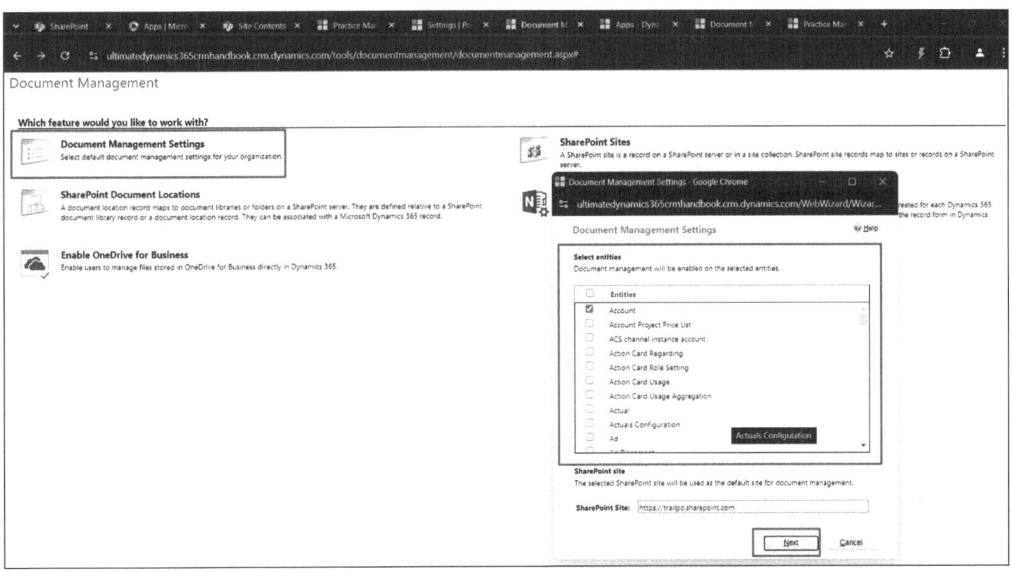

***Figure 6.5(a)**: Document Management Settings*

2. Select the entities where you want to enable document storage (for example, Accounts, Contacts, Opportunities), and Dynamics 365 will create corresponding document libraries in SharePoint for each selected entity.

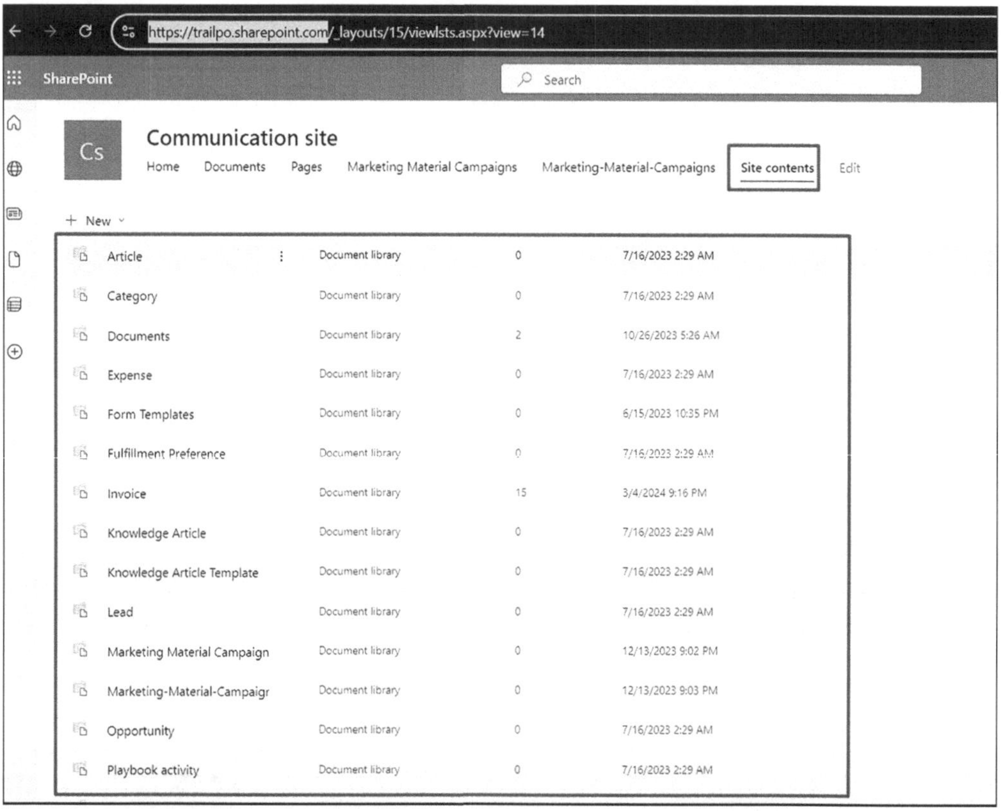

Figure 6.5(b): *Document Libraries created in SharePoint for synced entities*

For newly synced entities between Dynamics 365 CRM and SharePoint, a SharePoint document library is automatically created.

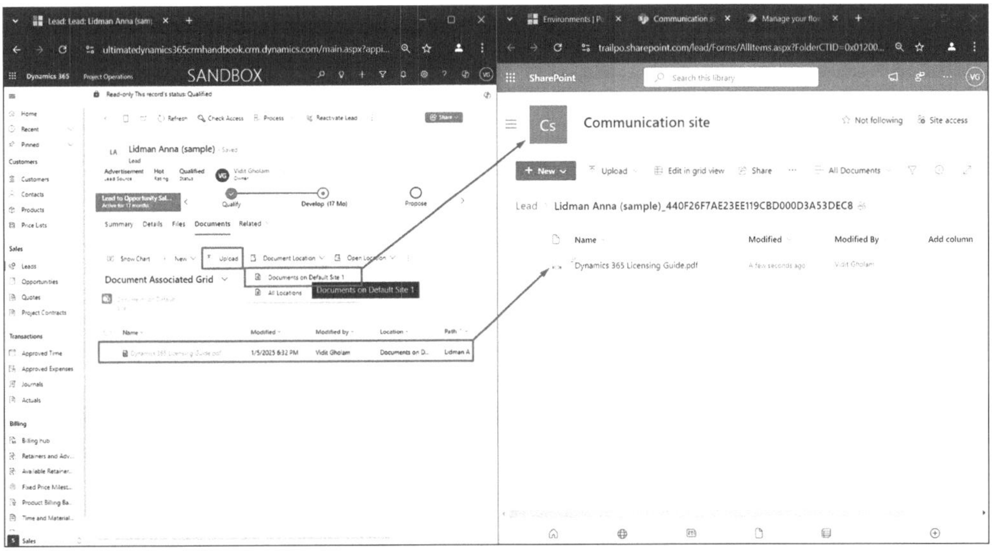

Figure 6.5(c): *Document uploaded from CRM into the SharePoint site*

Along with this, a document location record is created in CRM.

Figure 6.5(d): *Document location record created for the entity records in CRM*

Let us understand what document locations are in Dynamics 365 CRM.

Document Location in Dynamics 365 CRM

In Dynamics 365 CRM, document locations are records that link specific CRM entities, such as accounts, contacts, or projects, to a corresponding document library or folder in SharePoint. These document locations manage and store documents related to each CRM entity within SharePoint while still being accessible from within Dynamics 365 CRM.

Here's how they work:

1. When a SharePoint document library is created for an entity (such as `Accounts` or `Projects`), a document location record is automatically generated in Dynamics 365.
2. For every record within that entity (for example, a specific account or project), Dynamics 365 creates a folder in SharePoint and stores the link to this folder in the document location.
3. The document location helps Dynamics 365 internally track where documents for each record are stored in SharePoint, allowing seamless access to files directly from the CRM interface.

In short, document locations are the connectors between CRM records and their associated document storage in SharePoint. They help users upload, access, and manage documents directly from Dynamics 365 while utilizing SharePoint for storage.

Now that we have covered how to document locations link CRM records to SharePoint for seamless document management, let us move on to another important feature: managing Word templates in Dynamics 365 CRM. This allows you to create standardized documents such as quotes or invoices with just a few clicks.

Managing Word Templates in 365 CRM

Dynamics 365 CRM offers a feature that allows users to automatically fill Word documents with data from CRM fields. This means you can create templates that can be used for different records in CRM. For example, if you want to make a Quote Summary document that shows details, such as the customer's name, quote line items, and amounts, you can easily map this information onto a Word document using the template feature. This makes it quick and easy to create accurate documents without even entering the information manually.

The first step to creating these templates is to download a blank Word document from CRM that includes XML mapping for the entity and its fields.

What is XML Mapping?

XML mapping is a way of connecting the data fields from Dynamics 365 CRM to specific spots in the Word document. When you download this blank document, it comes with special codes that match the fields in CRM. This helps Dynamics 365 know exactly where to put the right information when a document from the template is created, ensuring everything is filled in correctly.

1. **Go to the `Power Platform Admin Center`**: Select your environment and click on **`Settings`**.
2. **Access `Document Templates`**: Under **`Settings`**, find and click on **`Templates`**, then choose **`Document Templates`**.

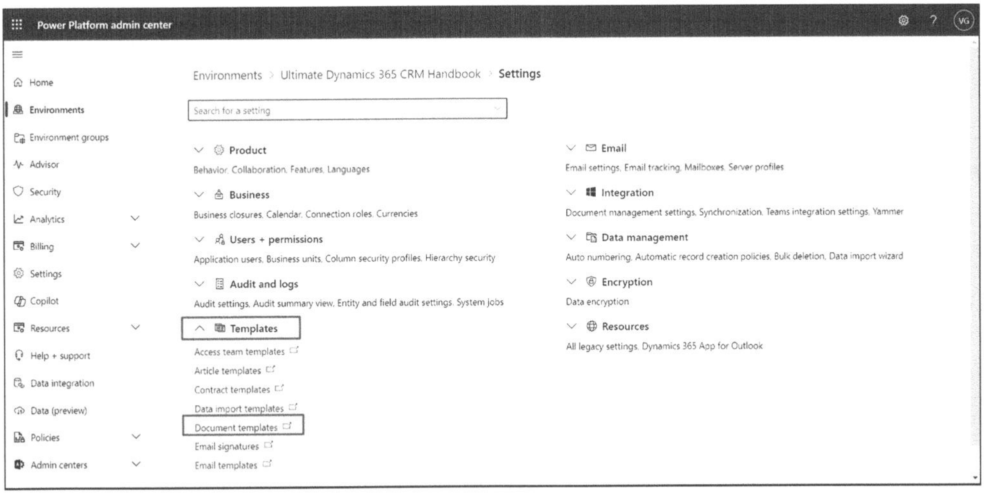

***Figure 6.6(a)**: Document Templates option in Power Platform Admin Center*

3. **Navigate to Template Settings**: You will be redirected to the document template settings area.

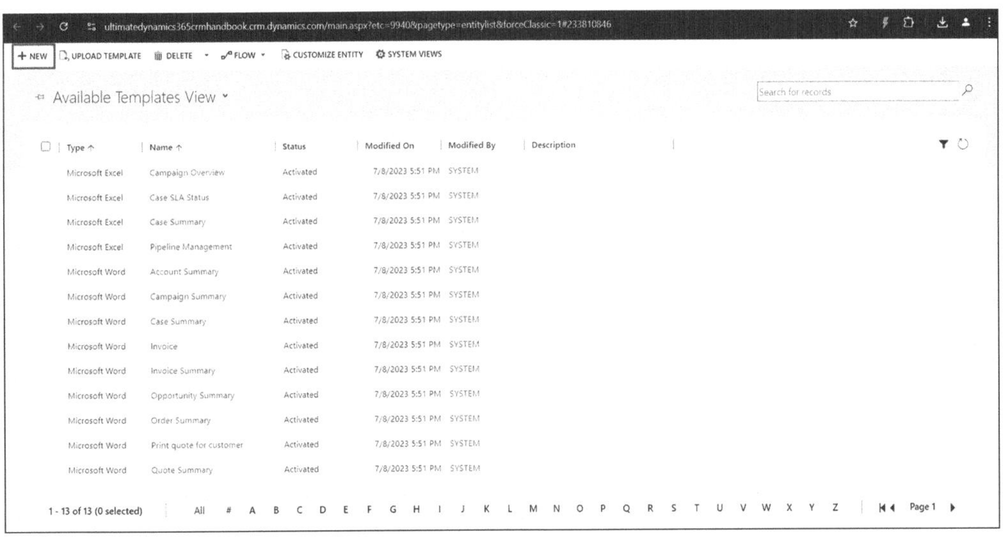

***Figure 6.6(b)**: Template Settings Dynamics 365 CRM*

4. **Create a New Template**: Click on **`New`**, choose **`Word Template`**, then select the entity for which you want to create the template. After that, click on **`Select Entity`**.

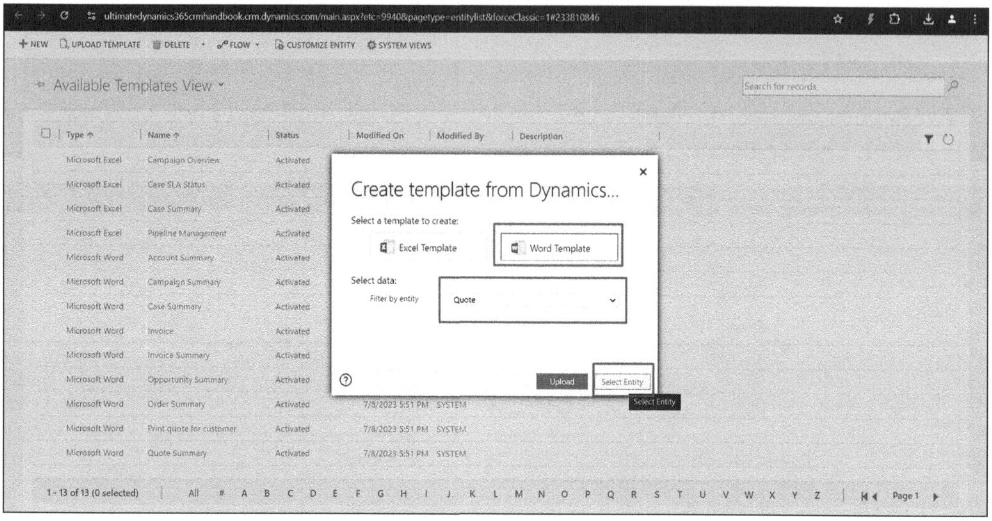

***Figure 6.6(c)**: Creating a word template Dynamics 365 CRM*

5. **Select Related Data**: Choose which related entity data you want to include (you can go one level deep). For example, in a Quote template, you can also pull information from the Opportunity related to the Quote.

6. **Download the Template**: Once your options are selected, click on **`Download Template`**.

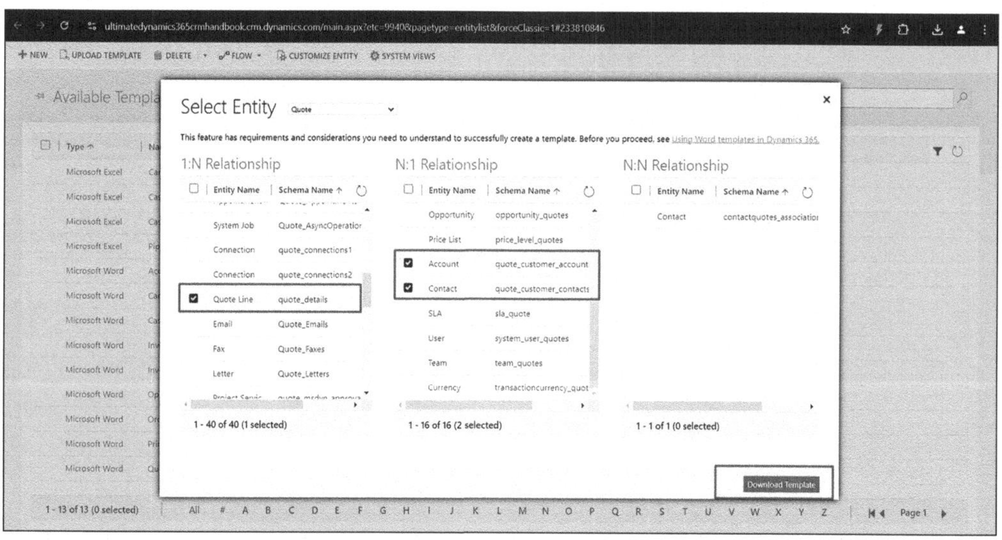

***Figure 6.6(d)**: Selecting Related Data*

7. **Open the Word Document**: Open the downloaded Word document and click on the **`Developer`** tab.

8. **Map the XML Fields**: In the **`Developer`** tab, click on **`XML Mapping Pane`** and select the **`Custom XML Part`** for the entity you downloaded the template for.

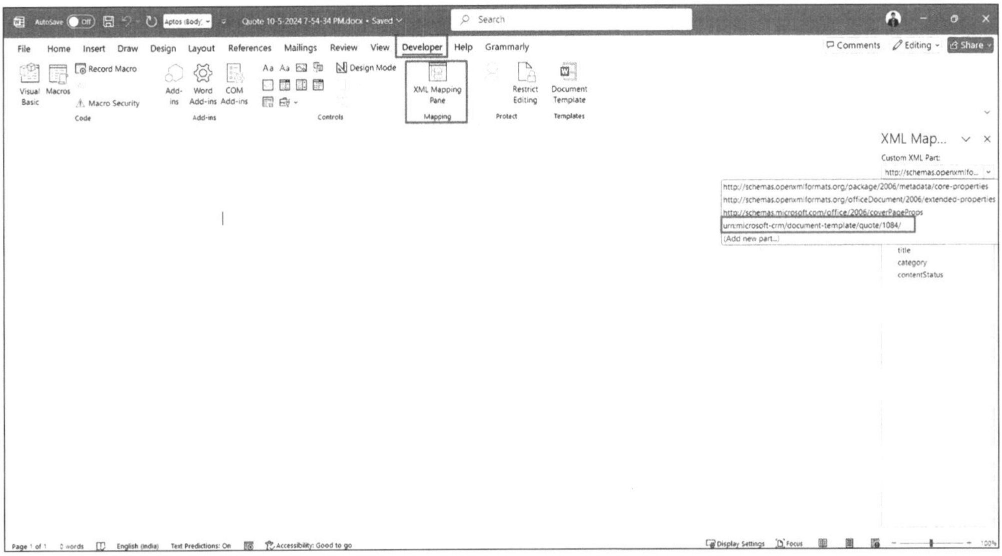

Figure 6.6(e): *XML Mapping in Word Template*

9. **Enable Developer Tab**: If the **`Developer`** tab is not visible, you need to enable it. Go to the **`File`** menu, select **`Options`**, then click on **`Customize Ribbon`** and check the **`Developer`** option.

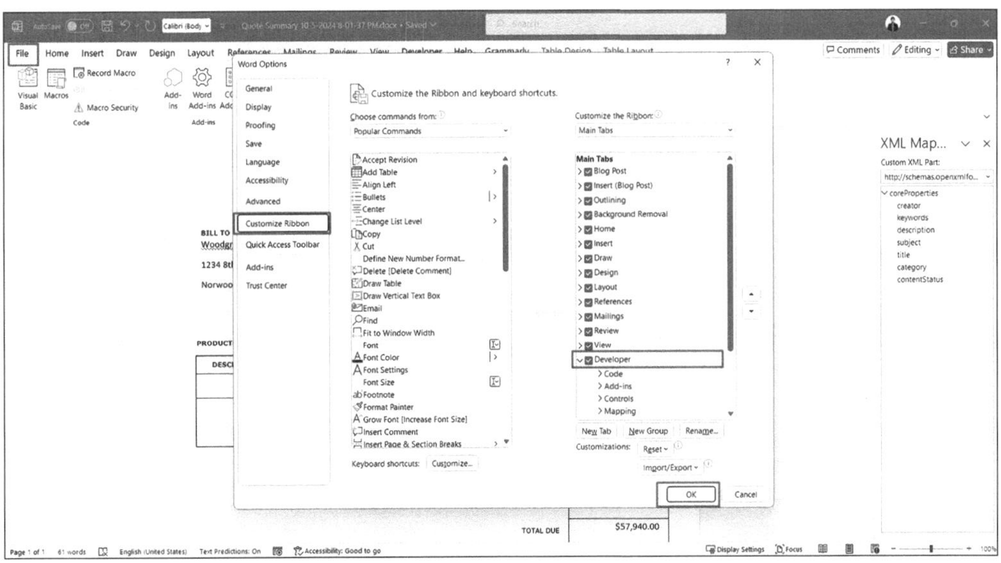

Figure 6.6(f): *Enable developer option in Word Template*

10. **View Entity Fields**: You will now see a list of all the entity fields (and related entity fields) you chose earlier.

11. **Map Fields to the Template**: The next step is to map these XML fields to the correct spots in your Word document.

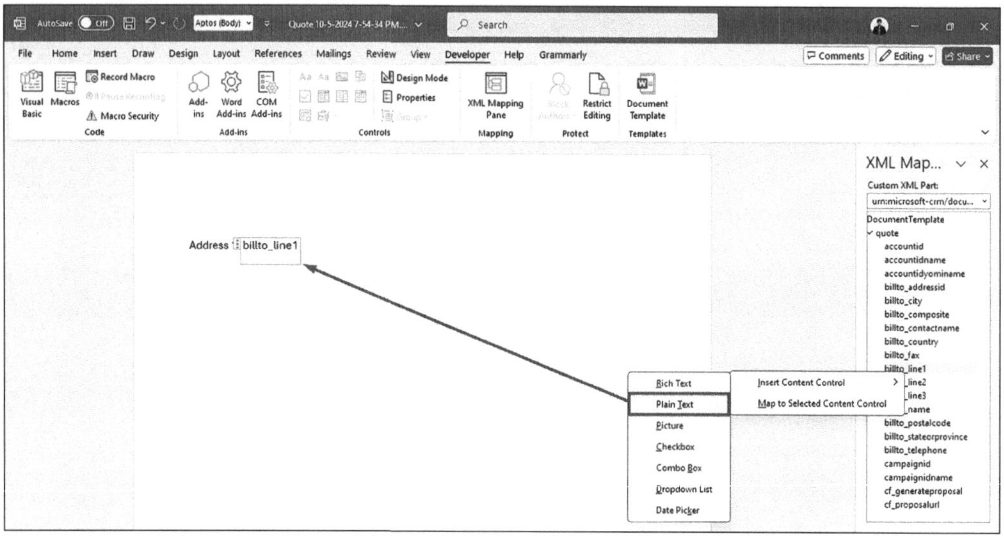

Figure 6.6(g): *Adding entity field mappings on the Word Template*

12. *Figure* 6.6(h) shows a completed Word template called **`Quote Summary`**. The template is fully mapped with fields from Dynamics 365 CRM, ready to be uploaded, allowing users to automatically generate a professional Quote Summary document based on the data in the **`Quotation`** record.

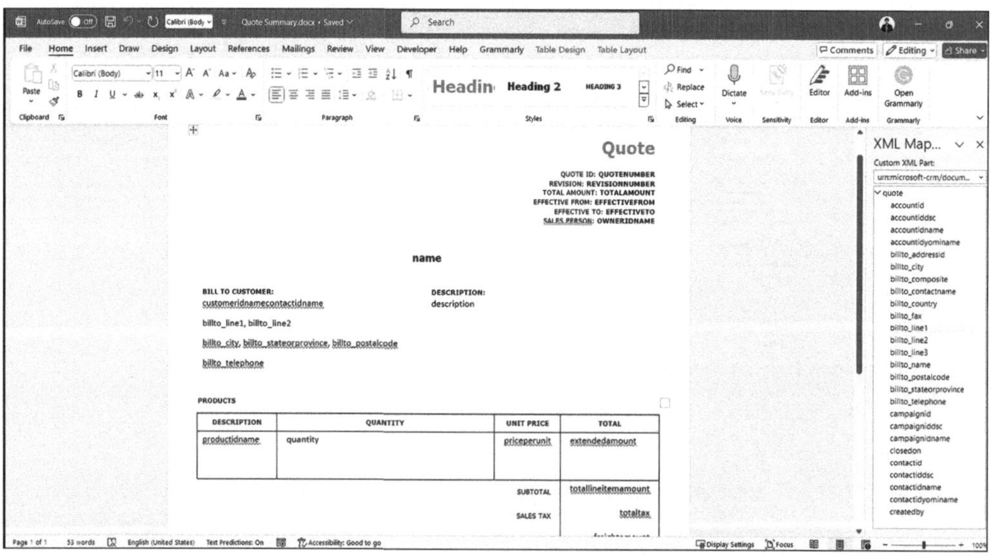

Figure 6.6(h): *Quote Summary Word Template*

13. **Upload the Template**: Once you have mapped everything in the document, upload it as a document template in Dynamics 365.

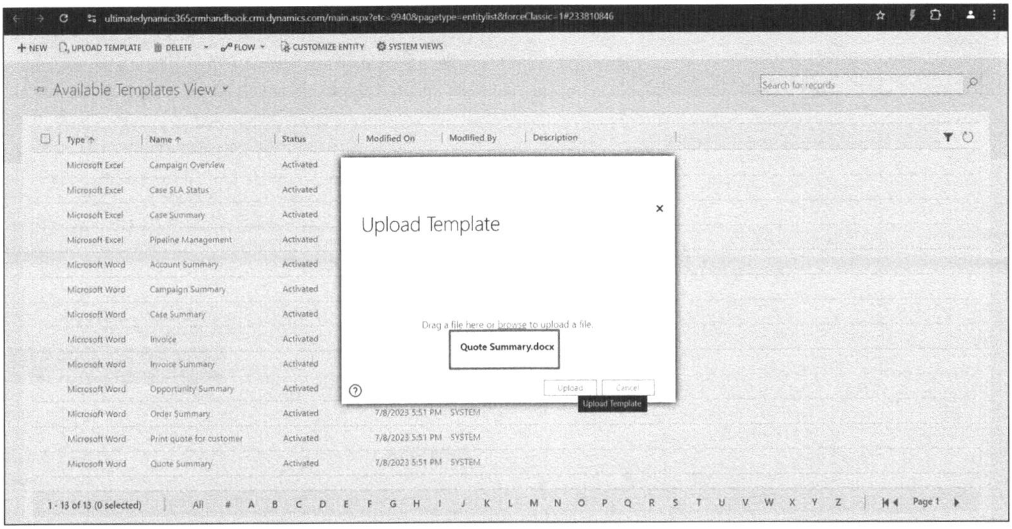

Figure 6.6(i): *Uploading the Word Template to Dynamics 365*

14. You can use see the uploaded document in the **`Template`** view. You can also open and download the template for future changes.

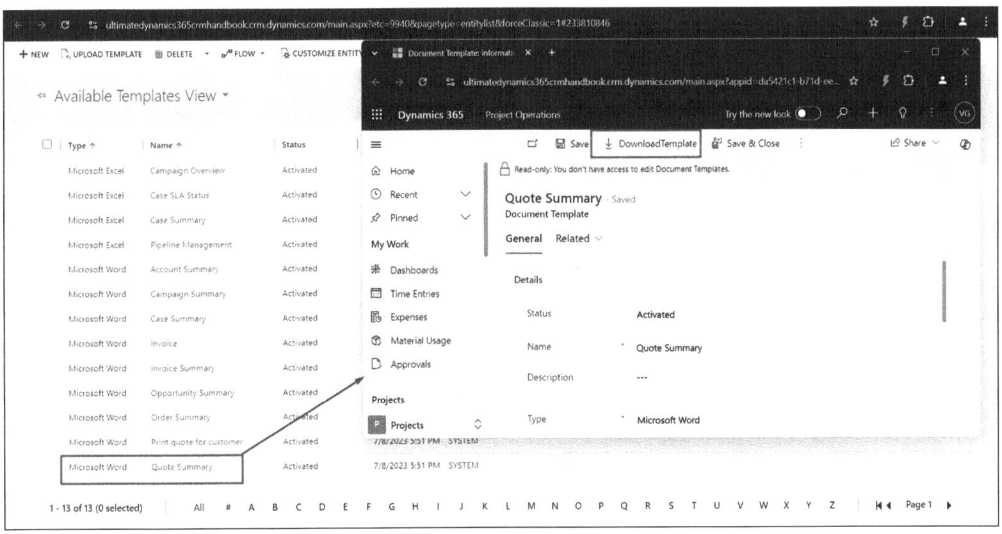

Figure 6.6(j): *Uploaded Word Template Summary*

Using the Word Template

Now that we have created and uploaded the Word template, it is time to use it:

1. **Go to the entity**: Navigate to the entity (such as Quotes or Accounts) for which the Word template was created.

2. **Find Word Templates in the Ribbon**: In the entity's ribbon at the top, look for the `Word Templates` option.

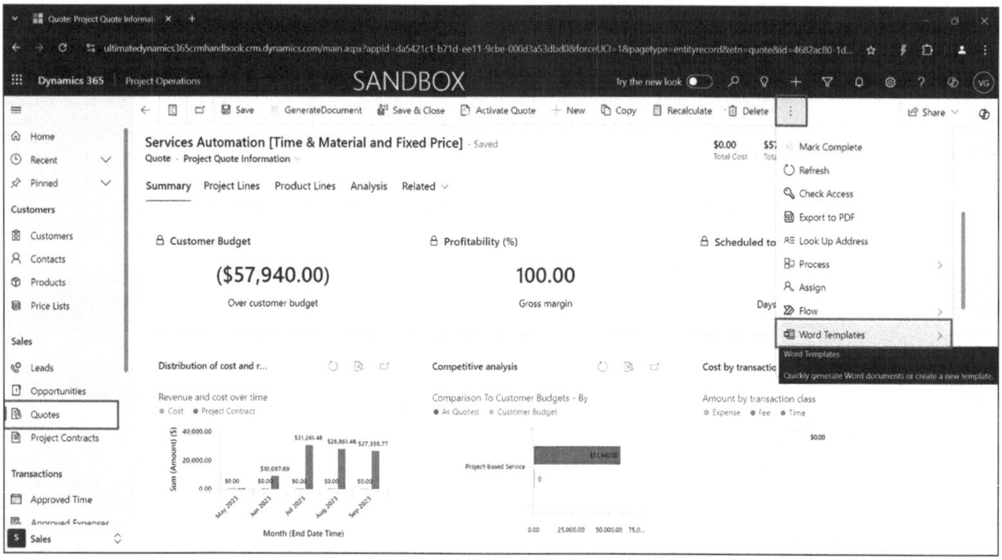

Figure 6.7(a): *Using the Word Template*

3. **Select your template**: Under `Word Templates`, you will see a list of all the templates available or uploaded for that entity. Select the one you want to use to generate the document.

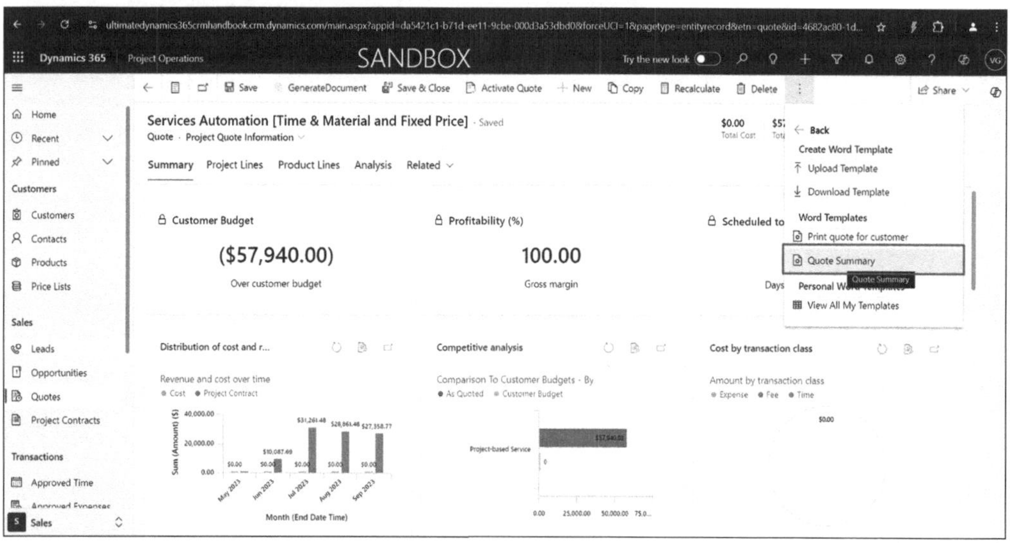

Figure 6.7(b): *Using the Word Template*

4. Your document will now be automatically generated with the mapped data from the selected entity.

5. Dynamics 365 also lets you generate PDFs directly from these Word documents. To do this, simply click on the **Export to PDF** option.

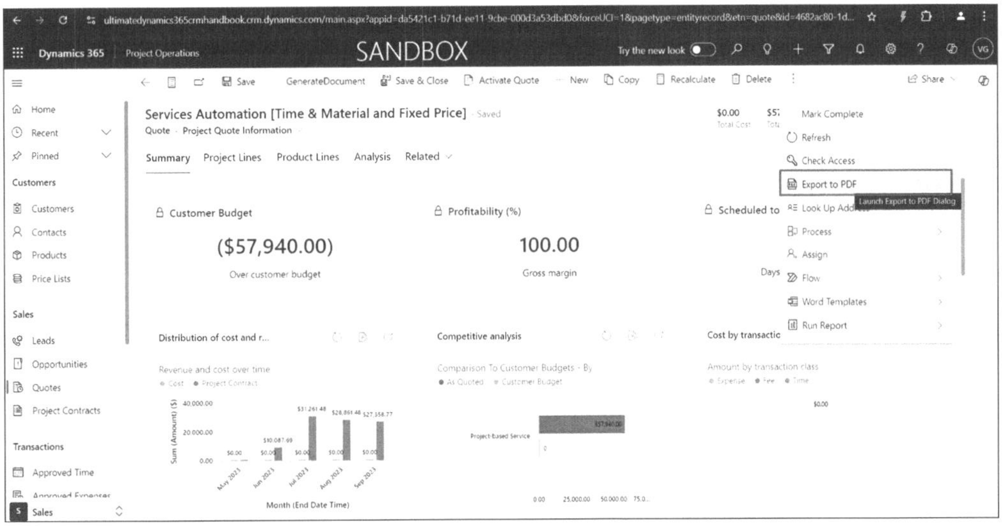

Figure 6.7(c): *Exporting Word Document Templates as PDFs*

6. You can select the **Word template** you want to generate a PDF from. You also have the option to view the generated PDF before downloading it.

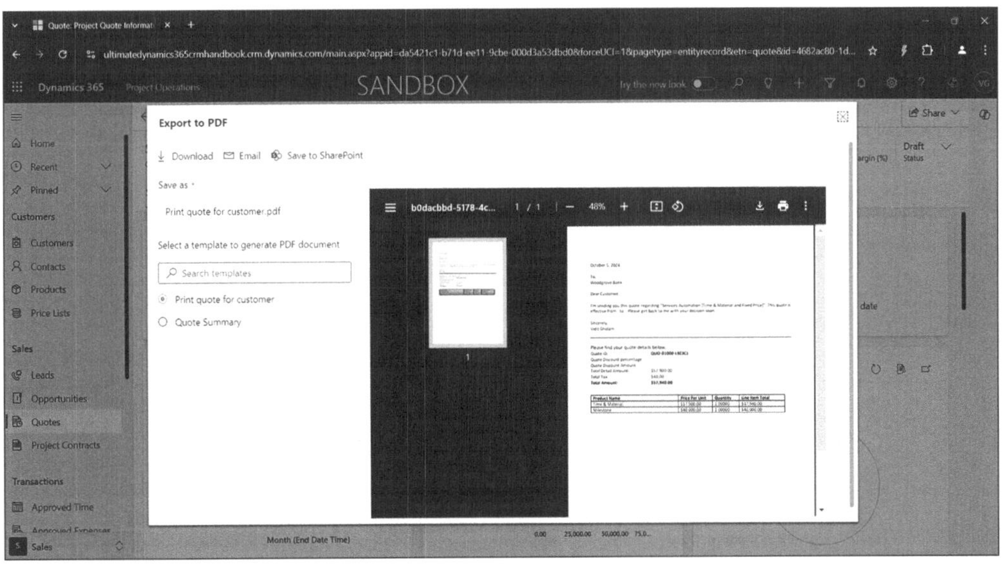

Figure 6.7(d): *Exporting Word Document Templates as PDFs*

7. This feature is available with Dynamics 365 Sales Premium, Enterprise, or Professional licenses. By default, it works with certain out-of-the-box (OOB) entities, but you can enable it for other entities, including custom ones.

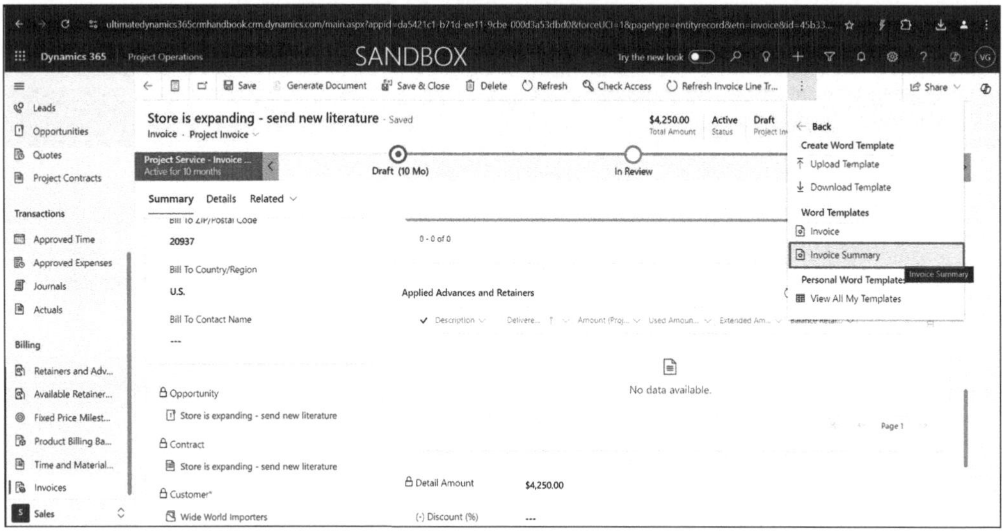

Figure 6.7(e): *Document Templates for Invoices*

8. Similarly, for invoices, you can create **`Invoice Summary`** templates just like the Quote templates. *Figures* 6.7(*e*) and 6.7(*f*) show examples of how an invoice summary template can be created and used in Dynamics 365.

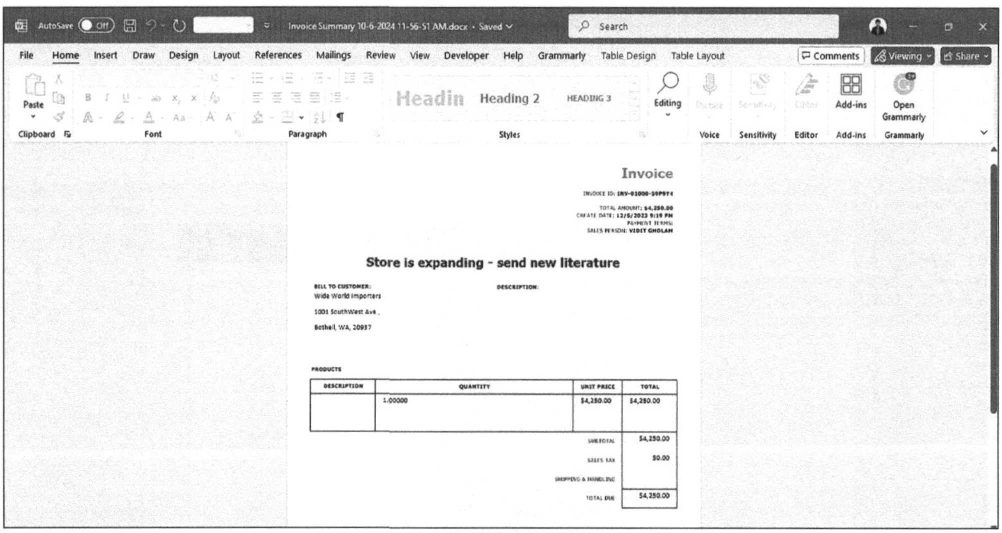

Figure 6.7(f): *Invoice Summary Document*

Generating document templates in Dynamics 365 is a simple and convenient way to create Word documents, but there's a limitation – you can only pull data from one related entity level deep. For example, when working with Quotes, you can include information from Quote lines, but not further details such as Quote line specifics or lead information from the Opportunity linked to the Quote.

If you need to access data beyond one level, such as getting Quote line details or pulling lead information, you must go beyond basic templates. In this case, you can customize the process using Power Automate flows to generate multi-level documents, allowing for more complex data retrieval and document creation.

Generating Quotation Documents Using Power Automate

In this section, we will explore how to generate more detailed Word templates using Power Automate. This approach will allow us to include data from multiple related entities, going beyond the limitation of standard Word templates in Dynamics 365.

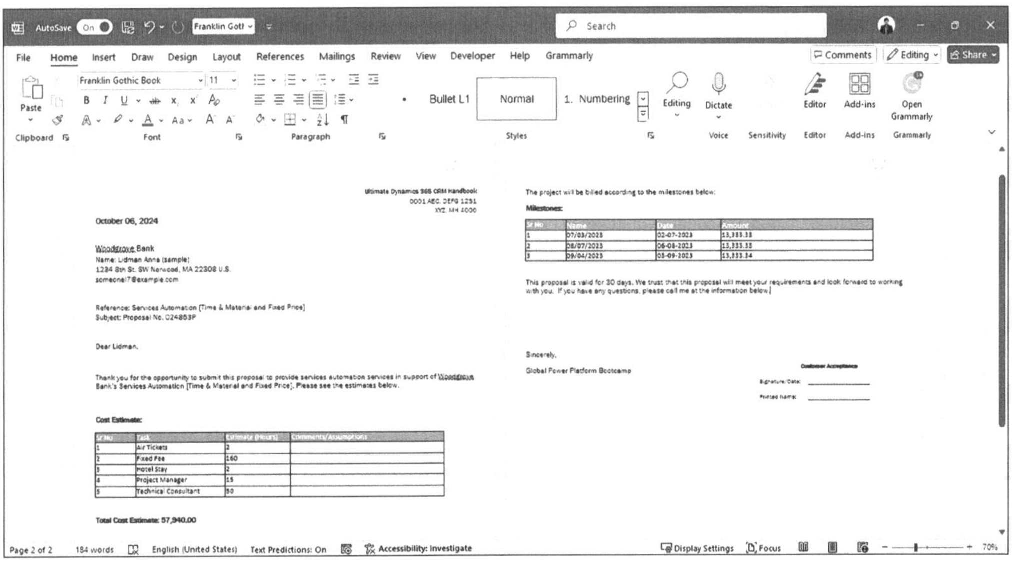

Figure 6.8: *Detailed Quotation Document generated using Power Automate Flow*

Figure 6.8 shows a detailed Quotation document generated using a Power Automate flow. As you can see, the document provides comprehensive information about both Fixed Price and Time and Material types of Quote lines. The data is dynamically inserted into tables within the Word document, making it easy to present structured details.

Now, let us take a look at the process flow to create the automation that generates this document:

Generating the Word Document Template for Power Automate

First step is to generate a word document template; this template does not need any

XML mappings from Dynamics 365 CRM. You can begin creating this template from a blank Word document.

We will use content controls in Microsoft Word to design this template. While we will cover this process in detail here, the blog referenced in **Reference 2** provides additional step-by-step guidance on creating a Word template with content controls and integrating it into Power Automate.

Content Controls in a Word Document: In Microsoft Word, "**`controls`**" refer to interactive elements or form fields you can insert into your document. These controls are ideal for creating dynamic documents, such as forms, surveys, and templates. Essentially, content controls allow you to capture dynamic input within a Word document.

Creating Word Template and Storing it in SharePoint

By following these steps, we will learn how to create a sample Word template that can be integrated into a Power Automate flow for dynamic document generation.

Step 1: Enable **`Developer`** tab in Word

Right-click on the ribbon in Microsoft Word and select **`Customize the Ribbon`**.

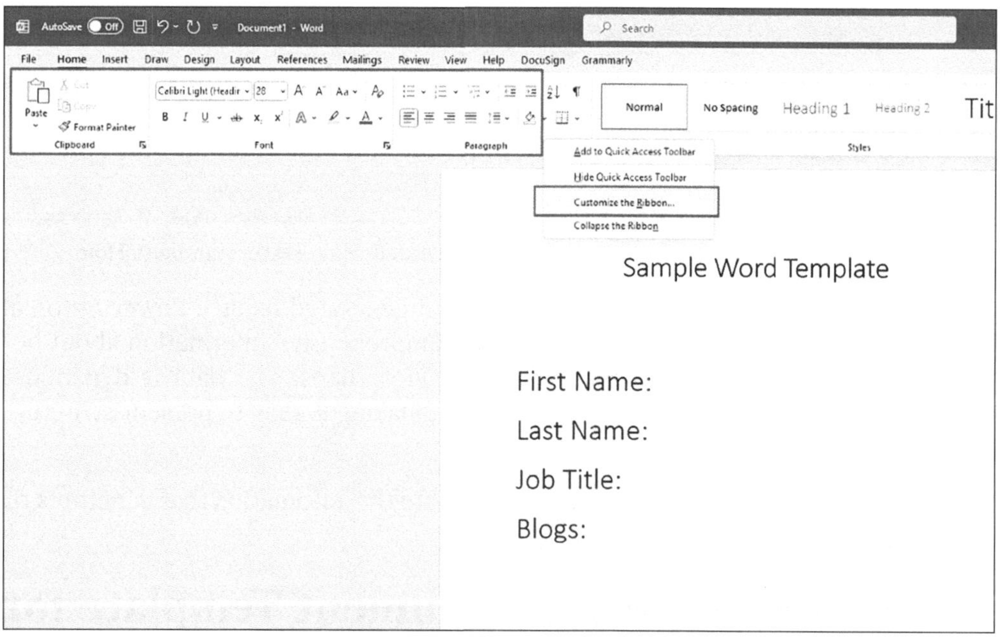

***Figure 6.9(a)**: Enabling Developer Tab in Word*

Step 2: Activate the **`Developer`** tab

In the **`Customize Ribbon`** window, check the box next to **`Developer`** to enable the **`Developer`** tab on the ribbon.

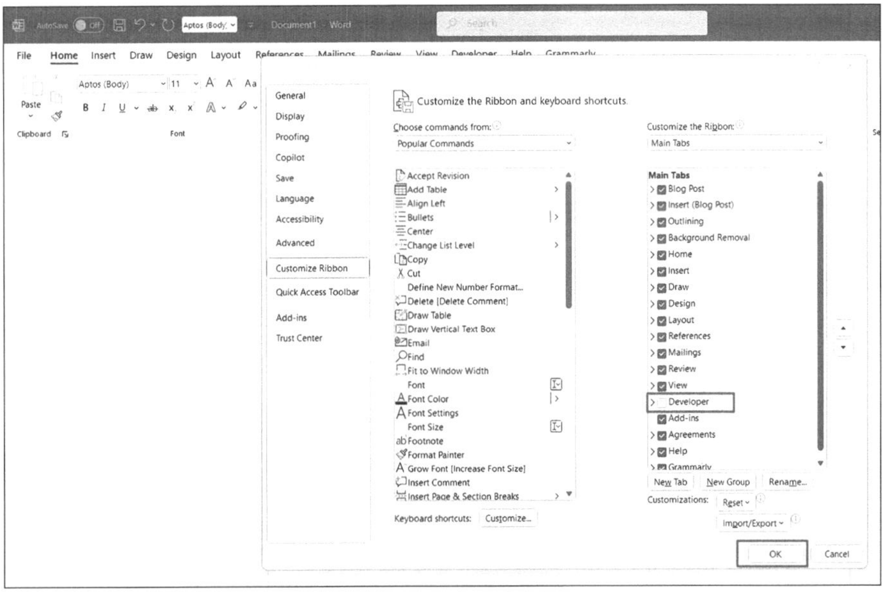

***Figure 6.9(b)**: Activating Developer Tab in Word*

Step 3: Access **`Content Controls`**

Once the **`Developer`** tab is enabled, you will have access to the **`Controls`** section on the ribbon. Here, you will find a variety of controls, such as **`checkboxes`**, rich text, plain text, repeating controls, and image controls.

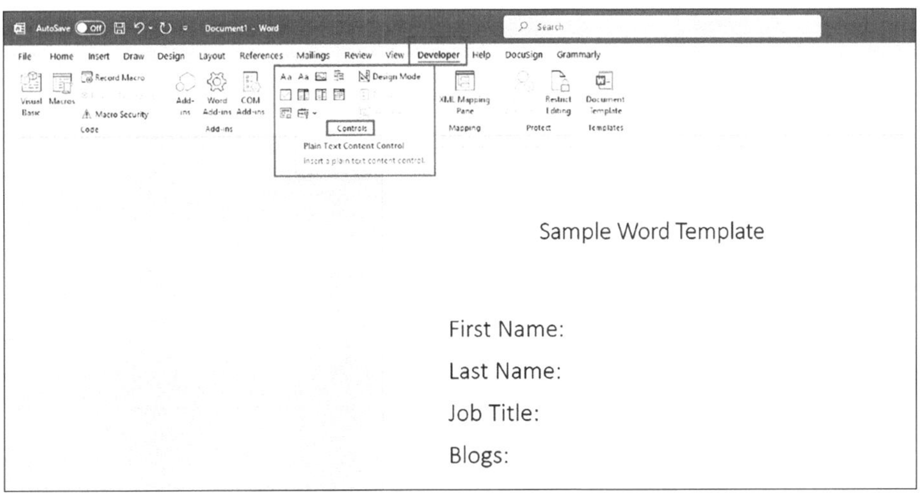

***Figure 6.9(c)**: Accessing Content Controls*

Step 4: Insert **`Plain Text Control`**

Insert a **`Plain Text control`** into your document, as shown in the following figure. Then, click on **`Design Mode`** to enable editing of the control.

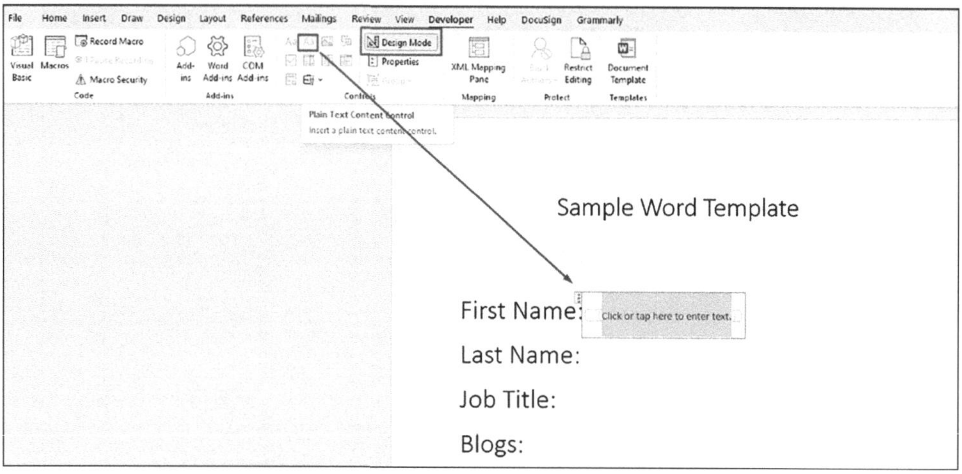

***Figure 6.9(d):** Inserting Plain Text Control*

Step 5: Set **`Properties`** for the **`Plain Text Control`**

Click on the **`Properties`** button for the plain text control you inserted in Step 4. Here, add a **`Title and Tag`** for the control. These values are important, as they will be used to input data into the **`Power Automate`** flow action.

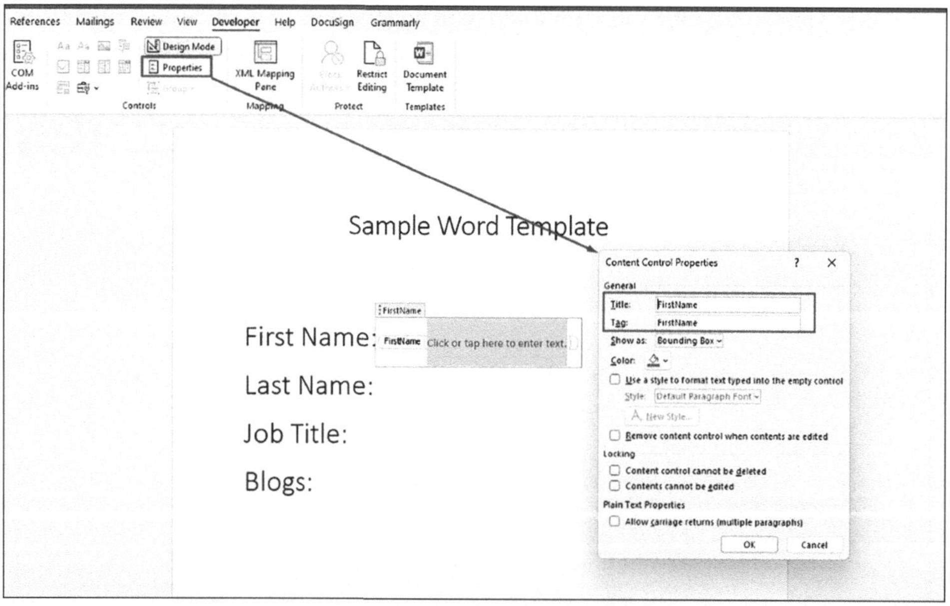

***Figure 6.9(e):** Setting Properties for the Plain Text Control*

At this point, your sample Word template should look similar to the following figure, with plain text controls and corresponding titles and tags for each control.

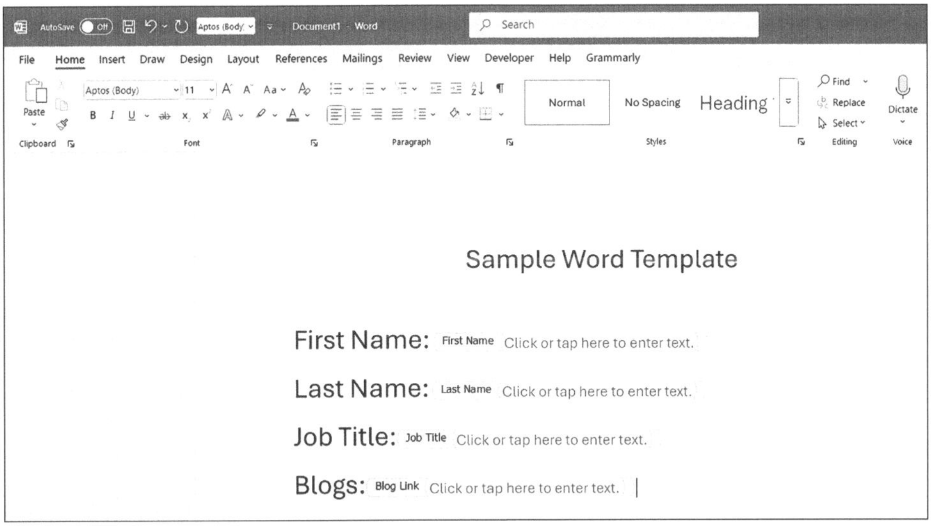

***Figure 6.9(f)**: Sample word document template with Content Controls*

Step 6: Save the Word Template

Save the Word template you created into a **`SharePoint`** document library. For this example, we have saved it in a folder within the default communication site.

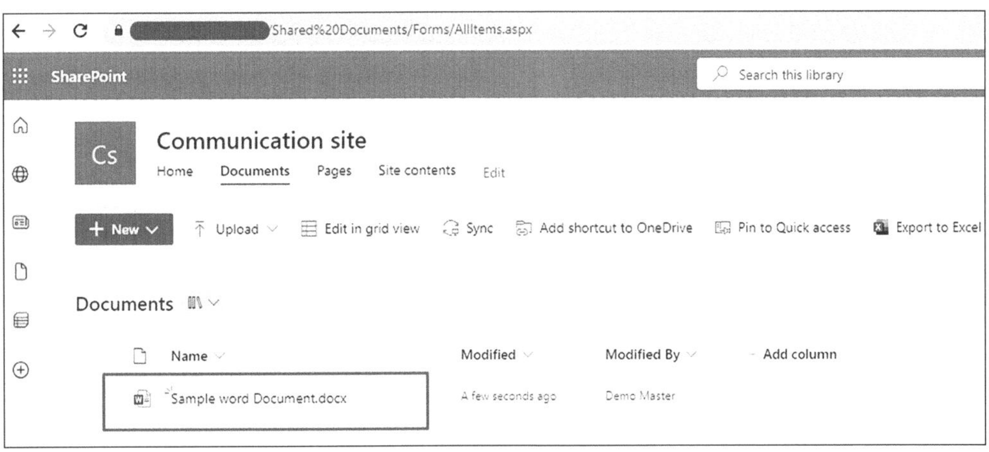

***Figure 6.9(g)**: Uploading the Word Template to SharePoint site*

Power Automate Flow

In this example, we will be using a manually triggered flow, where we will provide inputs to the flow.

Step 1: Add "**`Populate a Microsoft Word Template`**" Action

After setting up the flow inputs, search for the **`Populate a Microsoft Word Template`** action in the flow.

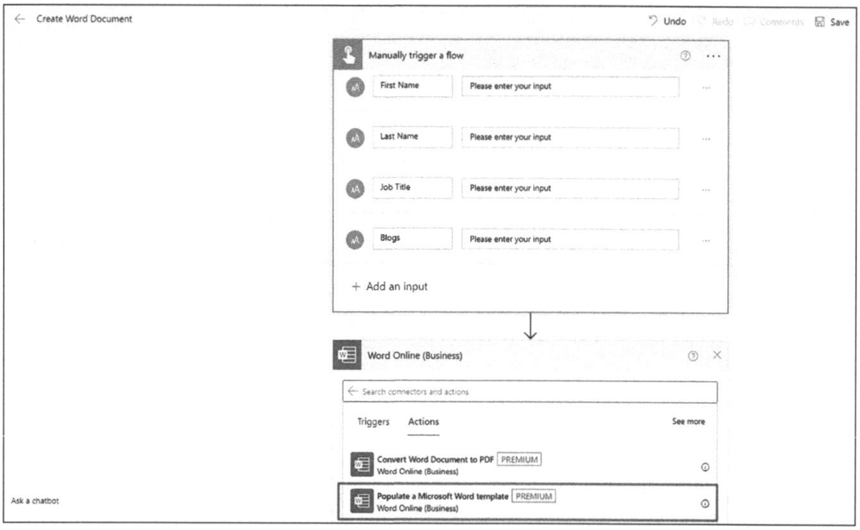

***Figure 6.9(h)**: Adding "Populate a Microsoft Word Template" Action*

Step 2: Select the **`SharePoint Location`** for the Template

Within the action, select the **`SharePoint`** location where you saved the Word template created in the previous steps. After selecting the template file, you will see all the titles and tags you applied to the content controls in the Word document.

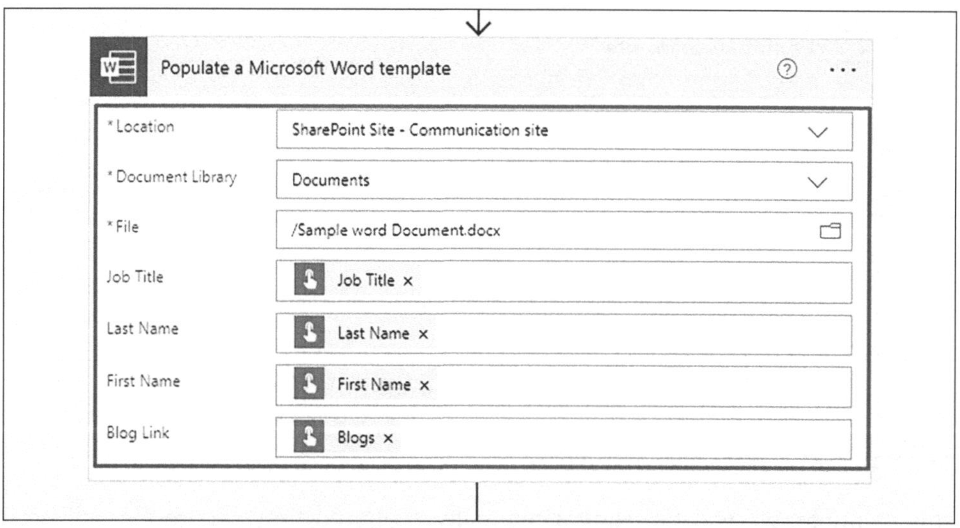

***Figure 6.9(i)**: Selecting the SharePoint Location for the Template*

Step 3: Generate and Store the Word Document

The **`Populate a Microsoft Word template`** step will generate the Word document with the dynamic inputs populated into the content controls. You can store this document in SharePoint or email it, depending on your requirements.

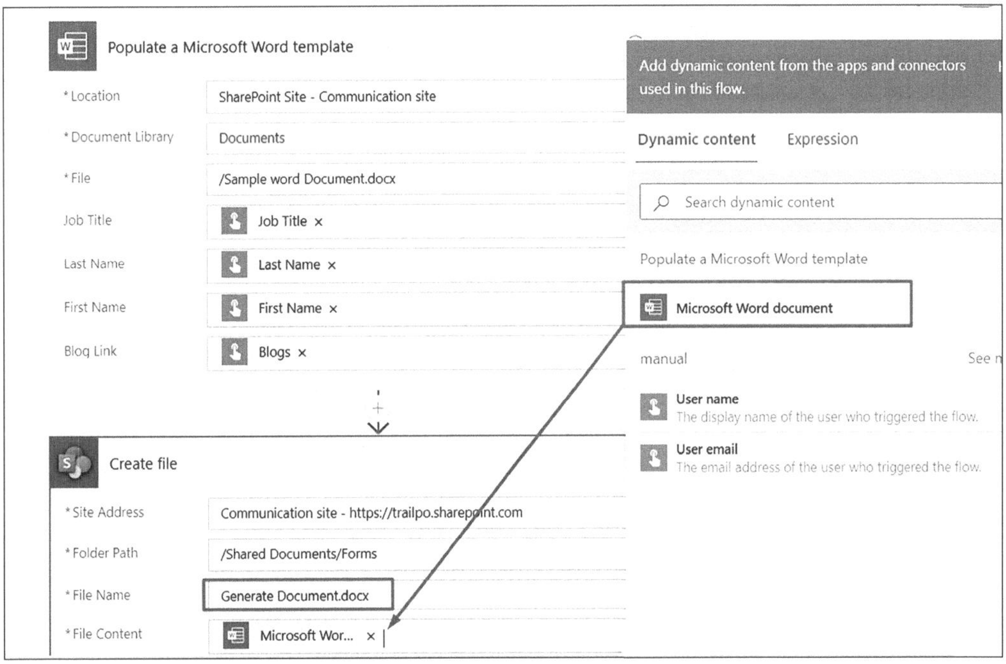

***Figure 6.9(j)**: Generating and Storing the Word Document in SharePoint*

Ensure the generated file with the .docx extension is named, or it will not open properly.

What we just saw is a sample Word template, while the actual template is shown in *Figure 6.9(k)*. You can also create templates based on your preferences and specific requirements.

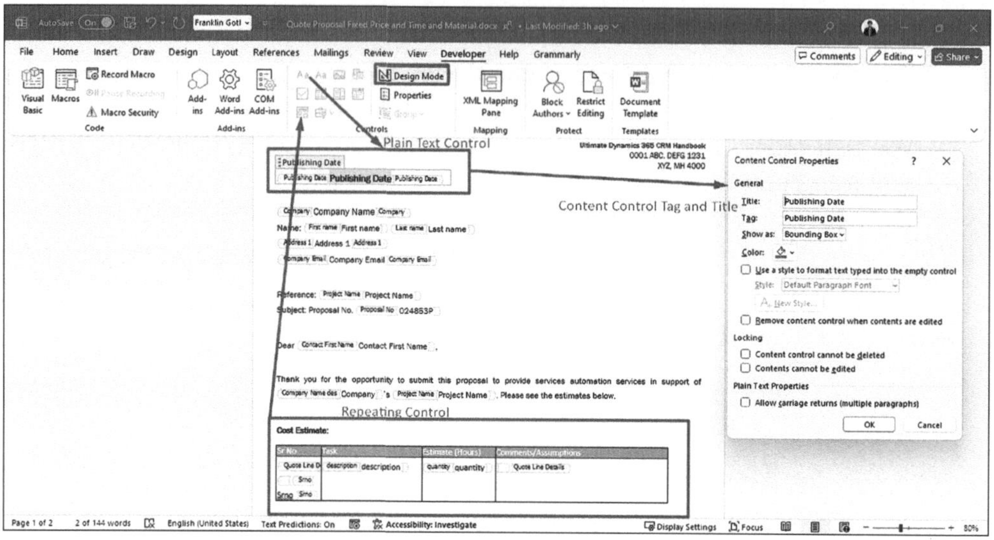

Figure 6.9(k): *Word document template for Power Automate Flow*

Note: *All figures in this section are sourced from the author's blog, "Power Platform Puzzles".*

1. We have also added tables as you can see in the document shown in *Figure* 6.8. **Reference 3** is a Blog that explains how to populate tables in a Word document with dynamic data.
2. *Figure* 6.9(*k*) shows the use of Plain Text and Repeating Word document controls to create the Word template. It also illustrates how tags and titles are added to the content controls, so they appear correctly in the Power Automate flow action. Detailed steps for setting this up are provided in **Reference 2** and **Reference 3**, which explain how to configure and utilize these controls in Word templates.

   Using these steps, you can successfully create a word document template to be used in Power Automate Flow.

Storing Generated Word Template in SharePoint

For this example, we are creating a detailed Quotation document and have prepared three different types of templates:

1. **Time & Material Template**: Used by Power Automate when the Quote contains only Time & Material (T&M) Quote Lines.

2. **Fixed Price Template**: Used by Power Automate when the Quote contains only Fixed Price Quote Lines.
3. **Fixed Price and Time and Material Template**: Used by Power Automate when the Quote contains both Fixed Price and Time and Material lines.

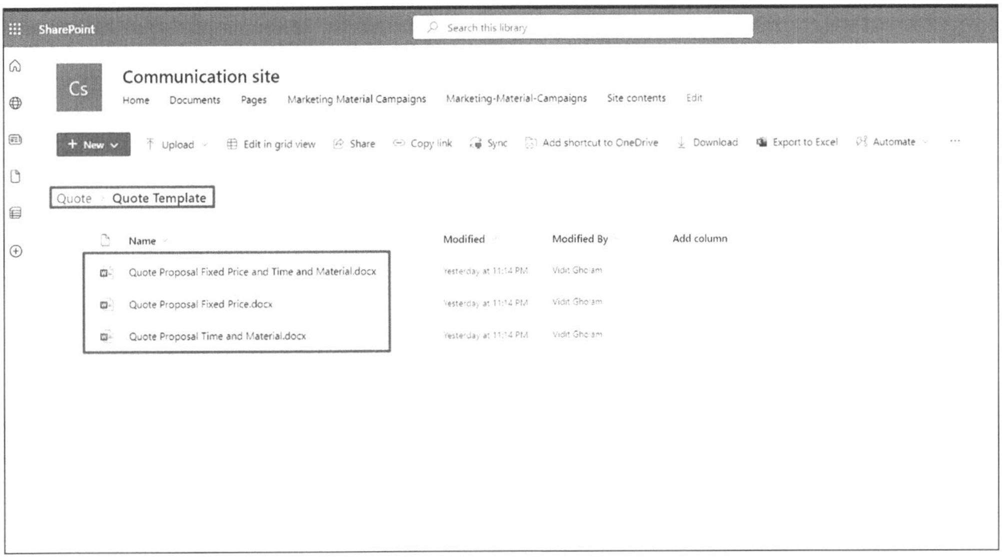

***Figure 6.10**: Word Templates Stored in SharePoint Online*

All three templates are stored in the SharePoint document library created for the Quote entity in Dynamics 365 CRM, inside a folder named Document Templates, as shown in *Figure 6.10*.

Power Automate Flow Trigger

Before creating the Power Automate flow, it is important to determine the trigger condition for the flow, as discussed in the earlier chapter.

1. In this example, the trigger for the Power Automate flow will be "**`When an HTTP request is received`**." This trigger will generate an endpoint and accept two input values:
    - **`EntityName`**: The logical name of the entity (for example, Quote).
    - **`RecordID`**: The GUID of the record that will be processed.

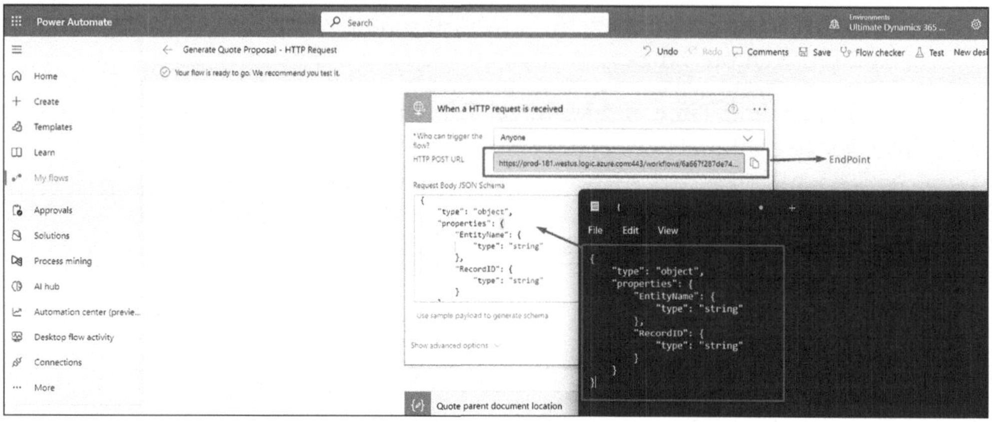

Figure 6.11(a): *Power Automate Flow Trigger*

2. The flow will be triggered by the user through a custom ribbon button on the Quote form. This button will be linked to a JavaScript function.

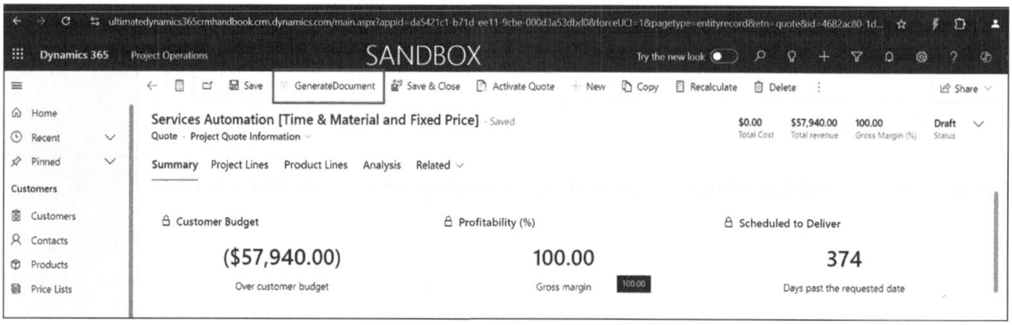

Figure 6.11(b): *Generate Document Custom Ribbon Button*

3. The JavaScript code tied to the custom button will call the HTTP request endpoint and pass the two parameters–**`EntityName`** and **`RecordID`**–to the flow.

   Note: *The* **`Xrm.Utility`** *object used in the script shown in Figure 6.11(c) is a utility that allows developers to perform common tasks, such as showing alerts, opening forms, and managing notifications in the user interface. It is part of the client-side scripting and makes it easier to interact with the system's UI. To learn more about how to use it and explore other features, users can refer to the Dataverse's Client Object Model referenced in Reference 5, which provides additional information for working with data and services.*

```
var TriggerFlow =
{
    Main: (executionContext) =>
    {
        var formContext = executionContext.getFormContext();
        //Strict Defined Parameters
        var RecordID = formContext.data.entity.getId().replace("{", "").replace("}", "");
        var EntityName = formContext.data.entity.getEntityName();
        //Find Plural Logical Name of the Entity and Call Flow
        Xrm.Utility.getEntityMetadata(EntityName, "").then(
            function (result)
            {
                Xrm.Utility.showProgressIndicator("Please wait a moment..Proposal is being generated")
                TriggerFlow.CallFlow({logicalEntityName: result.EntitySetName, CurrentRecord: RecordID});
            },
            function (error)
            {
                console.log(error);
            }
        );
    },
```

Figure 6.11(c): *JavaScript registered on the Ribbon Button*

a. *Figure* 6.11(c) shows the main trigger function in JavaScript. This function retrieves the **`formContext`** and uses it to access the **`RecordID`** and **`EntityName`** from the form. These values are then stored in variables. Additionally, the function initiates a process indicator to inform the user that the document generation process has started.

b. The main function then calls the **`CallFlow`** function, passing the **`EntityName`** and **`RecordID`** as parameters to trigger the Power Automate flow.

```
CallFlow: ({logicalEntityName, CurrentRecord}) =>
{
    var flowUrl = "https://prod-181.westus.logic.azure.com:443/workflows/      385ea8f7/trigger
    var inputdata = JSON.stringify({
        "EntityName": logicalEntityName,
        "RecordID": CurrentRecord
    });                                          Flow Inputs        Flow EndPoint

    var req = new XMLHttpRequest();
    req.open("POST", flowUrl, true);
    req.setRequestHeader('Content-Type', 'application/json');
    req.send(inputdata);
```

Figure 6.11(d): *Call Flow JavaScript Function*

c. The **`CallFlow`** function sends an HTTP POST request to the Power Automate flow trigger, using the **`EntityName`** and **`RecordID`** as part of the request body. It then waits for a response from the flow, either indicating the success or failure of the document generation process.

```
req.onreadystatechange = function () {

    if (this.readyState === 4) {

        req.onreadystatechange = null;

        if (this.status === 200) {
            var result = this.response;
            var proposalurl = result;
            var url = proposalurl;
            var confirmStrings = {
                text: "Proposal Generated Successfully",
                cancelButtonLabel: "Cancel",
                confirmButtonLabel: "Open Proposal"
            };
            var confirmOptions = { height: 120, width: 260 };
            Xrm.Navigation.openConfirmDialog(confirmStrings, confirmOptions).then(function (success) {
                if (success.confirmed) {
                    window.open(url, '_blank');
                }

                else { }
                });

            Xrm.Utility.closeProgressIndicator()

        }

        else if (this.status === 400) {

            var result = this.response;
            var alertStrings = { confirmButtonLabel: "Yes", text: "Error "+result, title: "Document was not generated" };
            var alertOptions = { height: 120, width: 260 };

            Xrm.Navigation.openAlertDialog(alertStrings, alertOptions).then(
                function success(result) {
                    console.log("Alert dialog closed");
                },
                function (error) {
                    console.log(error.message);
                }
            );
            Xrm.Utility.closeProgressIndicator()

        }

    }
```

Figure 6.11(e): *Call Flow JavaScript Function*

4. Once the flow processes the request, it will generate the document based on the Quote type.

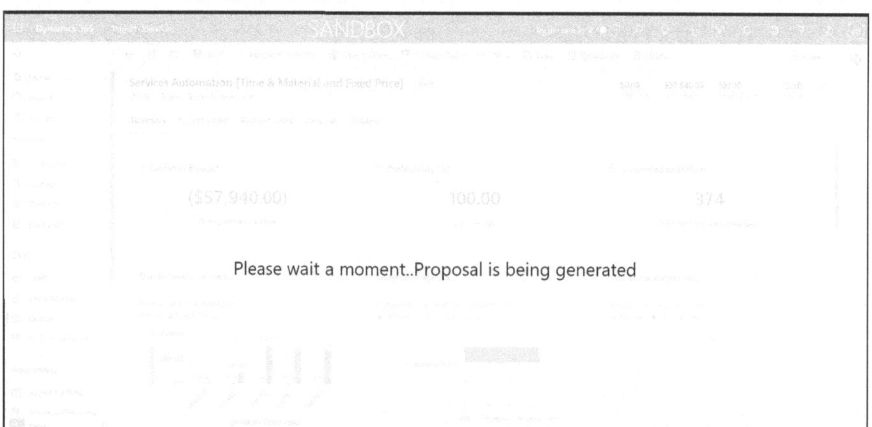

Figure 6.11(f): *Generating document generation progress indicator*

5. The flow will send a response to the JavaScript code, and a pop-up alert will notify the user that the document has been successfully generated.

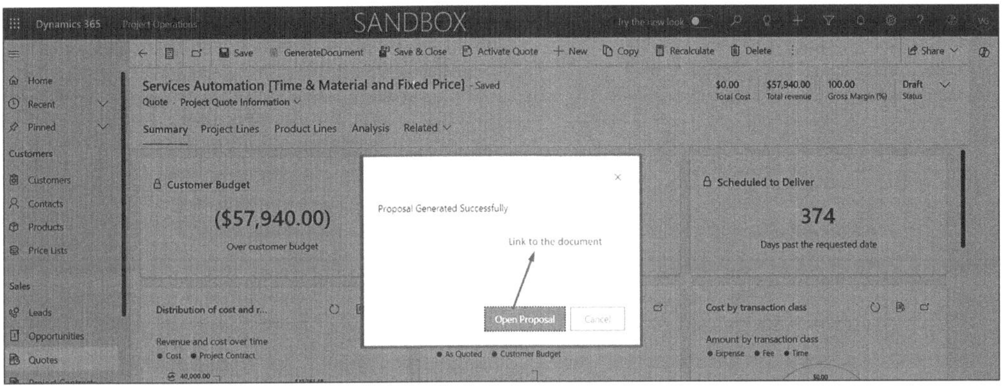

Figure 6.11(g): *Alert when document generation is completed*

Power Automate Flow

Figure 6.12 illustrates the entire process flow of the document generation process, and therefore, the Power Automate workflow.

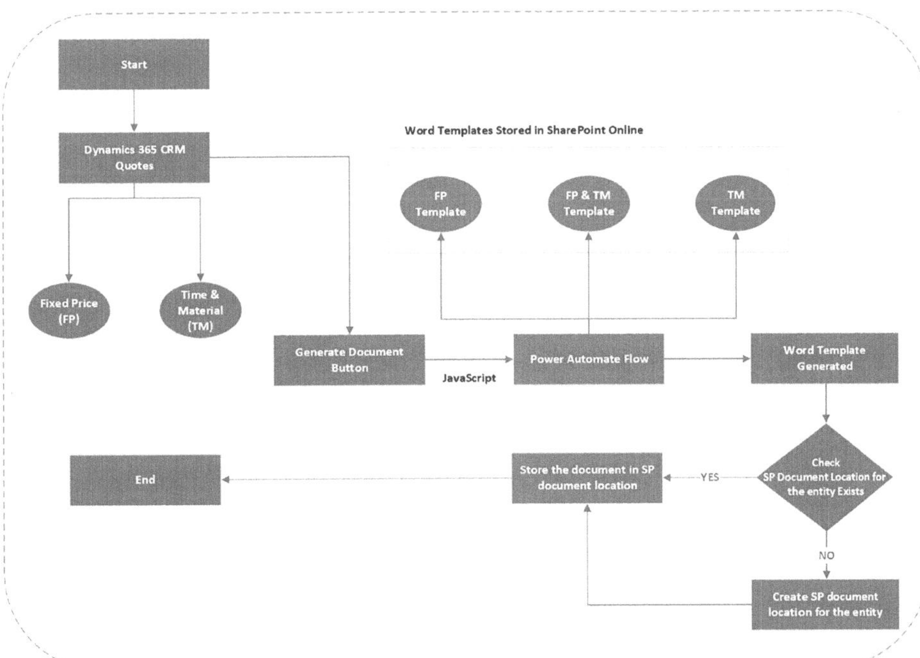

Figure 6.12: *Power Automate Process Flow Diagram*

1. Once the Quote is ready, the user clicks the "`Generate Document`" button.

2. This action triggers a Power Automate flow, passing the Quote GUID to the flow via JavaScript.

3. Using the Quote GUID, the flow retrieves data such as the project name and customer information, including address details. This is done through a series of GET actions, for example, retrieving the customer record based on the Quote ID, followed by extracting the customer details from that record.

4. These details are stored in variables to be used in the Word template.

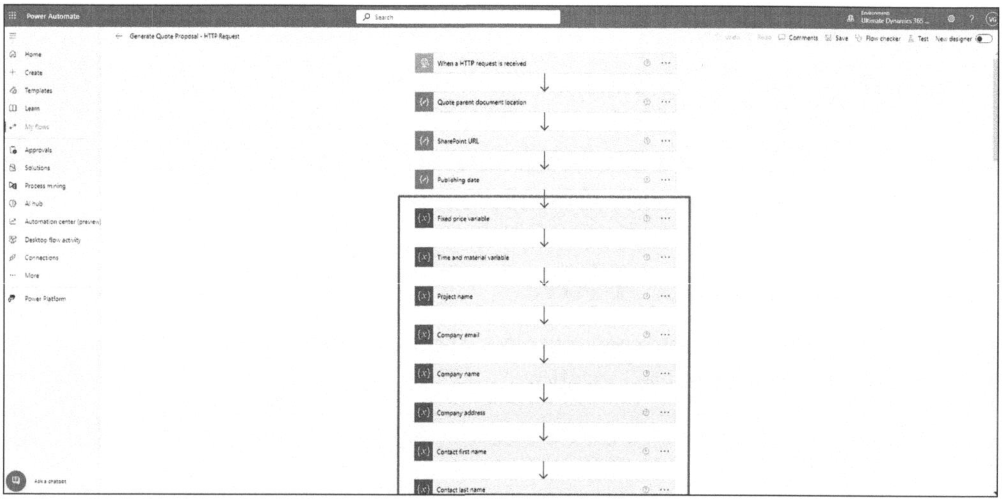

Figure 6.13: *Power Automate Flow to Generate Quote Proposal*

5. JSON arrays for the table values are prepared, as explained in **Reference 3**.

6. Depending on the types of lines in the Quote, the appropriate Word document templates are selected from the SharePoint Document Library.

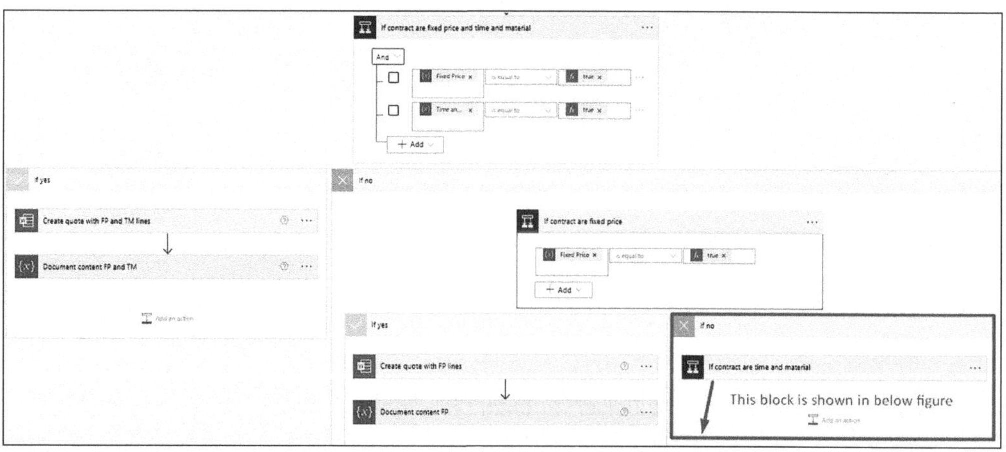

Figure 6.14: *Condition to pick the word template based on Quote lines in the Quote*

7. The Word documents are generated using the "**`Populate a Microsoft Word Template`**" action in Power Automate.

Figure 6.15: *Populate a Microsoft Word Template Action in Power Automate*

8. *Figure* 6.16 demonstrates how the '**`Populate a Microsoft Word Template`**' action accepts input values and provides a clearer understanding of how tables are dynamically populated using JSON arrays.

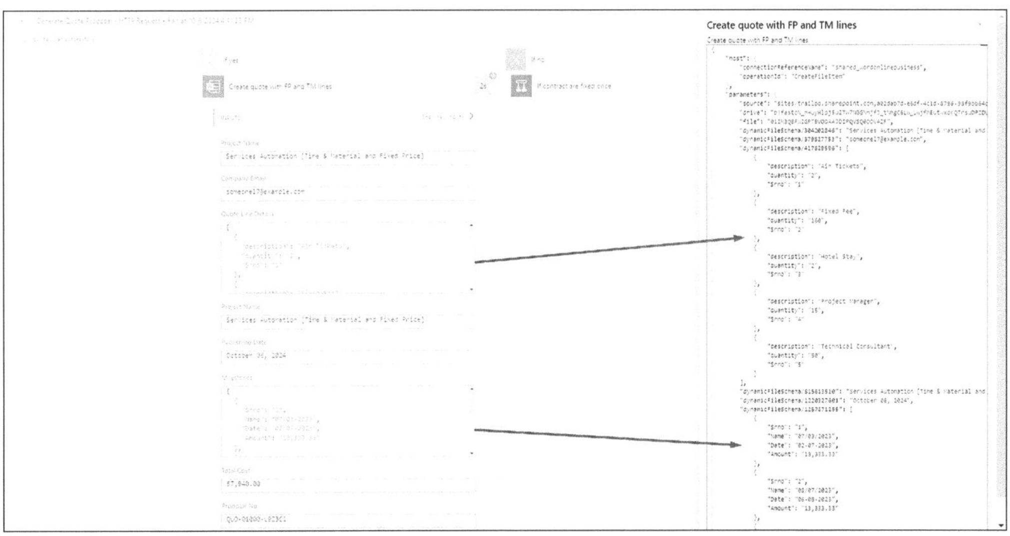

Figure 6.16: *Input to the Populate a Microsoft Word Template Action*

9. All generated documents are stored in the document location for the respective entity, which in this case is the Quote entity.

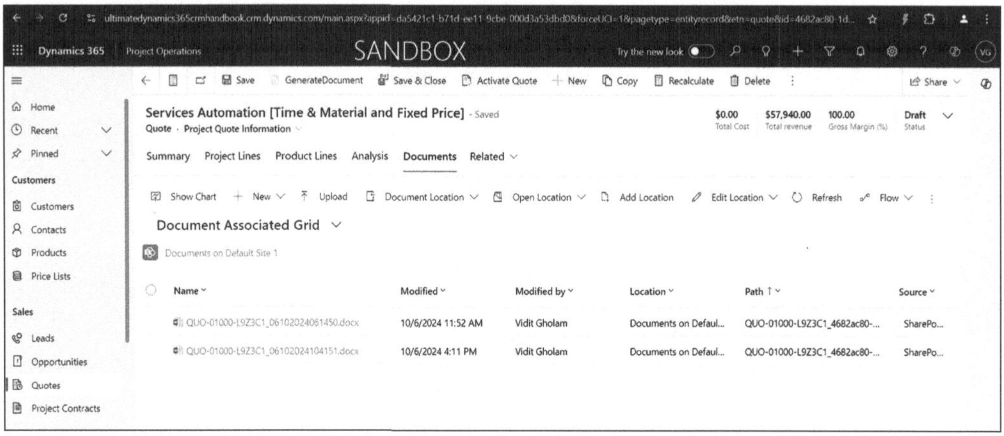

Figure 6.17: *Word documents stored in the document location of the respective entity*

10. The flow checks whether a document location exists for the Quote entity in CRM. If not, it creates the document location and saves the document there. Detailed instructions for generating document locations are provided in **Reference 4**.

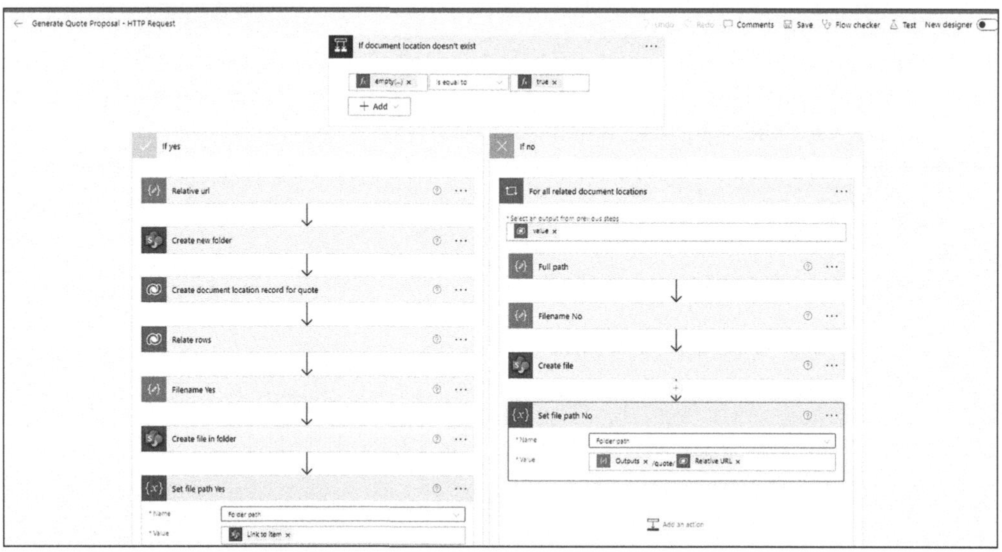

Figure 6.18: *Condition to check SharePoint Document location*

11. Finally, the SharePoint link to the generated document is sent back as a response to JavaScript, which then displays an alert to the user with a link to open the document.

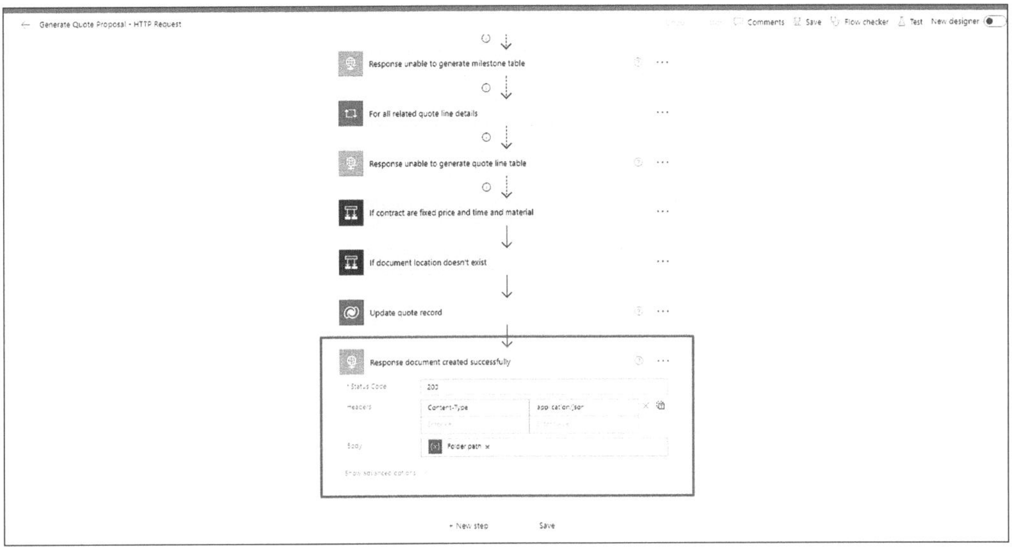

***Figure 6.19**: Response to the JavaScript*

Generating Invoice Documents Using Power Automate

We can follow the same process flow used for creating quotation templates with Power Automate. However, since invoices may require more detail or grouping within the document, we could consider using a Custom Action instead of processing everything inside the Word template. This Custom Action would extract all Word document tags and label values, generate JSON arrays through a plugin, and pass them to the flow as output parameters.

This approach can simplify the Power Automate flow, reduce execution time significantly, and make error logging easier. It also enables more complex logic, such as grouping similar expenses into a single table.

Figure 6.20 illustrates a detailed invoice document with Time & Material lines grouped by resources and expense lines grouped by categories. Building such complex grouping logic within a Power Automate flow can be challenging, which is why calling a Custom Action is recommended. This allows the complex logic to be managed within a plugin action using C#.

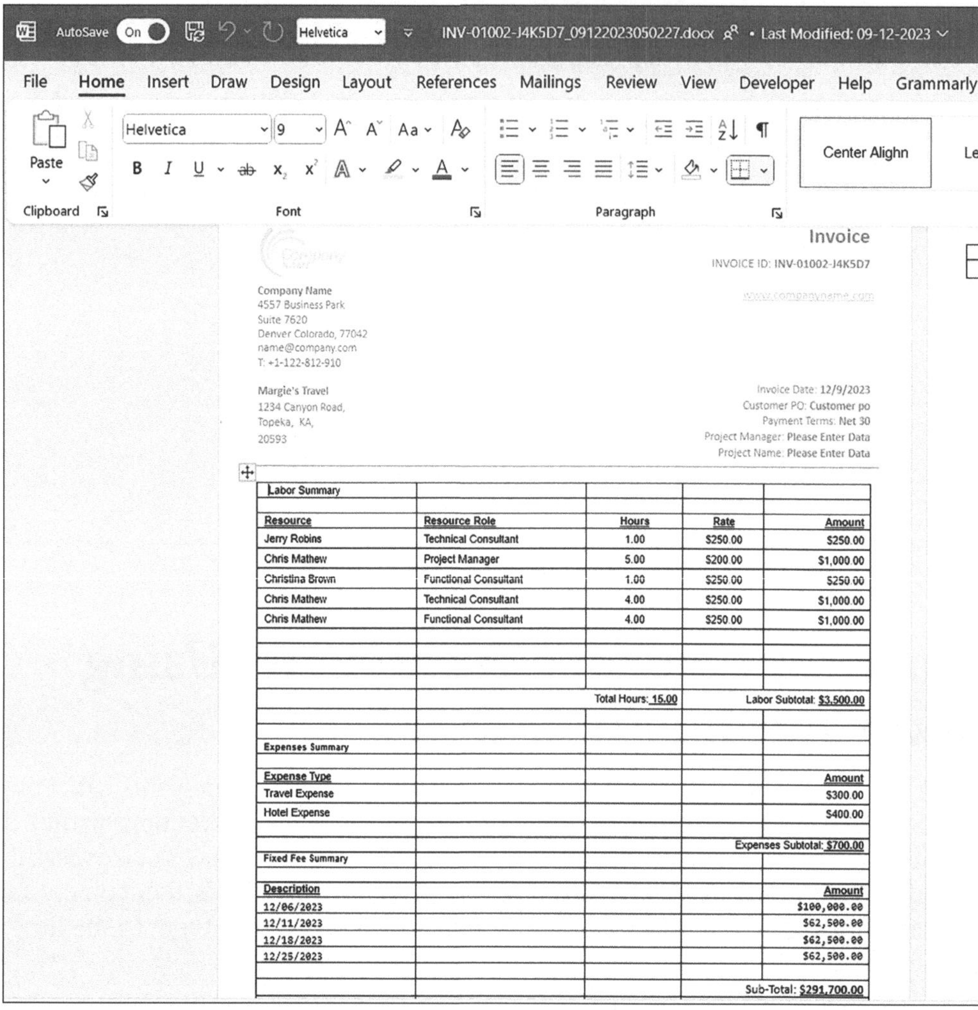

***Figure 6.20**: Invoice Document Template*

Actions in Dynamics 365 CRM

A Custom Action in Dynamics 365 CRM allows you to create reusable tasks that perform specific business functions. These actions can execute complex logic that is not possible with standard workflows.

You can trigger Custom Actions on demand, either from buttons in the user interface or programmatically. They accept input values and return output results, making them flexible for different scenarios.

Custom Actions can be combined with plugins, which are pieces of code written in C# that enhance their functionality. This means you can handle complex operations more easily.

You can use Custom Actions across different entities, allowing for consistency in processes. They are especially useful for automating tasks such as approval workflows or data updates.

In Dynamics 365 CRM, actions are classified into two types: **bound actions** and **unbound actions**. Bound actions are linked to specific entity records and operate on their data, requiring the record's ID as an input parameter. They are useful for tasks such as "**Approve Order**" or "**Add Note**" for individual records of entities. On the other hand, unbound actions are independent and do not tie to any specific record, allowing for greater flexibility. They can be called without requiring an entity ID and are suitable for operations such as "**Generate Report**" or "**Send Notification**."

Figure 6.21 illustrates a custom-bound action on the invoice entity that provides all the necessary inputs to the Word templates as output parameters.

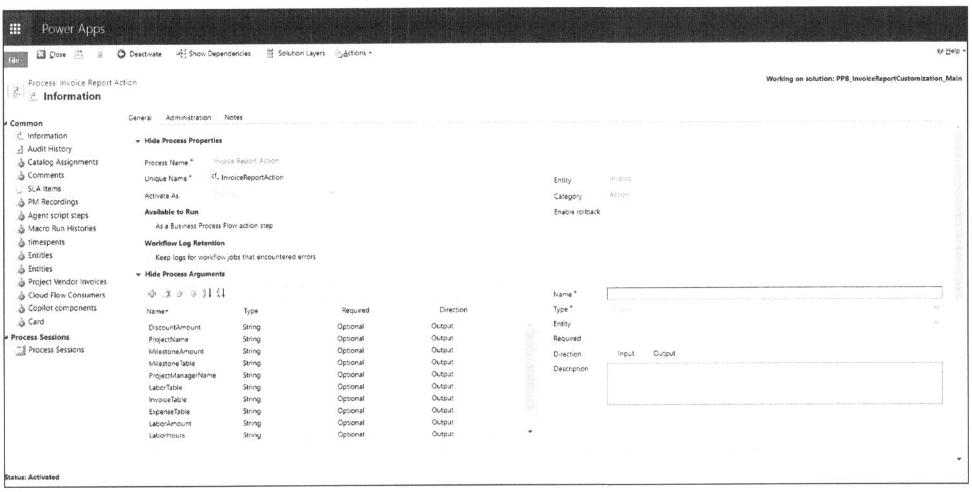

***Figure 6.21**: Custom Action in Dynamics 365 CRM*

You can invoke a bound action in a Power Automate flow using the '**Perform a bound action**' action.

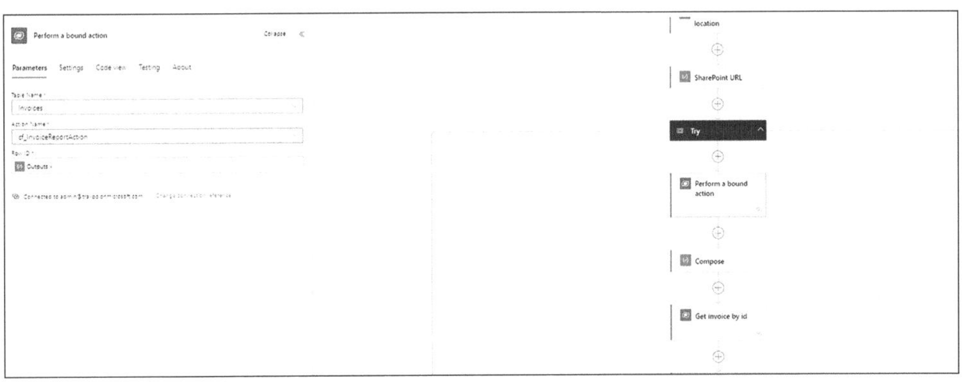

***Figure 6.22**: Perform a bound action Power Automate Action*

The output parameters are then utilized in the Word template, reducing the number of steps in the flow and making it simpler to manage.

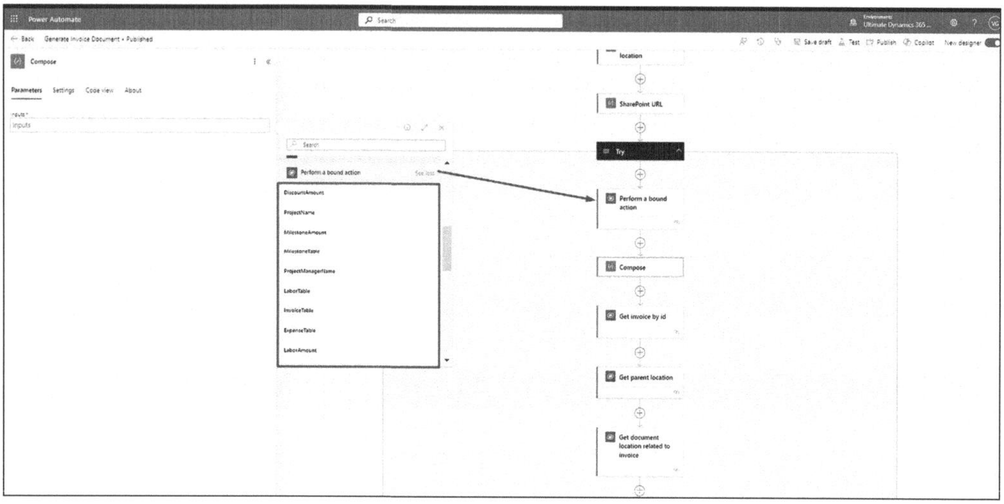

Figure 6.23: *Output of the Perform a bound action Power Automate Action*

This approach allowed for the creation of a detailed invoice document. The chapter explored various methods for working with Word templates and Power Automate, providing ideas for designing any logic that fits business needs. It also highlighted the flexibility of Dynamics 365 CRM.

Conclusion

In this chapter, we covered key aspects of document management in Dynamics 365 CRM. We discussed integrating with SharePoint Online for better collaboration, managing Word templates for consistency, and automating the creation of quotation and invoice documents using Power Automate.

In the next chapter, we will learn about customer engagement in Dynamics 365 Customer Service. We will explore connecting a Power Page Customer Self-Service Portal, managing cases and service requests, and setting up automated notifications and email templates. Let us make customer service smoother and more efficient together!

References

1. Create standardized Word Template in Dynamics 365 CRM https://learn.microsoft.com/en-us/power-platform/admin/using-word-templates-dynamics-365

2. Create word document using Power Automate Flow: https://powerplatformpuzzles.com/2023/07/30/create-word-document-using-power-automate-flow/

3. Dynamically populating tables in word document using Power Automate:

   https://powerplatformpuzzles.com/2023/07/18/dynamically-populating-tables-in-word-document-using-power-automate/#:~:text=In%20the%20word%20document%20the,in%20your%20word%20document%20template

4. Dynamically create SharePoint Document Location for D365 CRM entities using Power Automate Flow: https://powerplatformpuzzles.com/2023/07/10/dynamically-create-sharepoint-document-location-for-d365-crm-entities-using-power-automate-flow/

5. Client API Reference for model-driven apps: https://learn.microsoft.com/en-us/power-apps/developer/model-driven-apps/clientapi/reference

CHAPTER 7
Customer Service Management in Dynamics 365 CRM

Introduction

In today's competitive landscape, effective customer service is essential for building lasting customer relationships and ensuring satisfaction. Dynamics 365 CRM offers robust tools and features to help organizations improve their customer service processes, making it easier to meet and exceed customer expectations. This chapter focuses on the core components of customer service management in Dynamics 365, explaining how you can use its capabilities to simplify interactions, manage cases effectively, and empower your customer engagement team.

We will begin by discussing the Power Page Customer Self-Service Portal, a powerful way for customers to independently find answers to common queries, submit service requests, and track case progress–all of which can alleviate the load on your support team. We will also explore the process of managing cases in Dynamics 365 Customer Service, covering everything from creating cases to automating notifications that keep both your team, and your customers informed.

This chapter also includes practical guidance on setting up automated case assignments through a support email address, helping you to route customer requests efficiently to the right team members. Finally, we will walk through the process of creating and automating email templates, an essential tool for maintaining consistent and professional communication with your customers.

By the end of this chapter, you will be equipped with actionable insights and techniques that will transform your customer service management, enhancing both team efficiency and customer satisfaction. Let us begin with these essential components and see how they can drive your organization's success.

Structure

In this chapter, we will discuss the following topics:

- Introduction to Microsoft Power Pages
- Configuring a Power Page Customer Self-Service Portal
    - Portal Management Model-Driven App
    - Power Page Design Studio
    - Key Features of the Power Page Customer Self-Service Portal
- Managing Cases/Service Requests in Dynamics 365 Customer Service
    - Automated Case Assignments Using a Support Email Address
    - Automated Case Notifications
    - Creating and Automating Email Templates

Introduction to Microsoft Power Pages

Microsoft Power Pages is a feature within the Power Platform that enables users to build external-facing websites without the need for deep technical expertise. Power Pages are commonly used to create customer-facing portals, partner portals, or even internal business sites that integrate with Microsoft Dataverse. These portals allow for secure sharing of data with users who are outside of your organization while still connecting directly to your Dataverse or other data sources.

With Power Pages, you can build and design responsive websites using templates, page layouts, and a user-friendly drag-and-drop editor. It also supports advanced functionalities such as authentication (allowing users to sign in using Azure AD, LinkedIn, or other identity providers), secure data sharing, and form integration.

You can leverage Power Pages to create:

- **Customer Self-Service Portals** where users can access knowledge bases, submit service requests, and track cases.
- **Partner Portals** that help partners collaborate with your business on deals and projects.
- **Employee Portals** for internal team communication and information sharing.

Configuring a Power Page Customer Self-Service Portal

By setting up a Power Page Customer Self-Service Portal, organizations allow customers to manage their own service needs, which boosts customer satisfaction and aligns operations. This digital solution helps engage customers, keep them happy, and build loyalty, while also freeing up your team to focus on more complex issues and proactive support. Using Power Apps Portal also offers several benefits over creating a custom website from scratch. It allows for quick configuration and provides seamless integration with the Dataverse, meaning the same database can be used across both Dynamics 365 and Power Apps. Additionally, external contacts do not require Dynamics 365 or Power Apps licenses, making it cost-effective for organizations who need to provide access to external users. This simplifies management and reduces the need for extensive custom development, making Power Apps Portal a more efficient and scalable solution.

You can start building a Customer Self-Service Power Page by using the ready-to-use template. Follow these steps:

1. Go to https://make.powerpages.microsoft.com/.
2. In the templates section, search for "**`Customer`**" and select the **`Customer Self-Service Portal`** template.

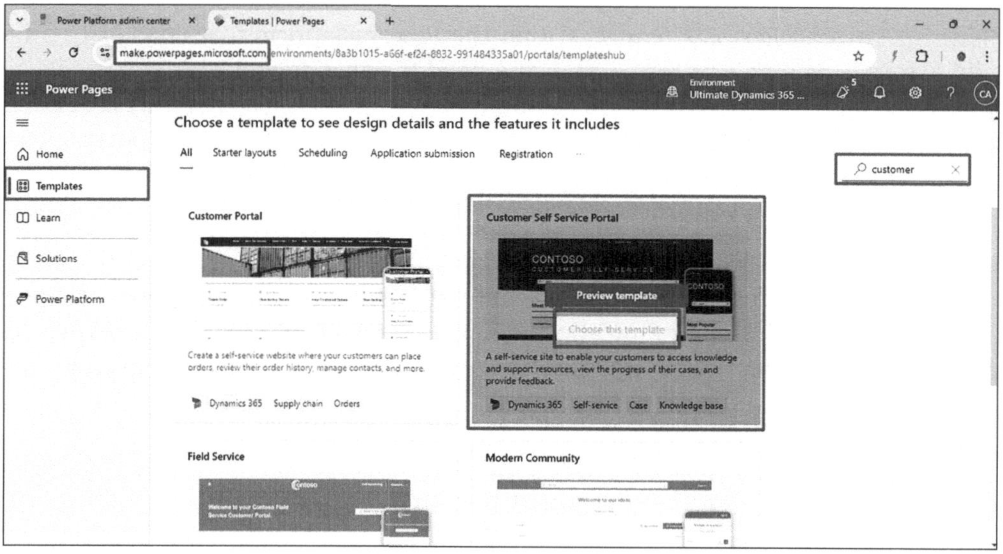

Figure 7.1: *Customer Self-Service Portal Template*

3. Name your website, set the website address, choose the language, and click **`Done`**.

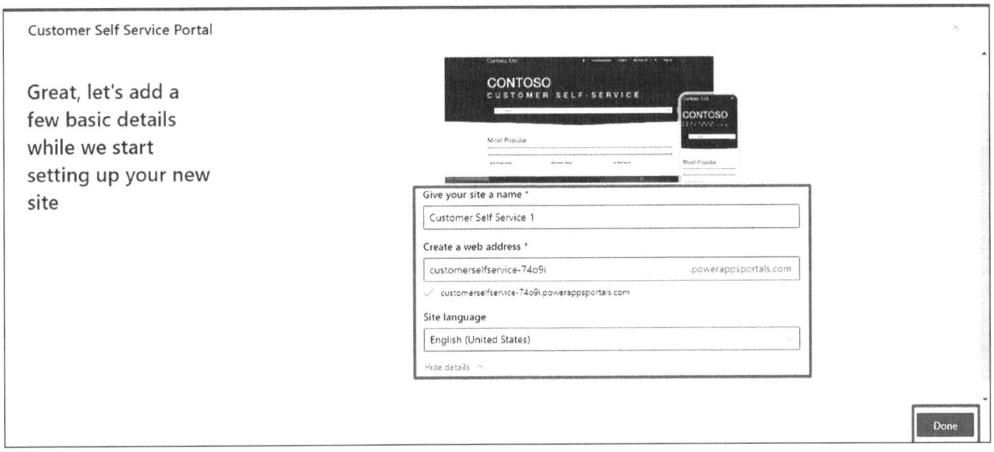

Figure 7.2: *Configuring a Customer Self-Service Portal*

4. The **`Customer Self-Service`** Portal's managed solutions will then be imported into your selected environment.

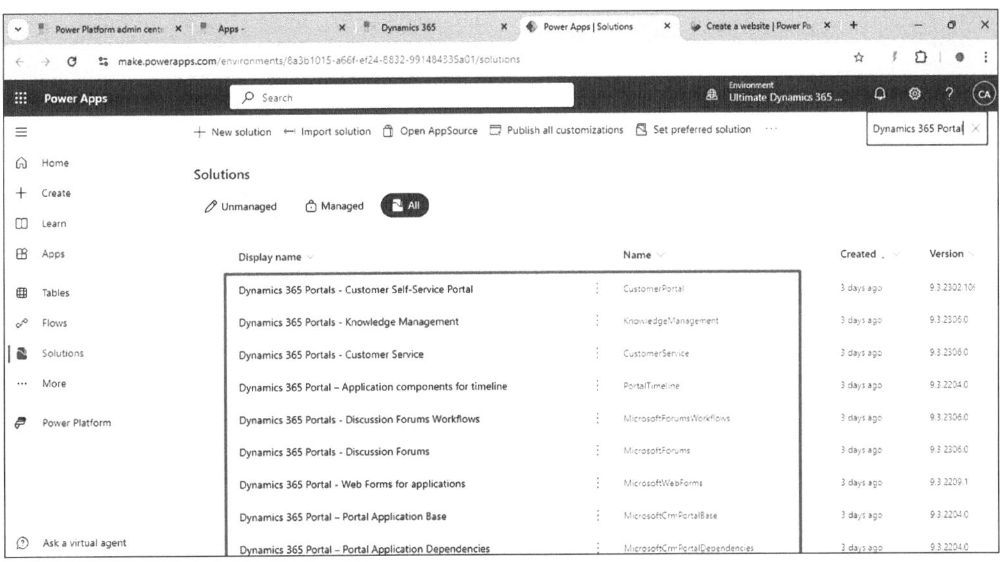

Figure 7.3: *Customer Self-Service Portal Managed Solutions Getting Deployed*

5. A new model-driven app called **`Portal Management`** will appear in your apps, containing all the portal settings.

6. Once configured, you can start customizing and building the portal in **`Power Page Studio`**.

Portal Management Model-Driven App

In Dynamics 365, the Portal Management Model-Driven App is a centralized application designed to help administrators and developers manage the settings and functionality of Power Pages.

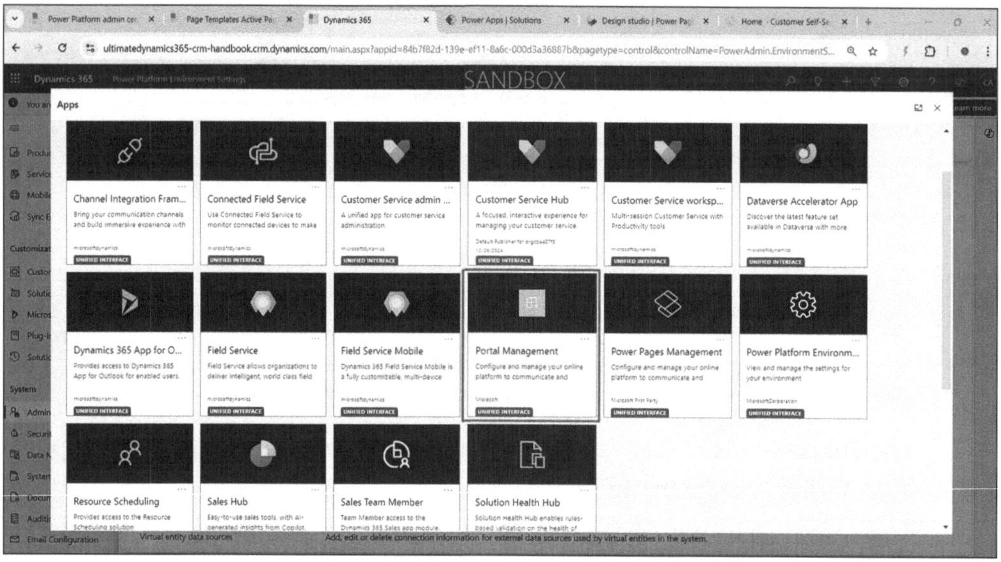

Figure 7.4: *Portal Management Model-Driven App*

Here is a summary of each main area within the **`Portal Management`** app, along with details about their roles in configuring and customizing a **`Power Page Customer Self-Service Portal`**:

Web Pages

What it is: This is where you manage the pages that make up your portal.

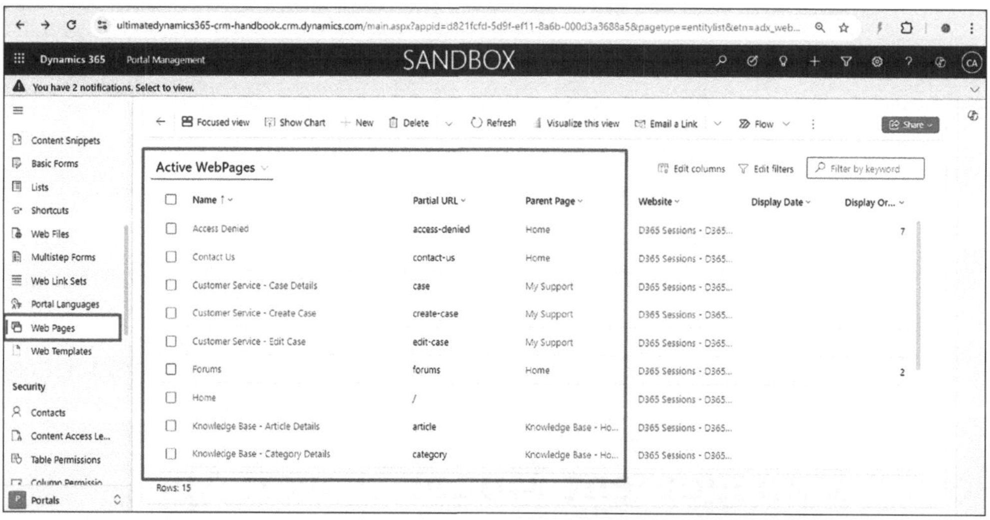

Figure 7.5: *Web Pages in Portal Management Model-Driven App*

How it Works: You can easily add, edit, or organize your pages here. This includes setting up page titles, links, and page templates. It is also where you control who can see what content. This makes sure users can navigate through your portal easily.

Web Templates

What it is: Web templates are the building blocks for your portal's design.

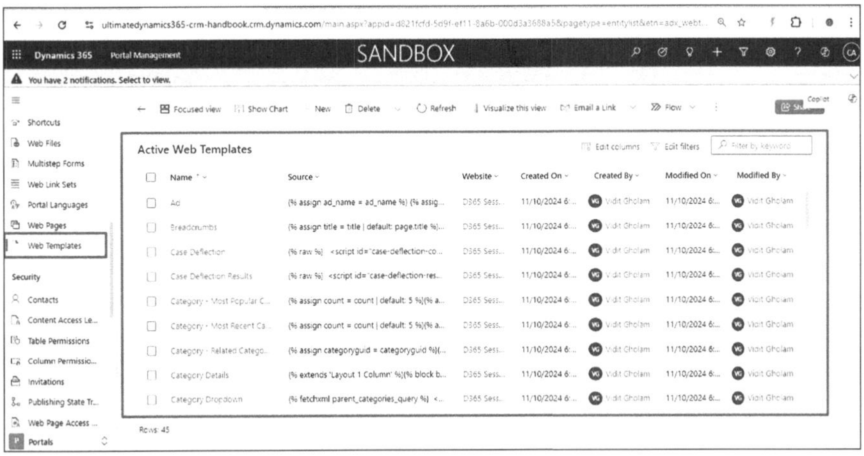

Figure 7.6: *Web Templates in Portal Management Model-Driven App*

How it Works: You can use these templates to create consistent page layouts, such as headers, footers, and navigation bars. This helps ensure that your portal looks uniform throughout, keeping your design aligned with your brand.

Site Settings

What it is: A central place to control key settings for your portal.

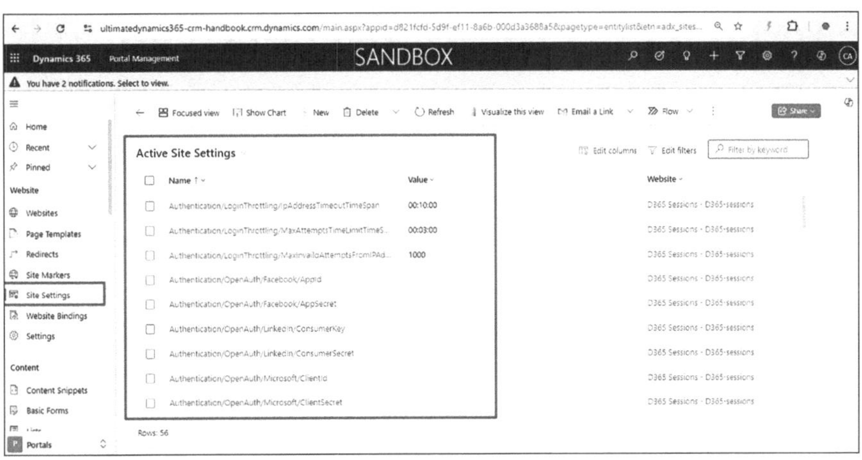

Figure 7.7: *Site Settings in Portal Management Model-Driven App*

How it Works: Here, you can manage important settings such as the portal's theme, login options, and security. You can also set up features such as CAPTCHA for extra security or adjust how fast the portal loads. This area helps you align the portal's settings with your organization's needs.

Content Snippets

What it is: Small pieces of reusable text or HTML for your portal.

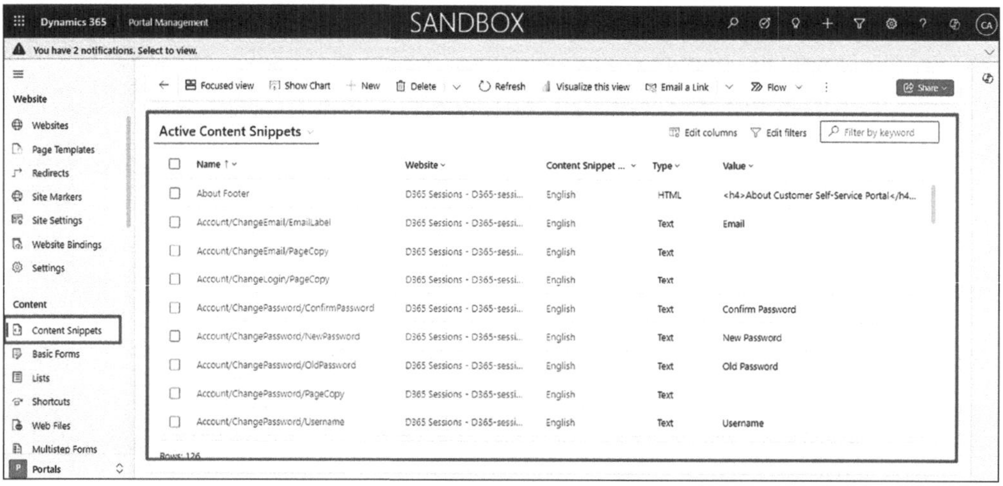

Figure 7.8: *Content Snippets in Portal Management Model-Driven App*

How it Works: If you have text or content that you want to use on multiple pages (for instance, a standard footer or header), you can store it here. That way, you do not have to update each page individually– just update the snippet, and it changes everywhere. It makes managing your content much easier.

Basic Forms (Entity Forms) and Lists (Entity Lists)

What it is: These are tools to display and interact with data from Dynamics 365 on your portal.

How it Works:

1. Entity Lists show a list of records, such as a customer's list of open cases, so users can see and interact with their information directly on the portal.

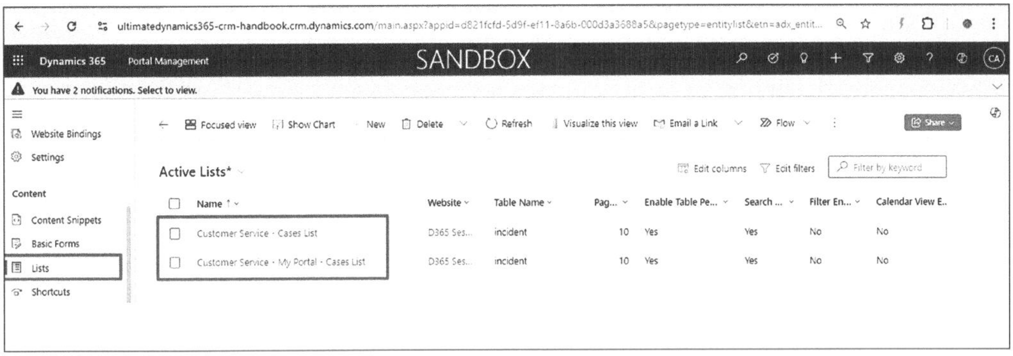

Figure 7.9: *Entity List in Power Pages*

2. Entity Forms allow users to fill out forms to create or update data. For example, customers can submit a support request.

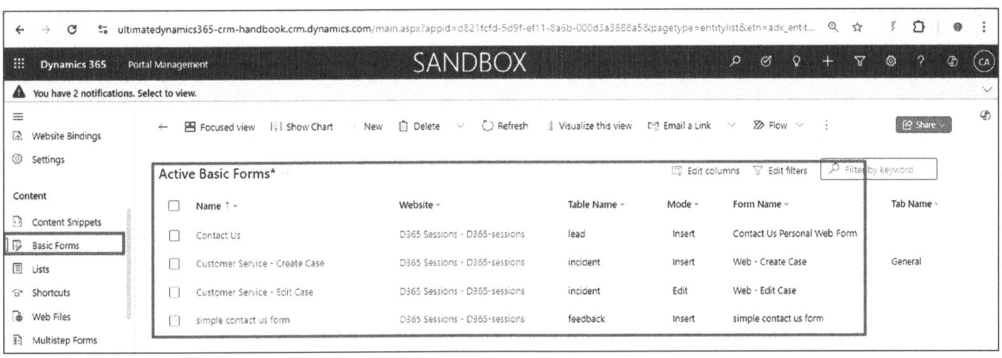

Figure 7.10: *Entity Form in Power Pages*

Web Roles

What it is: Web roles define who can access different areas of the portal.

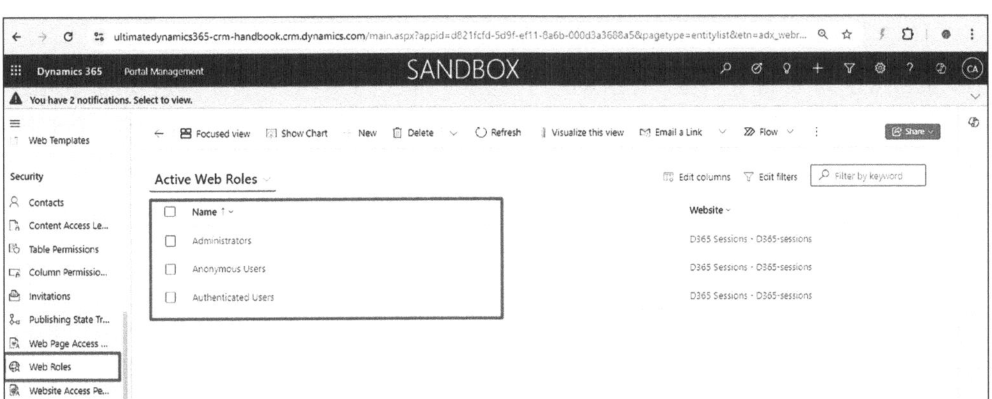

Figure 7.11: *Web Roles in Power Pages*

How it Works: You can assign roles to users (for instance, customers, admins, or support staff) and control what each role can see and do. This ensures that each user only has access to the parts of the portal they need.

Page Templates

What it is: These templates define how your pages will be structured.

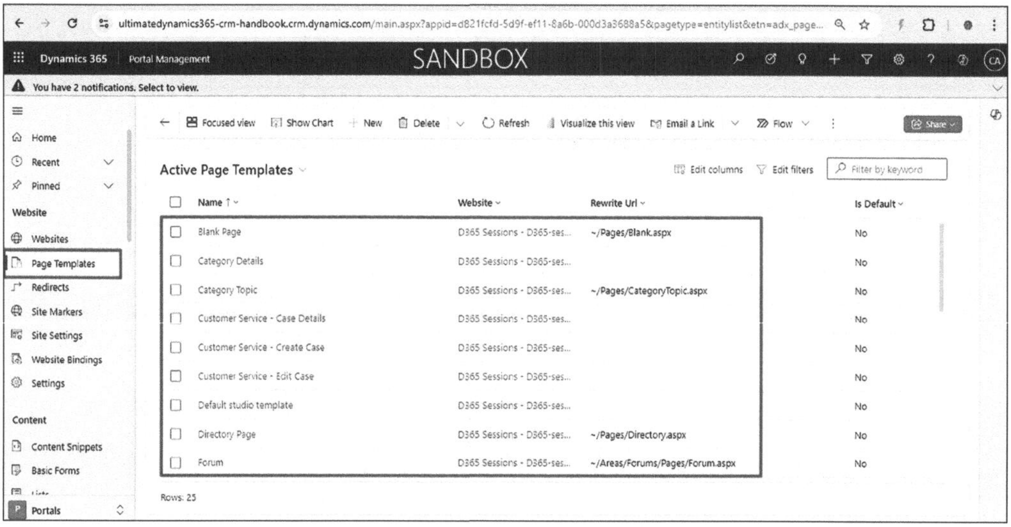

Figure 7.12: *Page Templates in Power Pages*

How it Works: Page templates help control the layout of your portal pages, ensuring that all your pages have a consistent look and feel. This works together with web templates to create a smooth, branded experience across the entire portal.

Content Access Levels

What it is: A way to control what content each user role can access.

How it Works: This feature lets you restrict access to certain pages or content, ensuring that only specific users can view certain information. For example, partners might see different content than customers. It is useful for providing tailored experiences to different groups.

Knowledge Articles

What it is: This is where you manage your portal's help content, such as FAQs or troubleshooting guides.

How it Works: You can upload articles to help users find answers to common questions. You can organize these articles by category, assign keywords, and track their publishing status. It is a great way to provide self-service support for your users.

Redirects

What it is: Manages how URLs are redirected to your portal.

How it Works: You can set up redirects if a page has been moved or if there is a broken link. This makes sure users do not end up on error pages and can always find the right content, improving their experience.

Power Page Design Studio

Power Page Design Studio is a web-based design and management tool for creating and customizing low-code websites or portals, specifically for customer engagement. It allows users to build, configure, and maintain portals connected to Dynamics 365 and other data sources. With Power Page Studio, you can easily create dynamic, branded experiences for customers, partners, and employees, offering them access to information, services, and interactions through a secure, user-friendly interface. Its drag-and-drop functionality and integration with Microsoft technologies make it an accessible tool for both technical and non-technical users.

Pages

What it is: Pages are the building blocks of your portal. Think of them as the individual web pages where you will display content, forms, or data to your users.

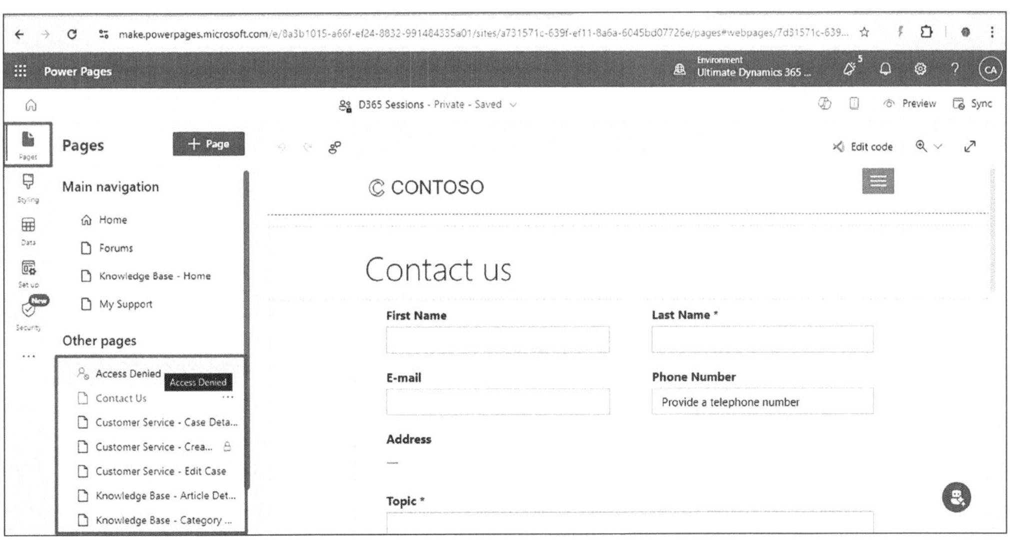

Figure 7.13: *Configuring Pages in Power Page Design Studio*

How it Works: In Power Page Studio, you can easily create and manage your portal's pages. For example, you can have pages such as "**Home**," "**Support**," or "**FAQ**." You can also organize them into a structure, where pages are linked together, and users can navigate smoothly. You will also have the ability to control who can see each page, making it easy to customize the experience based on user roles.

Components

What it is: Components are the elements you add to your pages to make them interactive and functional.

How it Works: This is where you get to make your portal come to life. You can add text boxes, images, buttons, forms, and even lists. For example, if you want customers to submit support requests, you can add a form that collects their information. Want them to see a list of their active cases? You can add a data list component. It is all about adding features that your customers can interact with easily.

Styling Workspace

What It Is: The Styling Workspace is where you can fine-tune your portal's appearance even further using custom code.

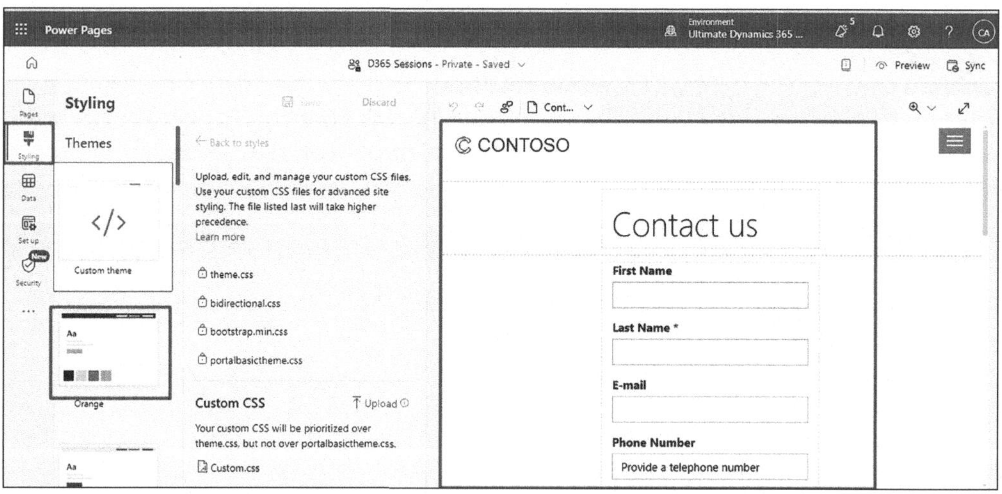

Figure 7.14: *Styling Workspace in Power Page Design Studio*

How it Works: If you want more control over how things look beyond basic themes, this is the place to be. The Styling Workspace lets you apply custom Cascading Style Sheets (CSS) to make specific adjustments, such as changing how a button looks or altering the layout of a page. It is perfect for when you need a more unique or detailed design for certain parts of your portal.

Themes

What it is: Themes control the look and feel of your portal. It is where you can style your portal to match your company's branding.

How it Works: Themes allow you to customize the colors, fonts, and general design to reflect your organization's identity. For example, if your brand uses blue and green colors, you can set those as the portal's primary colors. This ensures your portal looks professional and aligns with your company's branding, giving it a seamless and attractive design across all pages.

Data Workspace

What it is: The Data Workspace lets you connect your portal to the data from your Dynamics 365 environment.

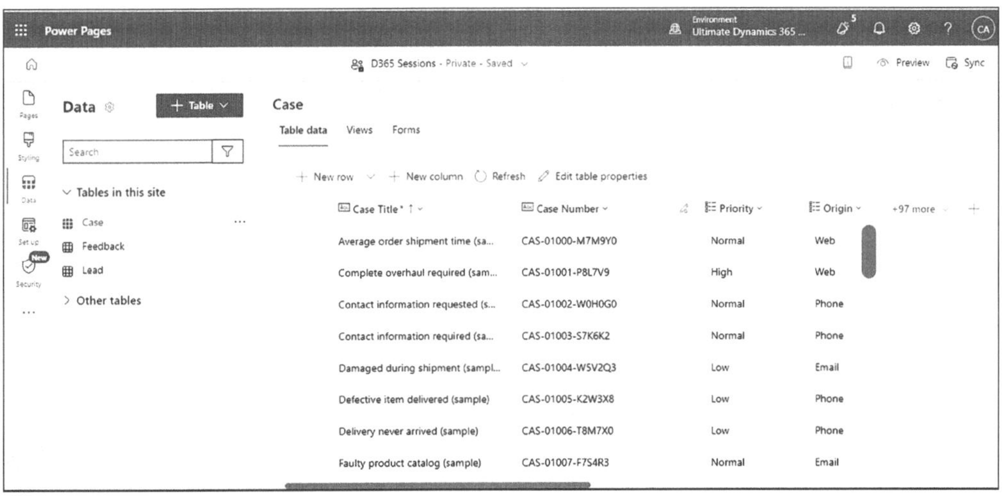

Figure 7.15: *Data Workspace in Power Page Design Studio*

How it Works: This is where you decide which data from your Dynamics 365 CRM should be visible to portal users. For instance, you might want customers to see their open cases, or you might want to display knowledge articles to help them solve common issues. The Data Workspace makes it easy to select which records, such as cases, contacts, or service requests, should appear on your portal. It essentially creates a live connection between your CRM data and the portal, so everything stays updated.

Security Workspace

What it is: The Security Workspace helps you manage who has access to what on your portal.

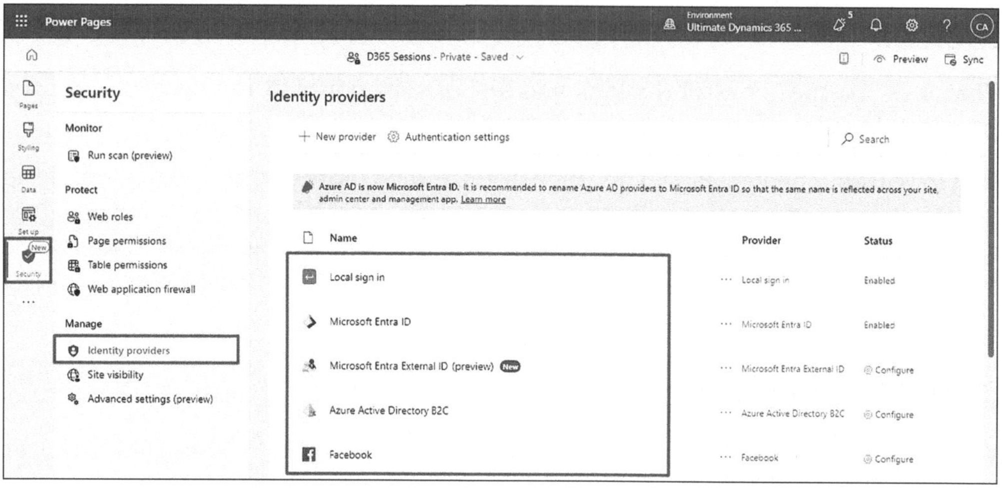

***Figure 7.16:** Security Workspace in Power Page Design Studio*

How it Works: Not everyone needs access to every page or piece of data. In this section, you will set up web roles (such as customers, employees, and admins) and decide what each role can see or do. For example, you might want only customer service agents to access certain administrative pages, while customers only see their own cases. This keeps your portal secure and ensures users can only see what they are allowed to.

Setup and Configuration

What it is: This is where you configure the overall settings for your portal, including things such as language, authentication, and site behavior.

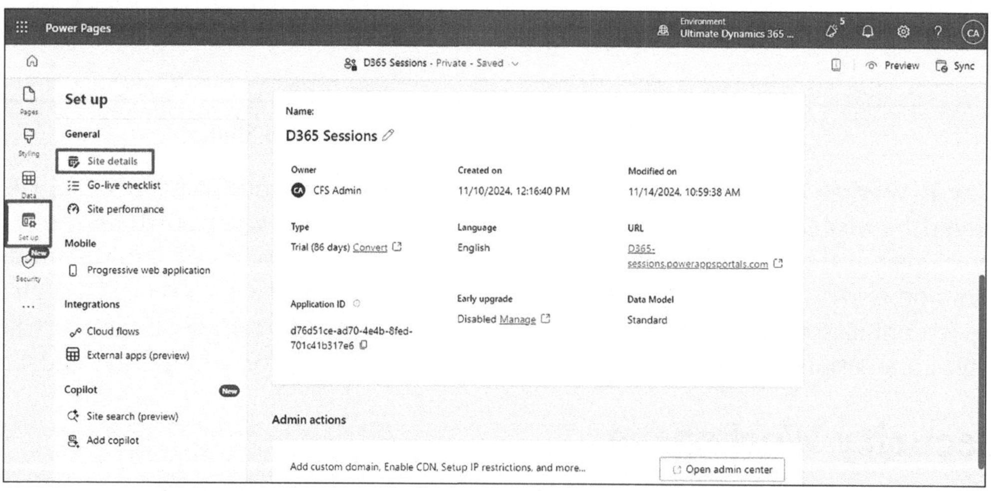

***Figure 7.17:** Setup and Configuration in Power Page Design Studio*

How it Works: This section lets you set up key aspects of your portal, such as choosing the default language for users (helpful for international customers), setting up authentication (for example, allowing users to log in via their Microsoft or Google accounts), and adjusting tracking and other technical settings. You can also customize general settings, such as enabling CAPTCHA for security or adjusting cache settings to improve site performance.

Preview Mode

What it is: Preview Mode lets you see how your portal will look and work once it is live.

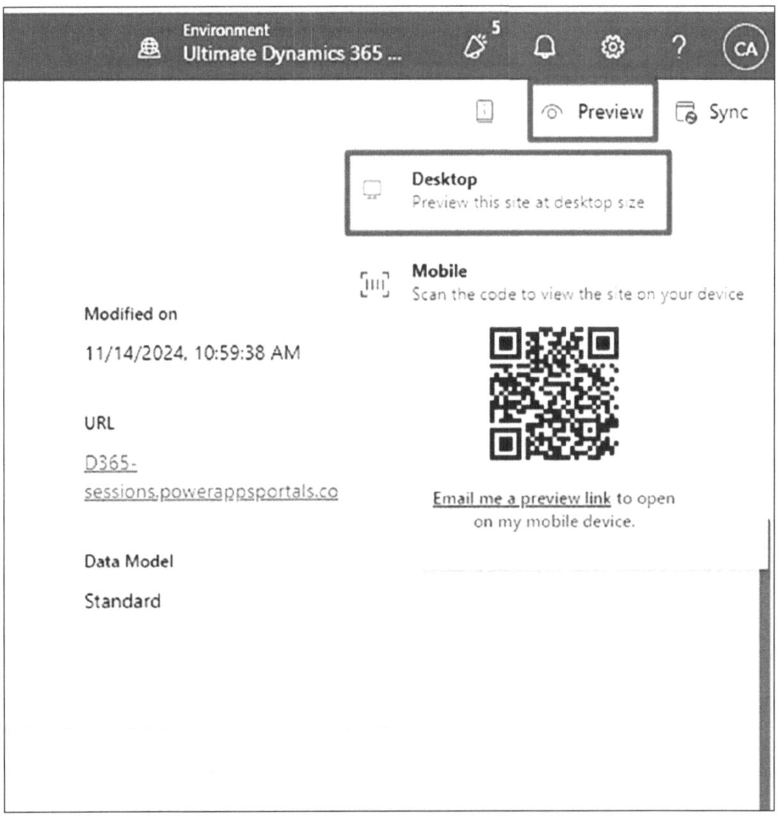

Figure 7.18: *Preview a Power Page Website*

How it Works: Before making your portal available to the public, Preview Mode gives you a sneak peek of how everything will appear to users. You can check the layout, test buttons, and forms, and make sure everything is working as expected. This step is crucial because it helps you catch any mistakes or issues before your customers start using the portal. It is your chance to make sure everything looks perfect and functions smoothly.

Key Features of the Power Page Customer Self-Service Portal

- **Self-Service Case Management:** Customers can create new cases, track the status of open cases, and review past interactions. This feature reduces the need for live support and provides customers with immediate access to their information.

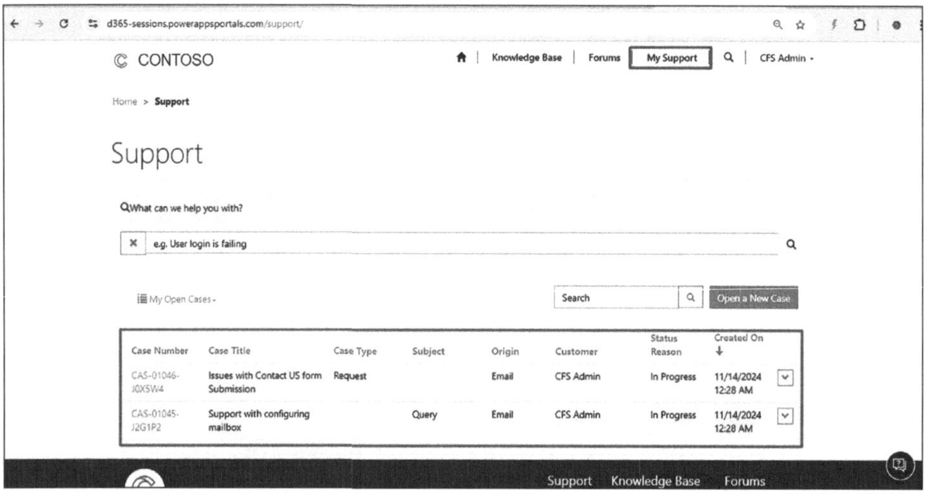

Figure 7.19: *Case Management in Customer Self-Service Portal*

- **Knowledge Base Access:** A centralized, searchable knowledge base allows customers to find answers to common issues, helping to resolve inquiries without direct agent involvement. **`Articles`** and **`FAQ`** pages can be tagged for easy searchability.

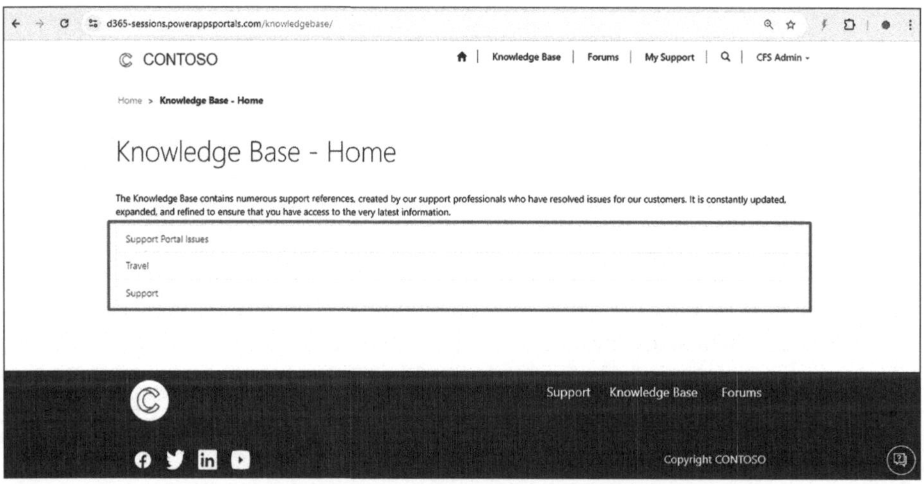

Figure 7.20: *Knowledge Bases in Customer Self-Service Portal*

- **Multi-Channel Authentication and Security:** The portal supports various authentication methods, providing secure, flexible access for different customer segments. This feature can help balance accessibility with data security and manage different customer access levels.

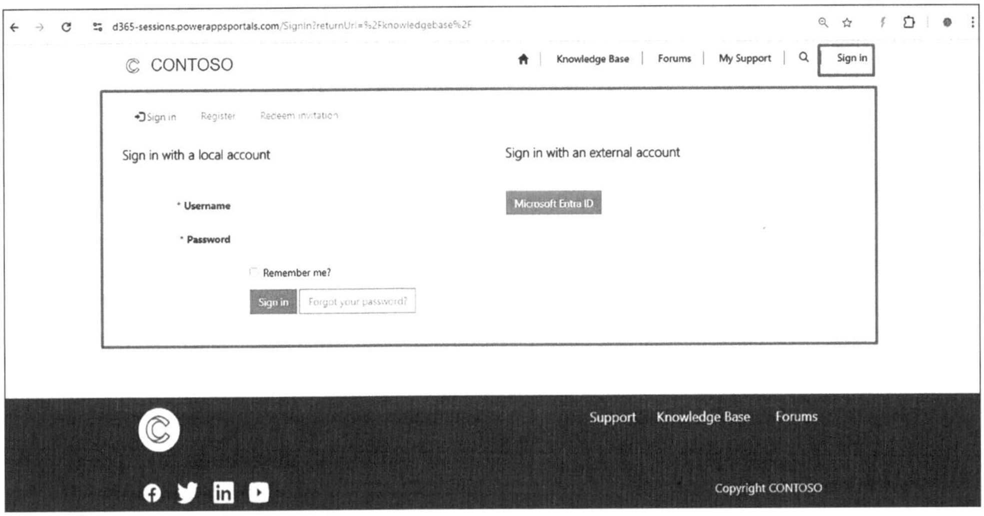

***Figure 7.21:** Authentication Options in Power Pages*

- **Real-Time Notifications and Updates:** The portal can send notifications for case updates, so customers receive immediate feedback on the status of their inquiries. Notifications can be configured to trigger automatically for specific actions, such as case assignments or case closures.
- **Customizable Branding and UX:** Customizable themes and page layouts allow the portal to align with your organization's brand. A simple, intuitive user interface enhances the customer experience by making navigation easy and accessible.
- **Integrated Insights and Analytics:** Built-in analytics track customer interactions, such as page visits, search terms, and cases created. Insights from portal usage can help your organization identify common customer issues, allowing for proactive customer service improvements.

Note: *When you create a portal, it starts as a trial portal, which is valid for 30 days. During this time, you can explore its features, test configurations, and decide if it meets your business needs. If the trial expires without being converted to a production portal, the portal will become inactive, and you will lose access to it. To avoid this, make sure to convert your portal to a production environment before the trial ends.*

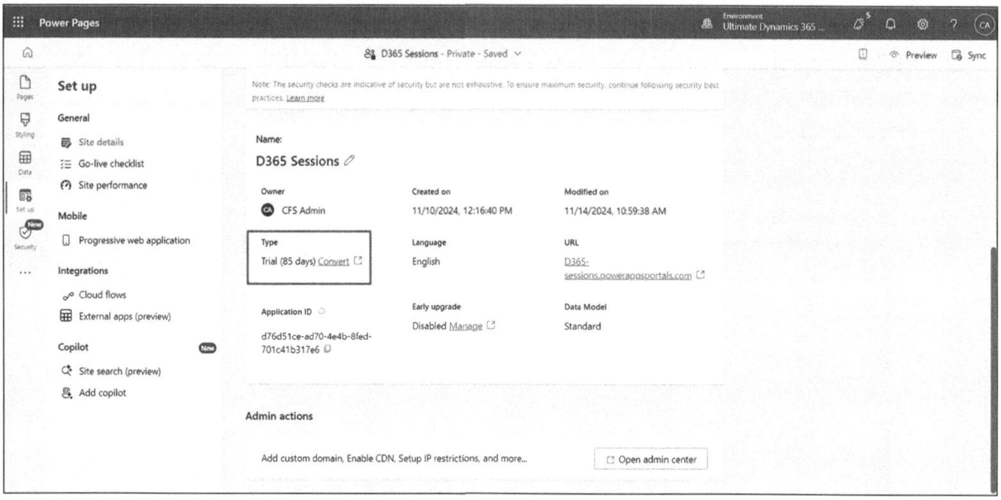

Figure 7.22: *Converting a Trail Power Page*

You can extend the trial two more times (30 days each)—with a maximum trial period of up to 90 days.

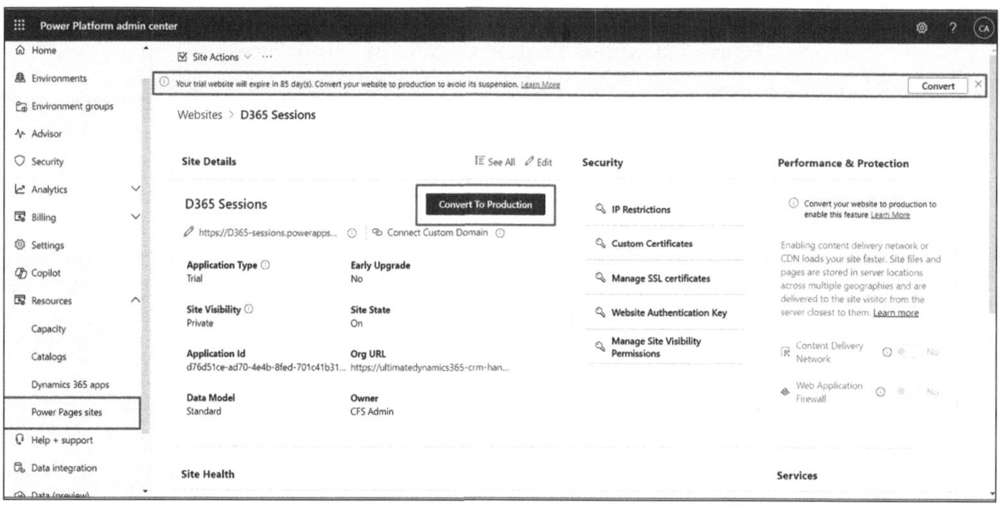

Figure 7.23: *Power Page Site Settings*

To manage all the licensing capacities for your portal, you can use the Power Platform Admin Center. This tool allows you to monitor and configure the portal's licensing details, such as the number of page views or logins available based on your license. As shown in *Figure 7.23*, the admin center provides a clear overview and control of your portal's usage, ensuring you stay within your allocated limits and can scale as needed.

With the portal now connected to Dynamics 365 Customer Service, all customer interactions, such as case submissions and inquiries, are captured in the Service Requests module. This connection ensures every service request is centralized, organized, and easy for your support team to access. From here, cases can be tracked, managed, and resolved efficiently, creating a smooth experience for both customers and support agents. Let us explore how you can effectively manage cases and service requests in **`Dynamics 365 Customer Service`**.

Managing Cases/Service Requests in Dynamics 365 Customer Service

No matter how advanced technology gets, customers still gravitate toward familiar ways to seek help—such as searching for a support email address. Even if companies provide AI-powered chatbots, self-service portals, or mobile apps, many customers prefer the simplicity and directness of email.

For example, if you own a smartphone from a leading brand such as Apple or Samsung and face an issue, your first instinct might be to look for their support email or phone number. It is a natural behavior because these traditional methods feel personal and reliable. This preference has been a constant in the customer service industry since the early days of support emails. Despite all the advancements, email remains a crucial touchpoint for addressing customer concerns, building trust, and offering a human connection when needed.

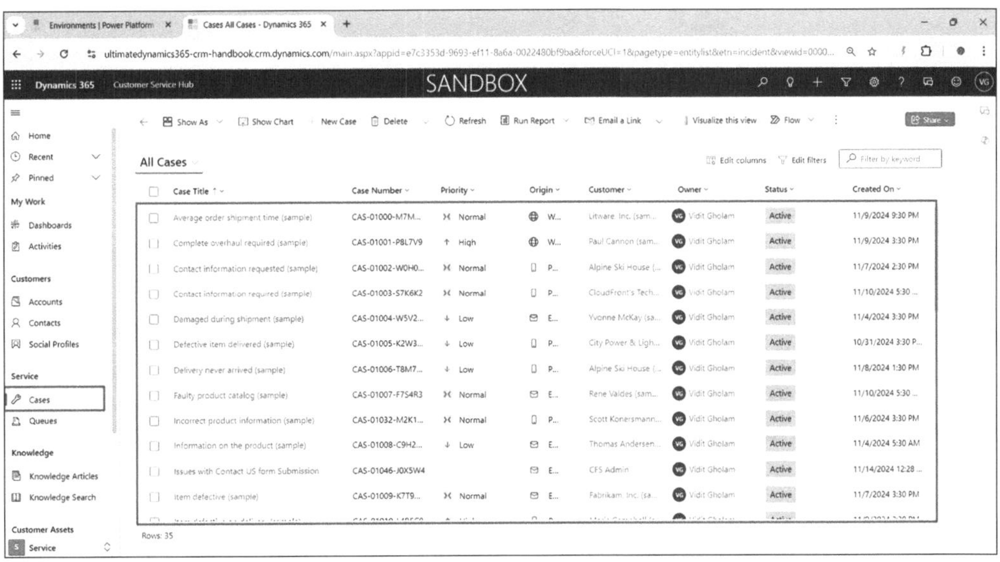

Figure 7.24: *Cases in Dynamics 365 Customer Service Hub*

Hence, we will now explore how to set up a support email address for your organization and configure it to automatically create cases in **`Dynamics 365 CRM`**. This approach ensures that every customer query sent to your support email is logged and tracked as a case, making it easier for your team to manage and resolve issues efficiently. Let us walk through the steps to get this set up!

Automated Case Assignments Using a Support Email Address

Setting up automated case assignments through a support email address is a smart way to make customer service smoother and more efficient. With this process, any query sent to your support email is automatically logged as a case in Dynamics 365 and assigned to the right team or agent. It saves time, cuts down on manual work, and ensures every customer request gets the attention it needs quickly.

Let us break down through a process flow how this would work.

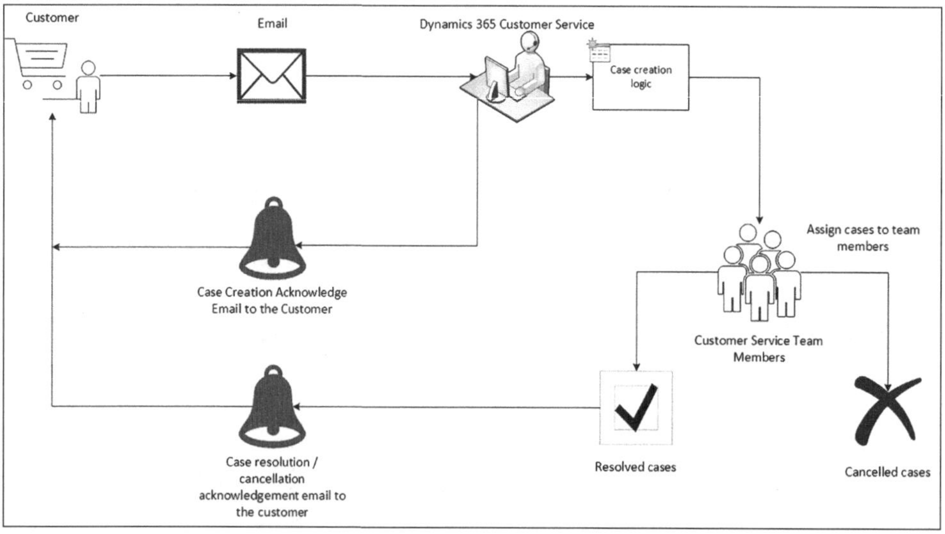

***Figure** 7.25: Automatic Case Creation Process Flow*

Your organization should have a dedicated support email address (for example, support@companydomain.com) to make it easier for customers to raise queries. As mentioned earlier, many customers usually prefer emailing over calling or using a support portal because it feels more convenient and direct for logging their service requests. Here is how a support email can streamline service management:

- **Support Email Address**: Customers send their inquiries or issues directly to the designated support email.
- **Automatic Case Creation**: Emails sent to the support address are automatically converted into cases in the Service Request Management System (SRMS). This is often handled through support queues or queue management features.

- **Case Assignment**: Once a case is created, it is assigned to the appropriate customer support team member for resolution.
- **Acknowledgment Emails**: Customers receive a confirmation email acknowledging their support request has been logged.
- **Team Notifications**: The assigned team member is notified about the new case and any required actions based on the established SLAs.
- **Defaulter Reporting**: A defaulter report can be generated internally to track any team members who may have missed service request deadlines.
- **Case Closure Notifications**: Customers are notified when their case is resolved or canceled, keeping them informed at every stage.
- **Email Tracking**: All communication via email is automatically tracked within the system to maintain a complete record of the conversation.
- **Service Request Management Portal**: For selected customers or based on company policy, a service portal can be provided. This portal allows customers to raise, track, and manage their service requests easily.

Creating a Support Mailbox for Case Creation

Let us walk through the steps to create a support mailbox for automatic case creation:

1. **Create a Shared Mailbox in Microsoft Admin Center:** Start by setting up a shared mailbox for your support email (for example, support@yourdomain.com) using the **`Microsoft Admin Center`**.

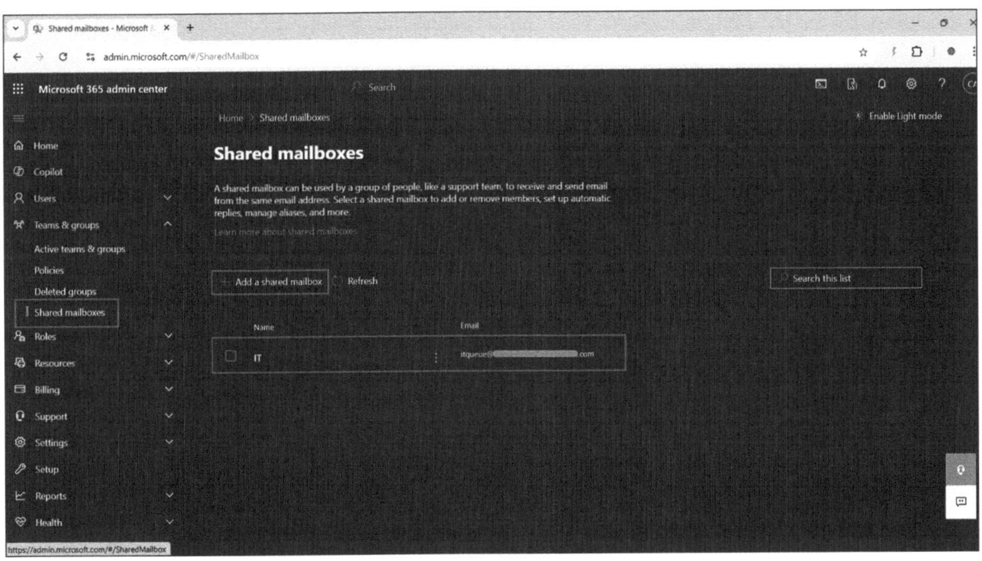

Figure 7.26: *Creating a Share Mailbox in Microsoft Admin Center*

2. **Set Up a Queue in the Target Environment:** In the designated Dynamics 365 environment, go to Power Platform Environment Settings (**`Advanced Settings`**) to begin creating a Queue.

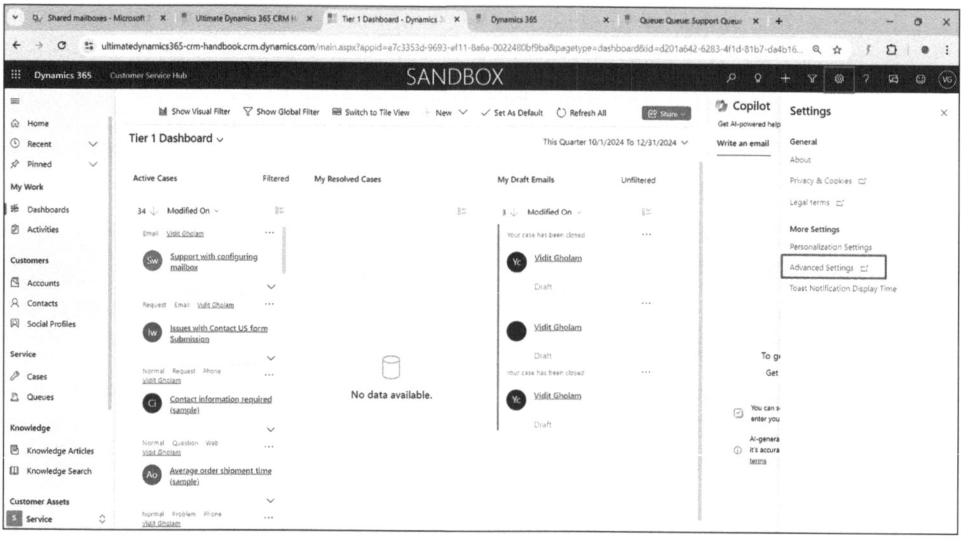

Figure 7.27: *Advance Settings in Dynamics 365 CRM*

3. **Navigate to Service Management:** Under **`Service Management`**, select **`Queues`** and click on "**`Create New`**" to set up your **`Queue`**.

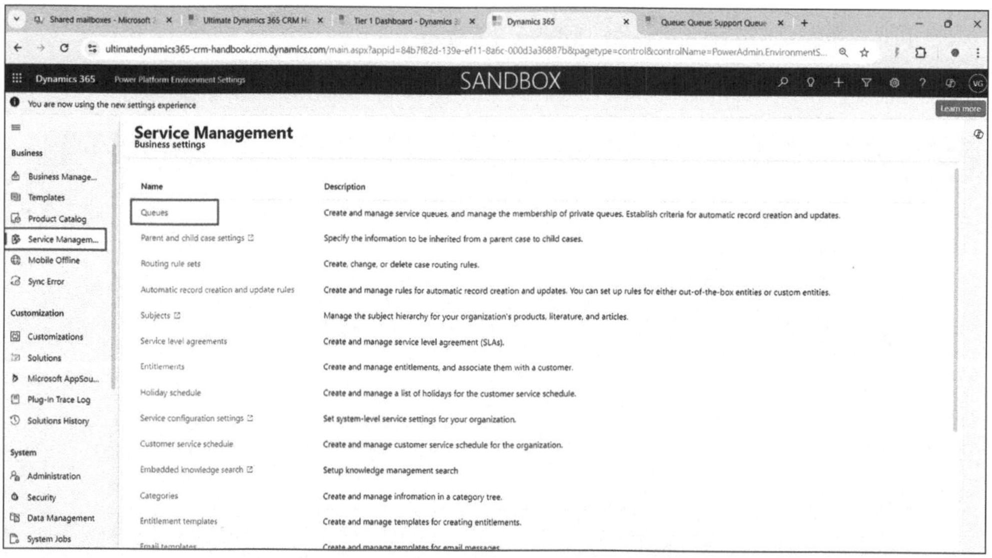

Figure 7.28: *Creating Queue in Service Management Settings*

4. **Mailbox Creation:** When you create the **`Queue`**, a corresponding Mailbox will also be created automatically.

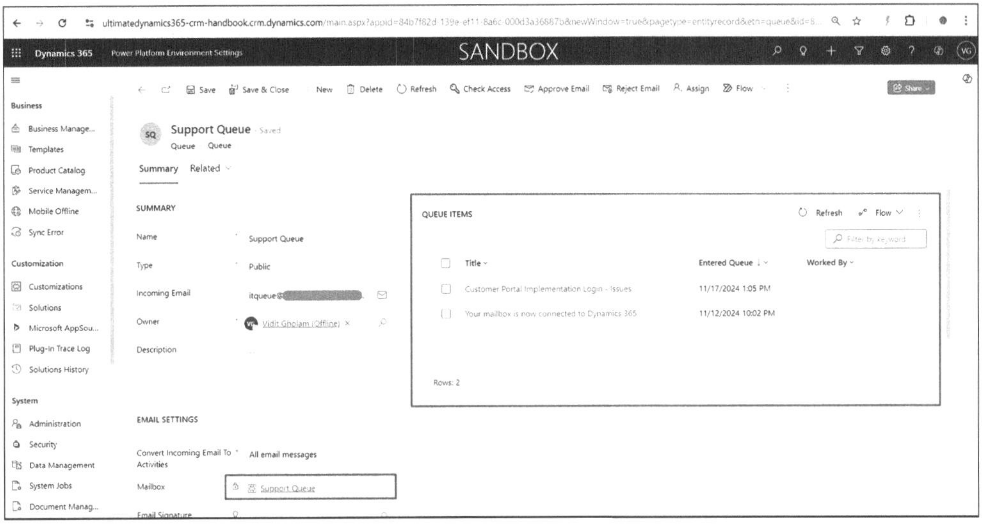

Figure 7.29: *Support Queue in Dynamics 365 CRM*

5. **Approve and Test the Mailbox:** Approve the mailbox, then test and enable it, as discussed in earlier chapters, to ensure it is ready for use.

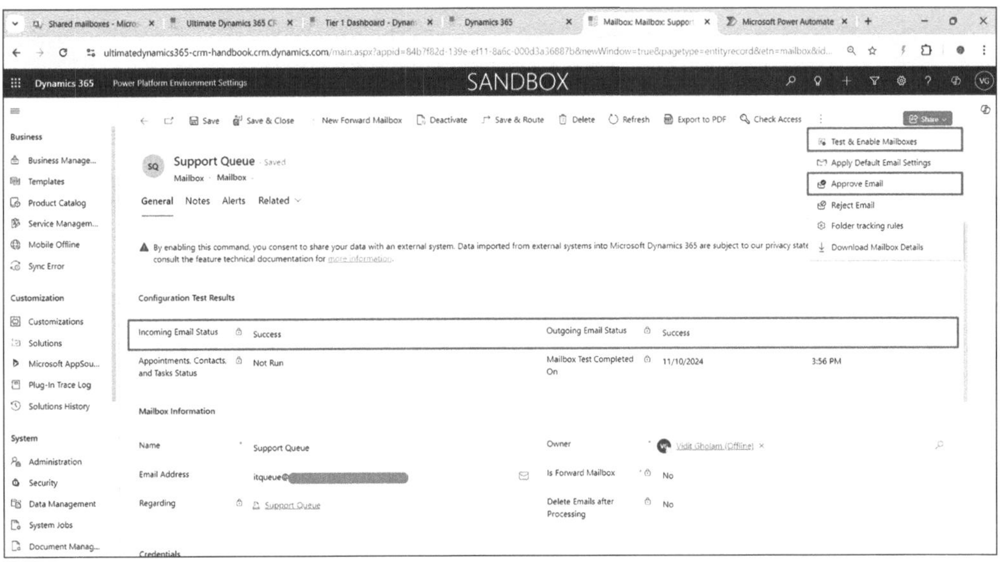

Figure 7.30: *Support Queue's Mailbox in Dynamics 365 CRM*

6. **Activate the Support Email:** Your support email address is now fully set up and linked to the **Queue**.

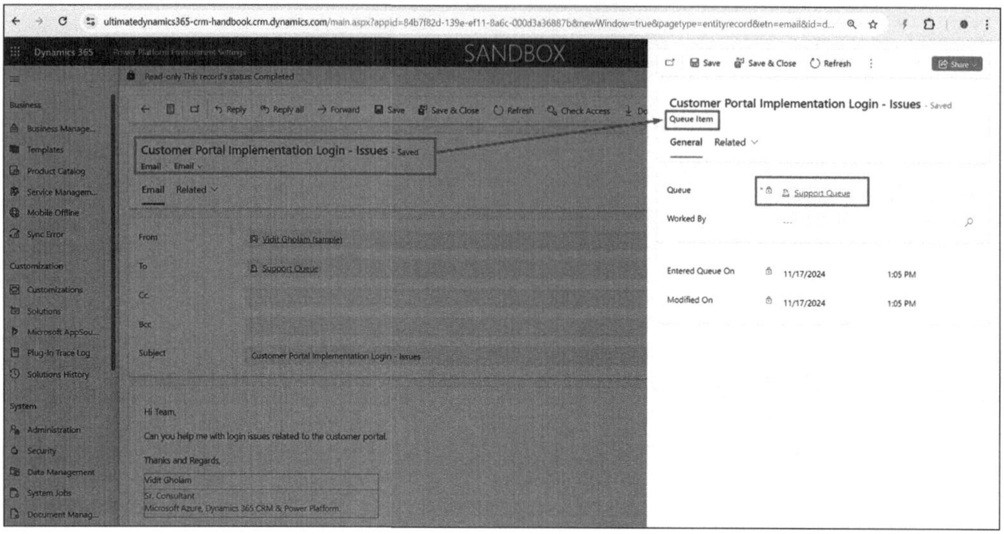

Figure 7.31: *Incoming Email Captured as a Queue Item in Dynamics 365 CRM*

7. **Queue Item Creation:** Any email sent to this address will automatically appear as a **`Queue Item`** in Dynamics 365, ready for case management.

8. **Case Creation:** Once an email is received in the Queue, you can use the Out-of-the-Box (OOB) functionality to convert it directly into a case. This streamlined process allows for quick and efficient case creation, as shown in *Figure 7.32*.

Figure 7.32: *Converting Emails to Cases in Dynamics 365 CRM*

9. **Custom Automation with Plugins or Power Automate**

For more advanced scenarios, you can write a custom Plugin or create a

Power Automate Flow that triggers whenever a Queue item is created. This automation can handle the process of converting the Queue item into a case, giving you flexibility to add custom logic or specific conditions as needed.

Automated Case Notifications

While resolving a case is crucial, keeping customers informed with regular updates is just as important, sometimes even more so. Frequent updates ensure transparency, build trust, and reassure customers that their issue is being actively addressed. Whether it is an acknowledgment when the case is logged, progress updates during resolution, or a final notification when the case is closed, these communications demonstrate a commitment to excellent service. Automated case notifications make this process effortless by sending timely updates to customers at key stages, keeping them in the loop every step of the way.

Creating notifications in Dynamics 365 CRM is straightforward, especially with the help of Power Automate. Let us explore some common process flows you can set up to send important notifications:

1. **Notification for Case Creation:** Alert the customer or team when a new case is logged.

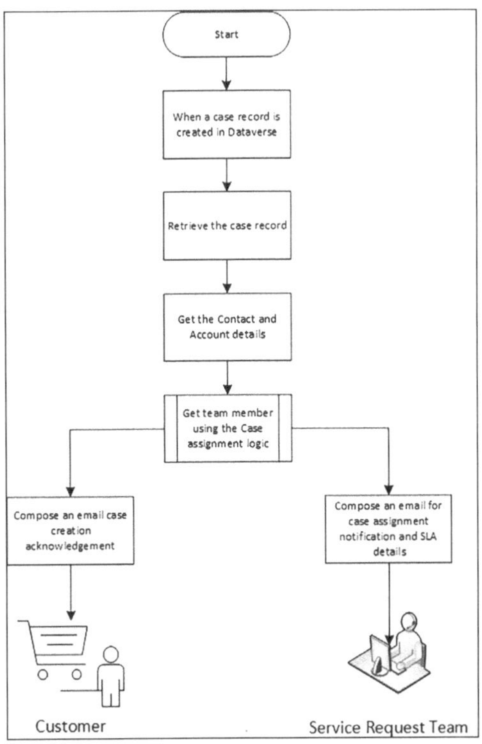

Figure 7.33: *Power Automate Notification for Case Creation*

a. **Trigger the Flow**: Start with a Dataverse trigger that activates when a case record is created.

b. **Retrieve Case Details**: Use a "`Get`" action to fetch all relevant details about the case.

c. **Fetch Customer Information**: Retrieve the customer and contact details to gather information such as the customer's name, email address, and other relevant data.

d. **Case Assignment Logic**: Implement logic for assigning the case. For example, you could create a lookup field on the customer record for the "`Responsible Person`." Based on the customer, the case can be assigned to the user specified in that field. You can design different assignment logics to suit your business needs.

e. **Send Notifications**:

    3. Compose an email with the gathered details to send a case creation acknowledgment to the customer.

    4. Notify the service request team with the case details and inform them about the case assignment.

This flow ensures that both customers and the internal team are promptly informed and ready to act.

2. **Notification for Case Assignment or Reassignment:** Notify the assigned team member or agent when a case is assigned or reassigned.

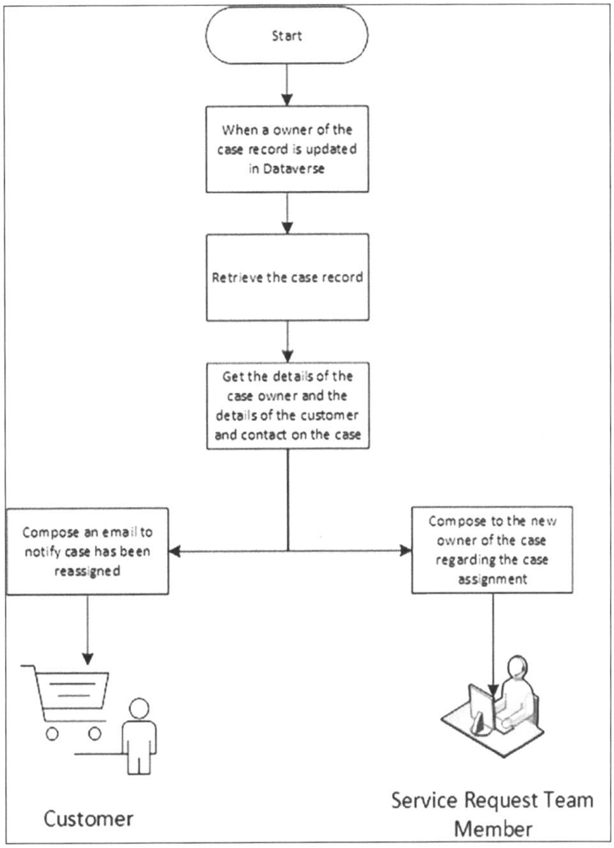

Figure 7.34: *Power Automate Notification when a Case is Assigned*

Notifying team members when a case is assigned to them and informing customers when a case is reassigned is a key part of effective communication in customer service. Here is how you can set up this flow:

a. **Trigger the Flow**: Use a Dataverse trigger that activates when a case record is updated. Configure the trigger to monitor changes specifically in the Owner field of the case entity.

b. **Retrieve Case Details**: Add a "`Get`" action to fetch the entire case record, ensuring you have all relevant information.

c. **Fetch Owner and Customer Information**: Retrieve details about the new owner (team member), the customer, and the customer's contact information, including name and email address.

d. **Send Notifications**:

   i. Compose and send an email to the customer, informing them that their case has been reassigned to a new team member.

ii. Send a notification to the team member, alerting them that a case has been assigned to them, along with any necessary details for follow-up.

3. **Notification for Case Cancellation:** Inform the customer when a case has been canceled.

4. **Notification for Case Resolution:** Send a final update to the customer when their case is resolved.

The final set of notifications is for when a case is resolved or canceled. These updates are crucial for keeping everyone informed, whether the case is marked as resolved or canceled by the customer through a portal or by the support team after communication with the customer.

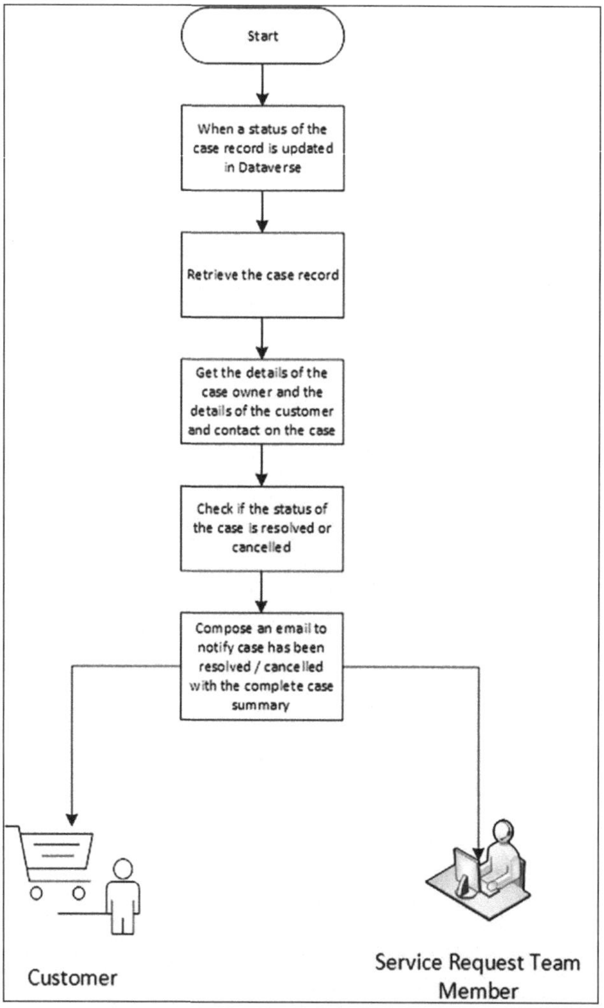

Figure 7.35: *Power Automate Notification when a Case is Canceled or Resolved*

Here is how the flow works:

a. **Trigger the Flow**: Use the same Dataverse trigger for updates to the case record. This time, configure the trigger to activate when there is a change in the status field of the case.

b. **Retrieve Case Details**: Fetch the full case record to access all necessary information.

c. **Check the Status**: Verify if the status field indicates the case is resolved or canceled.

d. **Send Notifications**:

   - Compose an email to the customer, informing them about the resolution or cancellation of their case.
   - Notify the team member assigned to the case, providing confirmation of the updated status.

Creating and Automating Email Templates

Email templates in Dynamics 365 Customer Service are pre-designed email formats that save time and ensure consistency when communicating with customers. There are two types of email templates: global templates and table-specific templates. Global templates can be used across any entity in the system, making them ideal for general communications such as notifications or reminders. They are easier to manage when you need to send the same message to different types of records.

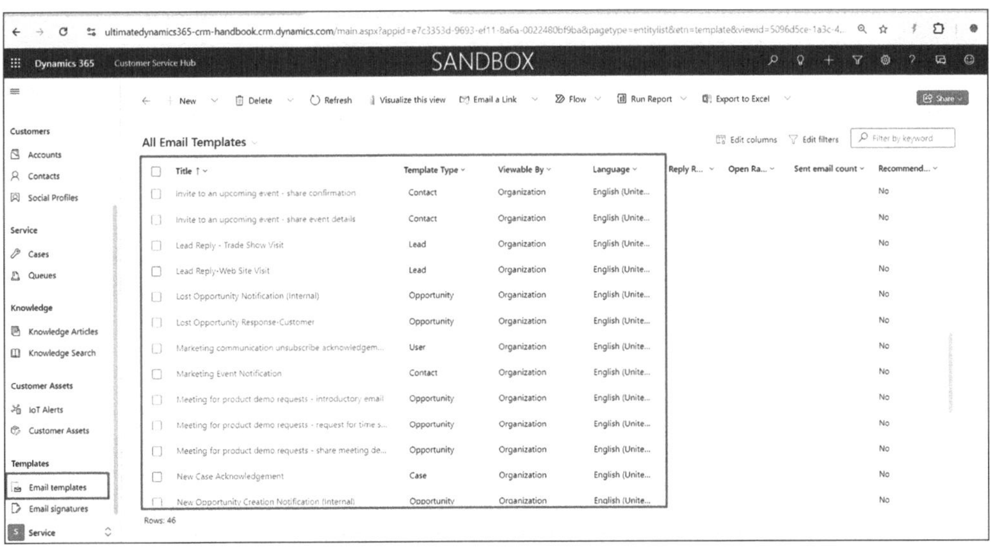

Figure 7.36: *Email Templates in Dynamics 365 Customer Service*

On the other hand, table-specific templates are tied to a specific entity, allowing you to include data unique to that entity, such as a customer's name or a case number. You should use global templates for consistent messages across records and table-specific templates when you need personalized, entity-specific communication.

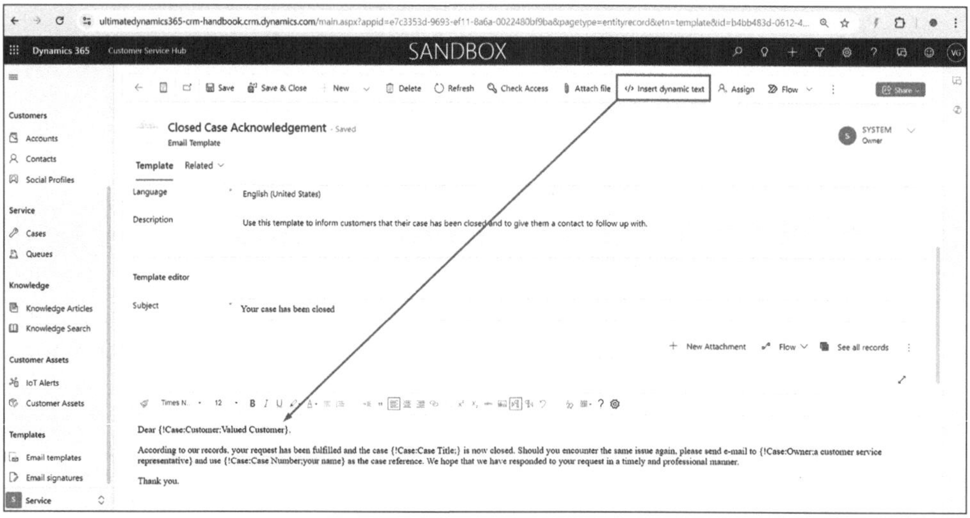

Figure 7.37: *Adding Dynamic Content to Email Templates in Dynamics 365 Customer Service*

These templates are incredibly helpful for several reasons:

- **Consistency**: They ensure your messaging is uniform and professional across all customer interactions.
- **Efficiency**: Instead of writing emails from scratch, team members can quickly use a template, speeding up response times.
- **Accuracy**: Dynamic fields pull in the correct information directly from the system, reducing errors and improving personalization.
- **Customer Experience**: Quick and clear communication reassures customers that their issues are being handled efficiently.

Email templates are especially useful for common scenarios, such as case acknowledgment emails, updates on case progress, or notifications about case resolutions. By setting these up in advance, your team can focus on delivering exceptional service while the system handles routine communication.

Using an email template in Dynamics 365 is straightforward but can involve multiple steps. For instance, if you want to send a case closure acknowledgment email, the process looks like this:

1. Create a new email record from the Timeline on the case record.

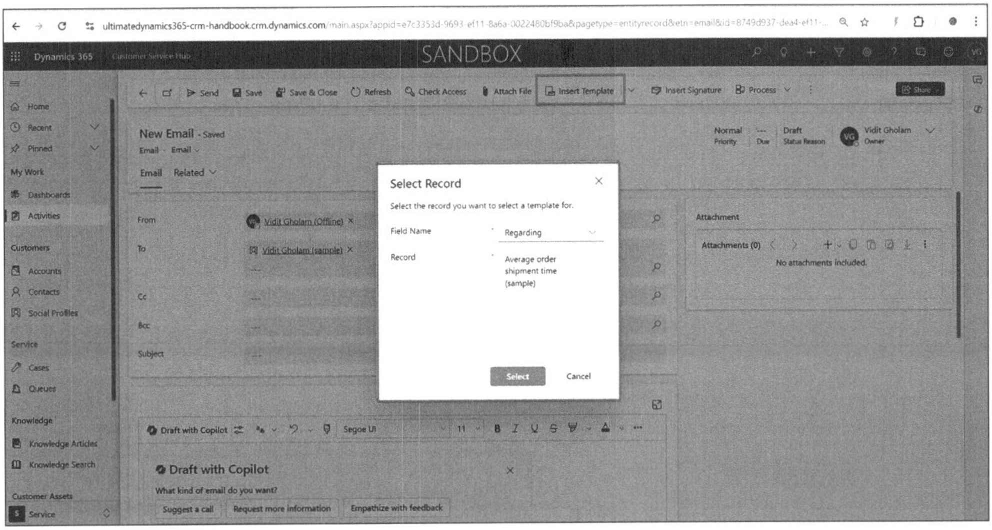

Figure 7.38: *Using an Email Template in Dynamics 365 CRM Customer Service*

2. Insert the email template into the email.
3. Search for and select the correct email template.

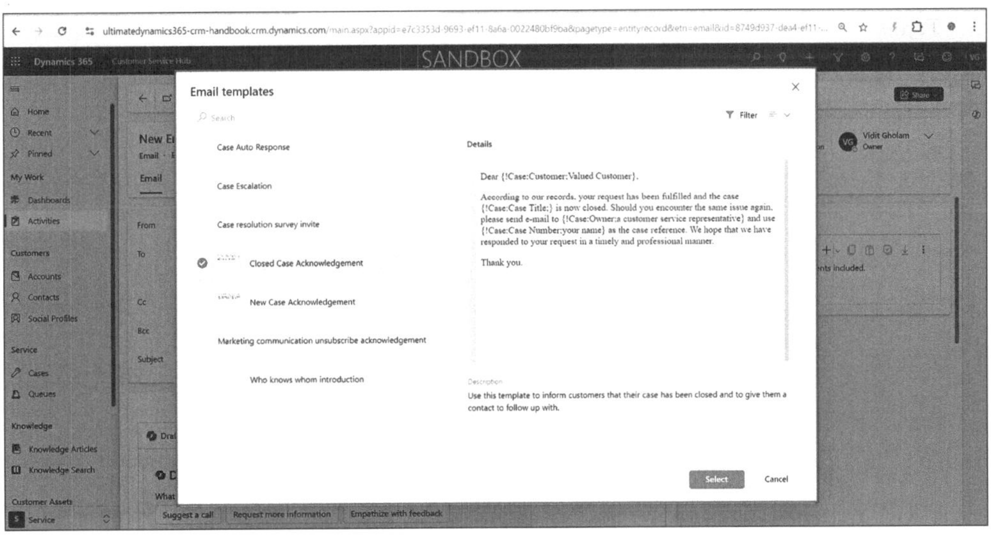

Figure 7.39: *Using an Email Template in Dynamics 365 CRM Customer Service*

4. Import the template content into the email.

While this ensures that your emails are consistent and accurate, it can become a time-consuming process, especially when you need to send a large number of emails.

With the power of Power Automate, sending email templates can be done in just a single click! Instead of manually navigating through multiple steps, you can automate the process for efficiency and ease.

For instance, in this example, the flow is designed as an HTTP-triggered flow, which can be activated through a JavaScript function linked to a button on the case form. Here is how it works:

1. The button is placed directly on the case form, giving users a convenient way to trigger the flow with just one click. (We used a similar approach for generating documents in *Chapter 6, Document Management in Dynamics 365 CRM*. You can check that chapter for the JavaScript example.)

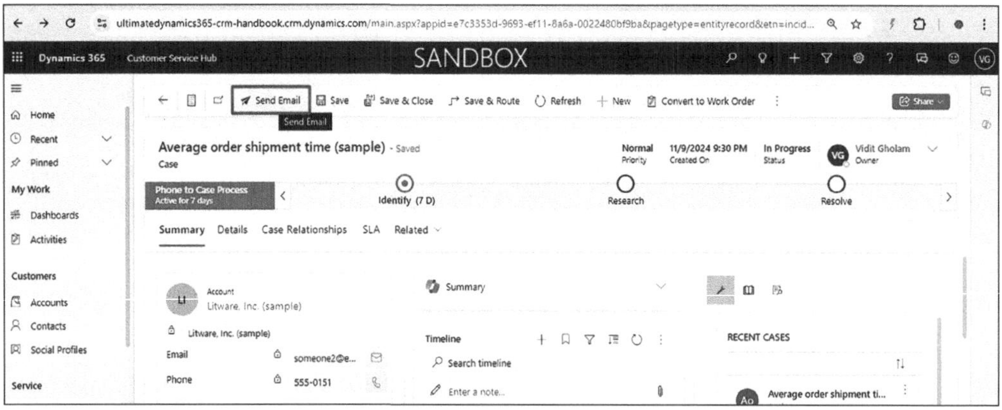

***Figure 7.40:** Send Email Button to Generate and Send Email Templates Automatically*

2. When clicked, the JavaScript function triggers the HTTP request to start the flow.
3. The flow automatically selects the appropriate email template, pulls in the required details, and sends the email seamlessly in the background.
4. To achieve this, pass the GUID of the email template record to the flow.
5. Use the InstantiateTemplate unbound action to generate the email content from the template.

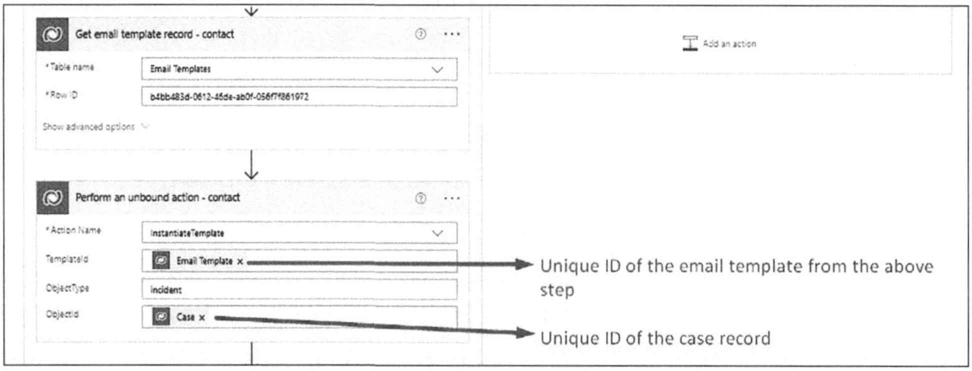

***Figure 7.41:** Power Automate Actions to Process an Email Template*

6. Parse the output of the unbound action using the provided schema.

```
{
    "type": "object",
    "properties": {
        "@@odata.context": {
            "type": "string"
        },
        "value": {
            "type": "array",
            "items": {
                "type": "object",
                "properties": {
                    "@@odata.type": {
                        "type": "string"
                    },
                    "subject": {
                        "type": "string"
                    },
                    "description": {
                        "type": "string"
                    }
                },
                "required": [
                    "@@odata.type",
                    "subject",
                    "description"
                ]
            }
        }
    }
}
```

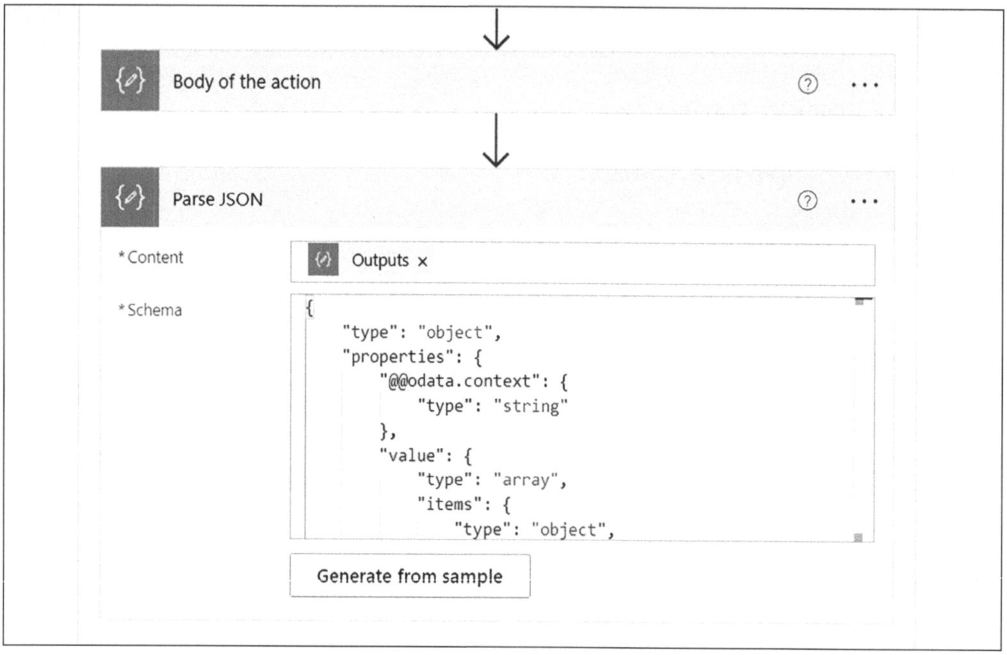

Figure 7.42: *Parsing the Output of the Unbound Action to get the Description and Subject from the Email Template*

7. From the output, retrieve the description (email message content) and subject generated by the template. These can then be used to create a new email record directly within Power Automate.

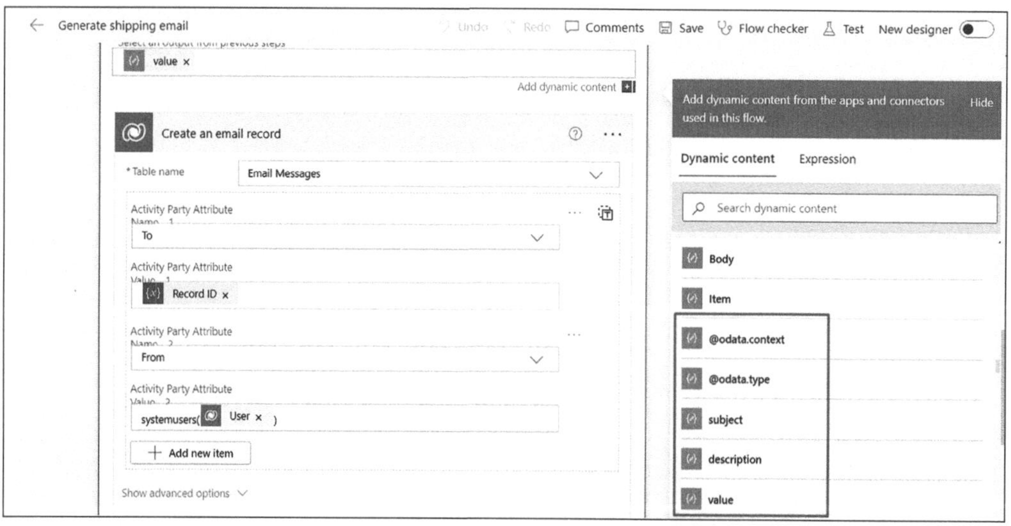

Figure 7.43: *Creating an Email Record from the Parsed Outputs*

This process ensures that email templates are used effectively and automatically without manual intervention.

Conclusion

In this chapter, we explored how to enhance customer service management in Dynamics 365 CRM. From configuring a Power Page Customer Self-Service Portal to automating key processes such as case assignments, notifications, and email templates, we covered tools and techniques that empower both customers and support teams. By implementing these features, organizations can provide faster, more transparent, and more efficient service experiences.

In the next chapter, we will shift our focus to the integration capabilities of Dynamics 365 CRM. We will explore how Dynamics 365 connects with third-party platforms, including financial and marketing systems, using tools such as Azure Integration Services. These integrations enable a seamless flow of data across systems, further expanding the possibilities of CRM for your business.

References

1. Get Started with Power Pages: https://learn.microsoft.com/en-us/training/paths/power-pages-get-started/
2. Convert a Power Page Website: https://learn.microsoft.com/en-us/power-pages/admin/convert-site
3. Get Started with Dynamics 365 CustomerService: https://learn.microsoft.com/en-us/training/modules/get-started-with-dynamics-365-for-customer-service/
4. Create a Shared Mailbox: https://learn.microsoft.com/en-us/microsoft-365/admin/email/create-a-shared-mailbox?view=o365-worldwide
5. Microsoft Learn: https://learn.microsoft.com/

CHAPTER 8
Enhancing Dynamics 365 with Azure Integration Services

Introduction

In today's interconnected world, a system's true potential often lies in its ability to connect smoothly with others. Dynamics 365 CRM is built with robust integration capabilities, allowing businesses to connect it with various applications and platforms. This chapter introduces the main integration options available in Dynamics 365 CRM and shows how it can work hand-in-hand with other essential tools.

We will begin with Azure Integration Services, Microsoft's solution for managing and simplifying complex integrations. Then, we will explore ways to connect Dynamics 365 CRM with key platforms, such as financial and marketing tools, to support and improve everyday business activities. Whether your goal is to enhance collaboration, maintain consistency in customer information, or automate tasks across applications, this chapter will highlight the benefits and possibilities of integrating Dynamics 365 CRM with the tools your organization relies on.

Structure

In this chapter, we will discuss the following topics:

- Introduction to Microsoft Azure
    - Azure Integration Services with a Focus on Azure Functions
    - Creating and Deploying an Azure function
- Integrating Dynamics 365 CRM with Other Platforms

Introduction to Microsoft Azure

Microsoft Azure is a leading cloud computing platform offering a range of services to help businesses build, manage, and deploy applications across the globe. By using Azure, companies can access powerful resources such as virtual machines, data storage, AI tools, and integration services without the need for heavy on-premises infrastructure. Azure's flexibility makes it a popular choice for organizations looking to enhance their digital operations, including integrating with systems such as Dynamics 365 CRM.

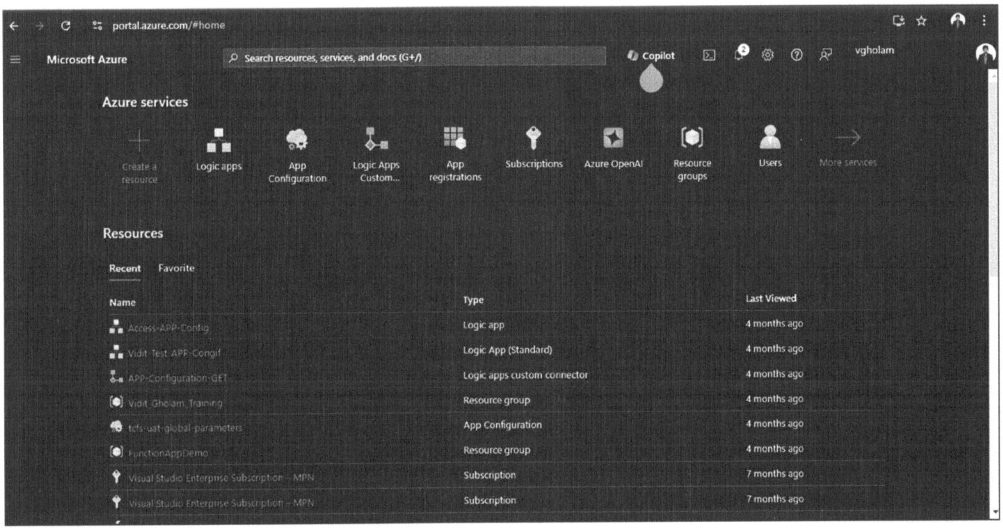

Figure 8.1: *Microsoft Azure Portal*

Getting Started with Microsoft Azure

To start using Azure:

1. **Sign Up for an Azure Account**: Head to the Microsoft Azure website(https://azure.microsoft.com/) to create an account. Azure provides a free trial that includes credits to explore its range of services.

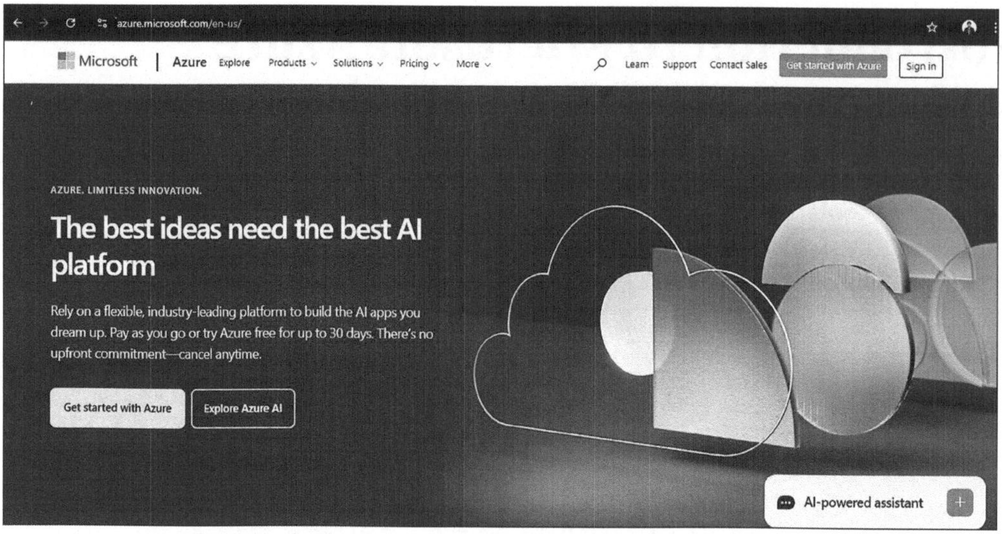

***Figure 8.2**: Microsoft Azure Website*

2. **Explore the Azure Portal**: The Azure Portal is where you can create and manage all resources. Subsequent to logging in, you will find a user-friendly dashboard that simplifies the setup and management of resources.

3. **Leverage Azure Documentation and Learning Resources**: Microsoft offers an extensive library of documentation, tutorials, and learning paths on Microsoft Learn. These guides help you understand everything from basic setups to advanced configurations.

4. **Start with Simple Services**: Begin with basic resources such as storage, databases, or a virtual machine, then move on to advanced services, including those in Azure Integration Services.

Azure Integration Services with a Focus on Azure Functions

When it comes to integrating Dynamics 365 CRM with other applications, Azure Integration Services provides the essential tools. One of the most versatile components in this suite is Azure Functions, which allows you to run small pieces of code (known as "functions") that respond to specific triggers or events. Azure Functions is serverless, meaning you do not need to manage any infrastructure, making it a cost-effective solution for many integration needs.

Here is how Azure Functions fits into integration and automation:

1. **Trigger-Based Automation**: Azure Functions can be triggered by various events, such as changes in a database, a new file upload, or HTTP requests. For

example, when a new lead is added in Dynamics 365 CRM, an Azure Function can be triggered to check the data, enrich it, or pass it to another system.

2. **Processing Data**: Azure Functions is ideal for processing data and performing lightweight transformations earlier than it reaches its final destination. For instance, you might have a function that cleans data received from another platform prior to updating it in Dynamics 365 CRM.
3. **Scalable and Cost-Effective**: Functions only run when triggered, and you only pay for the time the function executes. This makes them efficient and scalable for integration scenarios where resources should be used only when needed.
4. **Integration with Other Azure Tools**: Azure Functions can work seamlessly with other Azure services, such as Azure Logic Apps and Service Bus. Logic Apps can coordinate workflows, while Azure Functions handles specific, custom code as part of those workflows. For instance, a Logic App might trigger an Azure Function to validate customer data in advance of passing it to Dynamics 365 CRM.
5. **Flexible Coding Options**: You can write Azure Functions in various languages such as C#, JavaScript, Python, and more, giving developers the flexibility to work with languages they are comfortable with.

Other Components in Azure Integration Services:

- **Logic Apps**: Designed for workflow automation, Logic Apps let you build workflows visually, connecting Dynamics 365 CRM with other applications without extensive coding.
- **Azure Service Bus**: This messaging service is excellent for reliable communication between applications that operate independently but need to exchange information regularly.
- **Event Grid**: Ideal for real-time event-based integrations, where actions need to be triggered across systems quickly and efficiently.
- **API Management**: Allows you to expose APIs securely for use across various platforms, enabling access to Dynamics 365 CRM data for mobile or web applications.

Azure Functions, together with these other services, provide a flexible and robust foundation for integrating Dynamics 365 CRM with other tools, making it easier to manage and automate cross-platform workflows and processes.

Creating and Deploying an Azure function

Let us learn how to create and deploy an Azure function to create an account in Dynamics 365 CRM.

Create an Azure function project in Visual Studio:

1. Open Visual Studio.
2. Go to **`Create a New Project`**.
3. In the search box, type **`Azure Functions`** and select it from the options.

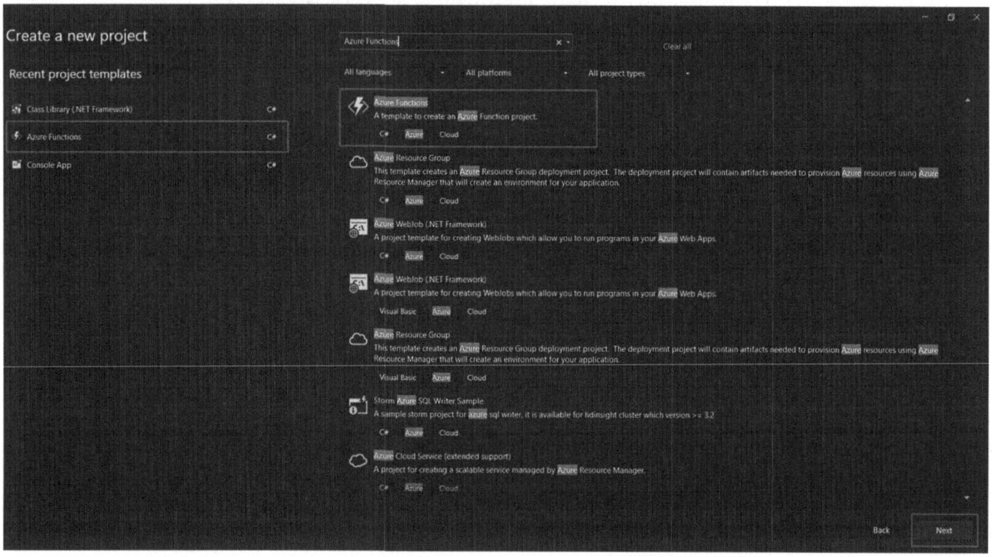

Figure 8.3(a): *Creating an Azure Function Project in Visual Studio*

4. Set the project name and location as desired, then click **`Next`** to continue setting up your **`Azure Functions`** project.

Figure 8.3(b): *Creating an Azure Function Project in Visual Studio*

5. Select the function worker as .NET 8.0 Isolated (Long Term Support). The function would be an HTTP triggered function, choose the access rights function.

6. A Functions Worker is the runtime environment that processes and executes the code in an Azure Function. Essentially, it is the component that listens for events (such as HTTP requests, messages in a queue, or changes in data) and runs the function in response. When you create an Azure Function, you choose a worker runtime (such as .NET, Node.js, Python, and so on) based on the language and platform you want to use.

   For example, when you select .NET Core as the worker for your function, it means the function code will be executed within the .NET Core environment. The worker handles the task of managing the function lifecycle, scaling resources automatically based on the demand, and ensuring the code executes efficiently and securely. This allows you to focus on writing the business logic for your function without worrying about managing servers or infrastructure, as the Functions Worker takes care of the execution behind the scenes.

   If you are creating an Azure Function in .NET, you need to choose a Functions Worker with .NET Core or higher versions of the .NET framework because these versions are cross-platform and support more modern development features, making them more efficient and scalable in the cloud environment.

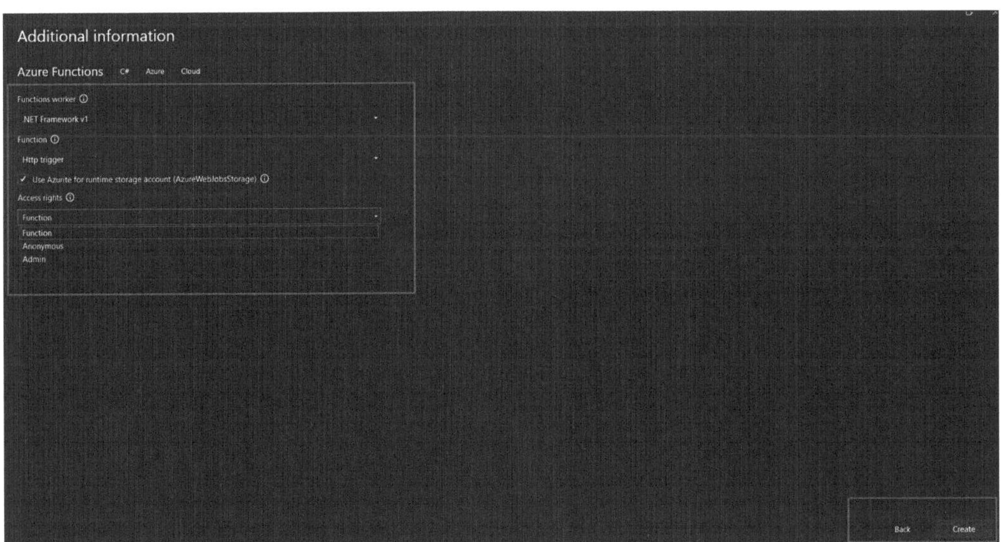

***Figure 8.3(c)**: Creating an Azure Function Project in Visual Studio*

7. Once your Azure Function project is created, you will see a default structure in Solution Explorer.

   a. **`local.settings.json`**: Stores configuration settings for local development.

b. **`Function1.cs` (or your chosen function name):** The main file where you write your function logic.

c. **`host.json`**: Used to configure the function app's settings.

d. **`bin` and `obj` folders**: Contain compiled files and build information.

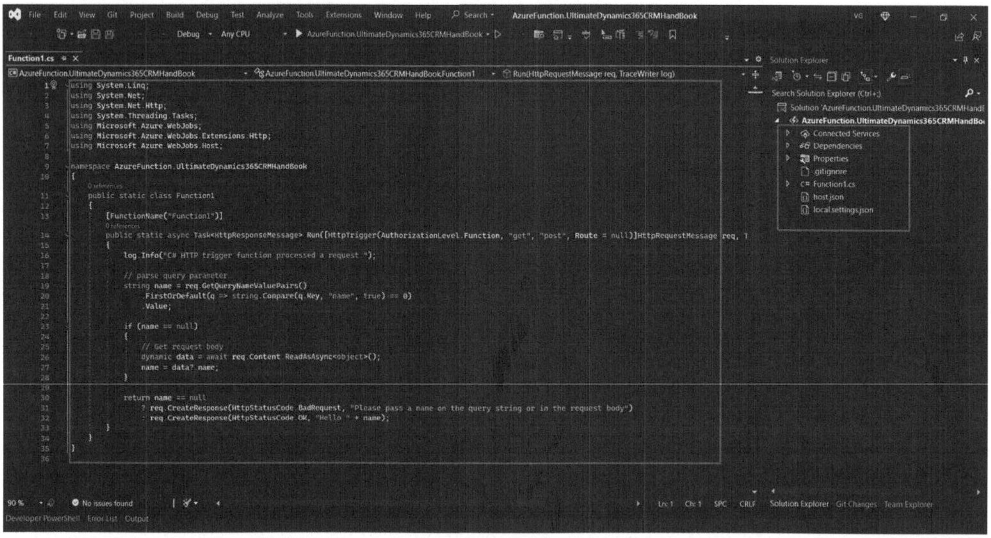

Figure 8.3(d): *Creating an Azure Function Project in Visual Studio*

8. To connect your Azure Function with Dynamics 365 CRM, you will need to add the **`Microsoft.CrmSdk.CoreAssemblies NuGet`** package:

    a. In Solution Explorer, right-click on your project.

    b. Select Manage NuGet Packages.

    c. In the NuGet Package Manager, search for Microsoft.CrmSdk.CoreAssemblies.

    d. Click Install to add it to your project.

    e. This package provides essential Dynamics 365 libraries that enable your function to interact with CRM data directly.

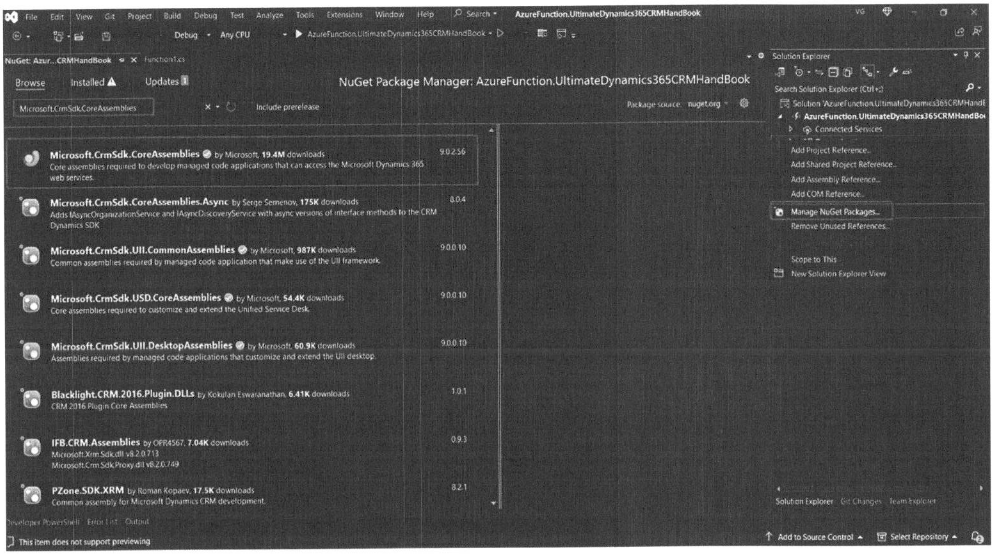

Figure 8.3(e): *Creating an Azure Function Project in Visual Studio*

9. The next step is to connect to Dynamics 365, which involves obtaining the organization's service. This connection can be established in two ways:

   a. **User ID and Password**: For tenants without Multi-Factor Authentication (MFA) enabled.

   b. **Client ID and Client Secret**: For tenants using MFA. The Client ID and secret are obtained from Azure App registration (Service Principal).

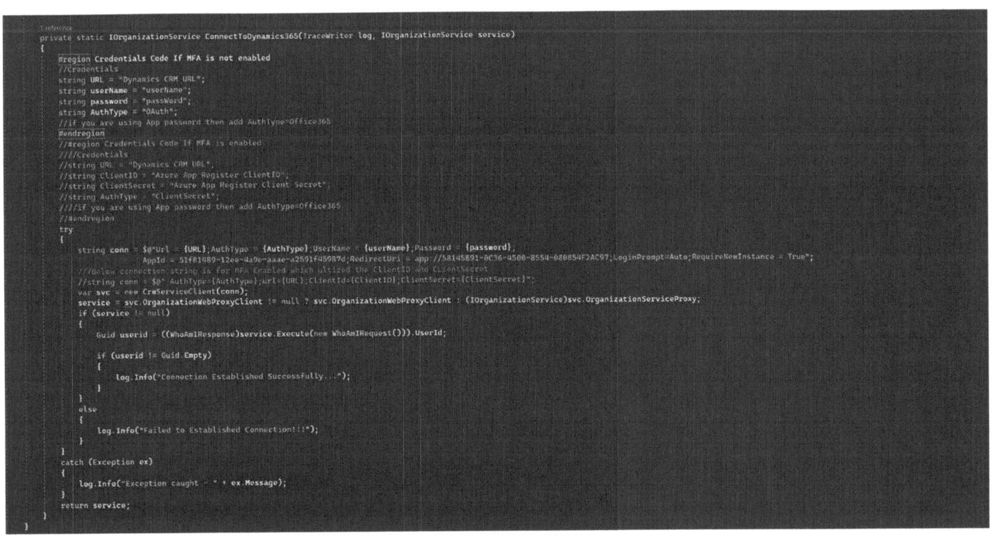

Figure 8.3(f): *Creating an Azure Functions Project in Visual Studio*

10. The code returns service using which we will be creating an account in Dynamics 365.

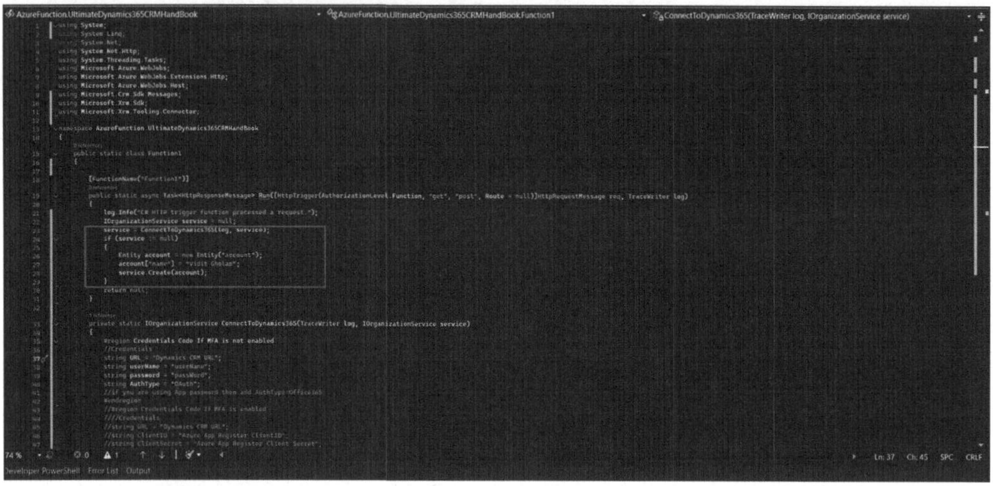

Figure 8.3(g): *Creating an Azure Function Project in Visual Studio*

11. To test the Azure Function locally:

    a. Run the function from Visual Studio. This will launch a local URL.

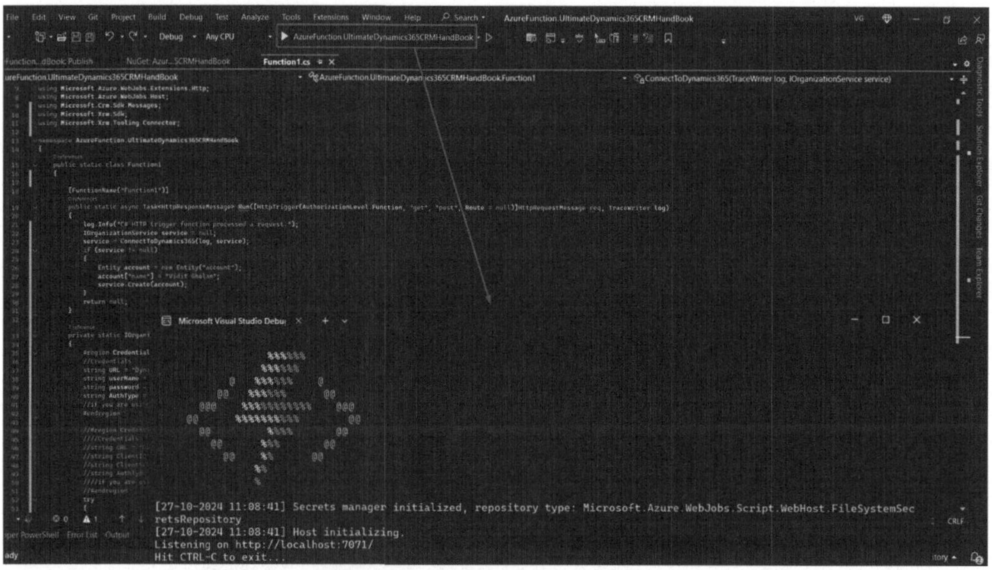

Figure 8.3(h): *Running an Azure Function Locally*

    b. Use Postman to send requests to this local URL.

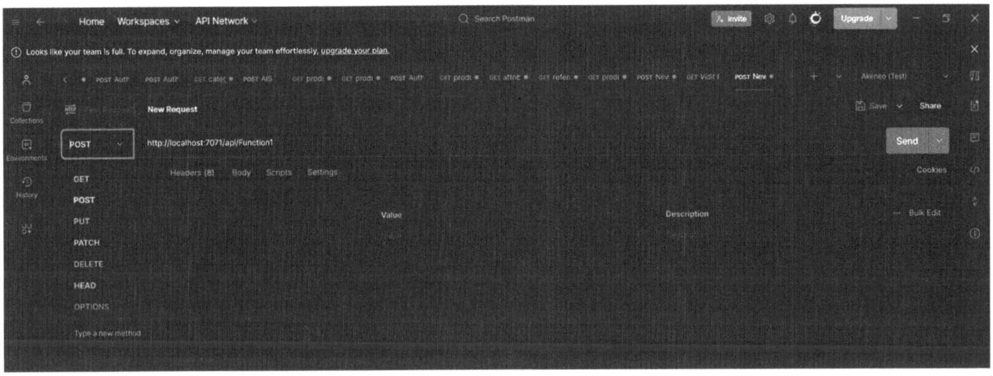

Figure 8.3(i): *Triggering the Azure Function via Postman*

Postman is an API testing tool that simplifies sending requests and viewing responses, making it useful for debugging and testing endpoints such as Azure Functions. To start using it, download Postman from the link in Reference.

c. Once installed, you can send HTTP requests to your function's local URL to verify its performance before deploying it live.

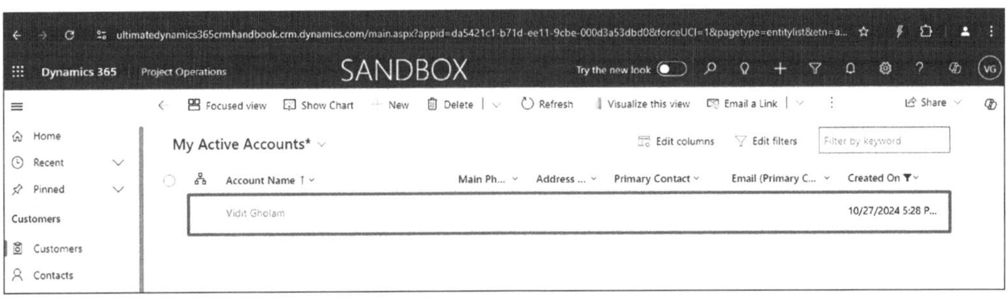

Figure 8.3(j): *Account Created via Azure Function*

You can now debug the function and check for any issues in real-time, adjusting as needed preceding deploying to Azure.

Now that you have created and tested your Azure Function, let us go over how to deploy it to the Azure portal:

1. Make sure you have an active subscription (trial or paid).
2. Go to portal.azure.com, search for **`Function App`**, and create a new app.

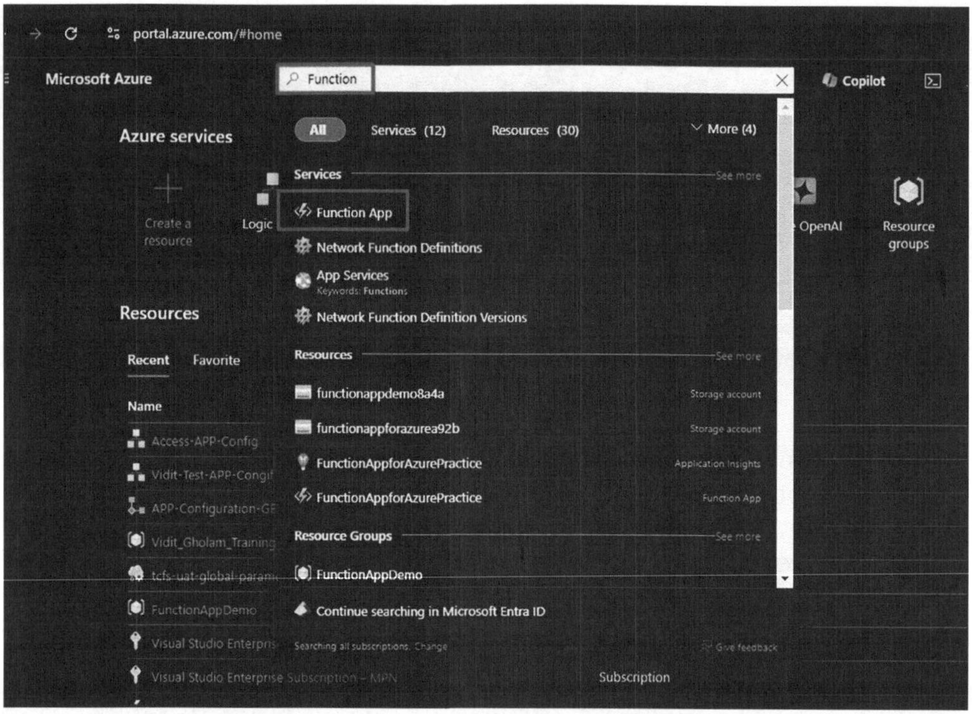

***Figure 8.4(a)**: Deploying Azure Functions on Azure Portal*

3. Select the Consumption Plan (or an alternative) for serverless hosting. This plan scales automatically, with billing based on usage. Other options include:

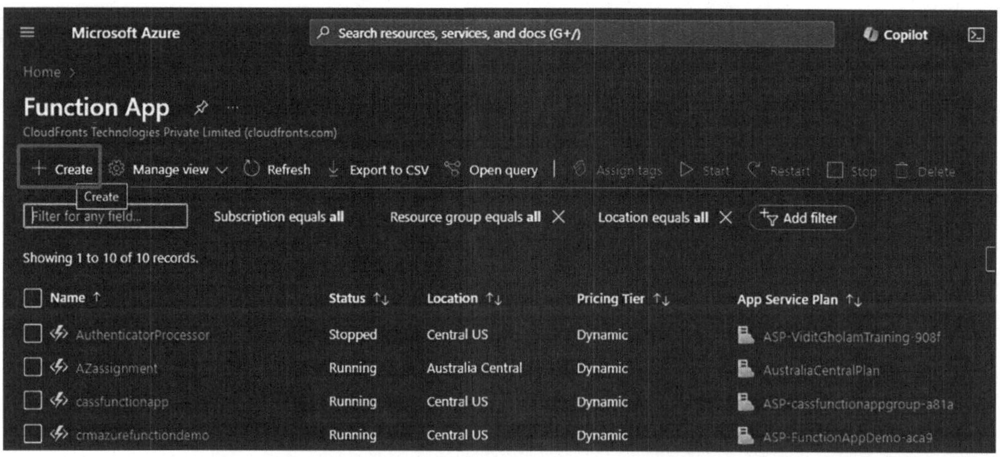

***Figure 8.4(b)**: Deploying Azure Functions on Azure Portal*

   a. **Premium Plan**: Offers advanced scaling, higher performance, and VNET integration.

   b. **Dedicated Plan**: Fixed cost with reserved VMs for predictable workloads.

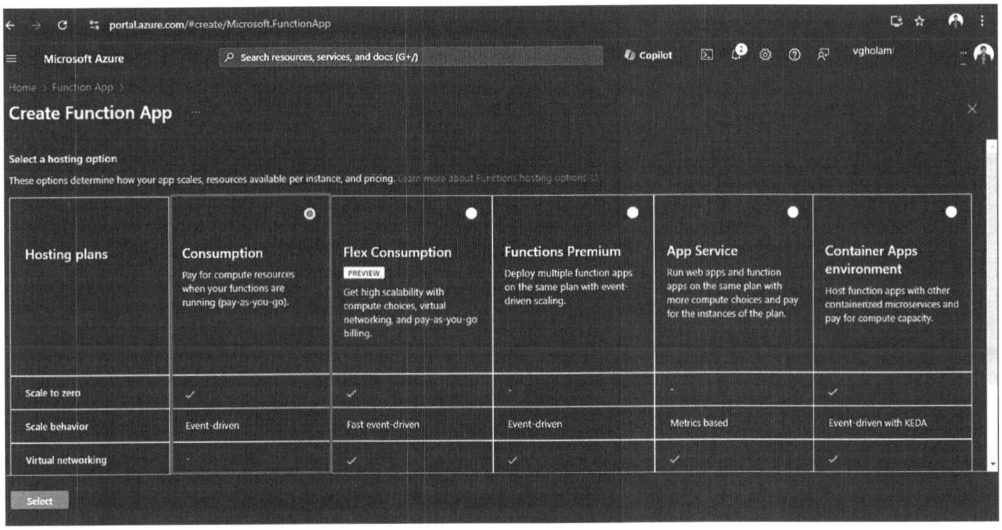

Figure 8.4(c): *Deploying Azure Functions on Azure Portal*

4. Choose an existing Resource Group or create a new one.

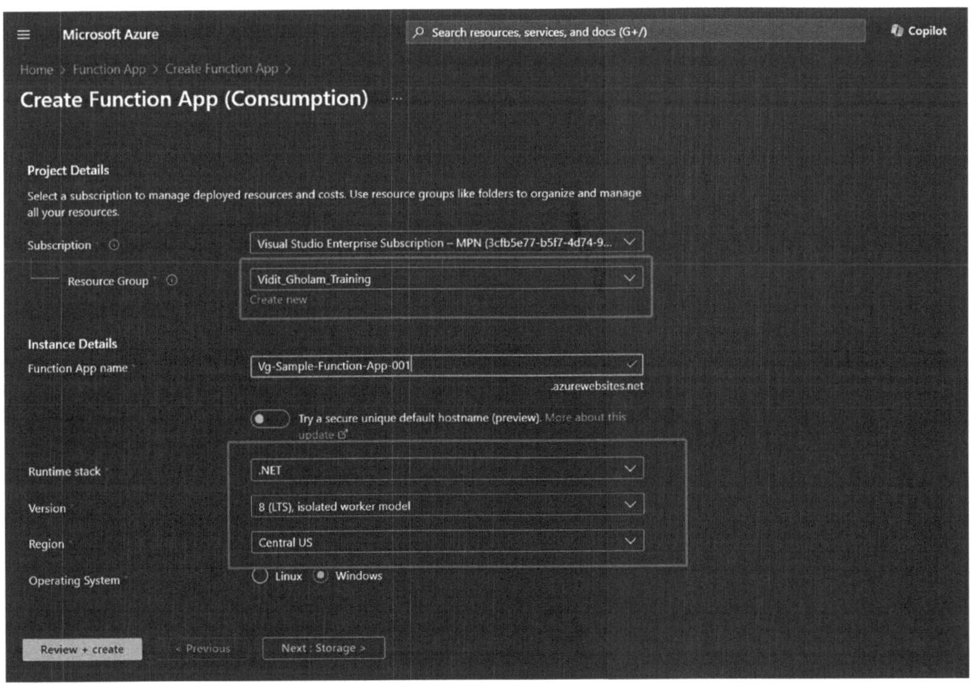

Figure 8.4(d): *Deploying Azure Functions on Azure Portal*

5. Name your function app, select the Runtime Stack (.NET and version), Region, and Operating System, then click **`Review + Create`**.
6. Review the details and create the function.

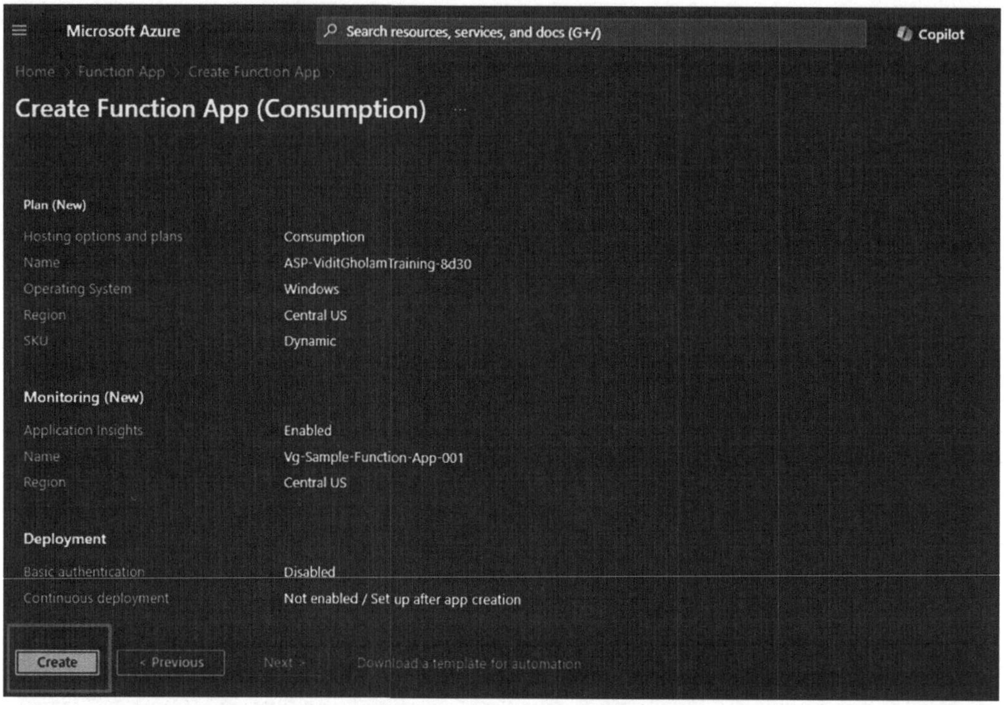

Figure 8.4(e): *Deploying Azure Functions on Azure Portal*

7. Once deployed, you are ready to publish the function from Visual Studio to the cloud.

8. Build the solution to ensure there are no errors.

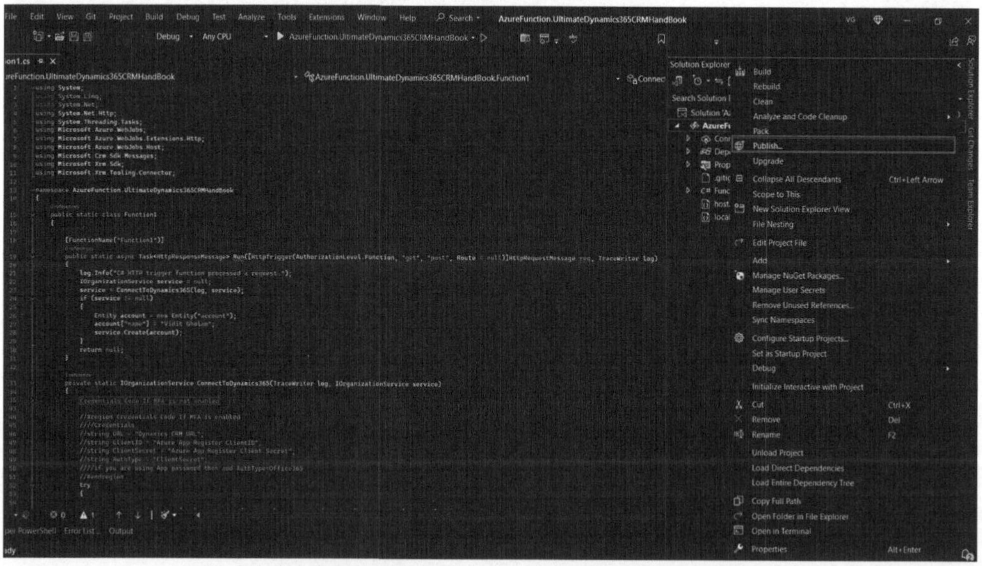

Figure 8.4(f): *Deploying Azure Functions on Azure Portal*

9. Right-click the solution and select **Publish**.
10. In the pop-up, select **Azure** as the target and click **Next**.

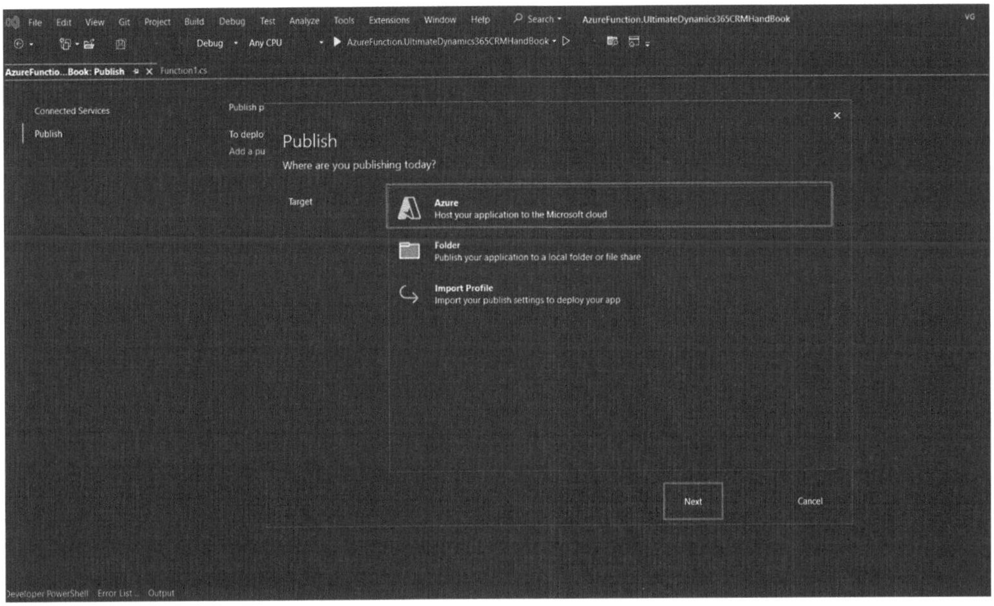

Figure 8.4(g): *Deploying Azure Functions on Azure Portal*

11. Confirm you are signed into Visual Studio with the same account as in Azure; your subscription and function app should be visible.

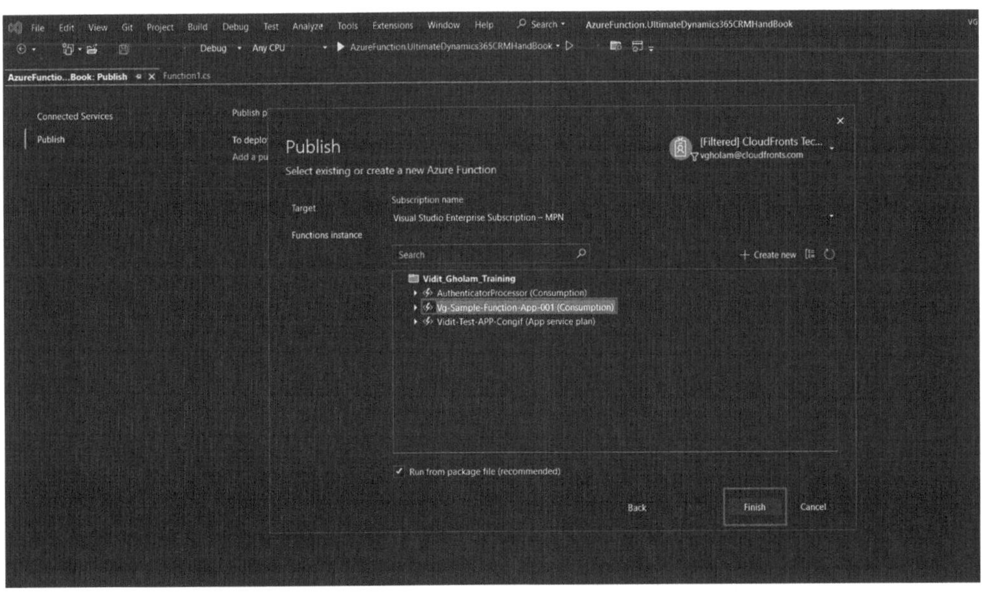

Figure 8.4(h): *Deploying Azure Functions on Azure Portal*

12. Select the **`Function App`** and click **`Publish`**.

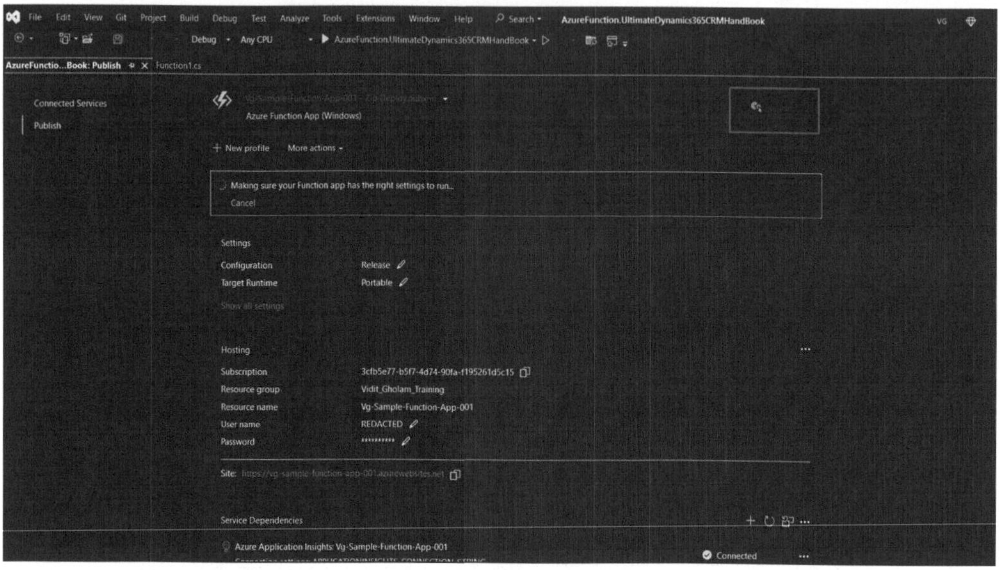

***Figure 8.4(i)**: Deploying Azure Functions on Azure Portal*

13. Subsequent to publishing, go to Functions under your function app in the Azure portal.

14. Open the function with the name you assigned in Visual Studio.

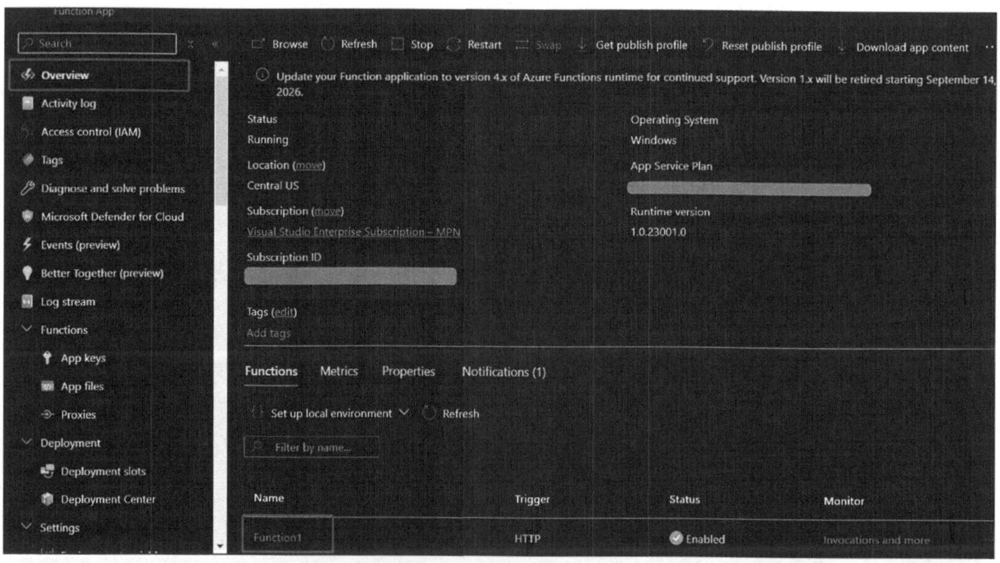

***Figure 8.4(j)**: Deploying Azure Functions on Azure Portal*

15. In the function, you will find URLs for POST, GET, and other requests.

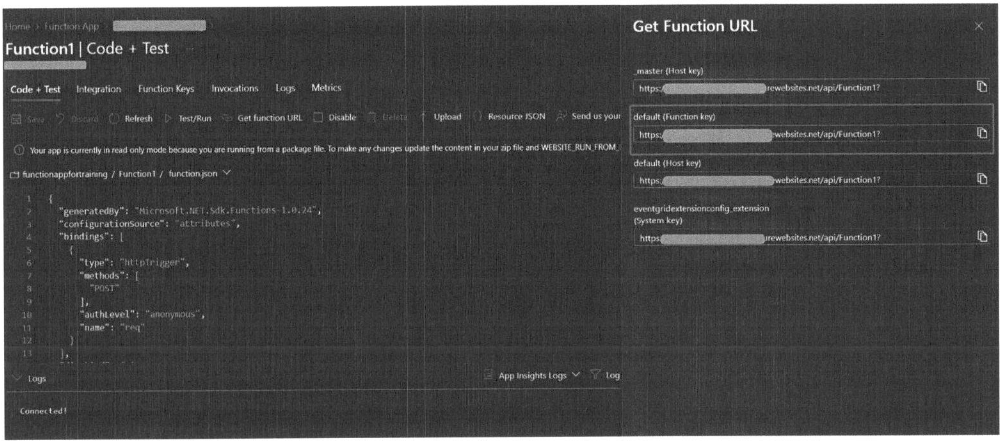

***Figure 8.4(k)**: Deploying Azure Functions on Azure Portal*

In summary, you can deploy an Azure Function using the steps outlined, enabling a scalable and efficient serverless execution. With this foundation in place, we now turn our focus to integrating Dynamics 365 CRM with other platforms, leveraging Azure Integration Services to enhance connectivity and automation.

Integrating Dynamics 365 CRM with Other Platforms

Integrating Dynamics 365 CRM with other platforms helps expand its capabilities across different business areas. For example, connecting with financial platforms enables the syncing of financial data, making invoicing and payments easier. Integrating with marketing platforms supports better customer engagement by automating campaigns, tracking leads, and gathering customer insights. Together, these integrations make it easier for teams to work with customer data in one place, improving efficiency and customer service.

When integrating two platforms, it is essential to clarify a few key points:

- **Source System:** Identify which platform (for example, CRM) will be the source.
- **Target System:** Define the target platform (for example, accounting software such as QuickBooks or Business Central).
- **Data to Sync:** Determine which data should sync, such as accounts, currencies, payment terms, or contacts.
- **APIs and Data Transformation:** Assess available APIs and any necessary data transformations to ensure smooth integration.

Let us explore the integration architecture that uses Dynamics 365 CRM Plugins and Azure Functions for a streamlined workflow. In this setup:

- Plugins within Dynamics 365 CRM can be used to trigger certain actions when data changes, such as creating or updating a record.
- Azure Functions act as scalable microservices that respond to the triggers, from other platforms, executing complex logic or sending data to other platforms as needed.

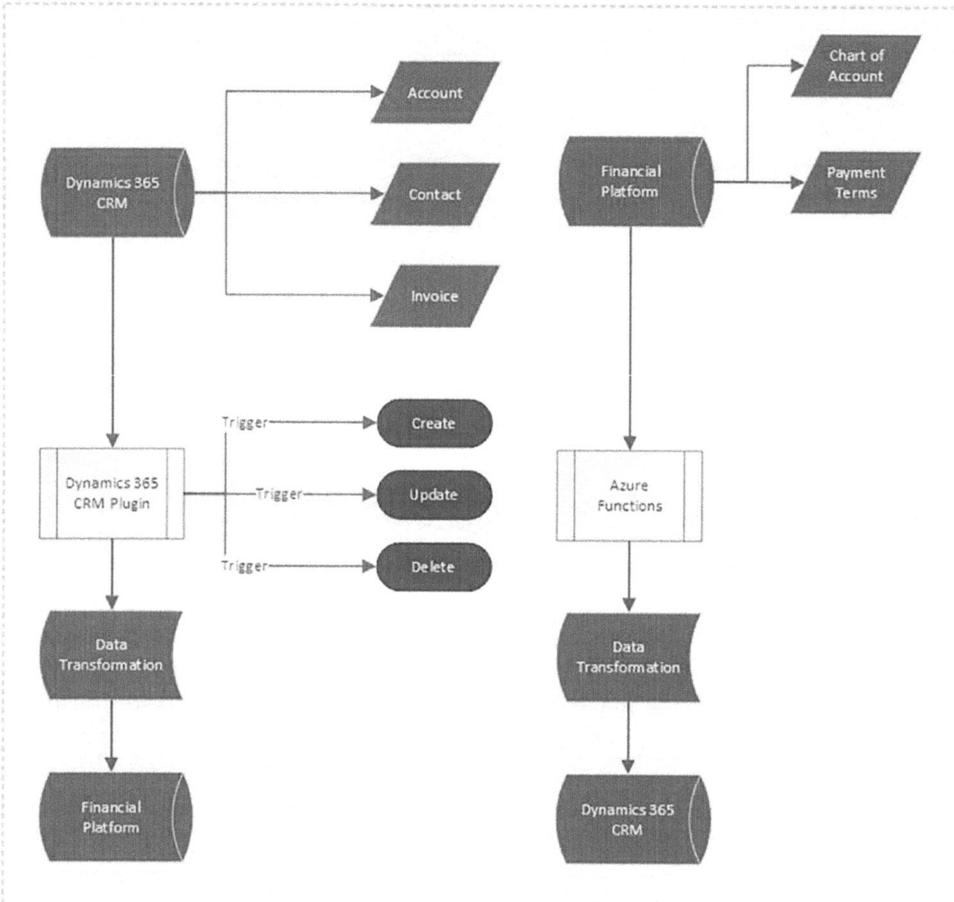

***Figure 8.5**: Integration Architecture D365 CRM to Financial Platforms*

For integrating Dynamics 365 CRM with financial platforms, consider the following steps:

Plugins: D365 CRM to Financial Platforms

1. **Source System**: Dynamics 365 CRM is the source.
2. **Data to Sync**: Accounts, Contacts, and Invoices are transferred from CRM to the financial platform.

3. **Triggering Mechanism**: A plugin is triggered when these records are created, updated, or deleted.
4. **Data Transformation**: The plugin converts records into Data Transfer Objects based on the financial platform's expected payloads.
5. **ID Mapping**: IDs are mapped between systems, such as storing the CRM account ID in the financial platform or vice versa.

Azure Functions: Financial Platform to D365 CRM

Azure Functions can act as an endpoint for Dynamics 365 CRM, accepting data from financial platforms.

- **Webhooks Integration**: Financial platforms that support webhooks can send data directly to an Azure Function via its URL.
- **Data Transformation**: The Azure Function processes and transforms the received data as required by CRM.
- **Creating Records in CRM**: The transformed data can then be used to create or update records, such as accounts, in Dynamics 365 CRM.
- **Master Data Sync**: This approach is ideal for syncing master data such as charts of accounts, currencies, and payment terms, which are often managed within financial platforms.
- **Bidirectional Updates**: Updates can flow both ways, such as marking invoices as paid in CRM when they are paid in the financial platform.

Similarly, for integrating Dynamics 365 CRM with marketing platforms or any other systems, you can utilize a combination of Plugins, Azure Functions, and Power Automate Flows.

- Plugins trigger actions based on events in CRM, such as creating or updating records.
- Azure Functions can receive and transform data from various platforms prior to sending it to CRM.
- Power Automate Flows enable seamless connections and automation between systems, allowing for efficient data synchronization without extensive coding.

It is important to know that Dynamics 365 already provides some powerful, ready-to-use tools that can save businesses time and effort, especially for tasks such as managing finances and automating marketing. Two key applications, Finance and Operations (F&O) and Customer Insights - Journey, are great examples of this. These applications are designed to be easy to use and provide all the features businesses need without having to build anything from scratch, which can be a huge benefit.

Finance and Operations (F&O) is a complete tool for handling financial tasks, such as accounting, inventory, and even manufacturing. It connects smoothly with Dynamics 365 CRM, which means all your customer information can work alongside your financial and operational data. So, if a sale is made in CRM, F&O can automatically handle the related financial processes, saving time and reducing errors. You get a single, integrated system for both front-end customer interactions and back-end financial management.

Customer Insights - Journey, on the other hand, focuses on marketing. It helps businesses understand their customers by collecting data from different places (such as CRM and social media) and then using that information to create personalized marketing campaigns. With Customer Insights, you can automate tasks such as sending emails or running campaigns based on customer behavior, all without needing a complicated custom setup. It works directly with Dynamics 365 CRM, so your marketing team always has up-to-date customer information to create better, more targeted marketing strategies.

Out-of-the-box (OOB) integration options for connecting Dynamics 365 CRM with Finance and Operations (F&O) and Customer Insights - Journey includes powerful tools such as Dual-write, which enables real-time data synchronization between CRM and F&O, ensuring consistency across sales, finance, and operations. The Common Data Service (Dataverse) unifies data across these systems, making it easy to share customer and financial information. Power Automate facilitates workflows, automating tasks between CRM, F&O, and Customer Insights, while the Customer Insights connector helps sync customer data for marketing personalization. Additionally, Azure Logic Apps and Azure Functions provide flexible, cloud-based solutions for integrating these platforms with other services, enhancing automation and data management.

Together, these applications and integration options make it much easier for businesses to manage their operations without needing custom development. They offer a simple, scalable solution that reduces complexity and helps everything run more smoothly, allowing businesses to focus on what matters most–serving customers and growing their business.

Conclusion

This chapter highlighted the integration capabilities of Dynamics 365 CRM, particularly through Microsoft Azure. We discussed how Azure Functions and related services enable seamless data exchange with financial and marketing platforms, enhancing operational efficiency. Understanding these integration methods allows businesses to utilize Dynamics 365 alongside their existing systems effectively.

In the next chapter, we will explore how Dynamics 365 CRM connects with familiar tools such as Microsoft Outlook, improving collaboration and productivity.

References

1. Get Started with Azure Functions: https://lcarn.microsoft.com/en-us/azure/azure-functions/functions-get-started?pivots=programming-language-csharp
2. Azure Function Documentation: https://learn.microsoft.com/en-us/azure/azure-functions/
3. Download Postman: https://www.postman.com/downloads/

CHAPTER 9

Integrating Dynamics 365 CRM to Outlook

Introduction

In this chapter, we will explore how Dynamics 365 CRM integrates with Microsoft Outlook and Teams to improve collaboration among users. By connecting these platforms, teams can enhance their workflows and communication.

We will start by configuring user mailboxes in Dynamics 365 for efficient email management. Then, we will discuss tracking emails through the Dynamics 365 App for Outlook to ensure important messages are recorded. Finally, we will demonstrate how to create emails and appointments directly within the CRM, making it easier for teams to stay organized and productive in their daily tasks.

Structure

In this chapter, we will discuss the following topics:

- User Mailboxes in Dynamics 365 CRM
  - Enable a User's Mailbox in Dynamics 365
- Creating Emails and Appointments in Dynamics 365 CRM
- Outlook Email Tracking Using Dynamics 365 App for Outlook

User Mailboxes in Dynamics 365 CRM

In Dynamics 365 CRM, a user mailbox plays a crucial role in managing email communications directly within the platform. It enables users to send and receive emails, track important interactions, and link emails to specific CRM records, improving overall workflow efficiency. The users can easily manage their correspondence without switching between applications by having their mailboxes integrated. Server-Side Synchronization (SSS) is the feature that makes this mailbox integration possible. It automates the synchronization of emails, appointments, tasks, and contacts between Dynamics 365 and an email server such as Microsoft Exchange, ensuring that communication is consistently updated across both platforms. SSS runs in the background, so users do not need to worry about manually updating records or switching between different systems. Additionally, users can configure personal options to specify what types of data should be synchronized, such as choosing to sync only emails linked to specific CRM records or choosing to exclude certain types of communication. This flexibility allows users to maintain control over their data, ensuring that only relevant information is synchronized while optimizing overall workflow.

Enable a User's Mailbox in Dynamics 365

Follow these steps to enable a user's mailbox in Dynamics 365 easily:

1. **Access Email Configuration**: To enable a user's mailbox, navigate to the **`Settings`** area in the selected environment within the **`Power Platform admin center`**. It is important to note that you can enable a user's mailbox in only one environment at a time within a Dynamics 365 tenant. From there, select **`Email Configuration`** to proceed.

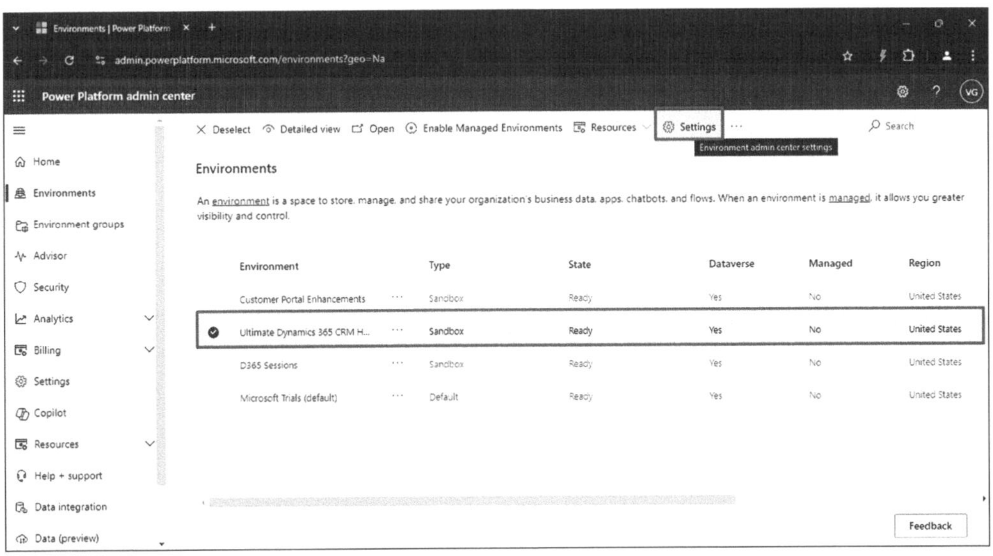

***Figure 9.1**: Enable a user's mailbox in Dynamics 365 – step 1*

2. **Select Mailboxes**: Within the **`Email Configuration`** section, click on **`Mailboxes`** to view the list of available mailboxes associated with users.

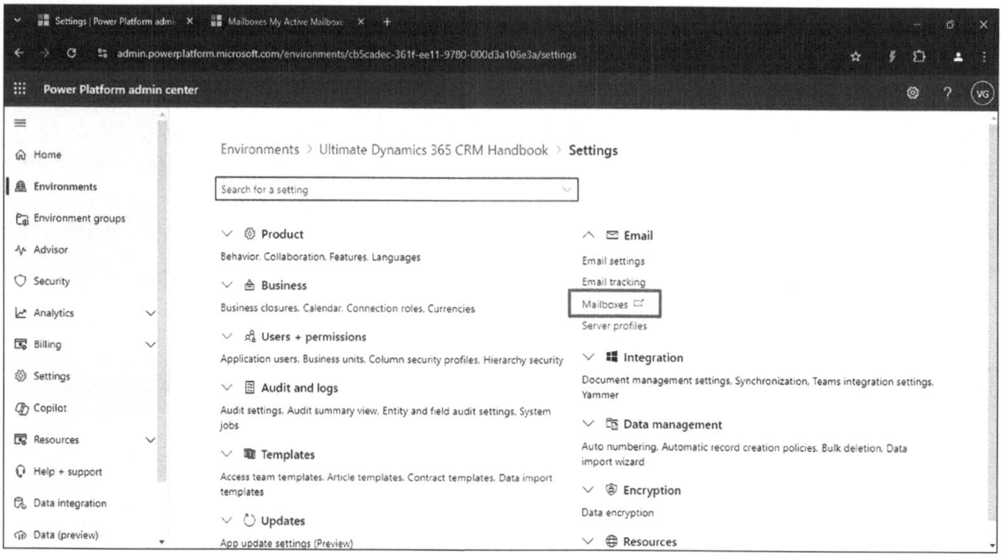

Figure 9.2: *Enable a user's mailbox in Dynamics 365 – step 2*

3. **Locate the User's Mailbox**: Find the mailbox you wish to enable. This might involve searching for the user's name or scrolling through the list.

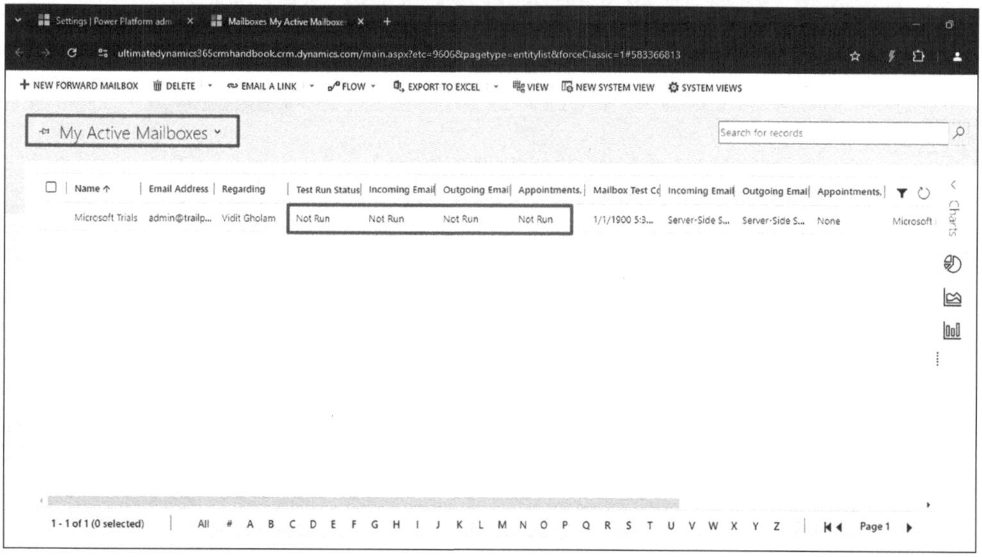

Figure 9.3: *Enable a user's mailbox in Dynamics 365– step 3*

4. **Edit Mailbox Settings**: Open the mailbox record for the selected user. Here, you will see various settings that control how email is handled.

5. **Set Incoming and Outgoing Email Options**: Configure the **`Incoming Email`** and **`Outgoing Email`** options according to your organization's requirements.

This may include specifying the email server settings and authentication methods.

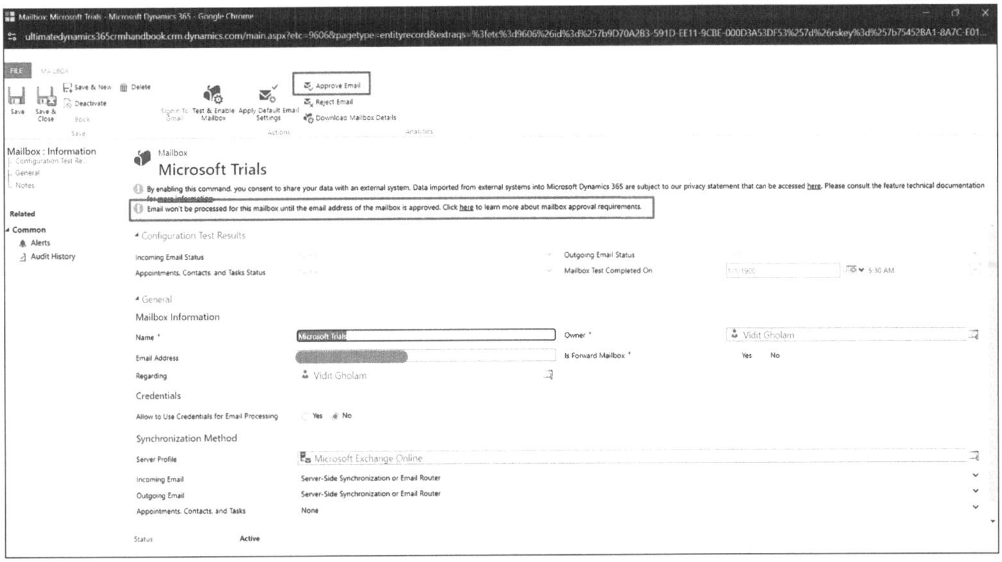

Figure 9.4: *Enable a user's mailbox in Dynamics 365 – step 4*

When enabling server-side synchronization (SSS) for a user mailbox in Dynamics 365, several options can be configured on the mailbox settings tab. Here is a breakdown of some of the important option.

a. **Email Server Profile**: This defines the connection between Dynamics 365 and the email server (for example, Microsoft Exchange). It specifies the server settings and authentication method used for email synchronization. This is important for ensuring that the system can securely communicate with the mail server.

b. **Incoming Email**: This option controls the synchronization of incoming emails from the user's mailbox to Dynamics 365. When enabled, emails sent to the user are automatically captured and associated with the relevant CRM records, such as contacts or cases.

c. **Outgoing Email**: This setting manages the synchronization of emails sent from Dynamics 365. It ensures that emails created within the CRM (for example, via case management or sales) are sent through the configured email server and recorded properly within the system.

d. **Appointment Synchronization**: This option enables the synchronization of calendar appointments between the user's Dynamics 365 account and their email server (for example, Outlook). Any scheduled meetings or appointments will be automatically synced, ensuring they appear in both systems.

6. **Approve the Mailbox**: To enable the mailbox for use, click the **`Approve Email`** button. This step is necessary to confirm that the mailbox is set up correctly and is ready for use in Dynamics 365.

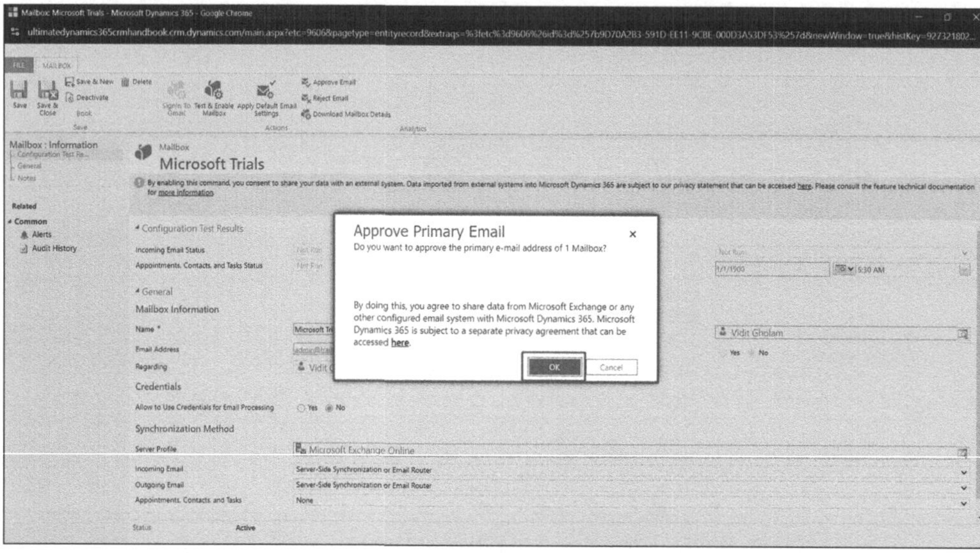

***Figure 9.5**: Enable a user's mailbox in Dynamics 365– step 5*

7. **Test the Configuration**: After approval, it is a good practice to test the mailbox functionality. Send a test email from Dynamics 365 to ensure that emails are being sent and received properly.

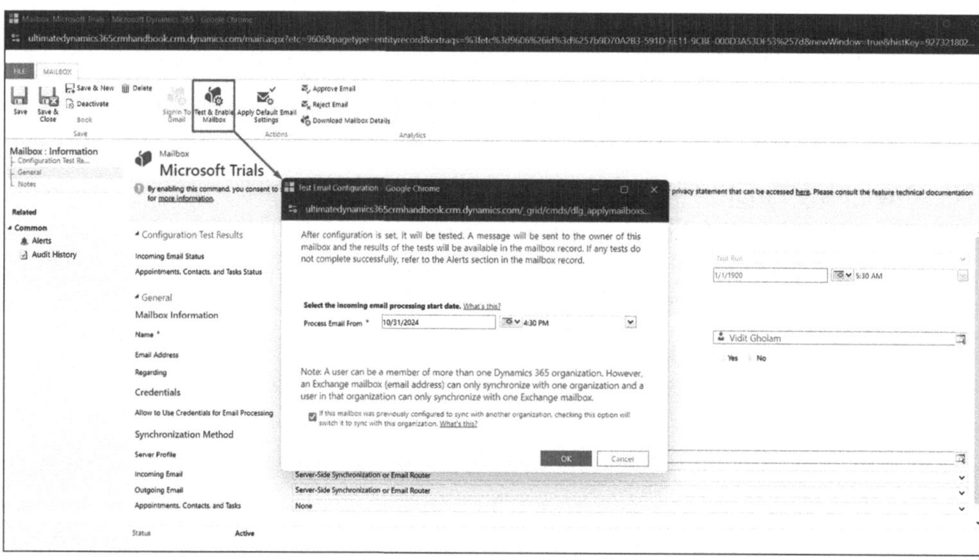

***Figure 9.6**: Enable a user's mailbox in Dynamics 365– step 6*

8. Once you have tested and enabled the mailbox, the status of incoming and

outgoing emails will change to **Success** from **Not Run**. If the mailbox is not enabled properly, then you will receive an alert message in the alert section, and the status for both incoming and outgoing emails will show as **Failed**. This feedback helps ensure that the mailbox is configured correctly and functioning as intended.

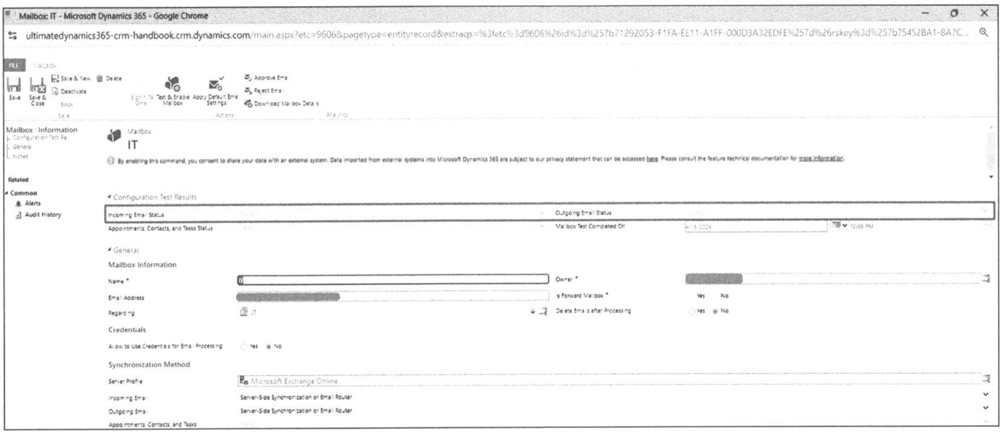

***Figure 9.7**: Enable a user's mailbox in Dynamics 365- step 7*

Creating Emails and Appointments in Dynamics 365 CRM

Now that mailboxes are enabled, let us see how to create and send emails and appointments from Dynamics 365 CRM. Emails and appointments are activity-type entities in Dynamics 365 and are available in the timeline section for many standard entities, such as accounts, contacts, cases, and invoices.

To send an email, select the Email activity from the entity's timeline, draft your message, add recipients (such as a customer or customer contact), and send it directly.

Let us walk through an example using the Case entity.

1. On the **Timeline** of a Case record, click the **Add** button and select **Email**.

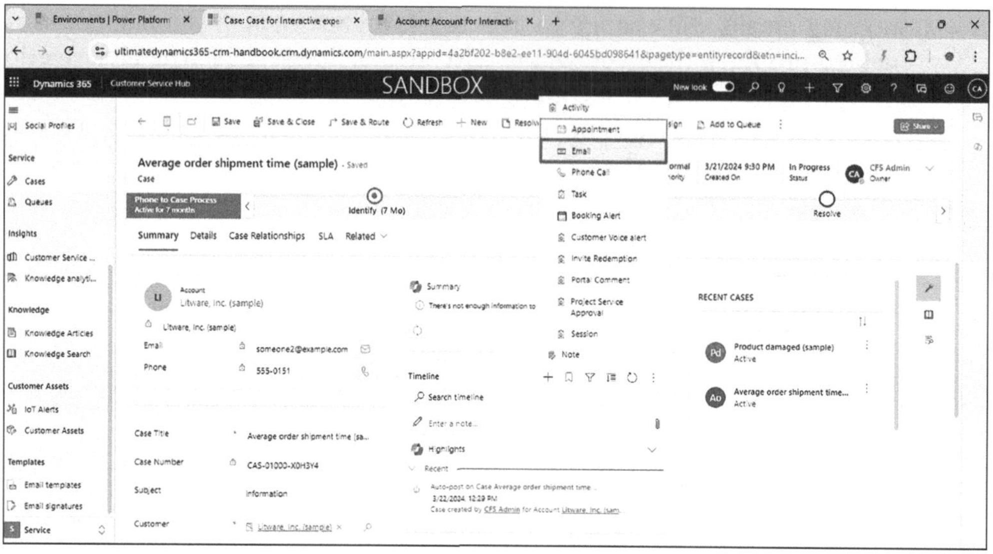

Figure 9.8: *Create an Email Record from the Timeline on a Case form*

2. This opens a new email record. Here, the **From** field automatically shows the owner of the **Case**, while the **To** field displays the customer linked to the **Case**.

3. You can adjust the **From** field by choosing from available entity options, as shown in *Figure* 9.9.

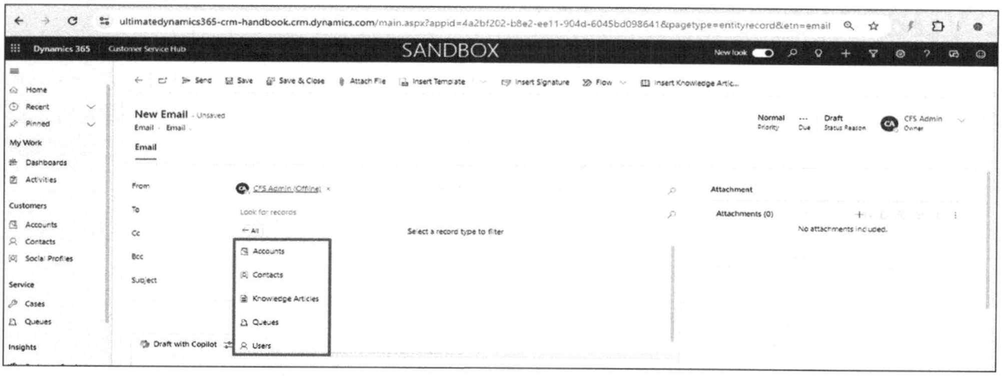

Figure 9.9: *Available to parties on the email record*

4. The email will initially be in **Draft** status. Add your email content in the body section or select an email template if you have one ready (we covered creating templates in *Chapter 7, Customer Service Management in Dynamics 365 CRM*). Once your message is prepared, simply click the **Send** button to deliver the email.

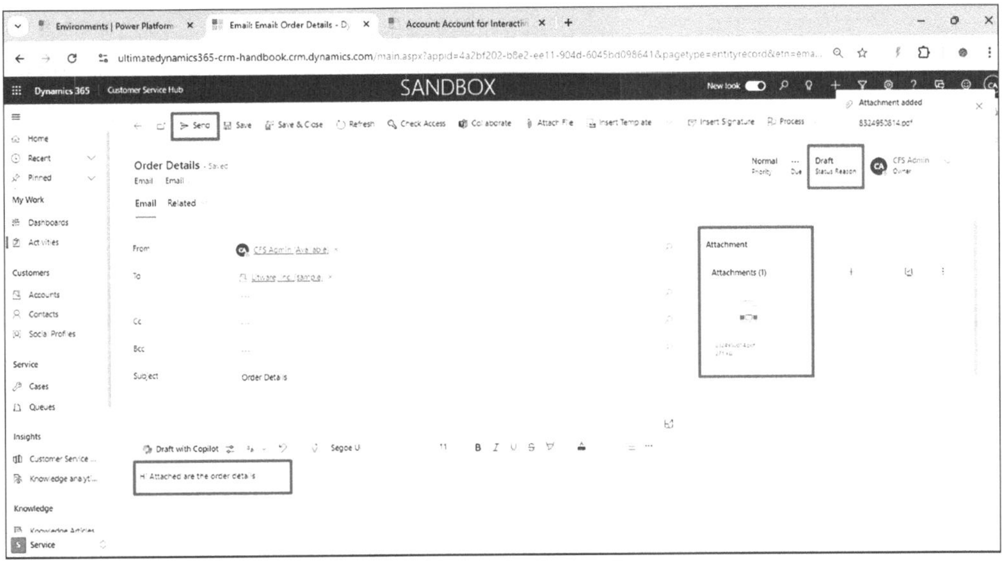

Figure 9.10: *Creating a draft email in Dynamics 365 CRM*

5. The email is sent in the context of the user listed in the **From** field of the email record.
6. If the user's mailbox is not properly configured, an alert will appear, and the email status will display as **Pending Send**.

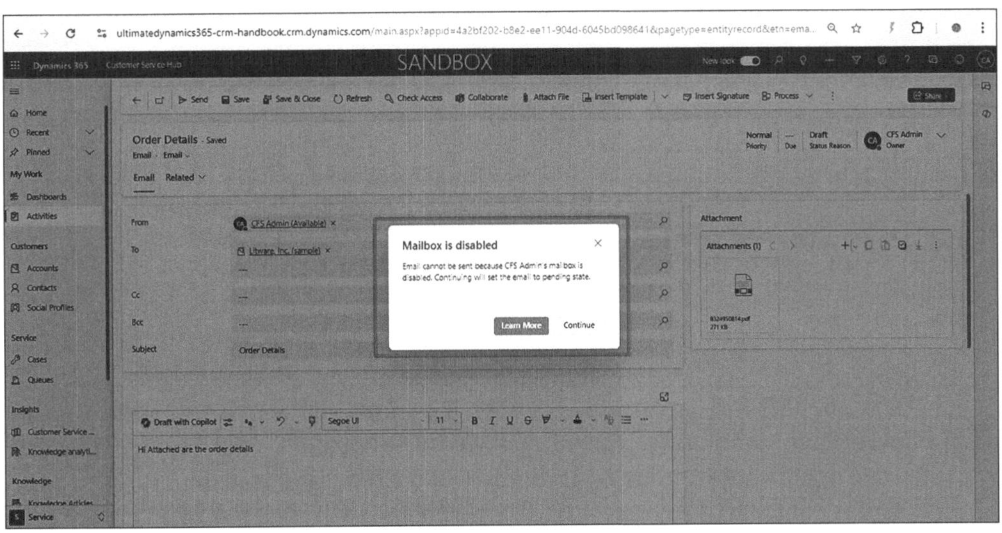

Figure 9.11: *Emails with pending sent status*

7. This email will remain in pending status until the mailbox is correctly configured. Once resolved, the email will be sent automatically.

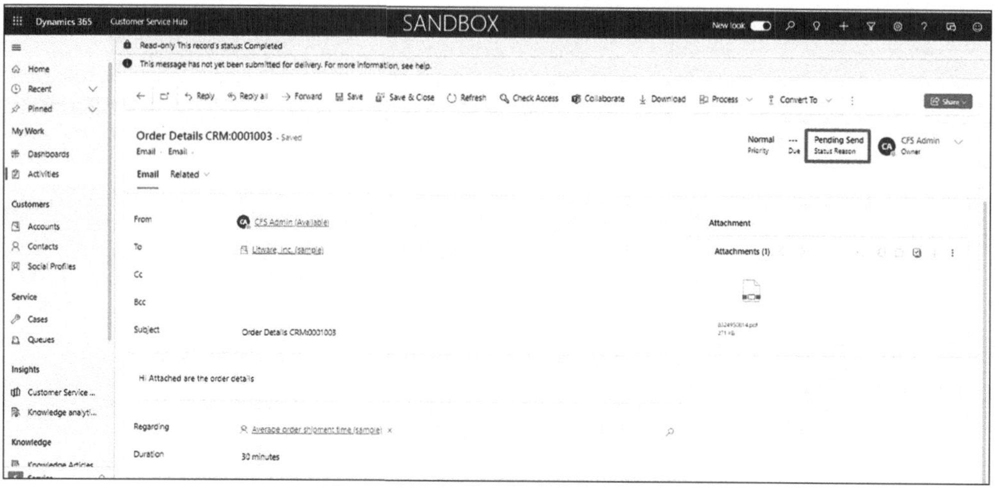

Figure 9.12: *Emails with pending sent status*

8. Pending emails can be sent at any time once the configuration issue is fixed.

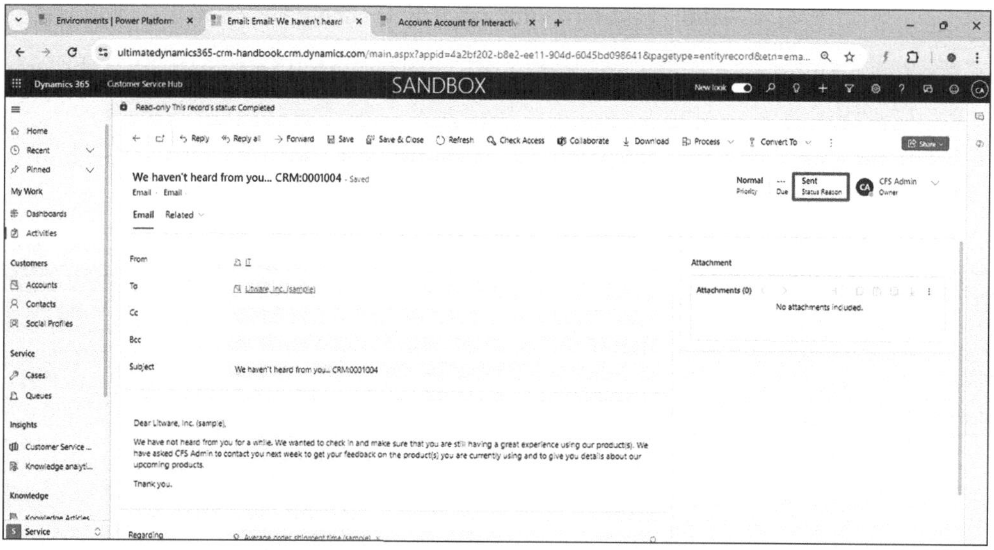

Figure 9.13: *Emails with sent status*

9. All email activities are tracked in the Timeline of the Case record. You may notice that a tracking number, such as "**`CRM:0001004`**," is automatically added to the email's subject line by Dynamics 365 CRM. This tracking number allows CRM to automatically associate any replies with this number back to the original Case record, keeping the entire communication history organized and visible within the **`Timeline`**.

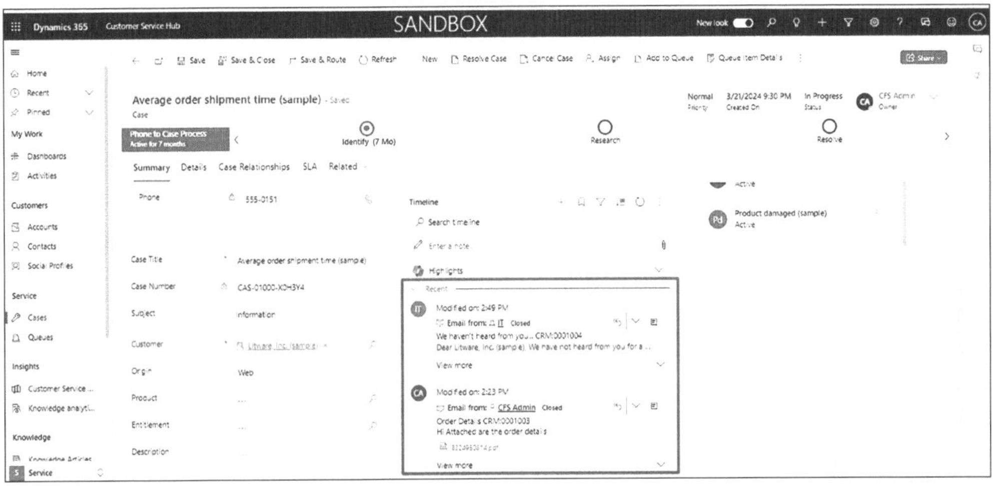

Figure 9.14: *Emails tracked on the timeline of the case entity*

10. This feature ensures continuity in tracking interactions related to specific records.

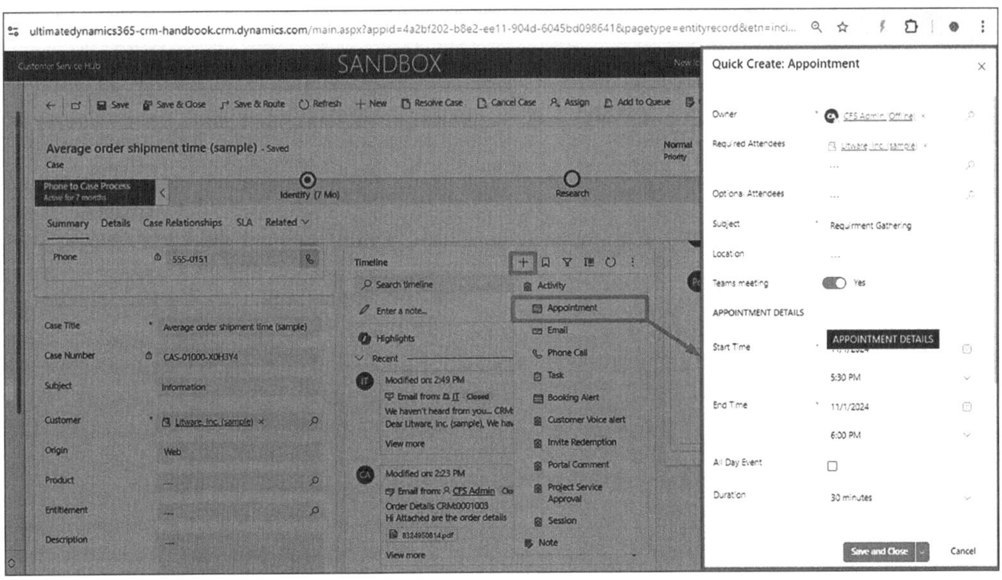

Figure 9.15: *Creating Appointments in Dynamics 365 CRM*

11. Similarly, Appointments can be created directly from an entity's Timeline, and they will automatically sync to the user's **`Outlook`** calendar. This keeps schedules aligned, as appointments created in Dynamics 365 appear in Outlook without manual entry, coordinating and keeping all activities easily accessible within both platforms.

Outlook Email Tracking Using Dynamics 365 App for Outlook

The Dynamics 365 App for Outlook is an integration tool that connects your Dynamics 365 CRM system with Microsoft Outlook, enabling you to view and interact with CRM data directly within the Outlook interface. By installing this app, users can track emails, schedule appointments, and view relevant CRM records such as contacts, leads, opportunities, and cases right from their Outlook inbox.

The main purpose of this app is to bridge the gap between Outlook and Dynamics 365, ensuring that all communications and activities related to CRM records are captured without needing to switch between different applications. With the Dynamics 365 App for Outlook, users can easily track emails, log interactions, and even create new records in Dynamics 365 directly from their Outlook interface.

To enable the Dynamics 365 App for Outlook add-in, simply assign the "*Dynamics 365 App for Outlook User*" security role to the user in Dynamics 365 CRM.

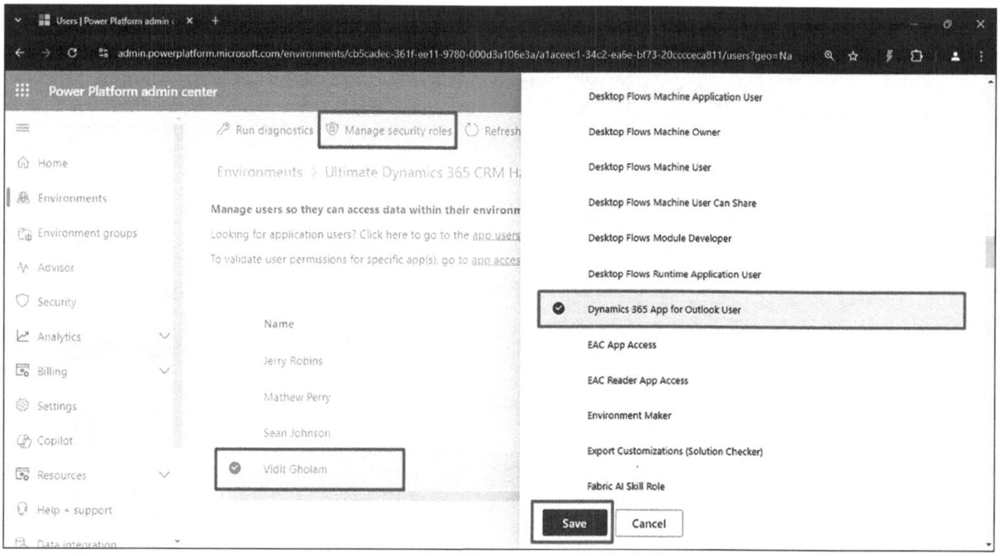

Figure 9.16: *Dynamics 365 CRM App for Outlook User Security Role Assignment*

Within a few minutes, the add-in will appear in the user's Outlook add-in list, making it available for tracking and managing CRM activities from Outlook.

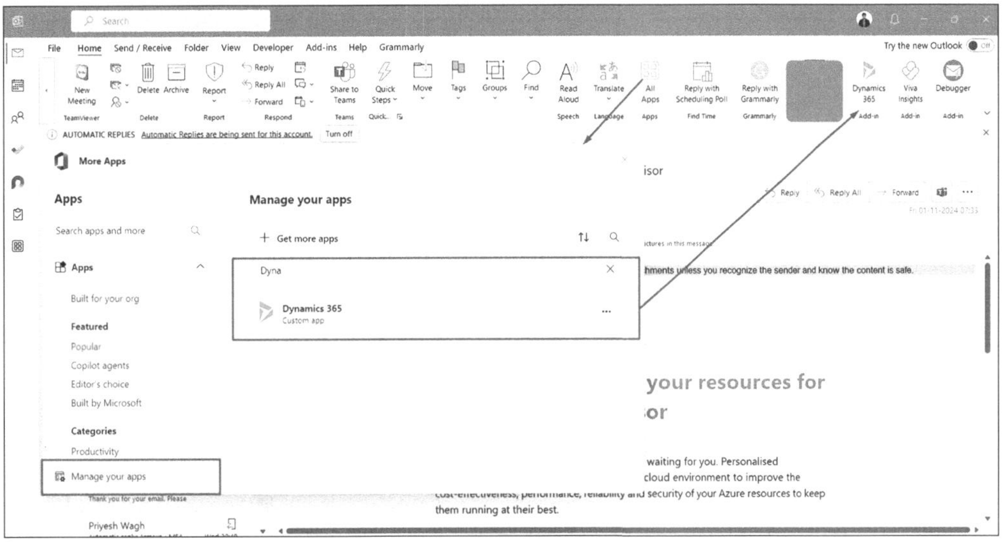

Figure 9.17: *Dynamics 365 App for Outlook*

Figure 9.17 shows the Dynamics 365 App for Outlook add-in. Once this add-in is added, you can easily track any email related to any Dynamics 365 record. Here is how to do it:

1. **Open the Email:** Select the email you wish to track in Outlook.
2. **Launch the App:** Click the `Dynamics 365` icon in the Outlook ribbon.

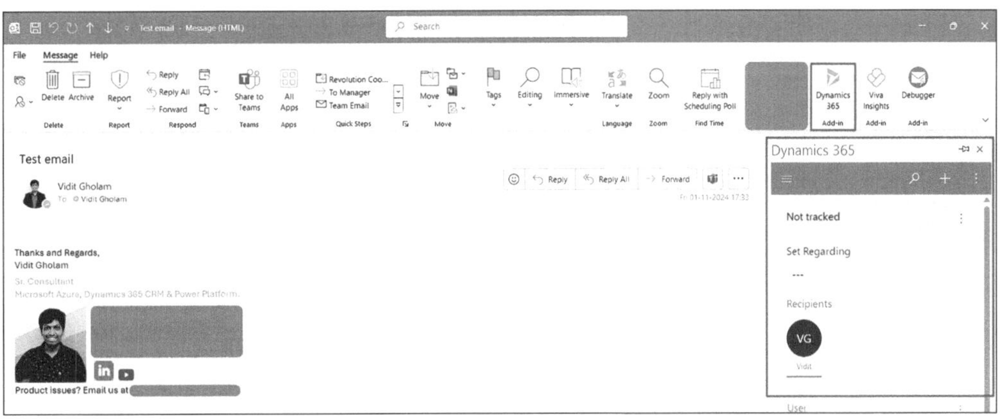

Figure 9.18: *Launching Dynamics 365 App for Outlook add-in*

3. **Track the Email:** Choose the relevant record to associate with the email.

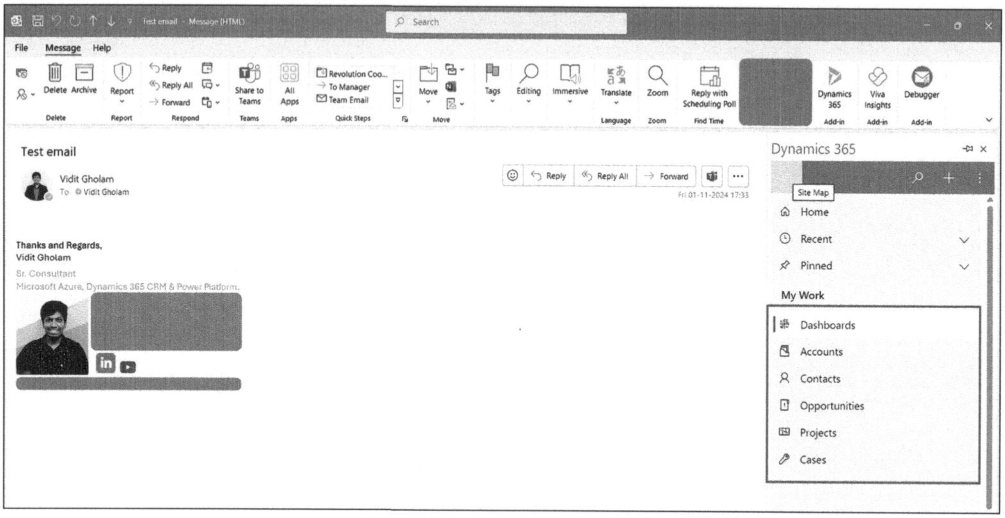

Figure 9.19: *Site map of the Dynamics 365 App for Outlook add-in*

4. **Set Regarding:** Click **`Set Regarding`** button to complete the tracking process.

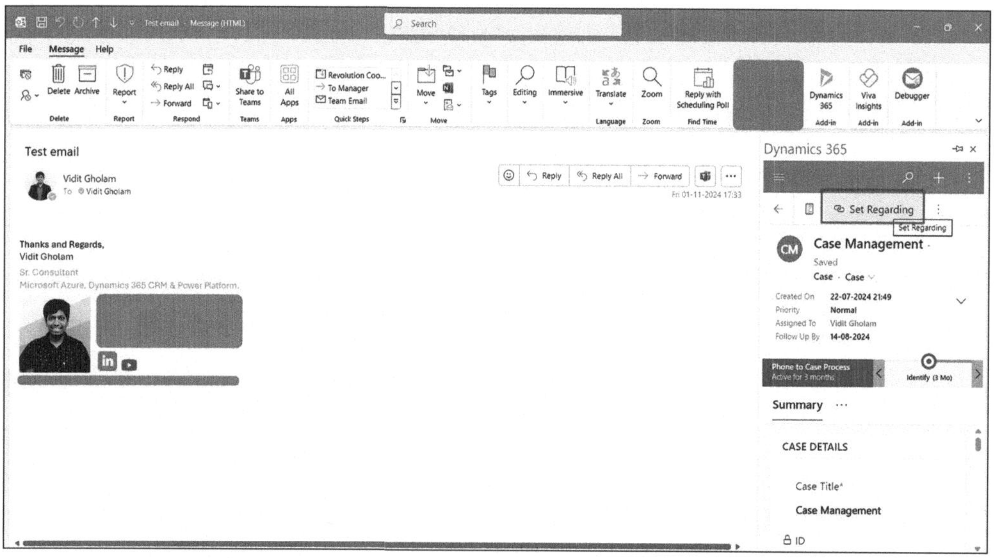

Figure 9.20: *Tracking Outlook emails using Dynamics 365 App for Outlook add-in*

5. The email will be tracked on the timeline of the corresponding Dynamics 365 record. This keeps all communications organized and easy to find, allowing users to see all interactions related to a specific record in one place.

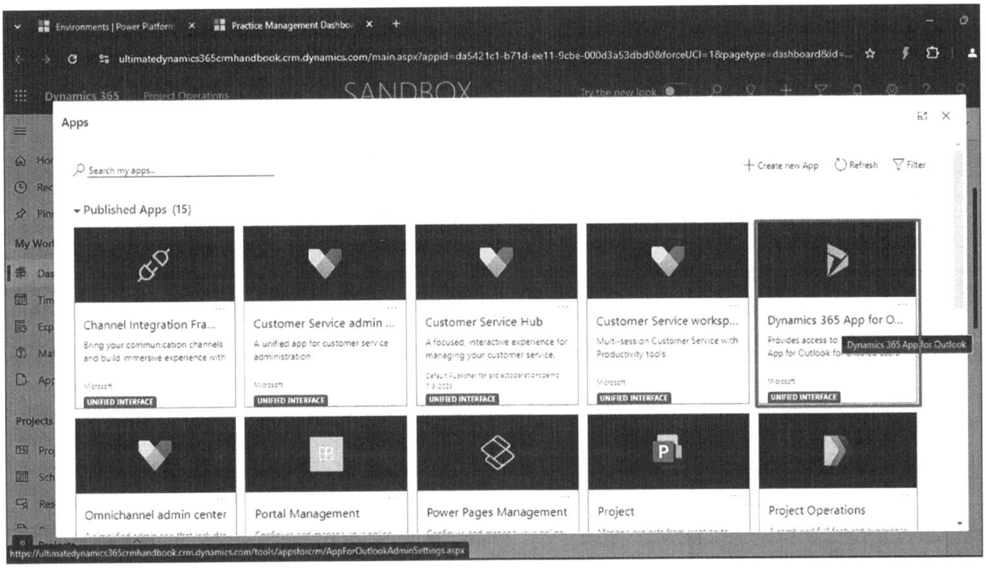

Figure 9.21: *Dynamics 365 App for Outlook Model Driven App*

6. Dynamics 365 App for Outlook add-in shows a Model Driven App, so you can customize the entities, forms, and views from the model- driven app as shown in *Figure 9.21*.

Conclusion

In this chapter, we explored the functionality of user mailboxes within Dynamics 365 CRM, including how to enable them and create emails and appointments. We also discussed the integration with Outlook through the Dynamics 365 App, allowing for easy email tracking. This understanding enhances communication management within Dynamics 365, enabling users to keep all interactions organized and accessible. As we move forward, we will look into the AI Copilot capabilities available in Dynamics 365 CRM, further improving user experience and efficiency.

References

1. Connect to Exchange Online: https://learn.microsoft.com/en-us/power-platform/admin/connect-exchange-online
2. Mailbox requires an approval by an Office 365 administrator alerts occur after selecting Test & Enable Mailbox: https://learn.microsoft.com/en-us/previous-versions/troubleshoot/dynamics/crm/alerts-about-mailbox-requires-approval-by-office-365-administrator
3. Overview of Dynamics 365 App for Outlook: https://learn.microsoft.com/en-us/dynamics365/outlook-app/overview

CHAPTER 10
AI Copilot Capabilities in Dynamics 365 CRM

Introduction

In this chapter, we will explore the AI Copilot capabilities available within Dynamics 365 CRM. This innovative tool is designed to enhance productivity across various functions, including Sales, Project Operations, and Customer Service.

We will begin with instructions on setting up Copilot for each of these functions, followed by an overview of its key features and benefits. Copilot can provide valuable insights, assist with decision-making, and automate repetitive tasks, making daily operations easier. Additionally, we will discuss how Copilot can be utilized for Sales tasks directly within Outlook, allowing users to access important information right from their inbox. This chapter aims to equip you with the knowledge to effectively use AI Copilot to improve your workflow and the overall customer experience in Dynamics 365 CRM.

Structure

In this chapter, we will discuss the following topics:

- Copilot in Microsoft Dynamics 365 CRM
- Setup Copilot for Sales, Project Operations, and Customer Service
- Copilot Capabilities in Dynamics 365 CRM
- Using Copilot for Sales in Outlook

Copilot in Microsoft Dynamics 365 CRM

As the name suggests, Copilot in Dynamics 365 CRM is designed to work alongside you, assisting with daily tasks and enhancing productivity. It provides intelligent recommendations, summaries, and insights directly within the CRM, making it easier to manage leads, track customer interactions, and generate relevant data insights.

Acting as a "*copilot*," it enables users to streamline tasks, prioritize actions, and stay on top of key activities, ultimately improving the CRM experience with proactive, AI-driven support.

Setup Copilot for Sales, Project Operations, and Customer Service

Microsoft Copilot is a generative AI chatbot developed by Microsoft based on the GPT-4 series of large language models. It was launched in February 2023 as Microsoft's primary replacement for the discontinued Cortana1. Initially introduced as Bing Chat, it was integrated into Microsoft Bing and Microsoft Edge. Over the course of 2023, Microsoft unified the Copilot branding across its various chatbot products1.

At the Build 2023 conference, Microsoft announced plans to integrate Copilot into Windows 11, allowing users to access it directly through the taskbar1. In January 2024, a dedicated Copilot key was introduced for Windows keyboards1. Copilot utilizes the Microsoft Prometheus model built upon OpenAI's GPT-4 foundational model and has been fine-tuned using both supervised and reinforcement learning techniques1.

List of Copilots in Dynamics 365 CRM

Here are some of the Copilots available in Dynamics 365 CRM:

- **Copilot in Dynamics 365 Sales:** Helps sales teams be more productive by providing quick summaries of opportunity and lead records, preparing for meetings, and reading the latest news about accounts.
- **Copilot in Dynamics 365 Customer Service:** Assists agents in delivering exceptional customer care by drafting contextual answers to queries in both chat and email and providing an interactive chat experience over knowledge bases and case history.
- **Copilot in Dynamics 365 Customer Insights:** Provides insights and analytics to help businesses understand their customers better and make informed decisions.
- **Copilot in Dynamics 365 Project Operations:** Simplifies project planning by generating task outlines, forecasting budgets, and creating project timelines.

These Copilots are designed to enhance productivity and efficiency across various business operations within Dynamics 365 CRM.

In the rapidly evolving landscape of business technology, Microsoft Copilot stands out as a transformative AI-powered assistant integrated within Dynamics 365 CRM. Designed to enhance productivity and efficiency across various modules, Copilot leverages advanced artificial intelligence to provide real-time insights, automate routine tasks, and facilitate seamless collaboration. Whether in Sales, Project Operations, or Customer Service, Copilot empowers teams to work smarter, respond faster, and achieve more, making it an indispensable tool for modern enterprises. In this chapter, we will be covering some features of Copilots in Sales, Project Operations, and Customer Service Apps.

Copilot in Sales Hub

Microsoft Copilot in Dynamics 365 Sales is an AI-powered assistant designed to enhance sales productivity and efficiency. It offers several key features, such as:

- **Quick Summary**: Sales teams can interact with Copilot using predefined prompts to get quick summaries of opportunities, leads, and accounts.
- **Embedded Experiences**: Copilot provides embedded insights directly within the Sales Hub, such as opportunity and lead summaries and recent changes to records.
- **Email and Meeting Assistance**: It helps in drafting emails, preparing for meetings, and staying updated with the latest news about accounts.

Copilot Prompts in Dynamics 365 Sales

Most copilots in Dynamics 365 work by using predefined prompts, which are built-in commands or questions that guide the AI in providing the right responses or actions. These prompts help the AI understand the user's needs and automate tasks efficiently. For example, a user might ask Copilot to "*generate a report on sales performance*," and the AI will know how to fetch the necessary data and create the report. Prompts can also be more complex, allowing users to get insights, perform data analysis, or trigger workflows. These predefined prompts make it easier for users to interact with the AI without needing to understand complicated commands. Essentially, they offer a simplified way to access powerful functionalities, boosting productivity and decision-making.

Get Info Prompts:

- **Get info from SharePoint**: Retrieves answers from documents stored in SharePoint.
- **Get latest news for account**: Displays recent news related to a specified account.
- **Show files from SharePoint**: Lists files associated with a particular record from SharePoint.
- **Show my pipeline**: Presents a view of open opportunities, ordered by the estimated close date.
- **Summarize file**: Provides a summary of a specified document.

Ask Questions Prompts:

- **What's new with my sales records**: Lists sales records updated in the past seven days.
- **What's newly assigned to me**: Identifies leads and opportunities assigned in the last 15 days.
- **What's changed for record type**: Details updates to account, lead, or opportunity records in the past week or since the last sign-in.

Stay Ahead Prompts:

- **Prepare for sales appointments**: Summarizes notes from the past three months and the latest email thread related to a record.
- **Show emails that need follow-up**: Lists emails awaiting your response.

Throughout this chapter, we will explore various Copilot features in Sales. For more detailed information on the latest features or updates, please refer to the link in **Reference 2**.

Setting Up Copilot for Sales

In Dynamics 365's Sales Hub,

1. Go to **`App Settings`** > **`Copilot`**.
2. Enable relevant features, including chat and embedded experiences.

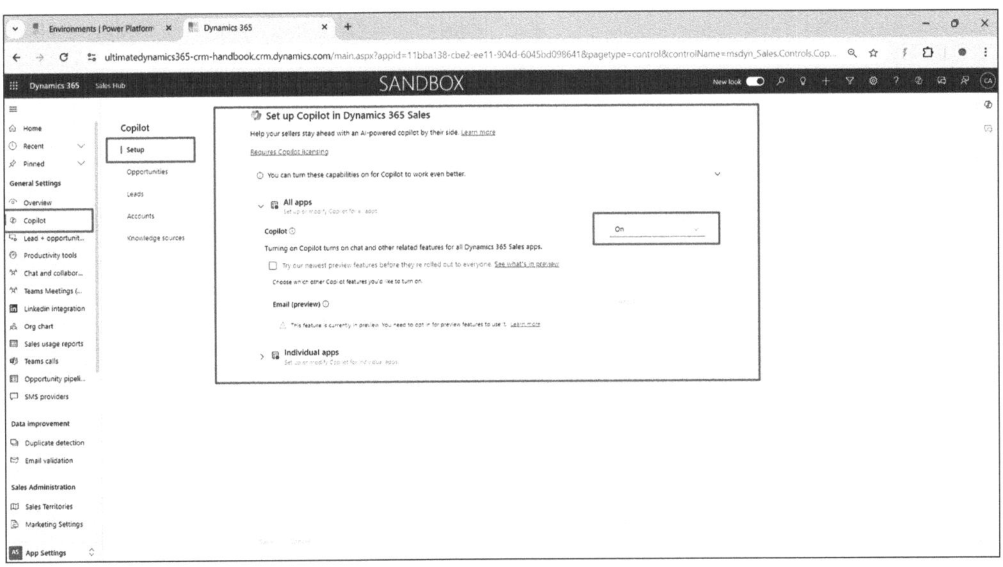

***Figure 10.1**: Copilot settings in Sales Hub – step 1*

3. You can enable Copilot across all Dynamics 365 apps or choose specific apps

where you want it activated. This flexibility allows you to adjust Copilot's AI assistance to the exact areas where it is most needed.

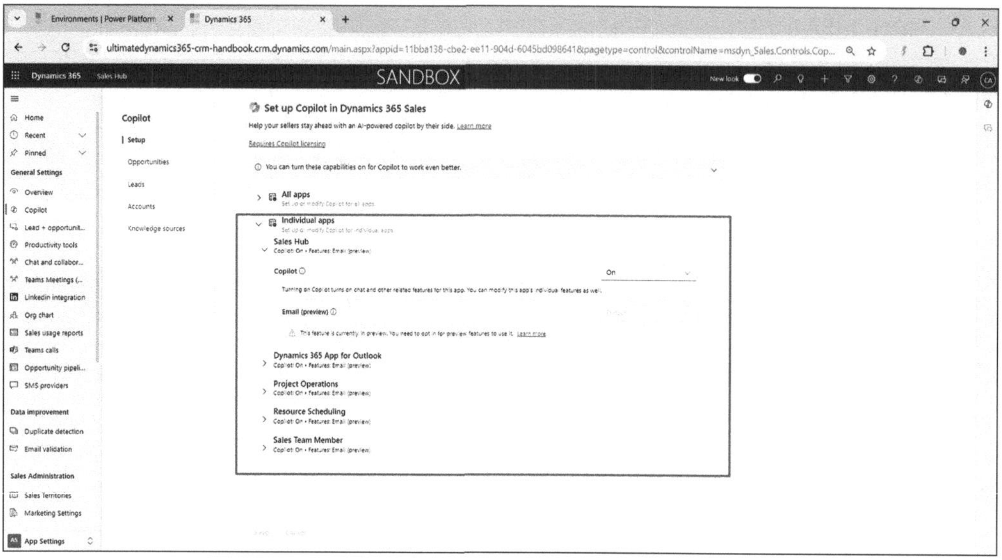

Figure 10.2: *Copilot settings in Sales Hub – step 2*

4. You can choose specific data points or fields from relevant entities for Copilot to pull data from, ensuring it uses the most critical information.

5. In **`Sales Hub`**, Copilot is designed to work only with a selected set of entities, allowing for focused assistance on relevant records and interactions.

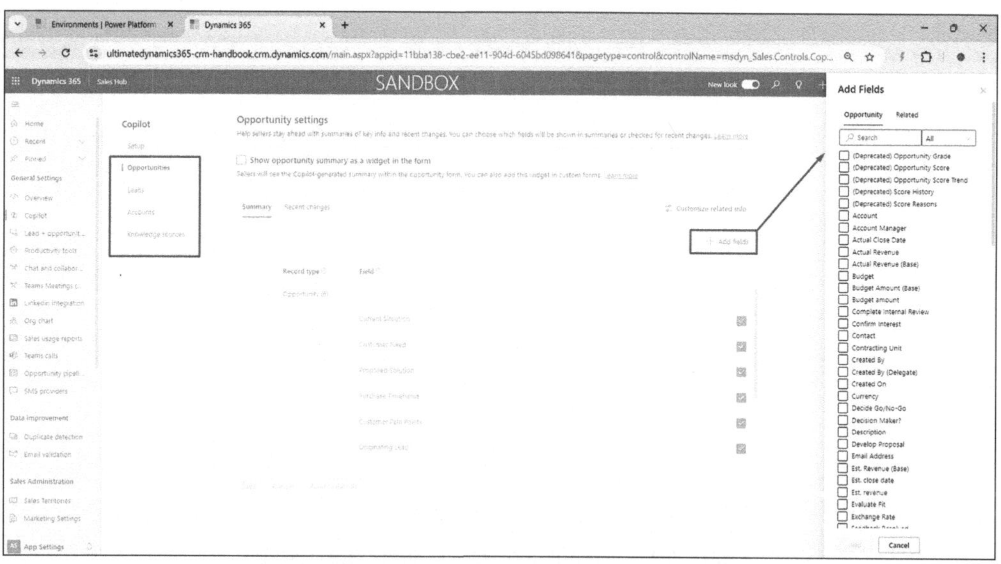

Figure 10.3: *Copilot settings in Sales Hub– step 3*

6. Turn on audit history for tables, such as lead, opportunity, and account, allowing Copilot to offer contextual insights based on past interactions and updates.

Copilot in Project Operations

In Dynamics 365 Project Operations, Copilot assists project managers and teams by streamlining project management tasks:

- **Project Insights**: Copilot offers AI-driven insights for project tracking, resource allocation, and risk management.
- **Time Entry and Reporting**: It simplifies time entry and generates detailed project reports, helping teams stay on top of project timelines and budgets.
- **Collaboration Tools**: Integrated with Microsoft Teams, Copilot enhances collaboration by providing real-time updates and notifications.

Setting Up Copilot for Project Operations

To configure Copilot for Project Operations, follow these steps:

1. Configuring `Project Operations Copilot` is simple; in the project operations model-driven app, under settings, click on `Parameters`.
2. Under the active parameter, open the `Default` parameter.

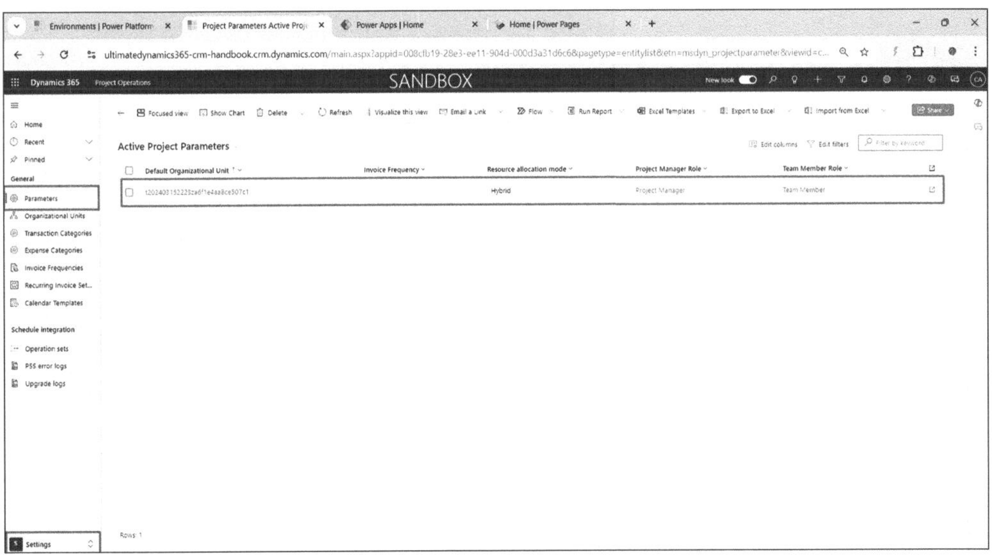

Figure 10.4: *Enabling Copilot in Project Operations – step 1*

3. In the ribbon area, click on `Feature Control`.

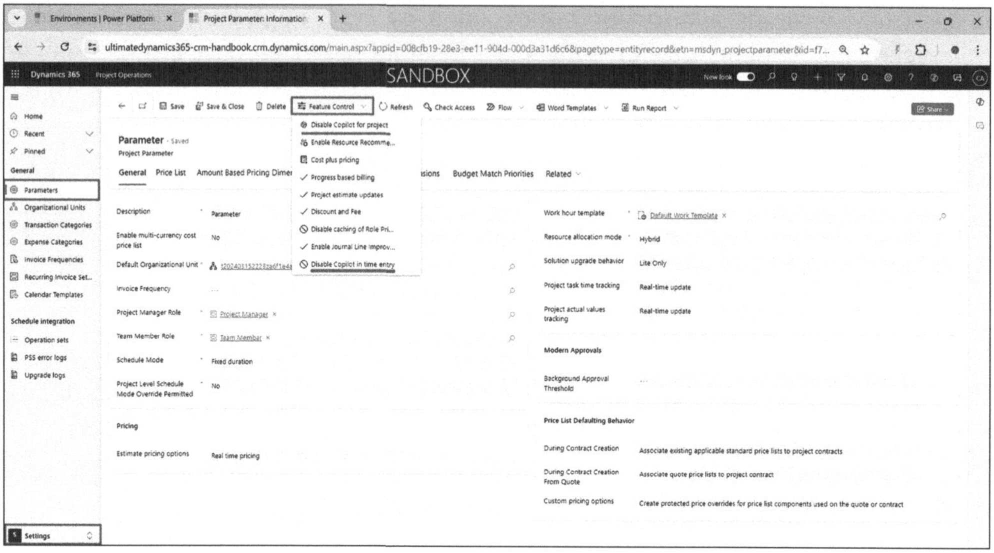

***Figure 10.5**: Enabling Copilot in Project Operations– step 2*

4. In the feature control, you will have options to enable and disable project operations Copilot.

Throughout this chapter, we will explore various Copilot features in **`Project Operations`**. For more detailed information on the latest features or updates, please refer to the link in **Reference 3**.

Copilot in Customer Service

Copilot in Dynamics 365 Customer Service revolutionizes customer support by leveraging AI to improve service delivery:

- **Case Management**: It assists agents in managing cases more effectively by providing quick access to relevant information and suggesting the next best actions.
- **Natural Language Processing**: Copilot uses advanced natural language processing to understand and respond to customer queries, making interactions more efficient.
- **Automated Responses**: It can generate automated responses and help in creating knowledge base articles, reducing the workload on customer service agents.

Setting Up Copilot for Customer Service

To enable Copilot in Customer Service, follow these steps:

- Open the **`Customer Service admin center`**.

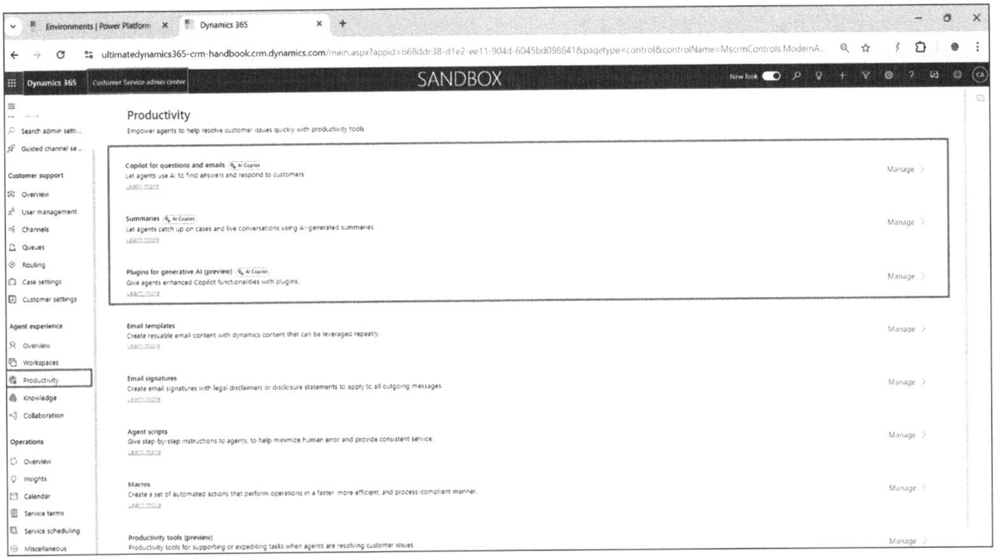

Figure 10.6: *Enabling Copilot in Customer Service– step 3*

- Under **Agent experience** in the **Productivity** section, you will find various AI Copilot options to enhance agent workflows.

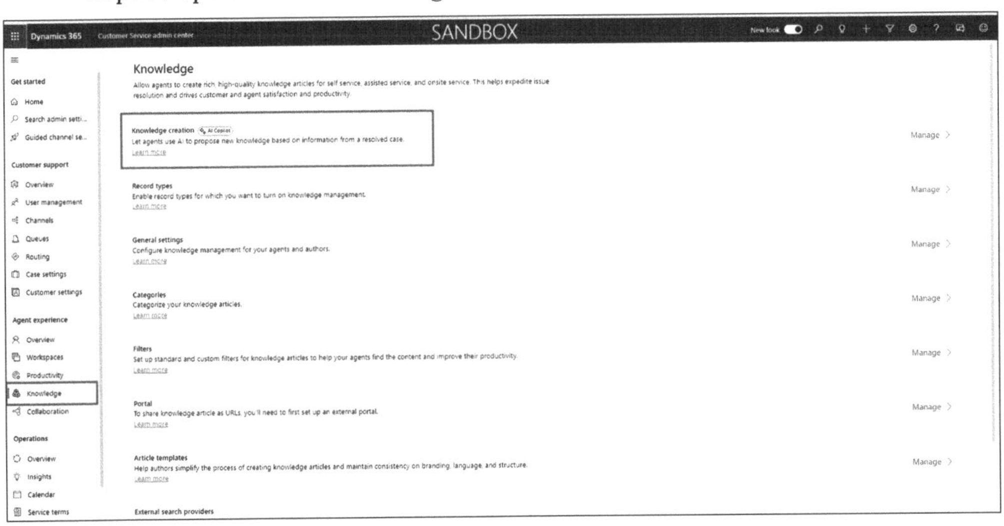

Figure 10.7: *Enabling Copilot in Customer Service– step 4*

- In **Agent experience** under **Knowledge**, you will find the Copilot feature specifically for knowledge creation, which helps agents generate and manage knowledge articles effectively.

These copilots integrate seamlessly into their respective modules, providing AI-driven assistance that enhances productivity, efficiency, and overall user experience in Dynamics 365 CRM.

Copilot Capabilities in Dynamics 365 CRM

With Copilot now set up, let us explore some of its features in Dynamics 365 CRM and review the key capabilities it brings to each area.

Summarize Lead Using Copilot

In Dynamics 365 CRM, Copilot can help generate a lead summary by analyzing relevant customer data. Copilot provides a concise overview of each lead, highlighting key details, such as recent interactions, account history, and any related activities. It assists sales teams by summarizing potential opportunities, guiding follow-ups, and suggesting personalized actions based on AI insights. This automated summary feature allows users to quickly understand lead context and prioritize actions, enhancing engagement and efficiency in lead management.

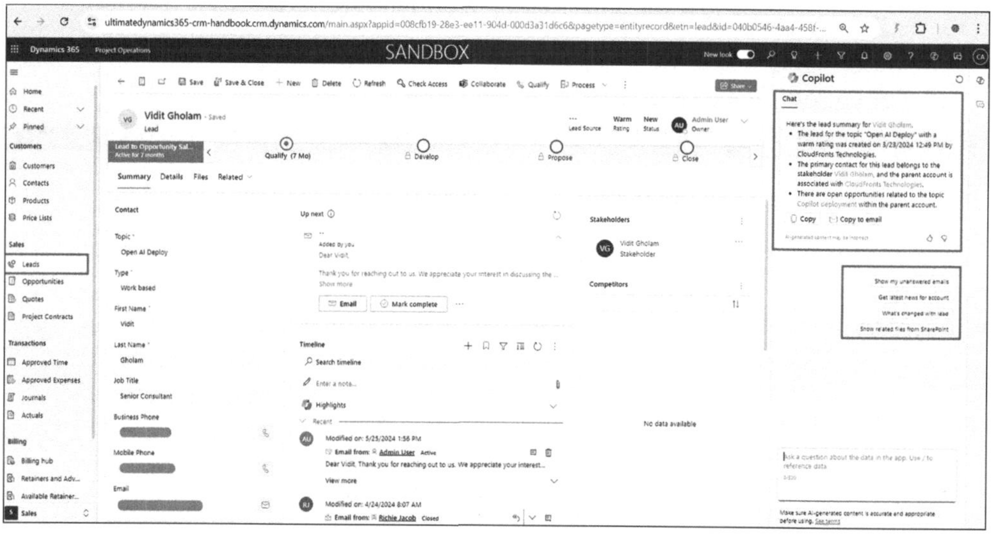

***Figure 10.8**: Lead Summary using Copilot in Dynamics 365 CRM*

Using Copilot in Dynamics 365 CRM, you can ask specific, predefined questions about a lead record, allowing you to get quick insights and important information without navigating through multiple fields.

Summarize Opportunity Using Copilot

With Copilot in Dynamics 365 CRM, you can quickly access opportunity summaries, offering a concise overview of critical opportunity details. Copilot pulls together key information, such as deal size, close date, recent interactions, and important notes, providing a snapshot that helps sales teams prioritize opportunities.

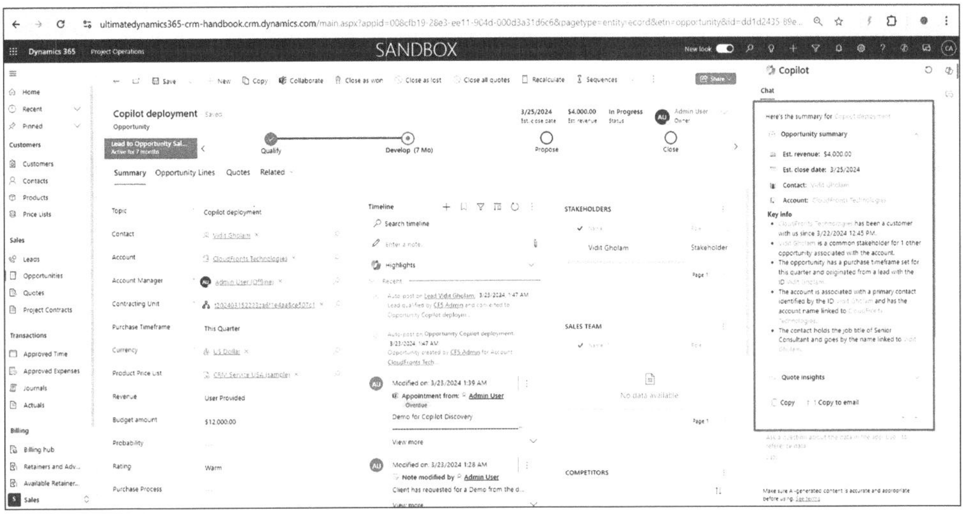

***Figure 10.9**: Summarize Opportunities using Copilots in Dynamics 365 CRM*

By analyzing and presenting data from related customer interactions, Copilot enables sales representatives to identify key engagement points and take informed actions, making it easier to manage and advance opportunities efficiently.

Creating Emails Using Copilot in Dynamics 365 CRM

Creating emails using AI Copilot in Dynamics 365 CRM enhances the email composition process. With Copilot, users can leverage AI to generate email drafts based on predefined templates, past communications, and contextual information from the CRM.

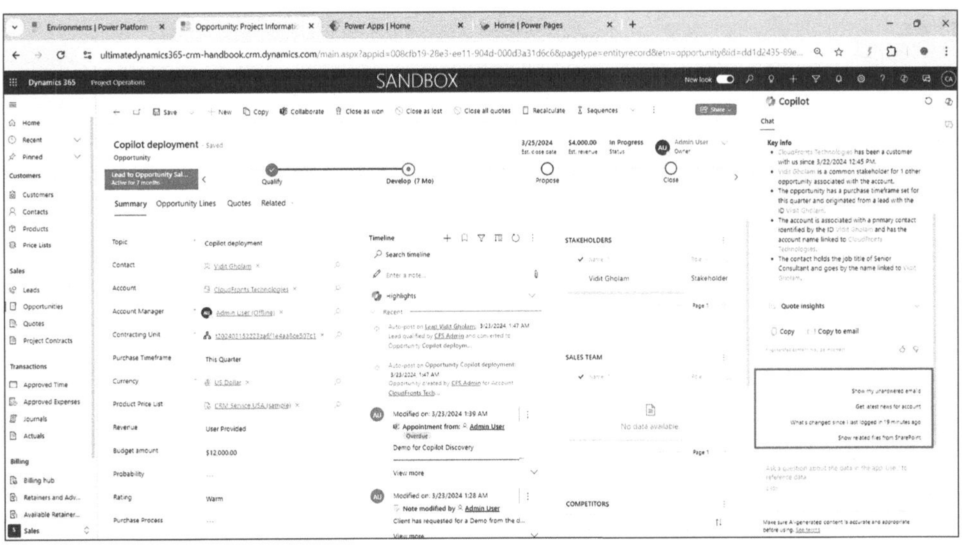

***Figure 10.10**: Creating Emails using Copilot in Dynamics 365 CRM*

For example, the Opportunity summary feature in Copilot provides users with the capability to automatically draft an email, as shown in *Figure* 10.10.

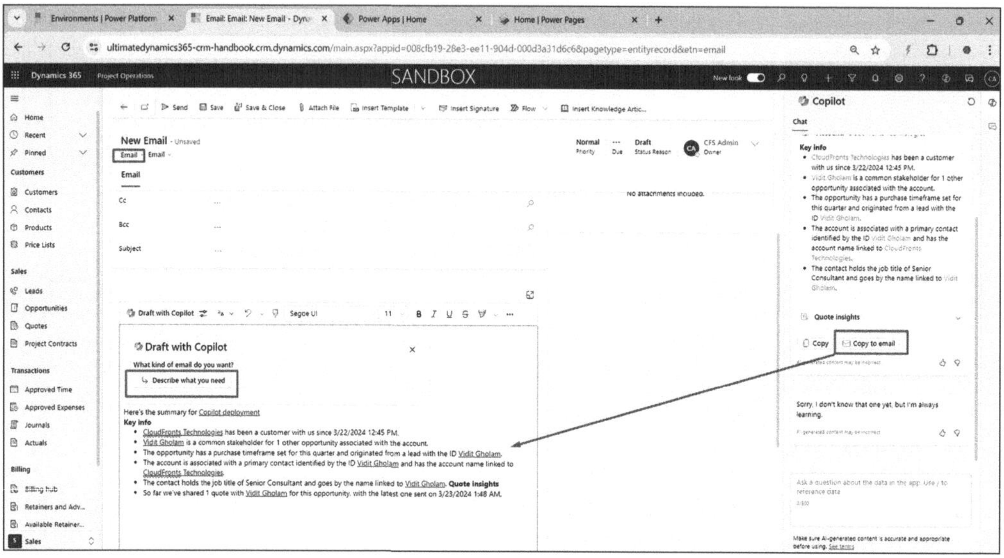

***Figure* 10.11**: *Creating Emails using Copilot in Dynamics 365 CRM*

This capability allows for quicker responses and more personalized messaging, as Copilot can suggest relevant content and even adapt to the tone needed for different audiences. By simplifying the email creation process, sales and customer service teams can maintain effective communication while saving time and effort.

Timeline Summary Using Copilot in Dynamics 365 CRM

AI Copilot makes it easy to see all the activities related to a specific record in Dynamics 365 CRM. It shows a simple timeline of past interactions, such as emails, calls, and meetings. This helps users quickly understand what has happened with a customer.

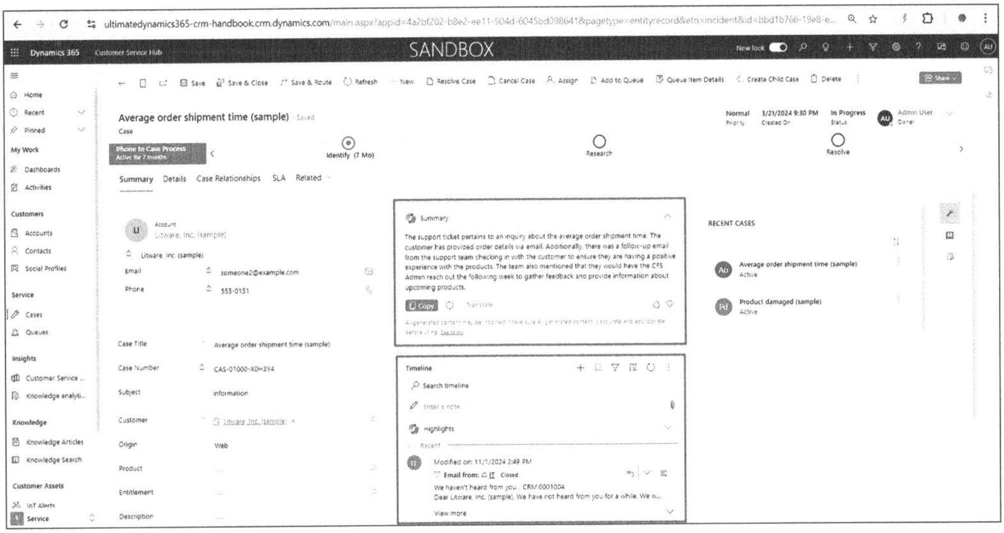

Figure 10.12: Timeline Summary using Copilot in Dynamics 365 CRM

Copilot can also point out important updates and suggest next steps based on the activities, making it easier to stay on top of customer relationships and ensuring nothing important is missed.

Creating Project Tasks Using Copilot

Using Copilot in Project Operations allows for the automatic creation of project tasks based on the project description.

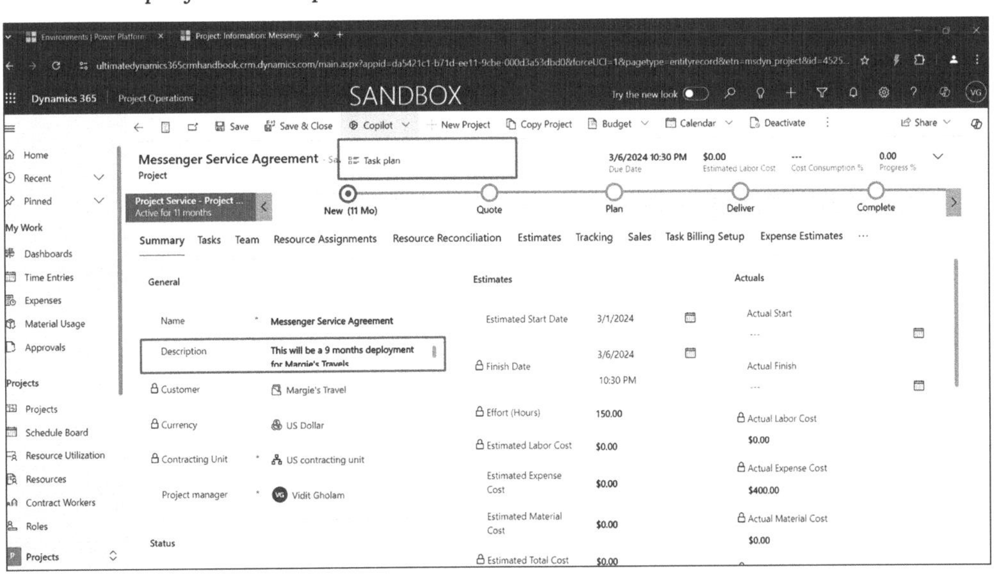

Figure 10.13: Creating Project Tasks Using Copilot– step 1

1. When you click on the "`Task Plan`" option from the ribbon in the project interface, tasks are generated automatically.

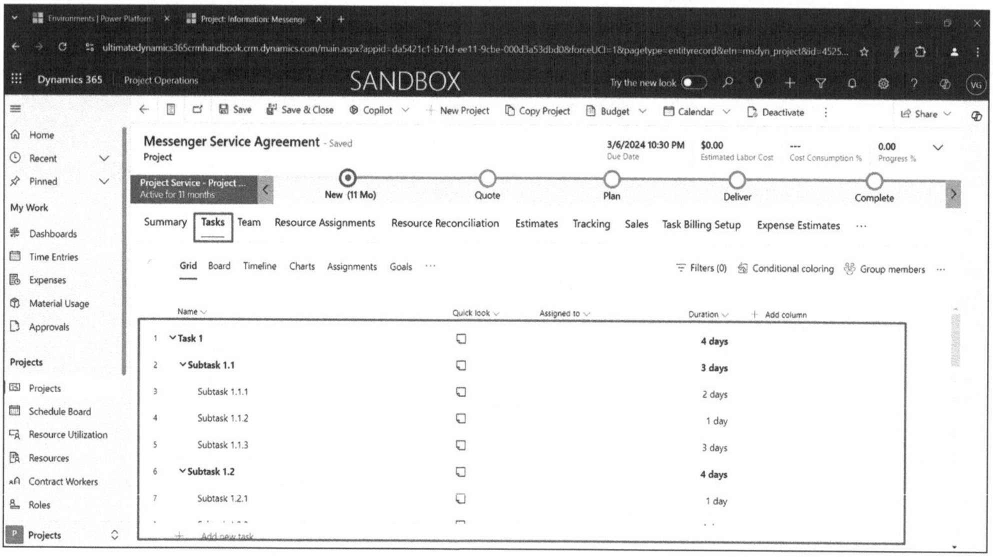

Figure 10.14: *Creating Project Tasks Using Copilot– step 2*

2. This feature enhances project management efficiency by streamlining the task creation process.

Using Copilot for Sales in Outlook

Copilot for Sales in Dynamics 365 Outlook is like having a helpful assistant right in your inbox! It makes replying to emails a breeze by suggesting quick responses related to the conversations. Plus, you can edit CRM records without leaving Outlook. It allows users to access relevant CRM records and update information without switching applications. Additionally, Copilot offers insights into customer interactions, helping users make informed decisions.

Using Copilot for Sales in Outlook provides several features that improve user efficiency and engagement. Here is a detailed overview:

- **Draft Replies**: Copilot assists users in composing quick and relevant replies to emails based on the context of previous conversations and the CRM data associated with the contact. This speeds up the response time and ensures that messages are personalized. For a working example, please refer to the link in **Reference 9**.

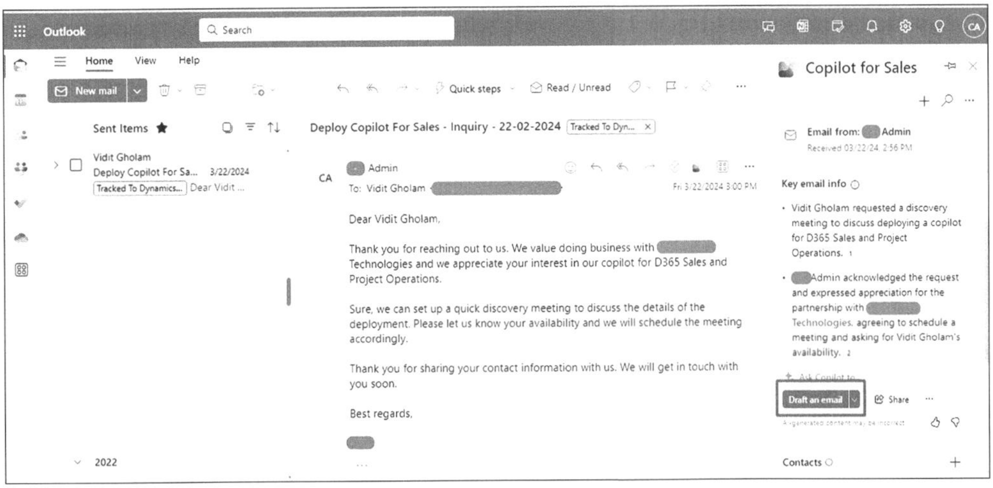

Figure 10.15: *Draft Email replies using Copilot for Sales in Outlook*

- **Editing CRM Records**: Users can easily edit Dynamics 365 CRM records directly from their **`Outlook`** interface. This integration allows for real-time updates to lead and opportunity information without switching between applications.
- **Task Management**: Users can create tasks and set reminders based on email interactions. This helps in managing follow-ups and ensures that important actions are not overlooked.

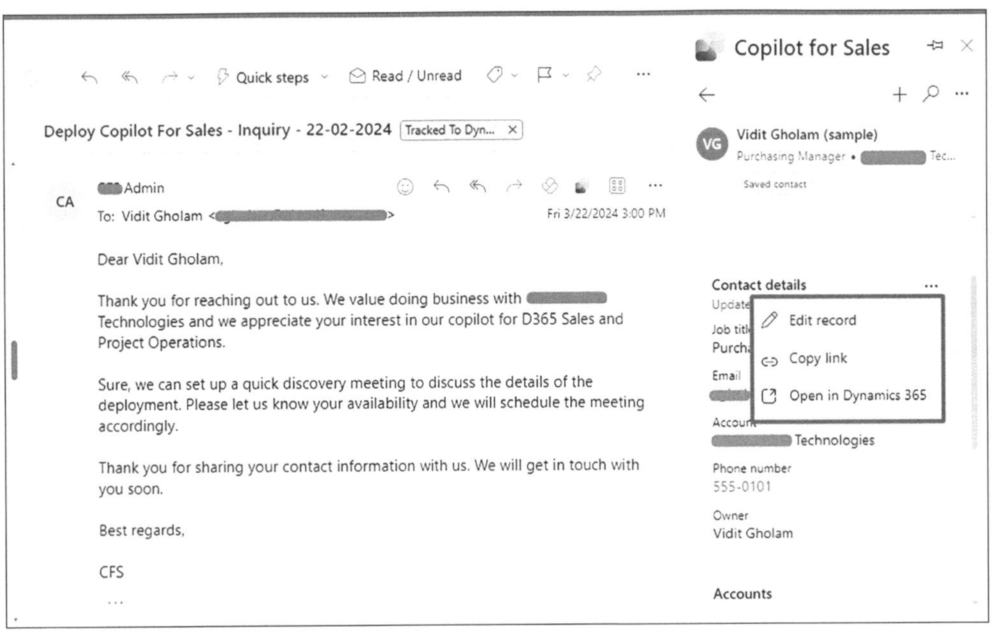

Figure 10.16: *Editing Dynamics 365 CRM records using Copilot for Sales in Outlook*

- **Access to Customer Insights**: With Copilot, users can access essential customer data while drafting emails. This feature ensures that sales representatives have all relevant information at their fingertips, helping them tailor their communication effectively.

- **Integration with Dynamics 365**: The connection between Outlook and Dynamics 365 allows users to keep track of all customer interactions, including emails sent and received, directly in the CRM.
- **Collaboration Tools**: Copilot facilitates easy collaboration by allowing users to share information and documents within Outlook, linking them directly to CRM records.

Installing Copilot for Sales in outlook

To install Copilot in Outlook, you must be an M365 Global Administrator.

1. Visit admin.microsoft.com and go to the **`Settings`** section.
2. Click on "**`Integrated apps`**" and select "**`Get apps`**."

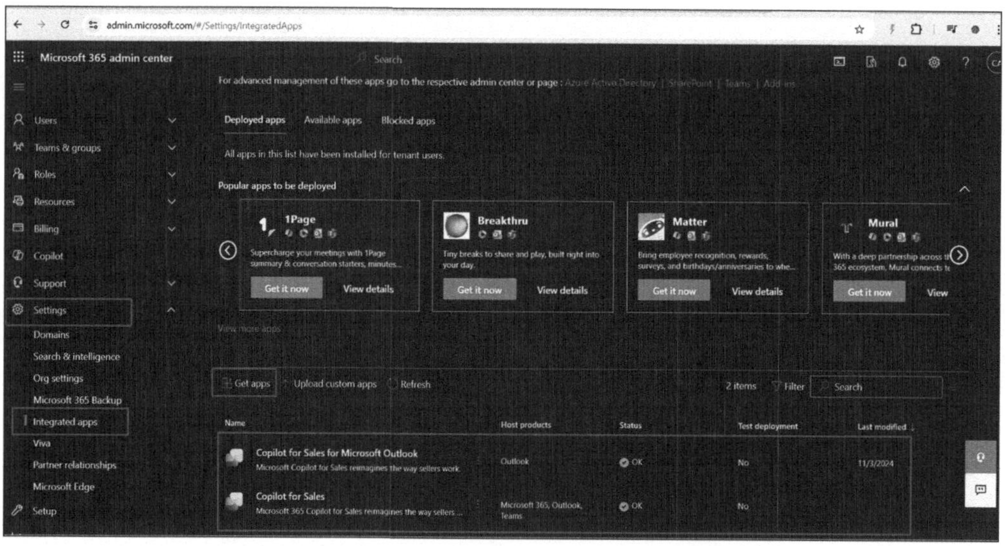

Figure 10.17: *Installing Copilot for sales in outlook– step 1*

3. Search for "**`Copilot for Sales`**" and install it.

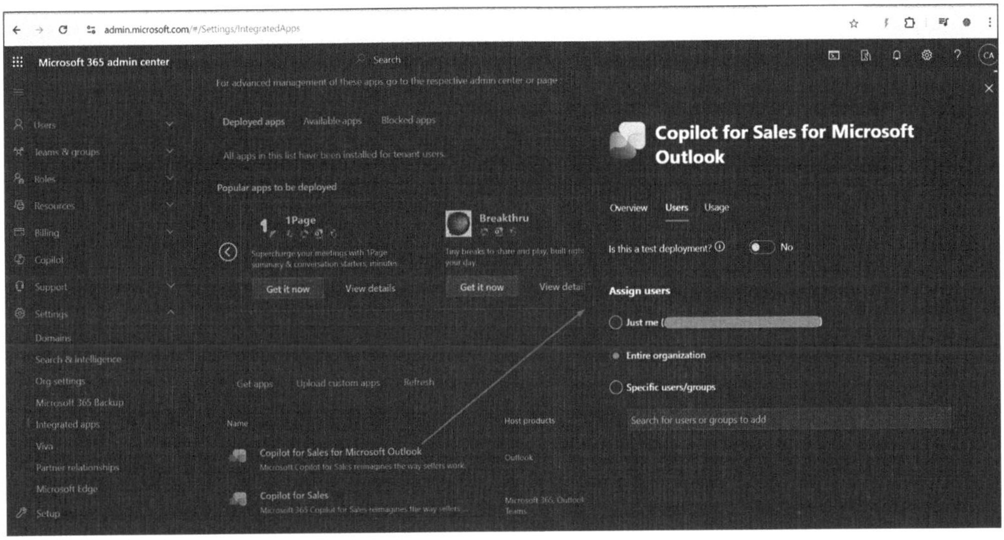

Figure 10.18: *Installing Copilot for sales in outlook– step 2*

4. After installation, you can assign Copilot to all users or specific users as needed. For a complete installation guide, refer to link in the **Reference 9**.

Note: *The logos and names of Copilot may change over time, so it is important to stay updated on the latest developments before any deployment.*

Conclusion

This chapter has provided an in-depth look at the capabilities of AI Copilot within Dynamics 365 CRM, covering its setup for various applications and its integration with Outlook. As we transition to the next chapter, we will explore practical business use cases and the future potential of Dynamics 365 CRM. Additionally, we will discuss various certification paths available for professionals, providing insights into exam structures and sample questions to aid in preparing for these valuable credentials.

References

1. Copilot in Dynamics 365 Sales Overview: https://learn.microsoft.com/en-us/dynamics365/sales/copilot-overview

2. Copilot Prompts in Dynamics 365 Sales: https://learn.microsoft.com/en-us/dynamics365/sales/copilot-prompt-guide

3. Copilot Features in Dynamics 365 Project Operations: https://learn.microsoft.com/en-us/dynamics365/project-operations/project-management/copilot-features

4. Ask Questions of Copilot in Dynamics 365 Sales: https://learn.microsoft.com/en-us/dynamics365/sales/use-sales-copilot
5. Welcome to Microsoft 365 Copilot for Sales: https://learn.microsoft.com/en-us/microsoft-sales-copilot/introduction
6. Turn on and Set up Copilot in Dynamics 365 Sales: https://learn.microsoft.com/en-us/dynamics365/sales/enable-setup-copilot
7. Microsoft 365 Copilot for Sales Deployment Guide for Dynamics 365 Customers: https://learn.microsoft.com/en-us/microsoft-sales-copilot/deploy-viva-sales-d365
8. Draft an Email Message with Copilot in Outlook: https://support.microsoft.com/en-us/office/draft-an-email-message-with-copilot-in-outlook-3eb1d053-89b8-491c-8a6e-746015238d9b
9. Install Copilot for Sales (admin-deployed): https://learn.microsoft.com/en-us/microsoft-sales-copilot/install-viva-sales

Chapter 11
Business Use Cases, Future Scope, and Certification Paths

Introduction

In this final chapter, we will explore practical applications and the promising future of Microsoft Dynamics 365 CRM. This section highlights real-world business use cases, showing how organizations use Dynamics 365 CRM to enhance efficiency, improve customer satisfaction, and support growth.

We will also review the available certification paths, designed to help you build specialized skills and earn recognition in today's evolving tech landscape. Covering certifications such as the Dynamics 365 Sales Functional Consultant Associate and Power Platform Solution Architect, this chapter provides a clear guide for advancing your career and expanding your expertise in Dynamics 365 and Microsoft Power Platform.

To support your certification journey, we have included sample exam structures, multiple-choice questions, and case studies. These resources will give you an idea of the exam format and content, helping you prepare confidently for success.

Structure

In this chapter, we will discuss the following topics:

- Business User Cases of Dynamics 365 CRM and Future Scope
- Certification Paths
    - Microsoft Certified: Microsoft Power Platform Solution Architect
    - Microsoft Certified: Power Platform Developer Associate

- Certification Example Structure
- Sample MCQs and Case Studies

Business User Cases of Dynamics 365 CRM and Future Scope

Understanding the business use cases and future scope of Dynamics 365 CRM is essential for professionals and organizations alike. By exploring the platform's practical applications, companies can use its features to enhance customer relationships, improve processes, and drive growth. Knowing how Dynamics 365 is applied across various industries helps decision-makers identify the specific tools and strategies that align with their unique needs and goals. Additionally, insights into the platform's future scope prepare organizations to stay ahead of technological advancements, enabling them to adapt to changing market demands, integrate data more effectively, and build cohesive digital ecosystems. In a rapidly evolving digital landscape, this knowledge allows businesses to make informed investments in their CRM strategies, empowering them to deliver exceptional value to customers and achieve long-term success.

Here are several detailed business use cases of Dynamics 365 CRM, along with insights into the platform's future scope:

Sales Process Automation and Forecasting

Use Case: Many organizations struggle with efficiently managing and forecasting their sales processes. Dynamics 365 CRM provides powerful tools for automating sales processes, helping businesses streamline lead management, track interactions, and organize follow-ups. For instance, sales teams at a manufacturing company can use Dynamics 365 to prioritize leads by leveraging AI-driven insights and customer behavior data. This enables them to focus on the most promising prospects, making their sales efforts more targeted and effective.

Features in Dynamics 365 Sales for Optimizing Sales Processes:

- **Lead and Opportunity Management**: Efficiently capture, track, and manage leads and opportunities through every stage of the sales pipeline, ensuring no opportunities are missed.
- **AI-Driven Insights**: Use predictive analytics to gain insights into customer behavior, helping prioritize high-value prospects and improving decision-making.
- **Sales Forecasting**: Automatically generate sales forecasts based on historical data and current pipeline, enabling more accurate and data-driven decision-making.

- **Sales Process Automation**: Automate repetitive tasks such as sending follow-up emails or scheduling meetings, saving time for sales teams to focus on higher-value activities.
- **Relationship Tracking**: Track every customer interaction, from meetings to emails, ensuring sales teams have a 360-degree view of customer relationships and history.
- **Customizable Sales Workflows**: Tailor the sales processes to meet the specific needs of the business, ensuring flexibility and adaptability in different sales environments.
- **Collaboration with Teams**: Integrate with Microsoft Teams to enhance collaboration across the sales team, enabling seamless communication and information sharing.

Figure 11.1: *Image is generated using Microsoft Designer (designer.microsoft.com)*

Impact: By automating routine sales tasks and analyzing customer data, sales representatives can focus on building relationships and closing deals. This approach leads to higher productivity, improved conversion rates, and more accurate forecasting, helping the business to set realistic sales targets and manage resources effectively.

Customer Service and Support Optimization

Use Case: Organizations in industries, such as retail, hospitality, and telecommunications, face the challenge of meeting high customer service demands. Dynamics 365 CRM offers a centralized platform that allows customer service teams to access complete customer histories, track service requests, and resolve issues across various communication channels, such as email, chat, and social media.

For example, a retail company can use Dynamics 365 to give customer service representatives a full view of each customer's previous interactions.

This enables them to respond faster and provide more tailored assistance, ultimately improving the customer experience.

Features in Dynamics 365 Customer Service for Support Optimization:

- **Case Management**: Efficiently manage customer inquiries, track case progress, and ensure timely resolutions.
- **Omni-channel Support**: Handle customer issues across multiple channels, including email, chat, phone, and social media, all from within the same platform.
- **Knowledge Management**: Provide customer service teams with access to a comprehensive knowledge base, enabling them to quickly find answers to common customer questions.
- **Service Level Agreements (SLAs)**: Define and monitor service expectations, ensuring customer enquiries are resolved within the agreed-upon timeframes.
- **Queue Management**: Organize and prioritize cases by severity or urgency, ensuring that critical issues are addressed promptly.
- **Reporting and Analytics**: Track and analyze service metrics to identify areas for improvement and enhance service quality.

Figure 11.2: *Image is generated using Microsoft Designer (designer.microsoft.com)*

Impact: This holistic approach to customer service improves customer satisfaction and loyalty. The platform's case management tools also allow companies to categorize and analyze recurring issues, providing insights that can lead to better policies, proactive issue resolution, and even the development of new services based on customer needs.

Marketing Campaign Management and Customer Engagement

Use Case: For companies looking to expand their reach and improve customer engagement, Dynamics 365's marketing features are invaluable. For example, a financial services firm launching a targeted campaign for new products can use Dynamics 365 CRM to segment audiences, design personalized email campaigns, and track engagement metrics such as open and click-through rates. Additionally, Dynamics 365 Customer Insights and Customer Insights - Journey play a pivotal role in enhancing these efforts.

Features of Dynamics 365 Customer Insights - Journey:

- **Customer Segmentation**: Automatically segment customers based on various criteria, such as behavior, demographics, and purchase history, enabling tailored marketing efforts.

- **Personalized Campaigns**: Create highly personalized journeys that respond to customer actions, improving engagement and conversion rates.
- **Multi-Channel Engagement**: Deliver marketing content across various channels, such as email, SMS, web, and more, while tracking interactions at every touchpoint.
- **Customer Behavior Insights**: Gain valuable insights into customer behavior, which can inform campaign strategies and enhance customer engagement efforts.
- **Journey Orchestration**: Orchestrate marketing campaigns with advanced workflow tools, ensuring customers receive timely and relevant messages based on their preferences and actions.
- **AI-Driven Recommendations**: Use artificial intelligence to suggest the next best action for customer journeys, further optimizing the marketing process.

Figure 11.3: *Image is generated using Microsoft Designer (designer.microsoft.com)*

Impact: The CRM's integration with Microsoft Power BI provides deep insights into customer behaviors, allowing marketers to continuously improve their outreach. By aligning marketing activities with sales data, companies can create more compelling campaigns that align with customer interests, ultimately increasing engagement and conversion rates.

Field Service Management and Mobile Workforce Enablement

Use Case: Industries such as utilities, healthcare, and construction often need to manage a large, mobile workforce. Dynamics 365 CRM's field service capabilities provide a range of features designed to streamline scheduling, dispatching, and real-time tracking of field agents. For example, a healthcare provider can leverage these tools to assign patient visits to nurses based on their proximity and availability, optimizing both time and resources.

Features of Dynamics 365 Field Service for Mobile Workforce Enablement:

- **Work Order Management**: Automatically generate work orders based on customer requests, service agreements, or routine maintenance schedules, ensuring field agents have all the necessary information at their fingertips.
- **Scheduling and Dispatching**: Use intelligent scheduling to assign field agents based on availability, skill set, and proximity to the customer, reducing travel time and increasing efficiency.
- **Real-Time Tracking and Updates**: Track the location of field agents in real-time, allowing for immediate updates on job progress and any potential delays, which helps in timely customer communication.
- **Mobile App for Field Agents**: Equip field agents with a mobile app that provides access to work orders, customer information, and real-time updates, allowing them to complete tasks efficiently in the field and capture necessary data on the go.
- **Inventory Management**: Manage parts and inventory in real-time, ensuring field agents have access to the right tools and materials needed to complete their tasks without unnecessary delays.
- **Customer Communication and Notifications**: Automatically notify customers about appointment status, delays, and technician arrival times, improving customer satisfaction and transparency.
- **All Under One System**: Use field service management with other Dynamics 365 apps, such as Sales and Customer Service, for a holistic view of customer interactions and a more coordinated service effort.
- **Mobile Workforce Collaboration**: Enable better collaboration between field agents and back-office teams with instant messaging, photo sharing, and document upload features directly within the mobile app.

***Figure 11.4**: Image is generated using Microsoft Designer (designer.microsoft.com)*

Impact: Real-time tracking and optimized scheduling not only reduce operational costs but also improve customer experiences. With mobile access to the CRM, field agents can view relevant customer details on the go, preparing them better for each visit and enhancing the quality of service delivered.

Future Scope of Dynamics 365 CRM

The future of Dynamics 365 CRM holds exciting potential as it evolves to meet the changing needs of businesses in a digital-first world. With advancements in artificial intelligence, machine learning, and cloud technology, Dynamics 365 CRM is expected to become even more integral in driving customer engagement, optimizing operations, and supporting data-driven decisions. As organizations seek smarter, more adaptable solutions, Dynamics 365 CRM's ongoing developments will provide businesses with the tools to remain competitive and responsive to both market trends and customer expectations.

- **Integration of Artificial Intelligence (AI) and Machine Learning (ML)**

  Dynamics 365 CRM will continue to integrate AI and ML features, enabling businesses to gain deeper insights and make smarter decisions. Using predictive analytics for sales and customer behavior forecasting is expected to become more sophisticated, helping businesses anticipate needs and trends with precision. This evolution will empower companies to offer hyper-personalized experiences that align closely with customer expectations.

- **Enhanced Cross-Platform Integration with Microsoft Ecosystem**

  As part of the Microsoft ecosystem, Dynamics 365 CRM will benefit from increased integration with tools such as Microsoft Teams, Power BI, and Azure. This cross-platform connectivity will make it easier for businesses to create seamless workflows that span multiple departments, from sales to customer service to finance. Such integrations will support more collaborative work environments and make it possible to centralize data and communication across all Microsoft applications.

- **Expansion of Industry-Specific Solutions**

  Microsoft has increasingly focused on delivering industry-specific solutions within Dynamics 365 CRM. As businesses demand more tailored functionalities, Microsoft will likely expand its offerings for specialized industries, such as healthcare, finance, retail, and manufacturing. This trend will help organizations address industry-specific challenges more effectively and comply with sector regulations.

- **Increased Role in Digital Transformation Initiatives**

  Dynamics 365 CRM is well-positioned to support digital transformation efforts by helping businesses migrate from legacy systems to cloud-based solutions. In the future, we can expect to see a greater focus on cloud adoption and digital workflows, particularly in companies looking to modernize and become more agile. Dynamics 365 will likely play a central role in helping these organizations enhance customer experience, improve data accessibility, and drive operational efficiency.

- **Focus on Enhanced Security and Compliance**

  As data privacy concerns grow, Microsoft will continue to enhance security and compliance features within Dynamics 365 CRM. This development is crucial for companies handling sensitive customer information, particularly in sectors such as finance and healthcare. The future will see even stronger data protection measures and compliance options, making it a trusted choice for companies with stringent data requirements.

Certification Paths

Microsoft certifications are essential for professionals looking to prove their expertise in industry-leading technologies, such as Dynamics 365 and Power Platform. These certifications help individuals enhance their job prospects, build credibility, and advance their careers by showcasing their skills to potential employers. Additionally, they ensure that certified professionals remain current with the latest tools, updates, and best practices, helping organizations achieve digital transformation efficiently.

Microsoft Certified: Power Platform Functional Consultant Associate (PL-200)

The Microsoft Certified: Power Platform Functional Consultant Associate certification is designed for individuals responsible for creating, configuring, and deploying solutions using Microsoft Power Platform tools, such as Power Apps, Power Automate, and Power Virtual Agents. This certification validates the skills required to gather business requirements, design solutions, and ensure the functionality of business processes.

The skills required for this certification are covered by the topics we learned through the Ultimate Dynamics 365 CRM Guide.

- Configuring and managing Microsoft Dataverse.
- Building applications using Power Apps.
- Automating workflows with Power Automate.
- Implementing solutions with Power Virtual Agents.
- Managing environments, security, and app lifecycles.

The certification is achieved by passing Exam PL-200, which tests knowledge in these areas.

Refer to the link in **Reference 1** for the study material and for scheduling the exam.

Microsoft Certified: Power Platform Developer Associate (PL-400)

The Microsoft Certified: Power Platform Developer Associate certification is designed for professionals responsible for developing and customizing Microsoft Power Platform solutions. This certification validates your ability to design and develop Power Platform solutions, integrate them with other services, and extend their capabilities using custom code. Key areas of focus include developing custom applications with

Power Apps, automating workflows with Power Automate, enhancing reporting with Power BI, and creating chatbots with Power Virtual Agents.

To earn this certification, candidates must demonstrate proficiency in designing technical solutions, configuring and customizing applications, and implementing business process automation. They should also have experience with development tools such as JavaScript, C#, and Power Platform APIs. The certification exam measures skills in areas, such as data integration, security management, and working with Power Apps components.

The skills required for this certification are covered by the topics we learned in *Chapter 4, Customizing Your Dynamics 365 CRM*.

- Customizing Entities (Tables), Fields (Attributes), Forms, and Views in Dynamics 365 CRM.
- Introducing C# Plugins in Dynamics 365 CRM.
- Using JavaScript's Web resources in Dynamics 365 CRM.
- Business Rules and Workflows in Dynamics 365 CRM.

The certification is achieved by passing Exam PL-400, which tests knowledge in these areas.

Refer to the link in **Reference 2** for the study material and for scheduling the exam.

Microsoft Certified: Power Platform Solution Architect Expert (PL-600)

The Microsoft Certified: Power Platform Solution Architect Expert certification is designed for professionals who lead successful implementations and focus on solving business and technical challenges using the Power Platform and Dynamics 365. This role involves responsibilities, such as envisioning solutions, gathering requirements, designing architectures, and implementing the solutions, while ensuring alignment with organizational needs. A solution architect should have a strong understanding of the Power Platform, Dynamics 365, related Microsoft cloud solutions, and third-party technologies

The certification exam (PL-600) tests your ability to perform key tasks, such as envisioning and analyzing requirements, architecting a solution, and implementing it across various environments. Key topics include designing integrations with other systems, implementing security models, and managing data strategies

To obtain the Microsoft Certified: Power Platform Solution Architect Expert certification, you must first pass the **PL-200** and **PL-400** certifications, followed by the **PL-600** exam.

Refer to the link in **Reference 3** for the study material and for scheduling the exam.

Microsoft Certified: Dynamics 365 Customer Service Functional Consultant Associate

This certification is designed for professionals who implement and configure solutions to manage customer service processes using Dynamics 365. The role includes configuring service management, automating service processes, and providing customer engagement capabilities.

The exam MB-230 tests skills in managing cases, queues, service level agreements (SLAs), and knowledge management.

Refer to the link in **Reference 4** for the study material and for scheduling the exam.

Microsoft Certified: Dynamics 365 Field Service Functional Consultant Associate

The Dynamics 365 Field Service Functional Consultant certification focuses on implementing and configuring field service solutions for organizations. It includes tasks such as managing work orders, and resources and dispatching field agents.

The exam MB-240 tests knowledge on configuring field service settings, creating schedules, and optimizing work orders and technician workflows.

Refer to the link in **Reference 5** for the study material and for scheduling the exam.

For more details on certifications in different modules, refer to the link in **Reference 6**.

Certification Example Structure

The Certification Exam Example Structure for Microsoft certifications typically follows a standardized format, designed to assess both theoretical knowledge and practical skills. Here is a summary of what you can expect in these exams:

- **Multiple-Choice Questions (MCQs):** These questions test your foundational understanding of key concepts, tools, and processes. You will be asked to select the most appropriate answer from a set of options. They focus on basic knowledge, definitions, and best practices.
- **Case Studies:** Case study questions simulate real-world scenarios where you need to apply your skills. You will be presented with a business situation or problem, and your task will be to choose or recommend the best solution based on the information provided. These questions assess how well you can analyze business needs and design appropriate technical solutions.

- **Drag-and-Drop or Hot Area Questions:** These are interactive questions where you might be required to organize information, place elements in the correct order, or select areas of an interface in response to a scenario. They test your ability to work with tools and interfaces, simulating real-world tasks.
- **Performance-Based Testing (PBT):** Some exams, especially those related to technical certifications, may include hands-on tasks where you demonstrate your ability to configure or implement solutions directly within the software environment. This may involve using virtual labs or sandbox environments to complete tasks that mimic actual job roles.

These questions are designed to test both the depth and breadth of your knowledge, ensuring you are well-prepared to apply your skills in a business context. Each Microsoft exam is structured to focus on a specific set of skills that align with the responsibilities of the associated certification role.

Note: *The exam structure outlined in the previous section is based on experience and may change over time. Microsoft certification exams are regularly updated to reflect new technologies, tools, and best practices, so it is important to review the official Microsoft certification page for the most current information. The format, including the types of questions, might evolve to better assess real-world problem-solving skills and practical knowledge. Always refer to the official resources for the most accurate and up-to-date details regarding the certification exams.*

Sample MCQs and Case Studies

Here are some MCQs sourced from learn.microsoft.com.

Multiple Choice Questions

1. An environment in Dataverse can contain all the following items except which one?
   a. Power Apps
   b. Power Automate flows
   c. Many instances of Dataverse databases
   d. A single Dataverse database
2. Security roles are used for all the following actions except which one?
   a. Limiting access to data
   b. Restricting access to an environment
   c. Restricting actions that users can perform on data
   d. Restricting printing of data a user can read

3. Which of the following options is NOT a type of security role?
    a. Basic User
    b. Global Security Role
    c. Environment Maker
    d. Delegate
4. Which feature in Dynamics 365 helps users to manage and automate customer service cases?
    a. Dynamics 365 Customer Service Hub
    b. Dynamics 365 Field Service
    c. Power Apps
    d. Power Automate
5. In Dynamics 365, what is the purpose of 'Service Level Agreements' (SLAs)?
    a. To provide customers with product specifications
    b. To measure the performance of the support team
    c. To integrate CRM with external ERP systems
    d. To track and manage customer orders
6. Which tool in Dynamics 365 is used for creating and sharing reports and dashboards across the organization?
    a. Power Automate
    b. Power BI
    c. Common Data Service
    d. Microsoft Teams

Answers

1. **Answer: C** - Many instances of Dataverse databases
   In Dataverse, an environment can contain a single database, but it does not allow for multiple instances of databases within the same environment. This keeps the data structure organized and manageable.
2. **Answer: D** - Restricting printing of data that a user can read
   Security roles in Dynamics 365 are designed to control access to data and actions on that data, such as viewing, creating, or editing. However, they do not govern actions such as restricting the printing of data.

3. **Answer: B** - Global Security Role
   Dynamics 365 offers various security roles, such as Basic User, Environment Maker, and Delegate. However, there is no security role called "Global Security Role" in the platform.

4. **Answer: A** - Dynamics 365 Customer Service Hub
   The Customer Service Hub in Dynamics 365 is designed to help support teams manage and automate customer service cases, providing tools for tracking cases, managing service requests, and ensuring timely resolutions.

5. **Answer: B** - To measure the performance of the support team
   SLAs in Dynamics 365 are used to track the performance of customer service teams against predefined targets, ensuring that service delivery meets the expected standards and timelines.

6. **Answer: B** - Power BI
   Power BI is the tool used within Dynamics 365 to create, visualize, and share reports and dashboards. It integrates with various Dynamics 365 modules to deliver actionable insights from data.

Case Studies

Here are some case studies sourced from learn.microsoft.com.

Case Study 1

Contoso Electronics, a global electronics distributor, has recently adopted Dynamics 365 Sales to improve its sales operations. The company wants to track sales opportunities, forecast revenue, and enhance customer engagement. Sales representatives need access to a clear, guided process for managing opportunities, while sales managers require visibility into team performance and pipeline health.

The company also aims to automate certain tasks, such as sending follow-up emails to customers after a sales meeting and creating alerts for high-value opportunities.

Question: Contoso Electronics wants to ensure that sales representatives are guided through each stage of the sales process. Which feature in Dynamics 365 Sales should they implement to achieve this?

a. Service Level Agreements (SLAs)

b. Business Process Flows

c. Power Automate

d. Customer Service Hub

Answer: **B -** Business Process Flows

Explanation: Business Process Flows guides users through defined stages of a process, helping sales reps follow consistent steps for managing opportunities from initial contact to close. This feature aligns well with Contoso's requirement to standardize the sales process for all representatives.

Case Study 2

Alpine Ski House, a sporting goods retailer, is implementing Dynamics 365 Customer Service to enhance its support for online orders. They receive a high volume of enquiries related to order status, returns, and product availability. The company wants to minimize response times and provide customers with accurate information quickly. Additionally, Alpine Ski House needs a way to automatically route incoming cases to the appropriate support team based on the type of inquiry.

The company also plans to track support team performance against response and resolution time targets.

Question: Alpine Ski House wants to ensure that support enquiries are automatically assigned to the right team based on the type of case. Which feature in Dynamics 365 Customer Service would help achieve this?

a. Knowledge Articles

b. Queues and Routing Rules

c. Business Process Flows

d. Marketing Lists

Answer: B - Queues and Routing Rules

Explanation: Queues and Routing Rules in Dynamics 365 Customer Service allow cases to be automatically routed to specific teams based on criteria such as inquiry type. This feature enables Alpine Ski House to efficiently manage high volumes of cases and ensure that each case reaches the right team promptly.

Conclusion

As we conclude this chapter, we have explored the transformative role of Dynamics 365 CRM across various business scenarios and its potential for shaping the future of customer relationship management. We have also outlined key certification paths covering essential certifications, such as Dynamics 365 Sales Functional Consultant Associate, Power Platform Solution Architect, and Power Platform Developer Associate that empower professionals to deepen their skills and validate their expertise. The certification exam structures, sample questions, and case studies provided offer insight into the types of knowledge and practical skills required to excel in these roles.

To our readers: Thank you for your journey through these chapters, exploring the depth of Dynamics 365 and Power Platform. As you advance in your learning or career, remember that the tools and knowledge you have gained here are just the beginning. Embrace continuous learning and innovation, as the evolving landscape of digital transformation will present new opportunities and challenges. We hope this book has been a valuable resource, and we encourage you to continue exploring, growing, and contributing to the field.

References

1. Microsoft Certified: Power Platform Functional Consultant Associate: https://learn.microsoft.com/en-us/credentials/certifications/power-platform-functional-consultant-associate/?practice-assessment-type=certification
2. Microsoft Certified: Power Platform Developer Associate: https://learn.microsoft.com/en-us/credentials/certifications/power-platform-developer-associate/?practice-assessment-type=certification
3. Microsoft Certified: Power Platform Solution Architect Expert: https://learn.microsoft.com/en-us/credentials/certifications/power-platform-solution-architect-expert/#certification-prerequisites
4. Microsoft Dynamics 365 Customer Service Functional Consultant: https://learn.microsoft.com/en-us/credentials/certifications/exams/mb-230/
5. Microsoft Dynamics 365 Field Service Functional Consultant: https://learn.microsoft.com/en-us/credentials/certifications/exams/mb-240/
6. Microsoft Certifications: https://learn.microsoft.com/en-us/credentials/browse/
7. Microsoft Learn: https://learn.microsoft.com/

Index

D

E